浙江省百项档案编研精品

英文文献中的
"温州"资料汇编（1876-1949 年）
THE COMPILATION OF MATERIALS ON WENZHOU
IN ENGLISH LITERATURE (1876-1949)

【第二辑】

《北华捷报》温州史料编译

（1876-1895 年）

THE COMPILATION AND TRANSLATION OF MATERIALS ON WENZHOU IN NORTH-CHINA HERALD (1876-1895)

温州市档案局（馆） 译编

社会科学文献出版社
SOCIAL SCIENCES ACADEMIC PRESS (CHINA)

目录

Contents

温州
《北华捷报及最高法庭与领事馆杂志》，1895 年 8 月 23 日 …………… 190
温州
《北华捷报及最高法庭与领事馆杂志》，1895 年 9 月 6 日 …………… 192
温州
《北华捷报及最高法庭与领事馆杂志》，1895 年 9 月 20 日 …………… 194
温州
《北华捷报及最高法庭与领事馆杂志》，1895 年 9 月 27 日 …………… 197
温州
《北华捷报及最高法庭与领事馆杂志》，1895 年 10 月 18 日 ………… 201
温州
《北华捷报及最高法庭与领事馆杂志》，1895 年 11 月 1 日 …………… 204
温州
《北华捷报及最高法庭与领事馆杂志》，1895 年 11 月 22 日 ………… 207
温州
《北华捷报及最高法庭与领事馆杂志》，1895 年 12 月 13 日 ………… 209

第二部分 英文文献

Islands off the Wenchow River, Wenchow River and Wenchow
The North - China Herald and Supreme Court & Consular Gazette, October 26, 1876 … 213
Wenchow
The North - China Herald and Supreme Court & Consular Gazette, April 5, 1877 … 218
Wenchow
The North - China Herald and Supreme Court & Consular Gazette, April 5, 1877 …… 220
Wenchow
The North - China Herald and Supreme Court & Consular Gazette, April 28, 1877 …… 221
Wenchow
The North - China Herald and Supreme Court & Consular Gazette, May 5, 1877 … 222
Wenchow
The North - China Herald and Supreme Court & Consular Gazette, June 9, 1877 … 224
Wenchow
The North - China Herald and Supreme Court & Consular Gazette, June 30, 1877 …… 225

Wenchow

The North - China Herald and Supreme Court & Consular Gazette, May 30, 1884 …… 327

Wenchow

The North - China Herald and Supreme Court & Consular Gazette, September 12, 1884 … 328

No Title

The North - China Herald and Supreme Court & Consular Gazette, October 15, 1884 … 329

Riot at Wenchow

The North - China Herald and Supreme Court & Consular Gazette, October 15, 1884 … 332

Wenchow

The North - China Herald and Supreme Court & Consular Gazette, December 17, 1884 …… 337

Railways in China

The North - China Herald and Supreme Court & Consular Gazette, March 18, 1885 …… 338

Riot at Wenchow

The North - China Herald and Supreme Court & Consular Gazette, December 22, 1886 …… 340

Hart's Peak—Wenchow

The North - China Herald and Supreme Court & Consular Gazette, April 6, 1887 …… 342

Wenchow

The North - China Herald and Supreme Court & Consular Gazette, June 17, 1887 … 343

Notes of A Trip to Wenchow and Its Neighbourhood

The North - China Herald and Supreme Court & Consular Gazette, February 10, 1888 …… 345

Chinese New Year Holidays At Wenchow

The North - China Herald and Supreme Court & Consular Gazette, March 2, 1888 … 349

Wenchow

The north - China Herald and Supreme Court & Consular Gazette, October 19, 1888 … 351

Wenchow

The North - China Herald and Supreme Court & Consular Gazette, October 26, 1888 … 353

Wenchow

The North - China Herald and Supreme Court & Consular Gazette, November 16, 1888 …… 354

Wenchow

The North - China Herald and Supreme Court & Consular Gazette, February 22, 1889 …… 356

The Disturbance At Wenchow

The North - China Herald and Supreme Court & Consular Gazette, July 3, 1891 ……… 358

Persecution of Christians At Wenchow

The North - China Herald and Supreme Court & Consular Gazette, February 26, 1892 …… 360

《北华捷报》简介与本书编辑说明

英国商人亨利·奚安门（Henry Shearman）于1850年8月3日在上海英租界创办周刊《北华捷报》（*North – China Herald*）；1856年后，随着商业广告增多，《北华捷报》开始增出英文广告日刊《每日航运新闻》（*Daily Shipping News*）。1862年后更名为《每日航运与商业新闻》（*Daily Shipping News and Commercial News*，又译为《航务商业日报》）。

自1859年起，《北华捷报》被英国驻沪领事馆指定为公署文告发布机构，得到上海工部局的资助和优先刊载工部局文告和付费广告的特权，因而一定程度上也反映了英国政府的观点，被视为"英国官报"（Official British Organ）。1864年7月1日，《北华捷报》将《每日航运与商业新闻》改为综合性日报独立出版。这时，该报馆改组为字林洋行，因而当时的中国人将这份"*North China Daily News*"英文日报译作《字林西报》。《字林西报》创刊后，《北华捷报》成为《字林西报》的星期附刊继续出版，其地位与影响力日益下降。1867年4月8日后增加商情并易名为《北华捷报与市场报道》（*North China Herald and Market Report*）

继续出版。1870年1月4日，《北华捷报与市场报道》增出期刊《最高法庭与领事公报》(*The Supreme Court and Consular*)，不久后两报合并，更名为《北华捷报及最高法庭与领事馆杂志》（*North China Herald and Supreme Court and Consular Gazette*）继续出版，一直到1941年12月。

为便于表达，本书以《北华捷报》统称该报纸；而本书则选取1876~1895年该报纸有关“温州”（Wenchow）的主要新闻报道和评论，并按照编年顺序加以编辑和翻译。

第一部分

中文翻译

junks cruising after pirates along
n-Chê sea coast, it seems that th
of Fukien and T'aichow are sti
nerous and as savage as ever.
nd its consort bound from Ningpo t
w laden with rice and sundries wer
y attacked near Wênchow by a co
pirates, who boarded the merchant
aving ransacked everything of valu
he latter, left them with twenty-fiv
nd seriously wounded. Stri
have been issued by the Governo
l, T'an, for the capture of the pirate
ite a large fleet of war junks is no
t it seems to be the universal opinio

chow as its Consul on the 12th inst.,
Parker taking leave on a new de-
ure, having first secured the last instal-
t of the indemnity that the authorities
ed to pay for losses sustained by
igners in the recent disturbances. To
be Mr. E. H. Parker's success in giving
ral satisfaction to foreigners and native
orities in regard to the questions raised
e riot to good luck, would be unjust to
accomplished officer. It was tact that
ted an amicable settlement

sitants of the so-called "C
ave put away their store-clo
ar. The rejoicings were co
uietness and decorum, the
of nastiness was eaten,
mount of tomtomming and fi
ulged in; in fact, everythi
accordance with "olo cu
Year's Eve most of the
ncipal thoroughfares were
ted with coloured lamps, a
re lighted in nearly all the
ty and suburbs. That this
usement did not result in a
onflagration is simply miraculous,
mmunity is by all right-thinking
ttributed to the special interven
ien Tien Ta Ti, the great Lord of
Heaven, or some other benevolen
hough here, as elsewhere, scoffers
ound who point to the saturated con
verything or to some other such c

cal Report
American

ang-ang, running as she
rt of the most influential
fter trip with improved
esults, seems now to have
o that point where if more
of necessity become m
g superfluity. As has bee
the impetus given by
y means of shipment has
nt export of al
ospects for tea

xpression, spread himself out over the
whole subject of the health, pestilence
amines, and topography of the place
Thirty-six closely printed pages have
not sufficed to relieve him of his whole
burden of knowledge, for at the begin
ning of his paper he says that he reserves
he medical
ccasion; but
f which he h
ully have th
hat we sho
uch a trifle
He begins
listrict in wh
and passing

the s
ay th
rejoici
d de
ness
omton
in fa
ce wi
Eve m
rough
colour
in m
burbs.
id no
mply
ll rig
spec
he gr
other
sewhere,
the saturated condition
some other such commo

To the Editor of the
NORTH-CHINA DAILY NEWS.

IR,—Although the subject of ra
China was ably discussed at a late
of the Shanghai Literary and De
iety the question was not so exha
reated as to preclude me from o
nall contribution, assuming that
be unacceptable to those who
ary (but not

During a fierce gale which raged at Wen
chow about a fortnight ago, several seriou
disasters occurred, attended in many case
with loss of life. Four large junks, lade
with poles, were upset and many other
dragged anchor or sustained other injurie
whilst a great number of small fishing craf
suffered a worse fate. The villagers on th
coast showed great barbarism. Instead o
affording succour, they busied themselve
with picking up wreckage thrown ashore
In the worst cases they even wrested th
poles away from the shipwrecked people
who in their exhausted state were made t
yield the logs to the merciless people
Owing to the unusually cold weather a
Wenchow there is considerable sufferin
amongst the poorer classes, who are no
provided with extensive wardrobes, an
specially amongst those who have a pre

(UNDATED.)

vastation that met ou
e river of Wênchow wa
les and miles the countr
vast expanse of wate
teads and graves, an
nds crowded with cattle
frowning background
a most depressing an
We passed too quickl
by the pen. Women an
roups, doubtless talkin
sses, while the men wer
In some places wher
he bridges were still standing only th
pper portion of their arches was visibl
ooking like mirages—water above, belo
nd around them! Great indeed mu
ave been the downpour to have caused suc
n inundation. It was a comforting chang
o turn one's gaze from the immerse
ountry to the numberless fishermen pu
uing their calling as if no such thing a
come troubles existed. The flooded cou

tically, it m
think the
mature, tha
where it m
needed; f
northern Ch
courses, and
is doubtful
ccessfully c
It was urge
yed by an i
of China,

be sent to Ta-c
Yo-ching-hsien
pirate-robbers
used considerab
ies of both this
how. Some tim
does plundered two
the Yu H'uan Bay
re) which caused the
to order one of his
against them. On
e of the bay the office
vessel decided to am
red a party of soldier

(FROM A CORRESP

Notice to mariners, also
d to feminine sphere
markable Peak on the
avigators see on their
Wênchow, having only
nd never named, has no
e denizens of Wênchо
Hart's Peak," in recogn
ices which the Inspecto
mperial Maritime Custo
y illuminating the coas
Formal recognition of the
y the Wênchowese, in pic-nic assembled
n the 22nd March, and that being th
irthday of the Emperor of Germany, nea
o the celebration of the Queen's Jubilee
nd within measurable distance of th
atal day of President Cleveland, th
ealth of those estimable rulers was drun

R OWN CORRES

ing, on ente
d some stragg
trawropes, the
that were d
ent the enemy"
ing. Had they resisted th
would have been as useless
A proposition that was mad
channel has been abandone
a panic was created by a p
quiring every family to bri
daring a basket of stones.
as secure as if they had
protection; the authorities
solicitous for their safety.
threw missiles, and others c

RIOT AT WENCHOW.

e *Yungning*, from Wênc
ed here on Saturday, b
culars of a riot which had
chow on the night of the
first intimation of this ri
hed up from Ningpo from informatio
lied by the *Yungning* on arrival a
port, though efforts had been made b
E. H. Parker, British Consul, and als

Macgowa
ow recen
put down
sumption
Southwaite
ld be tra

, which a reference to Mr. Dou
's table on the opposite page rend
ent. My views elsewhere publis

《北华捷报及最高法庭与领事馆杂志》，1876 年 10 月 26 日

瓯江附近的岛屿、瓯江与温州

瓯江附近的岛屿

岐头山①东北 10 英里处为头岙（Taou Island，今玉环岛）②，头岙（玉环）是温州东部最大的岛屿。岛上田畴垦辟，沿岸小村落繁多，其中最大的是东南角的开门村（今坎门镇）③。开门村附近是很好的锚地，也是躲避西北和东北向风浪的优良避风港。从前在外国人控制浙江和福建沿海武装贸易④的时候，这个村里住着几个外国人。⑤ 他们在当地建立据点，经常劫掠来往船队。但他们敌不过广东人，最后不得不离开转去北方。⑥ 岛上居民几乎全是福建渔民，⑦ 总能看到他们的帆船在岛周围行驶。

---

① 岐头山在瓯江入海口，属永嘉县。在海关术语中，Point 指“岬”，即突入海中的陆地，通常也是灯塔、桩标所在。参见陈诗启、孙修福《中国近代海关常用词语英汉对照宝典》，中国海关出版社，2002，第 538 页。

② 玉环岛别名头岙。为了便于理解，下文翻译时皆使用“玉环”这一习惯用法。参见林传甲总纂《大中华浙江省地理志》，浙江印刷公司，1918，第 49 页。

③ 按照发音与所指地理方位，开门村即今坎门镇。

④ 关于中国沿海海盗与贸易网络关系这一研究主题，可以参考 Robert J. Antony (ed.), *Elusive Pirates, Pervasive Smugglers: Violence and Clandestine Trade in the Greater China Seas*, Hong Kong: Hong Kong University Press, 2010。

⑤ 道光十九年，西洋番船停泊坎门，居民防守森严。参见玉环坎门镇志编纂办公室编《玉环坎门镇志》，浙江人民出版社，1991，第 6 页。

⑥ 咸丰九年，粤寇窜浙，邻郡皆陷。同治元年，粤匪攻城。参见《玉环厅志》，光绪六年刻本，卷 9；《永嘉县志》，光绪八年刻本，卷 8。

⑦ 光绪二十四年秋间，闽船来此捕鱼者约百艘。参见玉环坎门镇志编纂办公室编《玉环坎门镇志》，浙江人民出版社，1991，第 7 页。

瓯江河口以东 4.5 英里处，为虎豆山（今大门岛）① 与九麾山（今小门岛）②，二岛东偏北 2 英里处是鹿栖山（今鹿西乡）。鹿栖山的东面有一些小岛，北面则是北爿山屿与南爿山屿（Cliff Rocks）③。这些岛屿全都田地兴旺，住有福建渔民，岸边村庄无数。上述诸岛的东南方向有许多被称为“山穴”④ 的群岛，其中最大的是洞豆山（今洞头岛）、尾岙山（今东岙山尾）、半边山（今半屏山）和状元山（今状元岙）⑤，此外还有一些较小的岛。这些岛共同组成列屿，岛上开辟田地，人口繁盛。洞豆山西南是一处被称为黑牛湾（今洞头岛南部）⑥ 的优良锚地。这里可以补充淡水，港湾也名副其实。⑦ 黑牛湾之所以有名气，可能是因为虎头屿⑧。虎头屿是一座圆锥形岛，该岛西北半英里有一些礁石。从前广东海盗经常在这附近出没，几乎所有从这里经过的武装船队，都要和他们发生冲突。目前这

---

① 这里记载的“虎豆山”绝非今日虎头屿，据《玉环厅志》，凡是海中“山”名，必为大岛。根据前后文地理描述，虎豆山在瓯江河口东 4.5 英里，又在鹿栖之西，虎豆山必是大门岛无疑。大门岛，即黄大岙（隩）岛，“虎豆”可能是“黄大岙”的音转。另，孙中山在《建国方略》中将大门岛称为“虎头岛”。又，二战期间，日军同样称大门岛为虎头岛。“豆”与“头”通假。参见陈诗启、孙修福《中国近代海关常用词语英汉对照宝典》，中国海关出版社，2002，第 475 页；中山大学历史系编《孙中山全集》（第 6 卷），中华书局，2006，第 330～331 页；朱仁阳：《大门岛概述》，载《洞头县文史资料》（第 1 辑），1990，第 7 页。

② 依据前后文地理方位，此处九麾山应指小门岛，“九麾山”出处不明。

③ 瓯海关的北屿、南屿、茅草屿和珠坞都被称为 Cliff Island，可见这是一个相当随意的习惯性叫法。根据这里的地理描述，以及后文所说的建造灯塔计划，此处的 Rocks 也是复数形式，Cliff Rocks 指的应是北爿山屿、南爿山屿共同组成的群屿总称。参见陈诗启、孙修福《中国近代海关常用词语英汉对照宝典》。

④ “山穴”即“岙”。

⑤ 上述诸岛中文名，为原文照录，地理范围在今洞头区内。

⑥ 陈诗启、孙修福：《中国近代海关常用词语英汉对照宝典》，中国海关出版社，2002，第 447 页。

⑦ 大瞿岛远看像一头卧在海上的大黑牛，所以它前面的海域，被称为黑牛湾。参见林正秋编《浙江旅游文化大辞典》，中国旅游出版社，2012，第 287 页。

⑧ 虎头屿是进入航道的入口，现在建有国际灯塔。陈诗启、孙修福：《中国近代海关常用词语英汉对照宝典》，中国海关出版社，2002，第 456 页。

些岛上的海盗已经不多。如果温州对外开放贸易的话，这片水域的海盗必将遭到毁灭性打击。

有许多水道连通瓯江，但因为这些水道过浅，且沙线变化很快，致使海船只能走一条水道进入瓯江。因此，我在这里仅介绍外国商船前往瓯江所使用的这条水道。

这条东西走向的水道，在虎豆山（大门岛）与状元岙之间，水道宽约半英里。其中唯有两处险要之地，一处是沙隩①，低潮时水深只有1.5英寻②。另一处是虎豆山（大门岛）附近的青菱屿③，但青菱屿通常都露出水面，因此不难避开。虎豆山（大门岛）南岬④附近也有一块礁石，离海岸只有半链⑤距离，但因为有标桩明确的标示，所以很容易避开。

如果在南爿山屿附近最大的岩石上建造一处和西屿（Square Island，在福建连江县）⑥ 类似的灯塔，然后在沙隩建一处浮标，那么商船夜晚在这条水道航行时就不会遇到任何麻烦。关于浮标和灯塔，我建议用木料建造，因为当地木料比较便宜；另外使用昂贵的铁质灯塔与浮标，可能会诱使当地人来偷。相对便宜的材料，反而能保周全。

瓯　江

虎豆山（大门岛）西北偏西5英里处是岐头山，岐头山是通往瓯江的入口；岐头山西南偏西是灵冠山（今灵昆岛），这是瓯江无数岛屿中最大的一个。灵冠山东南方是一片绵延超过6英里的浅滩，岸边的浅滩一直延伸到尾岙山岛。灵冠山西侧是三座圆形的小山丘，其余都是低地，岛上有一些村庄。在瓯江北岸，从岐头山到磐石城突出的小山之间是一片低地，这片低地沿岸各村相当富庶。此河段水深在3到14英寻之间。过了北岸的

---

① 这里的沙洲，指“沙隩”。参见《玉环厅志·黄大隩图》，光绪六年刻本，卷首。

② 1英寻约合1.83米。

③ 参见《玉环厅志·黄大隩图》，光绪六年刻本，卷首。

④ 参见前文“岐头山（Wen-chow Point）”注释。

⑤ 1链 =1/10海里 =184.3米。此处半链约为92米。

⑥ 陈诗启、孙修福：《中国近代海关常用词语英汉对照宝典》，中国海关出版社，2002，第522页。

磐石城，还能看到4座岛屿。① 其中一座岛屿紧靠北岸，另外一座岛屿则几乎在瓯江中心②，且靠近茅竹岭③锚地，处于我们行船路线的北方。

接下来我们就到了地图上瓯江段所标示的茅草岑，如果温州对外开放贸易的话，这里会被定为海船锚地。

从茅草岑东炮台④到碎石码头（意译，今易通码头）⑤ 之间，坐落着一些小村庄。我们的地图上标明了这些村庄的名字以及它们的位置。这些村子里有一座极好的祠堂，可以用来建海关大楼；靠近祠堂的地方有两个优良的石制码头，其中一个240英尺长，15英尺宽；另一个120英尺长，10英尺宽。此处低潮时的水深介于2到14英寻之间；南岸边的锚地由东向西延伸超过1英里；春天时，这里每小时会涨潮3到5次，潮水落差有17英尺高。前文所说的沙洲构成了锚地北岸，那里是低平的沼泽地，上面只有很少的几座房屋，是建造船坞的理想场所。

在瓯江北岸，从磐石城一直到和温州府并排的大运河，是一连串的山丘，一直延伸到河岸边，几乎没有人开发过，看起来很荒凉。瓯江上另一群岛屿总共有6个，被当地人称为涂岛（今七都岛）。它们坐落在杨府山⑥北部，一条水道从这些岛的中间通往温州城。这些岛的周围都是浅滩，低潮时看起来像是一座大岛。从杨府山到温州城之间是低平、肥沃的耕作平

---

① 根据后文内容，这里指的应是今天温州茅竹岭北部附近的沙洲，可能是七都岛东部一部分。

② 这里所指并不是江心屿，只是七都岛附近江中的沙洲。

③ N. P. Andersen, “Reach in the Wenchow River,” *Reports on Trade at the Treaty Ports in China of the year of* 1868, Shanghai: Customs' Press, 1868, p. 54.

④ 这里指的应是茅竹岭炮台。温州共有4座炮台，即龙湾炮台、镇瓯炮台、茅竹岭炮台、状元桥炮台。参见温州文物处编《温州文物综录》，天马图书，1998，第78页。

⑤ 根据1868年温州港调查报告中的附图，这座码头的全称为Broken Stone Jetty，此图最西边缘处画出了码头位置，地点在杨府山以东、茅竹岭以西、状元桥正北。虽然没有标注中文名，但大概方位在今天温州易通码头一带。参见N. P. Andersen, “Reach in the Wenchow River,” *Reports on Trade at the Treaty Ports in China of the year of 1868*, Shanghai: Customs' Press, p. 54。

⑥ 陈诗启、孙修福：《中国近代海关常用词语英汉对照宝典》，中国海关出版社，2002，第466页。

原，散布着无数小村落。低潮时，上述杨府山北面的沙洲，就会贴近河岸。温州府地处瓯江南岸，城墙一直延伸到河岸。城的北面是一些小岛，其中一座小岛特别引人注目。这座小岛东西长约0.25英里，上面有一处宏伟的寺庙和两座古老的佛塔。①

城市上游的河流，自东向西流，河中也有许多小岛。此地风景如画，两岸绵延的高山一直延伸到河流的尽头。

温州城边有一条瓯江支流，自北向南流，总长大约100里，发源于荒凉的山区南溪（今楠溪）②。

温　州

温州府地处浙江省东南，北面和西面分别毗邻台州和处州，南面与福建省接壤，东部临海。总面积超过3500平方英里，人口大约300万。

温州府府治在永嘉县，坐落于温溪（即瓯江）南岸，距离河口约有20英里。城市位于一处很好的耕作平原上，四面环山，山距城约10英里。城墙最早建于4世纪，明太祖（洪武）于1385年下令扩建重修。城墙使用石头斜着建造，周长约6英里。街道又宽又直，平坦又干净。城市中的主要公共建筑是东门外的海关③、城市西南角的道台衙门以及位于城市中央的育婴堂。育婴堂建于1748年④，有100个房间。它的经费来源是捐款的利息收入以及政府提供土地获取的租金收入。根据创设记录，育婴堂收养的弃儿在2至300人之间。到了一定年龄，男孩子要么拜师学手艺，要么被领养；女孩则许配给别人做妻子，或者受雇成为女佣。西南门外面还有

---

① 今江心屿。

② "Map of ChehKiang," *China Imperial Maritime Customs Decennial Reports*, No. 1th, Shanghai: Statistical Department of the Inspectorate General of Customs, 1893, p. 363.

③ 这里指的是中国常关，并不是近代瓯海关，在1877年温州港规划图中，被标注为Native Custom House。参见"Plan of the Port of Wenchow," *China Imperial Maritime Customs Decennial Reports*, No. 1th, Shanghai: Statistical Department of the Inspectorate General of Customs, 1893, p. 387。

④ 温郡育婴堂，创建于乾隆十二年（1747），原文误。参见《郡守刘煜碑记》，《永嘉县志》，光绪八年刻本，卷35。

一处养济院①。该院建于14世纪，受到国家资助。每位接受救济的人每月可以领取1两半的补贴；但是看门人非常粗暴，除非饿得不行，一般很少有人会到这里来接受救济。

温州城边的岛屿上，有两座佛塔，令人好奇不已。这两座塔年代久远，宋朝最后一位皇帝“帝昺”② 曾逃到这里，躲避蒙古忽必烈可汗的追击，忽必烈是元朝的建立者。

1861年之前，温州是唯一允许茶叶出口的港口，这在某种程度让它成为周边地区的贸易市场。城市因为茶叶垄断贸易而繁荣。但1861年太平军攻占了整个温州府，为了防止茶叶落入太平军手中，就改成了现在的章程。该章程授权沿海任何一处海关分卡③都可以从事茶叶出口；从前聚集于此的庞大贸易，因而被分散到了所有沿海的小港口。④

温州的主要贸易是木材与竹子出口，货物从处州（Ch' u – chow）用木筏沿河运下。据估计，这两种贸易每年的总值不会低于200万银圆（$）⑤。从事此项贸易的商行与货栈位于城外西郊，那里堆放有大量竹子与木杆。

温州也会进口少量的糖和鸦片；鸦片主要由住在城里的福建商人从福

---

① 养济院在东福门外，洪武八年（1375）建。参见《永嘉县志·恤政》，《永嘉县志》，光绪八年刻本，卷2。

② 即宋怀宗赵昺，宋高宗赵构也曾在江心屿避难。

③ 这里所说的海关分卡，指的是原来温州常关（1865年改名为瓯海常关）下的分卡，在平阳、瑞安等地。参见陈诗启、孙修福《中国近代海关常用词语英汉对照宝典》，中国海关出版社，2002，第72页。

④ 这里指的是瓯海常关下的平阳、瑞安等地分割温州城的茶叶贸易，其所指仅在温州府内。

⑤ $是银圆标记，这里指墨西哥银圆，也被称为“鹰洋”，近代在中国流通极广。根据海关贸易报告，19世纪80年代，漕平银与英镑在当地没有金融市场，银圆又分为三种：一种是标准墨西哥银圆；第二种是当地仿造的“坤洋”，但已逐渐退出市场；第三种是某些人为了牟利，刮去银圆表面后的“糙洋”，也被称为“刮洋”。1882年，100海关两＝150.40墨西哥银圆。1891年，100海关两＝156.56墨西哥银圆。参见陈诗启、孙修福《中国近代海关常用词语英汉对照宝典》，中国海关出版社，2002，第691页；杭州海关译编《近代浙江通商口岸经济社会概况》，浙江人民出版社，2002，第418页。

州经陆路运来。

许多大商行为了便利，都将货栈设在运河沿岸。这样他们就能把货物直接运到货仓，以降低运输费用，也可以避免苦力滋事。

人们迫切地等待这座口岸开放对外贸易。温州人尊重外国人，不像许多其他开放口岸的人，会对外国人产生荒谬的观念。当欧洲人在大街上走的时候，妇女和孩子不会表现出害怕，也不会听到男人恶意的咒骂；甚至连骂人的词语番鬼、洋鬼子和红毛人，都变成了更体面的说法——番人。

状元桥是瓯江南岸的一个小村庄，在城市以南10英里处，瓯江的水深不足以支撑超过9英尺的船过状元桥。从河道入口到这个村庄的水道又宽又深，没什么阻碍，由于有一些浮标帮助标出了航道，无论多大的船只航行时都不会遇到困难。这里陡峭的河岸、落差巨大的潮水以及价格低廉的铁和木材，让状元桥成为海边一处最理想的船厂和兵工厂；宽敞的锚地，卸载货物的设施，还可以利用不同的运河往内陆运输这些货物，都足以证明它可以成为未来的外国租界。

《北华捷报及最高法庭与领事馆杂志》，1877 年 4 月 5 日

温州

海关已经任命了一批税务司到新的开放口岸任职。虽然已经指定了开设英国领事馆的官员，但我们尚未得到英国国旗已经升起的通知。虽然开设领事馆已然逾期，① 但我们推测，沿海和长江沿线前往福州和汉口的轮船，将会中途在温州和芜湖（Wuhu）停靠，我们很快就会看到此类轮船广告。与此同时，这些口岸的开放问题已经讨论许久，它们的贸易前景值得关注。令人好奇的是，这一时刻终于来到，至少这两处口岸②的本地人似乎要比外国人还要焦急。与温州人接触过的人都说他们比任何人都更友好，他们十分期盼能够和外国人开展商业往来。温州距离大海约 18 英里，坐落在流经浙江最富饶土地的河流岸边，这里应该成为声名显赫的贸易中心；并且它似乎也一直默默无闻地致力于此。问题是，交通设施的改善，频繁的轮船班次带来的人潮，到底会在何种程度上刺激温州贸易。目前洋布进口量据说达到了每年约 100 万银圆，鸦片则是介于 3000 到 4000 箱之间。温州还从上海和宁波进口了大量的棉花，从泉州③和台湾进口了糖；任何港口一旦进入贸易网络，都会向轮船提供货物。今年，因为洪水对本地农作物造成了破坏，所以温州进口了大量的大米。而这和平时恰恰相反，因为一般来说，温州都会出口大量的谷物。最主要的出口货物可能就是茶叶；这一新的市场会在多大程度上影响福州的贸易是一个很有趣的问题。目前，从平阳地区向上海和福州输出了大约 10 万担茶叶；现如今开放

---

① 条约规定温州开埠正式日期为 1877 年 4 月 1 日。杭州海关译编《近代浙江通商口岸经济社会概况》，浙江人民出版社，2002，第 409 页。

② 芜湖与温州在《烟台条约》签订后，同时开埠。

③ 陈诗启、孙修福：《中国近代海关常用词语英汉对照宝典》，中国海关出版社，2002，第 452 页。

了温州口岸，原来经陆路运往福州的白琳①茶，就可以替代为走水路运往温州。预计除了其他较少的货物之外，从这个地区会出口大约20万担的茶叶。丝绸是本地工业的特色产品，但仅限于中国人消费；丝绸原料一部分来源于当地邻近地区，但多数还是仰赖进口以满足本地生产商的要求；丝绸产品的出口据说高达约75万两白银。本地土药、明矾、木材以及纸张出口量非常大；据说铁将会是未来贸易的一种商品。本地人说，在青田县和泰顺（Taishan，原文误，应为Taishun）②有许多铁矿，他们希望在开放口岸后，可以得到允许开矿。正如我们之前说的那样，这里的水域足够广阔，可以让海轮③开到城市来；因此，英国人定居点已经选在了紧挨着城墙东北角的城外地区。靠近河岸的河面太浅，海轮无法进入；这里的贸易是否足够支撑码头和浮筒的建设，或者是否要建造灯塔，只有等到将来再决定了。之前对这条河流的报道，集中在城市下游10英里，认为这里是合适的租借地，这主要是因为在他们看来，很明显轮船无法在靠近城市的地方找到锚地；但事实证明这是错的，尽可能地靠近中国人的商业区所带来的好处不言自明。很幸运太平军没有占领温州，温州通商的环境异常好。这座城市洁净、道路整齐，人民富裕。一直都有人说温州人对外国人怀有善意；温州士绅对最近来附近勘察的官方旅客表现得很有礼貌，这与宜昌的士绅阶层所表现出来的恶意形成鲜明对比。④让我们祈盼开埠后的温州，能够让温州士绅们得偿所愿。

---

① 白琳茶，产在福建与浙江交界的福鼎。

② 原文“Taishan”，结合前后文，应为泰顺（Taishun）误写。泰顺产麻、铁、茶和药材。参见杭州海关译编《近代浙江通商口岸经济社会概况》，浙江人民出版社，2002，第409页。

③ 陈诗启、孙修福：《中国近代海关常用词语英汉对照宝典》，中国海关出版社，2002，第57页。

④ 光绪二年二月，内地会牧师在宜昌宣教，遭到打砸，宜昌府东湖县令熊銮，试图趁势将洋人驱逐出境，引起洋人不满。又宜昌关在选址时，占用城南景帝庙，也引起当地百姓不满，为后续宜昌教案埋下伏笔。参见《宜昌内地会滋闹教堂事略》，《万国公报》1877年第453期，第35~36页；《宜昌杂录》，《申报》1884年8月5日第3版。

《北华捷报及最高法庭与领事馆杂志》，1877 年 4 月 5 日

温州

一位通讯记者告诉我们，3 月 2 日这天，税务司好博逊先生搭乘海关巡逻船“凌风”号①已经抵达温州。从那时开始好博逊就一直在从事调查工作，直到 19 日才返回福州，去接其余的海关职员。锚地水很深，所有常规吃水的轮船都能够沿河而上，在温州城附近停靠——目前已经在北门外定好了海关大楼选址，此地面朝瓯江，对面就是最好的锚地。② 温州城市非常清洁，道路平坦，但却因为没能成为商业中心，而遭受失败的打击。主要的洋行都在南门外，似乎目前它们全部的“生意”，就是木材和木炭贸易——他们只能和茶叶贸易说再见。丝绸制品的产量不多，家具、雨伞、竹篮、垫子和棺材制造是目前雇用工人最多的行业。真的，没有哪个地方会像温州这样，有这么多寺庙，但得到妥善维护的却不多。

21 日美国领事罗尔梯③先生搭乘美国船只“宝洛司”号④从宁波抵达温州。根据报道，罗尔梯先生已经在邻近达文波测绘地点的上游地段，进行了租界地选址。低潮时许多渔民都会到这里晾晒舢板，未来想要在这里定居的人是否会留意这一事实，还另当别论。

---

① 陈诗启、孙修福：《中国近代海关常用词语英汉对照宝典》，中国海关出版社，2002，第 680 页。

② 即今望江码头。

③ 罗尔梯全名为“E. C. Lord”，为美国驻宁波领事，1875 年曾短暂回国休假。《申报》一般将其称呼为“罗君”。参见《总署收美使艾忭敏照会 · 光绪元年五月二十七日》，载黄嘉谟编《中美关系史料 · 光绪朝》（第一册），中研院近代历史研究所，1977，第 40 ~ 41 页。

④ 这是一艘美国炮舰，需要注意的是，历史上美国多艘兵舰都袭用此舰名。参见“The U. S. Gunboat *Palos*,” *The North - China Daily News*, 17 September 1884, 3。

《北华捷报及最高法庭与领事馆杂志》，1877 年 4 月 28 日

温州

截止到 11 日，外国社区已经住进了海关职员与传教士曹雅直①和蔡文才②，这两位传教士都是当地的老居民了。11 日这天，英国领事阿查立③乘坐“蚊子”号④抵达温州，使得社区得以稳固。他已经见过当地官员，我相信现在正忙着为之前所说过的领事馆选址。由于并未看到英国国旗在岸边飘扬，因此我认为他还没找到合适的地方。无论是对于外国人的出现，还是轮船现如今可以自由出入这个港口，这个城市的居民似乎一点儿都不关心。除了大米，他们看起来不想要任何东西。本地的鸦片供应充足，布匹从宁波经陆路运进温州。主要的商店都使用了煤油灯，火柴也便宜。至于茶叶，可能会签订一份合同以便从平阳地区输入毛茶⑤，但现在还没到季节。目前还没有外国商人，也没有外国商船出现。（4 月 18 日）

---

① 曹雅直是英国内地会传教士，1865 年初抵达宁波，1867 年 11 月入温州传教。参见沈迦《一条开往中国的船：赴华传教士的家国回忆》，新星出版社，2016，第 162 页。

② 蔡文才（Josiah Alexander Jackson），英国内地会传教士，19 世纪 70 年代在温州协助曹雅直工作，后赴处州传教。参见沈迦《一条开往中国的船：赴华传教士的家国回忆》，新星出版社，2016，第 162 页。

③ 阿查立（Alabaster，Chaloner），原为英国驻上海领事。李必樟译编《附录：外国人名中英对照表》，《上海近代贸易经济发展概况（1854—1898 年）：英国驻上海领事贸易报告汇编》，上海社会科学院出版社，1993，第 951 页。

④ 英国炮舰，从 1876 年开始驻扎在上海。参见“Her Majesty' s gunboat Mosquito anchored in the river yesterday morning,” *The North - China Daily News*, 8 July 1876, 3。

⑤ 毛茶（raw leaf）在海关贸易报告中，也被写作 Unfired Tea，指的都是没有炒过的生茶。

《北华捷报及最高法庭与领事馆杂志》，1877 年 5 月 5 日

新口岸

人们很难预料，商人是否会像天津和汉口开放时那样，涌向新的开放口岸。新开放口岸①相对来说不是那么重要的商埠，并且过往的经验已经证明，对于居住在小口岸的外国商人来说，新的贸易点的开辟，未必就意味着丰厚的贸易利润。新口岸可以让外国商品直接到靠近消费者的门户卸货，避免多次转运，以降低运费。同时相对于中国船运，用外国船可以规避厘金。但本地的经销商越来越倾向于直接去上海购买，用轮船运回货物后在自己的家乡销售，而不是在小口岸从外国商人手上购买。很明显，这样一来居住在此的外国商人就没有多少赚钱的机会。除非在特殊的季节——比如说，在汉口和福州茶季，当地除了一些代理商行，几乎没人会涉足外国茶叶贸易。大量的交易都是在上海完成，上海渐渐地成为商业中心，无论是何时、何地生产的外国货物，全都汇聚在上海，然后发往整个长江流域和北方口岸。即便考虑到所有情况，也必须承认新口岸的开放显然很不理想。上海洋商原本对新口岸怀有兴趣，预期可以在每地都建两三处洋楼，但目前看来，只有在温州的尝试成功了。我们目前对宜昌知之甚少，它的主要价值可能就是作为长江航道的起始点——至少对目前的航运来说是这样。宜昌下游不远是沙市，沙市原本只是用作短暂停泊②的港口，现在似乎成为主要贸易点。但我们可以预见，轮船公司很快将在宜昌建立航线，我们也会逐渐更多地了解到宜昌的商业潜能。温州与芜湖，土地富饶，水文优越，是天然的出口港，如果洋人的才能与资本能够支持其发展，两地

① 指 1876 年《烟台条约》中开放的一批口岸，包括增开宜昌、芜湖、温州、北海四处为通商口岸。

② 《烟台条约》规定，沙市并不是通商口岸，“不准洋商私自起下货物，今议通融办法，轮船准暂停泊，上下客商货物”。

贸易必定可观。但显而易见的是，外国人并不能指望在这些地方捡现成。在其他地方不幸赔了钱，想要在这里快速回本，恐怕不现实。两地的本土贸易都相当可观，如果外国人想要从中获利，那么就必须发挥其才智与资本，寻找到不一样的产品销售渠道。两地原本都是茶叶生产的天然出口市场，但这些茶叶现在都有了销往外国市场的其他途径，比如福州、宁波和镇江。今年温州商人已经签好合同，茶叶会依照老路，在温州出口。如果明年外商能继续投入资本，就能在温州建立起新的商业中心，考虑到运输距离的缩短，卸货价格也可能降低。对商人来讲，尽量靠近产地购买商品具有优势，尽量靠近销售地卸货具有类似的好处，这就是开放新口岸的目的——贸易地的多元化。本地销售商过去都是通过陆路，将货物运到价高的地方牟利，即便外国商人不打算在当地开展贸易，但也可以向中国人提供大规模轮船运输的服务，这将促使本地销售商在邻近港口集运货物。在太平天国叛乱之前，温州事实上已经是大宗茶叶交易的商业中心——邻近地区的产品都在这里汇聚，但贸易的集中却刺激太平军攻击温州府，生产商选择将贸易分散到附近的小口岸，此种情形一直延续至今。温州开放对外贸易，可能会吸引商业重新聚拢到这个旧贸易中心。

《北华捷报及最高法庭与领事馆杂志》，1877 年 6 月 9 日

温州

作为本报读者或其他出版物的读者，你们有充足的机会了解别人对温州的看法，以及诗歌是如何描述这个口岸的。因此我只需尽可能简略地记下目前关于此地的“八卦”①。

首先，我要告诉你们的事情，是一位美国人在沿河而下的途中，认出一艘中国改装帆船，其实是“曼打林”号②。他立刻跑到官府，郑重其事地描述了这艘船的真实身份，道台③立马扣押了这艘船。另一位居民，曾在长江贩货，也认识这艘船，但不敢十分肯定。诚然他们的意见构成了极好的初步证词，另外道台快速果断地做出决策，应该受到赞赏。

总体上讲，我觉得我可以报道说，这里的商业前景一片光明。但温州口岸在本年开放的时间太晚，已经错过了茶季，恐怕今年在茶叶贸易上难有作为。但也正因为如此，美好的希望总在将来。布匹生意无疑会开展起来，想要站稳脚跟和获取利润的商人应该紧跟成功的榜样，我想他们不会失望。目前商人几乎不考虑鸦片贸易，从宁波进口鸦片的走私船想要进来，目前来看困难重重，而且还要缴纳厘金。

---

① 原文作“gup”，应该是“gossip”的通俗写法。

② 也被译作“曼特林”号，船主是外国人，水手都是中国人，1873 年在航行途中船主被杀，船只与水手失踪。1877 年此船在温州被发现。参见《查办逃船》，《申报》1877 年 6 月 7 日第 2 版；《研究逃船》，《申报》1877 年 6 月 28 日第 2 版；“The Lorcha Mandarin,” *The North - China Herald and Supreme Court & Consular Gazette*, 30 June 1877，7。

③ 方鼎锐，字子颖，号退斋，江苏仪征人，1877 年任温处兵备道道台，兼任瓯海关监督职务，另有铜印关防，在 1877 年由礼部铸造。参见《浙抚谭钟麟奏温州通商征收事宜已遵章办理片》，载王彦威纂、王亮编《清季外交史料之光绪朝》，1931 年刊本，卷 10。

这里无疑是中国最干净（只要卫生预防和优点能够保持）、最健康的城市。迄今为止，天气一直凉爽宜人。似乎今年本地的鸦片种植要比往年减产5%左右，这将会导致印度鸦片进口的增加。

《北华捷报及最高法庭与领事馆杂志》，1877 年 6 月 30 日

温州

自从我上次写稿以来，温州已经连续下了 10 天大雨，洪水随之泛滥。河水大涨，有几天瓯江水流速度达到 7 节，但除了有几艘民船被冲出一段距离，我们没听到任何生命财产损失的消息。因为以上原因，当地河岸土壤松软，锚很难固定，即使是德国军舰“独眼巨人”号①也撤走了。相比最早的停泊地，德国船现在停得更远，也因此少了很多麻烦。

关于泥土，海军舰官在调查上游锚地的时候注意到了一个有趣的事实。一座岛下游约 0.75 英里处形成一处浅滩，浅滩横亘在瓯江里，海军的一艘船因之搁浅。虽然潮水强劲，人也使劲拉，但船仍迅速陷进泥里。桨手拼命划，可船仍以肉眼可见的速度，被泥巴裹着往上游走。考虑到这种现象，以及其他因素，表明瓯江航道水文变化极快，我们会在新的海图中予以标记。

德国炮舰的舰长和舰官，继续一天到晚不知疲倦地调查，几乎已经完成了对包括口岸水道上游界线和歧头山（下游锚地）之间河段的调查。我们知道“独眼巨人”号会继续调查，直到所有工作完成，或收到命令前往他地。

马因先生乘坐“征服”号②到了这里，他毫不犹豫地指认那艘三桅帆船就是“曼打林”号。这是第三个指认这艘疑船真实身份的欧洲人，船主

① 德国炮舰“独眼巨人”号在 1877 年 5 月 29 日至 7 月 21 日之间停靠温州，目的是勘测瓯江水文。参见赵肖为译编《近代温州社会经济发展概况：瓯海关贸易报告与十年报告译编》，上海三联书店，2014，第 55 页。

② “征服”号是瓯海关开关后，进入温州贸易的第一艘外国商船，为了进行纪念，江心屿被命名为“征服岛”（Conquest Island）。参见杭州海关译编《近代浙江通商口岸经济社会概况》，浙江人民出版社，2002，第 468 页。

目前没有任何能自证清白的可靠纸质文件，也无法巧言令色地说清这艘船现在为什么在他手上，船体的改装也让人生疑，这些无疑全都是破绽。与此同时，英国领事和道台都将这件事情汇报给了北京。值得注意的是，如果证明这艘船确实是“曼打林”号，那么此船在谋杀案后竟然在沿海地区做了这么久的生意①，中国政府无疑要承担未能“尽职调查”的责任。曾经无数外国人报告说见过此船，此船经常在温州进行贸易，现在外国人一进入温州，立刻就认出了它的真实身份，在英国领事的交涉下，终于将其扣押。中国人对外国人的说法予以种种否认，并不能让问题变得简单。这艘船曾在海上往返，公海上的外国人都能一眼认出，中国人显然早就知道了它的真实身份。

麻烦的是，这艘船现在已经破损，几乎一文不值。这无疑会影响到受害人的赔偿权益，同时也可以批驳所谓政府无责论。有人认为“政府除了进行尽职调查并逮捕罪犯，尽可能多地寻回被盗财产，并采取必要的步骤防止今后再发生这种罪行以外，不该为个人行为承担责任”。

贸易情况变化不大。我们注意到“征服”号在温州赚了 59000 银圆，人们估计船主会用这笔钱在温州购进货物，或兑付以前的进货款。所有人都会前往宁波，看起来中国人因为保守的性格，仍继续通过宁波购买商品，所改变的只是轮船运输代替了帆船运输而已。似乎只有通过触动天朝商人敏感的钱袋子，才能改变他们这种固执的做法。

多达 200. 5 箱的茶叶运到了上海市场。温州茶商报出的价格非常荒唐，并且他们认为只有在北方才能实现那样的高价。此事终将自行纠正。

① 1873 年海上命案发生，到 1877 年案发，已经过去 4 年。

《北华捷报及最高法庭与领事馆杂志》，1877 年 9 月 1 日

温州厘金章程*

1. 凡自欧洲、日本、广州、四川、汉口与福州输入商品，无论轮船、帆船、广东三桅船、白屁股船①、小艇，欲领洋货半税单照②，均须依本章程在局纳税。

2. 洋行进口货物必须向本厘金局提供进口货单，其格式与海关货单类似。有关洋行在口岸进行交易时，必须依照章程规定，按照本地商人应缴之当地税款，指导买客支付厘金，本地商人缴纳厘金之后，洋行才能交货。非法交易或具有非法交易企图者，依照章程之规定，处以三倍罚款。

3. 本地转运商从洋行处购买货物转运内地，无论水陆，都要接受厘金局分卡检查。各厘金分卡负责人会要求验看厘金存票③。若无存票，相关货物将被暂扣，等待汇报本局，然后决定是否处以罚款。

4. 当提供厘金存票时，相关货物要提交给本厘金局进行检查。如果包装、重量等相符，货物将被盖章放行。如果相关货物超重，则就此提出申请，并指定官员继续检查现场包裹，防止违法行径。

5. 针对土货出口，除茶叶和丝绸外，所有货物都按照海关税则的 3/10 征税。洋行转运土货出口免税，但（与本地人的）共谋行为一经发现，则将征收罚款。

---

* 1877 年温州厘金章程（*Lekin Regulation for the Wenchow District*），在当年就被废除，改为包税制。参见杭州海关译编《近代浙江通商口岸经济社会概况》，浙江人民出版社，2002，第 177 页。

① 一种白尾渔船，常见于舟山、宁波一带。参见马士《中华帝国对外关系史》（第 1 卷），张汇文等译，商务印书馆，1963，第 457 页。

② 洋船输入货物，虽然在开放口岸免缴在口厘金，但如果洋船进行转运业务，则需要交纳半税转运厘金。

③ 即缴纳转运厘金税后，由厘金局发给的收据。

6. 华商从洋行购买货物运往内地①，必须第一时间缴纳进口厘金税，洋商才能交货。立即前往内地转运，而不是在口岸存放的货物，必须缴纳全部税额，然后由本局颁发子口税票，持有税票的货物可以分批转运，在抵达最后子口之前无须缴税。针对（华商所持）土货，目前还不能以同样方式获取子口税票进行内地转运。因此华商进行土货转运，必须按照关税征收全额厘金。在洋货中夹带舞弊，将被视为走私行为。

7. 针对存放在外国洋行的所有种类的货物，条约规定，厘金局官员可以相度机宜，随时便宜设法办理，以杜弊端。按照此条，厘金局将指派一名官员对未售出的库存货物进行月度检查和登记。（条约第46款②有针对此种行为的规定）

8. 本地商人，在缴纳厘金税及获取存票后，必须认真填写此批货物将要运往的城市、街道等信息；如果货物经水路运输，还要提供水路路线的细节，以便进行全面检查，防止走私行为。

9. 如果洋行进口的货物在本口销路不畅，而需要再次出口，如果海关检查之后，证明这些货物同进口时一样完好无损，则将减免厘金税。（条约第45款③有针对此种处理的规定）

10. 最近的章程④指出，在外国租界内，洋货免于征收厘金税，但是超出定租界以外，将和土货一样征收厘金税。在外国租界的界限确定之

---

① 按照1877年《烟台条约》第三端第四节对1858年《通商善后章程》第七款的解释，“内地”指的是“不通商口岸，皆属内地”。参见褚德新、梁德主编《中外约章汇要（1689—1949）》，黑龙江人民出版社，1991，第202页。

② 指的是《天津条约》第46款规定，“中国各口收税官员，凡有严防偷漏之法，均准其相度机宜，随时便宜设法办理，以杜弊端”。参见褚德新、梁德主编《中外约章汇要（1689—1949）》，黑龙江人民出版社，1991，第139页。

③ 《天津条约》第45款规定，“英国民人运货进口既经纳清税课者，凡欲改运别口售卖，须禀明领事官，转报监督官委员验明，实系原包原货，查与底簿相符，并未拆动抽换，即照数填入牌照，发给该商收执”。参见褚德新、梁德主编《中外约章汇要（1689—1949）》，黑龙江人民出版社，1991，第139页。

④ 指《烟台条约》第三端第一节规定“所有现在通商各口岸，按前定各条约，有不应抽收洋货厘金之界，兹由威大臣议请本国，准以各口租界作为免收洋货厘金之处，俾免漫无限制”。参见褚德新、梁德主编《中外约章汇要（1689—1949）》，黑龙江人民出版社，1991，第201页。

前，现有厘金章程仍将继续执行。

11. 一旦外国人定居点的界线确定下来，如果发现中国商人的财产即本地商品也在租界内，将由本局进行裁定，地方当局采取此措施，是为了便于对本地商品进行管控。为了维护条约在涉及所有权方面的规定，如果本地商人和洋行共谋舞弊，或者洋行为厘金收入的诈骗行为提供保护，一经发现，将没收相关货物，并召唤洋行所在国领事，收取罚款。（参见条约第 48 款①）

按照宁波正在实施的厘金章程，起草了上述章程，以便符合本地情况；本章程乃遵循条约②规定拟成，在厘金税收总体利益之上，兼顾公平精神。

涉及鸦片章程

1. 将按照宁波的税收系统征收温州地区的鸦片厘金税，即每箱 40 两③。1 箱公班土④中有 40 个鸦片球，1 箱白皮土⑤中鸦片有 100 市斤。

2. 进口鸦片，将由海关进行检查，然后在海关关栈卸货，鸦片数量将汇报至本厘金局。一旦售出，买客须按照指示缴纳厘金，获得本厘金局提供的盖戳的放行单，此后鸦片才能交货。如有走私行为，将对走私的每担鸦片收取 1000 两的罚款。

3. 至于鸦片的厘金税，根据与洋行的协议，按照宁波的管理章程向他们收取厘金税。因此从征收的 40 两厘金中将会返还 5 两给相关的洋行中间人，1 两支付给本地牙商，其余总共 34 两上交厘金局。

温州的洋行还没有按照以上描述的方式缴纳厘金，目前没有必要退还上述厘金。

一旦洋行了解了这个问题，就会在适当时候进行考虑，同时也会颁布更为详细的运营控制措施。

---

① 《天津条约》第 48 款规定，“英国商船查有涉走私，该货无论式类、价值，全数查抄入官外，俟该商船账目清后，亦可严行驱除，不准在口贸易”。参见褚德新、梁德主编《中外约章汇要（1689—1949）》，黑龙江人民出版社，1991，第 139 页。

② 按照前文，指的是 1858 年《天津条约》与 1876 年《烟台条约》。

③ Tls.（Taels），中国古代银两单位，1 两 =50 克，此处应指 1 两白银。

④ 产自印度巴特拿，色黑，价高。

⑤ 产自印度马洼，价格低于公班土。

《北华捷报及最高法庭与领事馆杂志》，1877 年 9 月 1 日

温州

前几天这里的贸易突然遭到了打击，因为厘金局突然向我们征收很高的子口厘金税。当地政府颁布了一套荒谬的“章程”，还附上了税率表。此章程扭曲了条约中关于海关内容的条款，以便于章程的颁行。例如，条约有一条规定（原文如此），外国人和本地人一样要受厘金章程的制约。再有，另一条则说，厘金局官员每月将对洋行货栈检查两次，“通过检查海关陈明的货物内容，找出差异，看看哪些货物已经缴纳了厘金”等等。这和宁波现行的章程完全一致。一开始他们采取特殊的预防措施，防止公文流出，包括避免这些章程落入外国人手中。但是尽管如此，不久之后我们的官员就掌握了这些文件。中国人立即联合起来抵制这项敲诈勒索，结果导致当地贸易陷入停滞。当地洋行已经向上海发出命令停止发货，这使得我们最近失去了唯一进入温州进行贸易的轮船。本地华商威胁关闭店铺，最后道台撤回章程，对其做出修改。商人们还是不太满意，虽然已经逃过一劫，但我担心外国人还是会进退失据①。温州口岸的开放，严重损害了宁波厘金公会②的利益，他们担心甚至都实现不了相对较小的包税目标。

因此，宁波商人正在说服一两位温州商人加入他们，在温州同样开展厘金包税。现在要记住，宁波已经悄悄地允许他们这么干。他们已经获取征收较小税率的权力，并由此建立由所有当地进口商组成的包税公会，包税总额很容易通过极低的税率完成征收。③

---

① “Seylla and Chrybdis”，源自希腊神话，前者指海中的巨大礁石，后者指海中的漩涡，行船至此，左右为难。此处寓意左右为难，进退失据。

② 这里具体指的应是宁波匹头公会，该公会通过包认厘金税，垄断了宁波口匹头自由运销内地的权利。参见侯鹏《清代浙江厘金研究》，载周育民、侯鹏编《晚清国家与社会关系论例》，上海社会科学院出版社，2014，第 266 ~ 267 页。

③ 宁波厘金包税的意义，并不在于收税牟利，而是通过收税权，事实上垄断了内地转运贸易。外人因为在税收上的不平等待遇，很难涉足其中。

但是此刻，一名倒霉的外国人，竟胆大包天地进口了一大包货物，这些密谋者向他征收了理论上的全额税，在缴清税额之前他的货物只能被扣押。这怎么可能！这名外国人不断解释条约中规定的权利。但是，天啊，许多富人因此而濒临破产，证明这件事千真万确。并且令人感到奇怪的是，那些会因此受到影响的人，起初并不在意，也没有进行斗争，甚至没有向官府提出抗议。现在一切都太晚了，大胆的骗子已经站稳了脚跟，因此遍地痛哭与哀号。但即使这样，在有人催促他们奋力抗争的时候，他们却哽咽又坚定地回答：“不，贸易已经转移到本地人手中，他们的公会太强大了，现在再努力也不值得了。”看！这就是宁波人（据说，上头的厘金局官员自己就是他们中的一员）在这里的影响。感谢温州非比寻常的友善环境，再加上我们出众的经验与才干，我们乐观地希望能挫败这些阴谋家（截至目前，每一周都表现出更加公平的贸易前景）。我们会从这些狡猾的邻居手中，拯救我们的港口和我们自己。

（当地人中）流传着一种情绪，即通过这种方法把外国人赶出去。宁波的情况就是这样一种令人信服的证据。

这是我们第一次体会到，英国人现如今希望他们的政府能出面，干涉此项外国事务。许多期盼的眼睛都在注视着德国人和其他公使，据说这些人正在据理力争，以期不让《烟台条约》发生倒退，抵消其灾难性影响。

以上是目前有关我们这个口岸的所有“新闻”，此外由于厘金政策的消极影响，“征服”号已经撤回去了，这让我们深受打击，感到愤怒和失望。噢，威妥玛阁下①！威妥玛阁下！如果我们能对冲动与迟钝所能造成的长远影响有先见之明，哪怕只是预先略有留意，也能把我们从愚蠢的行为中拯救出来!!

Spes. ②

---

① 威妥玛（Thomas Francis Wade），1869 年至 1882 年任英国驻华全权公使，“威妥玛拼音”的创始人。

② 笔名，可能是“Speer”的缩写，“Spes.”有“希望”的意思。根据文章内容判断，此人是英国人，1877～1878 年在温州以“Spes.”的笔名于《北华捷报》发表通讯文章，1885 年再次以笔名“Spes.”在天津发表通讯文章。

《北华捷报及最高法庭与领事馆杂志》，1877 年 9 月 8 日

温州厘金章程

中国政府似乎又要故技重施，这种伎俩常常很有效果，尽管经常被曝光，但是每次使用仍有许多人受骗。目前正值各国在北京协商全面修订厘金税率①的时候，指望中国政府会在最近新开长江口岸与温州口岸问题上退缩，恐怕是不合时宜的。我们都清楚之前的历史，与中国交往有多么困难。中国人会一点一点地进行勒索，沟通越来越困难，直到最后连贸易都难以维持。接下来，原本的小事情就会升级成真正的争执。但战争是个难玩儿的游戏，中国政府现在更愿意尝试外交手段，这让他们很满意，并且夺回了曾经因为鲁莽所失去的东西。很明显，中国在接下来与德国公使的斗争中，必须花言巧语地放弃一些东西，才能避免一些更加难以承受的让步。中英烟台会议之前，这种外交把戏也占有一席之地，事实证明，对中国施加额外压力至关重要。不幸的是，我们现在的外交手段破绽百出。我们希望公使在条约中的用词能够完全准确，以防止被中国人利用，一两个模糊的词语，就像天堂守门人的剑②一样，能够转向任何方向，并被允许刺人。条约中用词的破绽与不明确，已经被中国人技术性地利用多次。但我们技巧娴熟的外交官并不在意最后结果如何，他们的目标，只是体面地从位置上退休。中外交涉已经变成一件简单的事情。德国公使会迫使中国

① 1876 年 3 月 25 日，德国公使巴兰德通知总理衙门，要求进行修改条约，并裁厘金。总理衙门的基本方针是若裁厘，则需要增加关税作为补偿，谈判在 1877 年达到高潮，且一直持续到 1880 年，以中德《续修条约》及《续修条约善后章程》签署告终。中德《续修条约》第八款规定对厘金问题另议，洋商的期望自此落空。参见王权《洋货内销与厘金问题（1861—1904 年）》，厦门大学 2008 年硕士学位论文，第 53 ~ 54 页。

② 圣彼得被称为天堂守门人，在《圣经》中，耶稣被围，圣彼得举剑刺伤其中一人，耶稣告诫他，收回他的剑，持剑的，必死在剑下。

政府做出一些让步，中国政府会以最开明的精神接纳这一立场，并且同意在某一特定的时候继续交涉。与此同时，中国政府很愿意增加障碍，这样一来就会有更大的能力让步，还能够因为有预谋地装作勉强同意的样子，而受到西方赞誉。这就像对彬彬有礼的裁缝所玩的一个老把戏。A 君欠了旧账，这位裁缝催促他快点还钱。A 君很情愿地答应了，约定了一个他能够还得起部分欠账的时间。与此同时，他想要买衣服，所以就找到了这个裁缝，订了几件新衣服。当要付款的时候，他只付了新做衣服一半的钱，但也算还了一部分钱。A 君很明显做好了两件事。以半价买到了衣服，同时他愿意答应裁缝的要求，以暂时减轻还钱的压力。他已经向裁缝履行了诺言，裁缝还能指望什么呢？这明显是裁缝的失误，如果这个裁缝允许 A 君这样出卖自己，任何一个明智的人都不应该批评 A 君。所以中国政府在发现必须要在某些事情上妥协后，马上就做出了新的侵害行为，希望当下一次“付款时限”到来的时候，和蔼可亲的公使先生能不去追究这最后的侵害举动，按照他们的要求，而非原状去处理。

《北华捷报及最高法庭与领事馆杂志》，1877 年 9 月 22 日

温州

现况相当不错，官员们对厘金税率的要求还算温和，并承诺会替代厘金税。在某些个案中，（受害者如果微不足道的话）中国人会强制缴纳厘金。同时因为自开埠以来就对进口商品征税，现在洋商们要求退还厘金的呼声也大量出现。需要重点指出的是，在外国人到这里之前，只有很少的情形下会征收名义上的厘金税，大多数情况下根本就不征收。[①] 所有对征收这种“军用税费”[②] 的热情，以及突然发现有必要征收它，都是在开埠外国人来了之后发生的。然而，当地官员似乎有点害怕——多亏了我们领事的能力——已经收回了所有布告，矫揉造作的章程[③]也被撕毁，现如今他们只是满足于发布空泛的税则。不管是通过人情还是花钱，我现在都搞不到厘金章程的中文原本了，但毫无疑问，即便是你上次刊登的简译本，也已经让当地官员们战战兢兢，懊悔不已。某天一位洋商卖给本地华商一些货物。在发现购买方属于受压力（需要缴纳厘金）一方的时候，他主动前往当局支付了厘金，并把厘金算到了价格里面。但是官员们焦急地反复告诉他，“他们绝不会从外国人手里攫取一分钱，除非北京授予他们强征厘金的权力”。不过这些官员最终还是从买家身上榨到了这笔钱。

与此同时，没有轮船进入温州。我们也不知道原因何在。这里的中国人说，他们在上海有大量的货物等待运输。今天美国炮舰“宝洛司”号来到这里，带给我们一些外部世界的消息。我们谁都不知道下一次再收到的

---

① 温州厘金局和瓯海关是在同一年成立。

② 厘金税起源于清廷对太平天国用兵时期，起初是一种临时性筹款方法。但此时光绪年间商埠厘金，与同治年间军事性厘金，在性质上已经发生重大变化，不可同日而语。

③ 指《温州厘金章程》。

消息是好是坏。霍乱疫情已经逐步减轻，当地的卫生优势——完美的排水系统和与众不同的洁净程度——让我们希望致命的疾病不会在当地蔓延开来。过去的十天一直都在下雨，本地人说此种令人愉悦的天气一直会持续到月底。我现在有义务，用一位通常的女性口吻结束这封无趣的信件，我会说（这确实是事实），“我们没有什么新闻，太乏味了”。所以为了下次能交好运，我现在要给自己署名 SPES。

《北华捷报及最高法庭与领事馆杂志》，1877 年 10 月 4 日

温州

很不幸，这里出现了霍乱，当地人中出现霍乱流行已被确认。每天的死亡人数为 35 人，但是据说在稳定地降低。令人开心的是，没有外国人感染霍乱，我们的领事还是一如既往地能干，他要求道台发布通告，呼吁民众遵循霍必澜①先生建议的卫生准则。明天将会举办巡行禳疫活动，官员们都希望能尽快带来好的效果。中国人一旦感染霍乱，除少数人会接受针灸治疗外，其他人几乎什么都不做，因此死亡率极高，几乎每个感染者都会死亡。通过以上描述，我并不认为这是最恶性的霍乱类型，我情不自禁地相信，如果进行治疗的话，定会明显增加康复人数。

谈到厘金，官员们陷入极度的不安之中。现在他们把布匹的税率降到了每匹 96 个铜钱，但即便如此也没人缴纳厘金税。鸦片名义上每担收取 40 两白银，现在也减少到 32 两，但是，唉！人们的愤怒并未平息。“这种税率太高了，史无前例，简直是勒索，为什么外国人来贸易我们就要被额外征税，又不是我们把外国人带来的！”这是当地商人对收税者的回复，同时官员们似乎也没有能力强制执行厘金征收政策。某天一名洋商想要运一些货去内地，他把货从仓库运到海关等待检查，一位自称厘金局官员的人在路上拦下了搬运的苦力，要求缴纳厘金。苦力们没有答应，并且告诉这位自封的官员起运货物的原因与目的地，这位官员随后鞭打了苦力，苦力们甩下货物回去找货主。货主立刻转回去追人，并抓住了这个冒失鬼。

---

① 霍必澜（Pelham Laird Warren，1845—1923），英国领事官。1867 年到中国，1877 年担任驻温州副领事官职务。初为英国驻华使馆翻译学生，历任英国驻温州代理副领事、驻台湾代理领事、驻台湾领事、驻汉口领事、驻汉口总领事等职。1900 年任英国驻沪代理总领事。1901 年 7 月至 1910 年底，任英国驻沪总领事。参见熊月之编《上海名人名事名物大观》，上海人民出版社，2005，第 302 页。

因为他无法准确地自证身份，就被扣押了起来，直到联系上厘金局。这是发生在大约上午9点的事，下午6点发现此人和厘金局还真有点关系，但厘金局的人不愿意认他。此人最终还是被释放。这名外国人发出了所有货物，并在货物上贴上纸条，标明了货主身份与发送地址。他告诉厘金官吏，如果拦下他的货物，他现在无法阻止，也会把货物留给他们，直到可以在别的地方采取措施保护自己，到那时，他会死咬厘金局要为扣留货物或其他行为所造成的损失负责。迄今为止厘金局的官吏并未采取任何措施，尽管人们看到一些官吏一手拿着雨伞，一手拿着利剑，但他们一看到外国人就匆匆离开了——我一直在查看4月份到6月份的海关贸易统计，我们这个口岸表现得不赖。与芜湖相比，尽管温州在交通条件上不利，但在布匹贸易方面却领先。虽然有一些卸货的过路轮船，但对温州来说，想要进行托运的货主必须要有耐心，等待机会出现。①

另一方面，过去的分析似乎已经得到证实，一个新的原色洋布（Shirtings）② 与洋标布（T－Cloths）市场已经形成。并且不像过去所预测的那样，温州并不仅仅只是宁波贸易的中转站。在贸易方面我们已经竭尽所能，但局面仍不受我们控制。在4月至6月的季度贸易报告中，我们注意到温州共进口了原色洋布和洋标布60705匹。去年宁波同季度进口了298553匹，今年同季度进口了306849匹，仅增长8296匹。我们有理由相信，在6月份之后的短暂时间内，如果一切畅通无阻，人们就会发现这种有利的前景以及不错的状况会变得越来越令人满意，但是现在，温州的厘金税毁掉了这一切。③ 这种厘金税在我们到来之前从未被征收过。

大雨连绵不断。我们担心“宝洛司”号会带回唱衰温州的消息。但请

---

① 这里是指温州在1877年货船运力不足，1877年温州开埠的9个月内，仅有23艘船只进港。参见杭州海关译编《近代浙江通商口岸经济社会概况》，浙江人民出版社，2002，第467页。

② 这里原文“Shirtings”指的是洋布，但根据上下文，作者实际说的应是“原色洋布”（Shirtings，Grey）。1877年温州原色洋布的进口量为34450匹，洋标布为41273匹。参见赵肖为译编《近代温州社会经济发展概况：瓯海关贸易报告与十年报告译编》，上海三联书店，2014，第80页。

③ 根据前文内容，温州在4月至6月共进口原色洋布和洋标布60705匹，而厘金局建立后，7月至12月仅进口15018匹。

记住，这是一个“最不寻常的年份”，为了让局面好转，我们全都生活在充满希望（Pes）[1] 的乐观状态中。

过去八天里，我们这里的天气非常糟糕。一天接着一天下雨，由于现在天气变冷，我担心尚未成熟的稻谷将要遭灾。

狩猎的季节到了，但是目前我们的猎人只捕捉到一些鹬。据说这个季节在下游锚地会有许多猎物，比如野鹅、野鸭、野鸡和鹿，甚至还有野猪。

一些外国居民住在城里，离海关很远。在中国城市的街道上行走是一件让人很不愉快和无聊的事情，尤其是在下雨天或坏天气。这里的轿夫很笨，一名外国人从上海订购了一辆人力车，但苦力却不知道如何拉车。我们社区的另一位成员想到了一个主意，即用驴来拉人力车。我很确定，你们这份日报的许多读者想象着这样一辆车，都会感到好笑，但是我可以向你保证，这是一种十分舒适的交通工具，并且我建议上海以及其他地方有人力车的人都雇用驴子而不是苦力，因为驴子毫无疑问要比苦力有许多优势。

美国炮舰“宝洛司”号于 14 日从上海到达温州，20 日将前往宁波。自从“欧罗巴”号[2]于 2 日离开温州去福州之后，我们没有见过除“宝洛司”号之外的任何一艘欧洲船。但我希望，一旦北方口岸冰封之后，我们这里能够经常有轮船来访，或许一个月可以来两次。(9 月 18 日)

---

① 文章作者在此通过谐音的方式署名，算是一个小把戏。

② 属于英国怡和洋行。

《北华捷报及最高法庭与领事馆杂志》，1877 年 10 月 11 日

温州

官员们发现，在评估支付的厘金税时，从总的匹数、包数和市斤数等中扣除 40% 的计税方法很方便。这样税收又基本回到了旧的税率。商人似乎有些赞成，有谣传说订单会像之前一样发往上海，贸易也将继续。正如加尔文主义者（Calvinists）① 说的那样，“上帝赐予的可能就是这样，所有的反对意见都将万劫不复”。厘金局局长已经被召回，但这到底是屈服还是更大的反击，现在还说不清。感谢德国和其他国家的努力，虽然厘金很可能注定要被征收，但我猜想人们必将拼死反抗。

霍乱并没有持续很长时间，现在已经完全消失。最多的时候，有一天死了 35 个人，这种高峰仅持续了两天。如果采取任何治疗方法，我想我们的死亡人数会减少很多。

“征服”号离开了我们，而且发誓说三个月内都不会回来。我希望这只是夸张的说法，因为瓯柑在未来 3~4 周就会准备好出货，那时轮船运费应该不错。但轮船必须在温州才行，这样才能从老式民船手上分一杯羹。我们听说各方都希望有轮船能来温州运输水果。自从厘金税开始征收以来，所有商品（比如藤条、枣等）都是通过民船从上海与宁波运来，因为这种做法可以逃税或者减税。似乎与外国人接触是征收厘金的主要理由，只要你避免和外国人接触，就不会被征收厘金。如果中国的外交官想到或者相信过往的条约，就会预测到这样的局面必将引起反弹。

---

① 基督教新教教派，16 世纪宗教改革运动时由加尔文倡导，故名。以其所著《基督教原理》为神学基础。有些主张沿袭路德派神学，有些则为它所特有。主张始祖亚当堕落犯罪后整个人类的本性全都败坏，故人们自己毫无办法自救，谁将得到救赎、谁将永远沉沦，早由上帝“预定”。参见任继愈主编《宗教大辞典》，上海辞书出版社，1998，第 360 页。

无论如何，温州是相当重要的茶叶口岸，我们心存自信的期望，下个季节好的茶叶会运到这里，要么用于出售，要么运往上海。茶农愿意以货易货，用茶叶换取布匹和鸦片，这些洋货都将有子口税票，茶叶也是，这样就不会被厘金局骚扰。据说外国人的到来很可能会刺激邻近地区的茶叶种植。让我们拭目以待吧。

撤销定期航班很不适宜，并且影响了贸易的恢复，而这种贸易正是这艘船逐渐建立起来的。但如果能够立刻带来收益，即便未来有风险，也别指望商人会疯癫到放过赚钱的机会。即便没有这些诱惑，但哪个商人又不是干劲儿十足呢？我坚定地认为，有一艘轮船会来到这里将水果运出去。

和之前一样，温州的新闻都很无趣，我感到很是不安，期望将来会更好，像往常一样署上我的名字。

Spes.

（10 月 4 日）

《北华捷报及最高法庭与领事馆杂志》，1877 年 10 月 25 日

温州

最末一次新闻后，目前唯一有价值的新闻是，茶叶厘金最后定在每箱 25 两，比海关子口半税要少。这当然会导致内地税收直接流入温州当局的口袋，脱离帝国财政①的控制。

我之所以说“最末”，是因为你想不到，为了获得想要的信息，我们得做多少工作，托多少人情。道台一直在生病，很明显已经不再适任，有传言说他很快要离职。好吧，即便来一个喜欢公开使绊子的，也比现在的道台好。即便他充满敌意，起码我们能看出来。本地茶商似乎在迫切地关注着我们的口岸，毫无疑问，只要有些资本，就可以在温州买到最好的“福州”茶，且至少在茶市之初，温州茶叶价格要低于市场价格。无论如何，都会有可观的茶叶运到这里，然后运往上海，甚至是福州。闽北茶叶在经陆路运往福州的过程中，要经过许多厘卡，但闽北茶叶运往浙江就不会存在这样的情况，因为一般都是通过海路运输。

除此之外我还要告诉你一件事，我敢说你听到一定会很高兴，闽浙两省当局目前正因为互相猜忌而进行斗争。从前福州是本区域内唯一的口岸与市场，福建因此调高了对浙江省的茶叶税。现在机会来了，浙江当局正在鼓励福建货物出省，走私运往温州。

温州的航运条件要优于福州，本地锚地广阔，能直通海上。即便是低潮时，水也够深，另外城市周围河网、运河密布，周边地区能轻易地直达温州城。

当然福州的既得利益问题可能在早期阶段，还是会对温州造成一定威胁，但凭借温州贸易的便利性，困难终将被克服。

---

① 这里指地方厘金侵夺中央财政。

我们的运动员们已经准备好了，希望能在冬季结束前呈上丰硕的成绩单。瓯柑已经成熟，我坚信这足够吸引轮船过来运输。

我期待着轮船的到来，期待着茶市①节日的到来，我仍然署上我的名字。

Spes.

（10月18日）

① 根据前文和读音，这里的“*Cha - ze*”可能是“茶市”的音译，但也无法完全确定。

《北华捷报及最高法庭与领事馆杂志》，1877 年 11 月 29 日

温州

我现在如同被拘禁的苦役囚犯，只能定期向外写信。作为囚犯来说，这里的日常生活还不赖，因为某些地理原因，① 我们如同被强制实施单独监禁，只不过监狱要大一些，好心的本顿维尔监狱②守卫肯定认为我们不需要这么大的活动空间。考虑到此种隔离完全是因为疏漏所造成的官方罪行，我们无须为此负责。我们可以确定的是，因为英国军舰“麻鹬”号到温州时没有带来任何信件，更不要说报纸了，无疑加重了我们的孤立之感。我们被告知，它出发前按时做了通告，但并没有看到邮政通告，因此也就没有寄送邮件。当然我们知道，因为人类所固有的善良，以及对遭受苦难的人道同情，让我们有权利期望这则消息能传达给相关邮政机构。我们当然还会记得，“麻鹬”号离开上海的那一天非同寻常，因为马会③即将开始，狩猎活动④也准备就绪。我们仍然情不自禁地希望，当人们知道我们是多么依赖担任职位的那些人给予我们帮助时，借助基督教徒的仁慈，他们可以抽出一点儿时间，为温州居民做出一个善意的、可以为他们带来不少欢乐的举动。在六周无聊的日子里，我们没有看过上海报纸，并且只

---

① 作者可能生活在江心屿上的英国领事馆附近。

② 英国一座著名监狱，位于伦敦，建于 1842 年。监禁准备流放的罪犯，同时是推行单人监禁制的模范监狱，许多新监狱都是仿照它的模式建立起来的。参见孙膺杰、吴振兴主编《刑事法学大辞典》，延边大学出版社，1989，第 172 页。

③ 1877 年上海秋季马会开始于 11 月 2 日。参见《赛马定期》，《申报》1877 年 11 月 1 日第 4 版。

④ “up - country trips”直译为“乡村之旅”，专指外国人在华的狩猎活动，为特殊用法。例如 1877 年 1 月的一场狩猎活动，在 13 天内共捕获猎物 1030 头，其中包括 851 只野鸡、64 头鹿、105 只鸭、9 只野兔和 1 只丘鹬。参见 *The North - China Daily News*，15 January 1877，3。

收到一封邮件。每个月的第二个星期六，我们都会派出信使，并约好回程的时间——但是，天啊！他们并没有带回任何信件。这就像拔示巴给大卫王生孩子一样①，只有我们可以找你，你却不会来找我们。引用一句讣告中的话，“朋友会友善地接受这点讽刺”。大约每个星期五，都会有一个特别信使从宁波抵达温州，但信件地址仍是填的海关以前的旧地址，请邮局②注意。

特别的事情就讲这么多，我们现在来说说一般的事情，这些事情可能更有趣。最近发生了一件让我们感到很受刺激的事情，一个中国佬③被公开地威胁和恐吓，他在之前卖了一些木材给洋行，并准备用外国船运输。说来精彩！这笔交易最后被告发，而告发者就是这名卖家自己，他因为害怕把木材卖给洋行，现在已经带着老婆和财产跑路了。首先我必须告诉你，这里的许多官员本身就拥有民船、店铺，一般也会直接参与贸易，或在其中参股。我举两个例子。镇台④自己就拥有一艘大帆船，在城里还有许多店铺。与此类似，一位温州府同知⑤也参与经商。接下来造成的结果是——出现了一种呼声，如果允许洋人购买木材等货物，并用外国商船运输，那么中国民船贸易必将被摧毁，这些显要也会受到波及。因此当上面提到的交易刚刚达成，木材只运了一部分时，一名心胸狭隘的官员来到卖主家里，威胁他如果再敢卖给洋人一根木头，或是与洋人有任何贸易往来，就要把他关进号子甚至杀头。我还要提一句，这批货的厘金已经按时缴纳，但却被官员无视。

---

① 拔示巴是大卫王最宠爱的妻子，两人的一个孩子病重，起先大卫王很是伤心，每天吃斋。孩子死后，大卫王立刻收起悲戚，人们奇怪地问其缘故，大卫王回答：“如今他死了，我干嘛还吃斋呢？难道能让他还魂吗？我能去找他，他却不会来找我了。”参见柯西多夫斯基著《圣经故事》，刁传基、顾蕴璞译，天津人民出版社，1998，第179页。

② 可能是“Letter Post Office”的缩写，但也不敢完全肯定。

③ 原文为“Chinaman”，是带有种族歧视意味的用法。

④ 镇台即总兵，此时镇台为温州镇总兵吴鸿源。一般地方上海盗、匪徒、走私事务，都是由温处道道台与温州镇总兵协同办理，因此总兵也容易借此营私。

⑤ 原文“Sub - Prefects”，意为知府的副手，应为温州府同知，但不知道这里明确指的是哪位。

归根结底我们要感激温州，让我们这么快就明确地见识到，中国人执行与解释《烟台条约》的真实想法。我们看到他们大胆地把厘金局建在海关旁边。我们发现所有货物，无论是落地销售还是转口销售，只要一上岸就会被收取史无前例的税费。然后，如果货物继续往内地运，就还要再缴一次类似的税。也就是说，第一次缴的税仅仅是一种额外进口税，其税负额甚至要超过合法的海关税。随后按照商品运输的远近，你还要再缴一次税，其总额与海关子口半税相当。因此，在货物到达农村的消费者手中之前，这些货物必定已经缴纳了两种进口税和一种运输税。① 海关和毗邻的厘金局都在唯一的码头上，就在北门②外，因此这种额外进口税就可以并且很容易与海关同时征收。毫无疑问，外国人的竞争已经让官商们③有所警觉。鉴于此种局面，我们唯一能够倚仗的，就是我们非凡的才干与勇气。在“征服”号被“驱走”之后，中国船主们无不得意扬扬。我相信关于厘金包税的约定已经达成。中国人倾向于使用这种操弄的手段，这样一来，包税商或名义包税商④几乎不用缴税，而外国人以及这些垄断者的敌人，必须全额缴纳公布的厘金税。温州包税的经营，是否会像宁波那样成功，尚有待观察。我甚至认为，鉴于外国人的某些影响力与经验，我们也许能幸运地进行反击，如果洋商们能发愤图强，温州包税的这种尝试（如果他们真敢这么干的话），从长远看来就会被挫败。然而官吏因为商业利益所在，必定会排斥外国人，这会增加他们要弄老把戏的诱惑力，同时还导致华商仅用最少的钱就拿到了包税权。当然，《烟台条约》应该被批准，任何抵抗都不会有效。想要留下的人，必须试着在这个“限制区”（我拒绝使用“租界”这个现代词语，我更喜欢这个老词）里尽可能让自己开心，因为他们将会在这里被幽禁，同时外面包围着无数厘金征税员，在英国女王的保护下展开狂欢。征税员们发现很容易开展工作，甚至比条约签订前还要容易。此种局面，天朝的胜利者可以凭借其出色的“外交手腕”

---

① 意思是货物被海关征一次税，又被厘金局征了两次税。

② 即望江门。

③ 这里指的是包税商。

④ 原文为“nominally purchase the right”，指“名义购买包税权利的人”，这里指的起初可能不是包税人，后来又加入包税公会，享受其垄断资源的商人，暂将其译为“名义包税商”。

而收获荣耀，他们将可怕的暴行，蒙上谦恭与真诚的外衣，这是一场排外主义的胜利，即便是最辉煌的战役也鲜有如此成果。过去因为我们在广州与天津的军事胜利，他们无法获得的，现在他们都拿到了。

因为抚台①要来温州，城市和郊区的大部分劳力都不得不换上军装。②从前我们把海军事务长称为“寡妇制造者”，看起来这种事情还在延续。当然，这些理想的战士必须承担这位大人停留期间的所有力役。你可以看见到处都是穿制服的人，他们在田野里穿行，搬运着货物，干着各式工作。这群人在一天当中的某个时段，需要前去听差，任务完成后，他们就可以各自去干自己的副业。顺便说一句，厘金作为一种紧要的军事税，就是要支付给那些当官的“寡妇制造者”。如果有善良的中国佬问官员为什么要征收厘金，官员定会自信满满地回复他：“这样做是为了巩固国家的军事地位，同时更多的证据表明，厘金的征收还远远不够。”

在与中国的外交中存在着许多明显不正常的事情，这不是件小事。中国处理与他国的外交，存在着大量的不道德特质。从北京的角度看，不仅要针对敌人，而且手段的卑劣程度，要与敌人的强大成正比。因此外交官必须花费大量时间去玩弄手段，以隐蔽欺诈与虚假。但中国这种欺骗的待人方式实际上相当滑稽，同样是这件事情，如果是各列强来做就会不同，列强会干得尽可能不露痕迹。

在过去数周，所有大型漕船都被强征到温州，以防抚台出其不意地到达，需要船只提供服务。这当然是件苦差，不高兴的船主挣不到什么钱，即使赚到的话也很少。

好像我们没有受到足够的折磨，我们的小社区又遭受到沉重一击，好博逊先生被从温州调到了打狗③。如果上天能赐福给我们，希望能派两名主官④到这个口岸来打开局面——他们必须要有才干，并且普遍受人爱戴。如果不是为了表达对好博逊的不舍之情，我们原本不应该臧否人物。后继者才最有资格，为两位官员所表现出来的谨慎、先见之明与坚定送上赞

① 抚台即巡抚，此时浙江巡抚是梅启照。

② 这里指的是“汛兵”，即绿营兵。

③ 今台湾高雄。

④ 指瓯海关税务司与英国驻温州领事。

誉。在温州开埠时，他们安排与详定了无数细节，充分体现了他们的责任感。我能够肯定的是，好博逊先生的名字，将一如既往地刻在这座口岸的深情回忆里。我确信我所写的，就是我所有同胞的心愿，以他们的名义，我祝愿前任能干、和蔼和受欢迎的税务司幸福长寿。

在向好博逊先生告别时，我们并未忘记迎接他的继任者①。这个继任者在中国生活并且服务了很长时间，而他的这种经历对他本身和这个口岸来说都大有裨益，所以他从现在开始会关注自己和这个口岸的命运。

你肯定会说：这封信中既有怒吼和中国人的邪恶，又充满哀悼之情，这就是一封灰心丧气的信。但物极必反，尽管磨坊转得慢，我们还是相信它磨出的东西，会超过预期。我天生的性格就是给人以安慰，我还是会继续相信（并且希望你也相信），我们所有人在中国的前景依旧充满希望。

——Spes.

---

① 继任者是马吉（J. Mackey），1877 年 11 月 8 日 ~1881 年 12 月 11 日在任。

《北华捷报及最高法庭与领事馆杂志》，1878 年 1 月 10 日

温州

在经历持续的温暖天气，以及大量降雨之后，冬天的寒冷终于占据上风，现在烤火变成了一件奢侈的事情。最近没有什么大事要说，上次我在信中提到的“木材案”，因为当地官员不愿意妥协，目前已经被提交给驻上海的德国领事，他现在可能会考虑采取进一步行动的必要性。

这里可能要提一下，温州政府已经尝试去寻找那名当地证人，甚至准备派出一队警察把他从避难的洋行中带出来。但洋商拒绝交出这名华商，并引用条约规定，要求出示授权令，警察只能撤退。我知道温州政府已经着手对这名不幸的华商展开反诉。据说罪名共有 7 条。通过相同的人，我们打听得知，现在的起诉包括与木材案无关的罪名，也与洋人无关。但我们有充分的理由相信，第一项罪名是指控他卖木材给洋人后，企图代买主走私。但这项指控很难成立，因为洋人没有缴纳厘金税的义务。我倾向于认为，尽管有相反的主张，但经过考虑后起诉书可能还是会指向与洋人的关系方面。

然而那名华商仍然待在洋行，如果对他还有第三次威胁，我强烈建议他继续待在洋行。

前几天发生了一件同样的事情，尽管不那么肯定。厘金官员去了这座城市的一个本地商人的商店，并且检查了他的账簿，发现他从一个外国人那里购买了洋货。他们暗中伺伏，发现这些货物是从外国人那里获得的，很有可能避开了厘金官员的警惕，因此对本地商人收取了非常重的罚款。

此事在中国商人圈子里引发了一场小骚动，他们开始认真讨论成立公会的事。商人们显然已经注意到，与洋人的直接往来，已经引发了温州官员的不满，并且已经开始整治某些参与对外贸易的个人。大多数时候“团结就是力量”，因此组成公会将更有效地抵制强权，远远好于单打独斗。

华商们并不会公开表态反对政府，以避免造成进一步的刺激，可能在一年之内，他们就会打着包税的名义组织公会，这样就可以在华商与厘金局之间达成协议。虽然不大可能调整税率，但却可以调和各方利益，甚至缓和某些偏见。我们立即与这些中国人取得了紧密联系，中英烟台会议提交给德比勋爵①一份备忘录，德比勋爵在政治上支持《烟台条约》的签订。英国反鸦片联盟的秘书②也给报纸写信。这两份文件罕见地指责了我们，事实上我们几乎没有得到任何支持。

我不想暗示任何受人尊敬与人格高尚的条约签订者，说他们不了解文件的实际情况，或去传播这些错误的印象。但必须要承认的是，备忘录与报纸信件这两件事确实可受指摘，我认为真相遭到了隐瞒。这份备忘录的主要观点在于，主张中国对洋货征收的税是合理的，其税额不超过其他国家，或与其他国家相等。从备注的主旨看，海关税将成为基本税收，而在鸦片问题上，厘金问题仍将留待讨论。这样的结果，会导致中国提出同时收取两种税的要求。

海关税从整体上讲，我想现在不会有人说不合理。待在中国的大多数人都会承认，与任何机构相比，中国海关组织体系近乎完美，税收也十分公正。但同时，我衷心希望海关子口半税——按照条约规定——仅仅通过同一机构征收。③ 我在中国温州写这封信，没有必要再去指出这里的“厘金”有多么不同寻常，其目标与结果是多么地不相符合，围绕厘金征收的腐败有多严重，当与几乎完美的海关系统相比时，厘金局的下面掩藏着如此之多的罪恶，以至于外国人不得不大声疾呼。海关的管理，不仅人格无可指摘，且充满睿智，切实地增加了税收，某种程度上也有利于国家；反观厘金局，是由一批欺诈犯与专门营私的人在管理，这是一群最下流的狡诈与偏执之徒，因此虽然增加的收入不多，却对广大公众造成沉重负担。

---

① 德比十五世勋爵，即爱德华·亨利·斯坦利（Edward Henry Stanley），1848 年入选英国下议院，1866～1868 年和 1874～1878 年，两次担任英国外交大臣职务。

② 英国反鸦片联盟的秘书是杜纳（Frederick Storrs Turner），他反对英国在印度和中国的鸦片倾销与售卖政策，1876 年出版了《英国在印度与中国的鸦片政策及其后果》（*British Opium Policy and Its Results to India and China*）。

③ 作者在这里表达的意思是，希望内地运输税仅仅通过海关征收。政出一门，裁厘入关，这也是海关总税务司赫德的主张。

遇事多想想积极的一面总是好事，但由于我们处在中国，知道事情的真实情况，这个格言就不能成立，相反很可能会对不知情者造成误导。谁能说出厘金的税率，或者是厘金的税收上限？我们知道在某些地方，在某些官员手上，厘金是按价的 7% 到 10% 征收。但我们也知道，由于没有对征收额度进行限制，可能会有人在里面上下其手或大发淫威。我们也意识到所有这些情况，取决于中国征税人的意愿与能力，也取决于我们的履约人在备忘录中或反鸦片联盟秘书所表现出的确凿无疑的无知。引用任何公布的关税都是荒谬的，因为厘金征收往往胆大包天，征税人会在权力的允许范围内，根据缴税人是谁，任意增加或减少税额。最后会挑选一批商人组成一个公会来保证厘金征收，这个包税公会的力量虽然不足以减轻官府对个体的盘剥，但却能带来他们更想要的结果，即不是“圈子”里的人会灾难性地遭到排挤。在正式成立法院之前，外国人任何的抗议与行动同样荒谬无用。假设在极少数情况下，就像最近在温州遇到的那样，你碰巧遇到一个本地人愿意牺牲他未来的前程，甚至愿意牺牲他的生命来帮外国人打官司——但中国众所周知的共谋、伪证和收买还是会使事情变得复杂化，你不能和他们讲什么法律形式，否则只会徒增烦恼。在中国当原告太难了。如果一个人坏到骨子里（这样相对较小的一部分人可能会毫不犹豫地采取利益交换的手段），那么我们很容易就能发现他的犯罪事实。但对于广大中国人，包括内陆地区来说，你想要揭发一个中国本地人的罪恶几乎不可能，更不用说他背后还有保护伞。中西之间两套司法调查体系完全相反，并且基于相反的根基，任何企图将这两套系统进行联合，或者换个技术术语进行混合的努力，都是不切实际的。① 在谎言被证实之前，总是假设那不是假话。在罪恶还没来得及实现之前，总是假设对方清白无辜。这种病态的绥靖只会适得其反，也只是在为另一种形式的腐败提供平台。

当指责外国人对中国人太过苛刻时，这实际是在老调重弹，而没有考

---

① 《烟台条约》第二端第三节规定，“至中国各口审断交涉案件，两国法律既有不同，只能视被告者为何国之人，即赴何国官员处控告；原告为何国之人，其本国官员只可赴承审官员处观审。倘观审之员以为办理未妥，可以逐细辩论，庶保各无向隅，各按本国法律审断”。参见褚德新、梁德主编《中外约章汇要（1689—1949）》，黑龙江人民出版社，1991，第 201 页。

虑现实中这种假设是否成立。老家那些善良的乡亲们，他们是真正拥有英国式仁慈和基督教感情的人，他们不仅将这种善良施惠于自己的同胞，而且还扩展至异教徒和野蛮人。只要逮住机会，他们总是对贬低自己的国家充满热情。但却忽视了关于中国本地人的一种事实，即中国本地人在道德上和政治上，实际存在着两种不同的阶级——一种是官吏阶级，另一种是被统治阶级。目前区别对待这两者很重要，特别是在英国获得的关于中国人的大部分公开信息都来自民间。我想任何一个公正的人都不会否认，后者有许多杰出的品质，且没有沾染明显的恶习。我这里指的当然是中国民间彼此的关系。因为他们的统治者在对待外国人的问题上，不断对民间进行欺骗与煽动，中国民间有时对我们的观察有所偏颇，因此引用他们的话并不公平。在读到那本有趣的小书《中国和中国人》① 时，其中有一句话令我印象很深，作者观察到中国人皈依时，并不会有负罪感，“他们不觉得与我们一样是同样的罪人，只因为他们生来不是罪人”。虽然目前还没有人对牧师的这句话进行评论，但它符合我对中国人整体道德观的认识，这与西方形成了鲜明对比。在中国人的社会里，恶性犯罪并不常见，盗案也不多，且他们相互之间展现出的仁慈无疑令人瞩目。但他们不会以我们的方式看待欺骗，中国人自己却熟稔这套把戏，在面对欺骗时，他们能避开恶果或减少损失。我们只有在很少的情况下才会去撒谎，并能理解这些善意的谎言，比如当听到表兄弟有孩子出生时装作很高兴，比如在听到祖母死亡时表达悲痛，比如我们会在贸易中善意地向买方让利等等。我们知道所有这一切的表演，都存在着一定的意义。但中国人进行类似表演的范围却要大很多。事实上在大多数情况下，他们会因为礼貌和权宜，说话模棱两可。但中国人也有自己的荣誉观，而且还很强烈。例如在达成协议后，即便只是口头协议，据我所知中国佬也很少会赖账，此外还可以在日益衰退的天朝人身上挖掘出其他许多闪光点。中国人温顺、好客，在没有遭受官府挑拨和欺骗时，善良且慷慨。他们不会手持大口径火枪，戴着猪鬃，烧死或踢死我们的妻子。如果中国老百姓是这样的，那中国的官员又

① 作者是倪维思（John Livingston Nevius），美国长老会牧师，本书于1869年出版。参见John Livingston Nevius, *China and the Chinese: A General Description of the Country and Its Inhabitants*, New York: Harper & Brothers, 1869。

如何呢？一切其他国家、一切统治阶级有或没有的恶习，似乎都集中在了中国的统治阶级和官吏身上。他们存在的根基，是最丑陋的暴政与毫无约束的狂妄。任何人事都能撼动他们的专制地位，只要有人愿意开始去改善人民的生活条件，或睁眼看世界，腐败的专制立刻就会被终结——一切好的或有益的事物，都是中国统治阶级仇恨的对象，因为这对他们来说是坏的和不利的。有人可能会问，如果中国人民品行端正，那些从中选取的官吏怎会如此糟糕？回答很简单：在成为官吏之前，他们要特别下功夫学习，并证明自己掌握了衙门里邪恶的潜规则，在以后的生活中，官吏会严格遵守这套潜规则。与中国的人民接触后，我们发现他们很迫切并且很高兴与我们交易。我们看到双方的贸易，让外国人访问的邻近地区立刻繁荣起来。但官府很快搅进来捣乱，每一次不幸的事件，每一次和谐交往被中断，都是起因于官府的嫉妒、偏执和傲慢。如果中国民间能够组成一个团体，自由地表达他们对中外交涉规则的意见，我想只要是在中国居住超过一年的人，都不会拒绝接受中国人民的意见。中国人民的利益与我们的利益紧密相连：中国官府对权力的贪婪，对掠夺的渴望，完全站在我们文明的对立面。我们的文明顺应于公众民意，而中国官府的倾向却是摧毁或阻碍这种民意。中国的朝廷被迫与列强打交道，朝廷中也不乏品德高尚之人，或许更为开明，所以我们也许不能像公开批评中华帝国其他地方的官吏那样来批评这些开明大臣。北京进行改良和进步的意愿可能很大，但中央权力明显不足，朝廷必须集中更多权力。这种情况也类似反映在中国长久以来存在的宗藩关系上，由于中国权力的衰落，看起来小公司们日益从大商业集团里独立出去。

关于鸦片问题，我并不认为对鸦片征收的厘金税额会引发多少抗议，这种特定形式的税收似乎没有被人特别注意，或者换个说法，鸦片进口与其他洋货进口的征税没什么两样。目前在中国直接的鸦片贸易，起码在一两个口岸，是被限制的。虽然中国政府目前还没有为打击鸦片贸易给出公正的理由，哪怕是明白无疑的感情用事的理由也没有。如果鸦片贸易能够按照中国人的期望带来大量收益，中国人就会开放国家，但他们也会向我们索要对等的交换条件。我倾向于认为，在短时间内英国贸易总体上会获利，即便是少数受到冲击的人，也会在其他口岸找到同样的机会，来壮大他们的资本和企业。

但印度政府对此最有话语权，我认为他们不会轻率地看待此事。对于支持反对鸦片贸易的言论，印度政府进行了辩护，读到后者的辩护让我非常开心。我不敢相信一个自称品德如此高尚的人，一个担任反鸦片联盟秘书职务的人，竟然不了解中国本地鸦片种植的数量。外国人忽视了在温州所发生的事实，却能够再一次从中得到教育。有些人自以为通过倾听与思考，然后发现，哦！中国的人道主义者和信徒们是希望摆脱鸦片的。你只要一到温州——请你记住，这虽然是一个新口岸，但温州在开埠之前就与宁波有自由的交通联系，而在宁波存在着大量外国鸦片的进口——我们发现本地鸦片种植遍地开花，鸦片田顺着瓯江一直延续到浙东。现在你做何感想？这里种的鸦片特别好，农民极其内行。因此中国鸦片能很顺利地与外国商品进行竞争，迄今为止几乎把外国鸦片挤出市场。本地人说，要不断种植罂粟，直到全省种满为止。秘书长先生一定会很高兴，因为这样宁波才能减少输入害人的白皮土。中国的罂粟种植似乎没有影响到其他作物的种植，罂粟十分美丽，很适合作为一种景观植物种植。现在狡猾的农夫已经看到了罂粟巨大的利润，他们不愿意放过任何一小块土地以种植罂粟。真的有谁会相信中国能够阻止鸦片种植，或愿意阻止这种安眠植物的种植吗？哦，当然不会相信。每个人都知道，长久以来，鸦片种植在名义上都是被禁止的，但这就为地方官吏提供了太多上下其手的机会，他们只会偶尔吹吹风，也乐得小心地睁只眼闭只眼。北京无疑会颁发禁烟告示，地方官吏肯定会张贴这些告示。整个地区的官吏都会为此高兴，他们很明白，这份告示让他们又多了一个进行盘剥的正当理由。如果反鸦片联盟能成功地让外国鸦片退出中国市场，一定会受到中国官吏的感激。如果不让中国百姓、官吏和其他人进行鸦片贸易，就像不让他们抽鸦片一样，他们宁愿选择牺牲，选择抵抗至死。中国中央政府对此完全无能为力，并且永远不会有人真的想要查禁鸦片。这是个无比脆弱的政府，不会去干犯众怒的傻事。

几天以前，德国帆船“长安”号抵达温州，带来了大量邮件。它会在新年那几天离开，同时带走一些海关职员。

《北华捷报及最高法庭与领事馆杂志》，1878 年 1 月 17 日

温州

道台已经严禁温州铜钱出口到其他中国口岸。一名洋商企图用外国船只汇寄铜钱到宁波，按照常规程序，这名洋商前往关栈取货盖章时，道台拒绝发货。我们有理由相信道台阁下反对铜钱出口的做法，是受到了某人给他建议的影响，我们拿到了这封回复给道台的信件，他在信里仅仅简单地认为其他商品的出口，会适应外部需求，且不会干扰本地需求，或导致本地需求的紧缩，但铜钱出口却不是这样，铜钱一旦出口，就再也无法收回（原文如此)，并且无法用其他任何一种方法收回。他对于条约完全嗤之以鼻，似乎在他来看，他提出的理由足以将这些条约弃置一旁。在这个案例中，洋商蒙受了双重损失，船只无法运货，只能用压舱物代替，同时这名商人原本的生意也泡汤了。我们完全能理解这名商人的抗议，他提出的索赔要求也已经受到关注，与以前一样，此事已经被提交到合适的地方处理。

今天这里在下雪，天气并不好。如果将来被问到温州的天气如何，是否总是下雨，我们可以像格陵兰诺的男孩①那样回答“有时也下点雪”。

---

① 源自于《曼兹关于特罗萨克斯、卡特琳湖、罗蒙湖等地袖珍指南》里的一段对话。参见 John Menzies，*Menzies' Pocket Guide to the Trosachs*，*Loch Katrine*，*Loch Lomond*，*Etc*，Edinburgh：Macpherson & Syme，1852，p. 97。

《北华捷报及最高法庭与领事馆杂志》，1878 年 3 月 14 日

温州

我们目前唯一的消息是，在温州市区中心发生了一场大火，许多房屋被烧毁。如果不是因为城内牢房的高墙把火隔开，大火可能会烧毁整个街区。这场大火发生在深夜，天亮时才熄灭。幸运的是，只夺去了一个男人、一个男孩和一个女孩的性命。火灾现场附近，现在贴满了耀眼的红、黄布条，这是附近的居民表达的对上天的感激，赖上天保佑，他们的财产才得以保全。他们相信，上天一定不会让火灾再次发生。(3 月 1 日)

《北华捷报及最高法庭与领事馆杂志》，1878 年 3 月 28 日

温州

现在人们对外国鸦片的需求特别旺盛。因为担心轮船输入鸦片，所以温州已经禁止来自宁波的鸦片进口。结果导致现在温州市面上鸦片缺货，本地存货很少（由于收成不好），鸦片价格因而空前高涨。人们原本对“欧罗巴”号怀有很大期望，愉快地认为它定会带来足够的货物。但结果令人失望，船上没有鸦片。通过鸦片目前如此高的价格，我们可以想象这种日常奢侈品在温州的存货量已经很低，人们现在的烟瘾如此之大，以至于愿意为之付出任何代价。为什么不能从南方运来鸦片呢？帆船每天都会运煤油到温州，这种商品的利润很高，市场需求也大。不久棉花也会运入温州，邻近地区每年都会消费大量棉花。帆船在运输中处于公认的劣势，轮船可以将其挤出贸易。每艘轮船都能增加温州的贸易量。可以得到证明的是，中国人对此心怀恐惧，他们在宁波和福建采取了有力行动，仍旧采用帆船进行运输——“拿骚”号①正在温州外港进行测量。“黑水鸡”② 号于周一离开温州，转往福州。（3 月 23 日）

① 英国测量船。

② 英国炮舰。

《北华捷报及最高法庭与领事馆杂志》，1878 年 4 月 20 日

温州

邮局送来了令人悲痛的消息，领事旗已经降下，这座小港口到处都弥漫着沉重的气氛。对我们其中一些人来说，梅辉立①先生是他们的朋友。对所有的人来说，他是一位有名望的学者，也是一位官员，所有人都尊敬他。现在还不知道，他的逝世对英国外交部和英国臣民会带来什么样的损失，他这个朋友的影响难以估量。他一生在每个部门的工作都近乎完美，这让他最亲近的人的痛苦难于言表。我们谨向为此噩耗难过的人们表达慰问（几乎我们所有的同胞皆在此列），在这种强烈的痛苦中我们感到无能为力。梅辉立在中国留给我们的回忆不会消失，作为负责、忠诚、才干和高贵的榜样，他将指引我们的未来，正如过去他的存在帮助和指引过我们一样。当时间抚平我们今日的悲伤后，留下的将会是安慰，而不是痛苦，而这份安慰对许多人来说将铭刻终生。

我们昨天看到了两则通告，感到非常高兴，通告上说会有两艘轮船从上海和福州驶来本港。毫无疑问，今年本地华商的贸易会更加活跃，即便是最沮丧的人都充满了希望。一些外地华商也赶来温州，他们说想要看看茶叶贸易的机会如何。同时也还有人赶来温州专门瞄准本地茶市场，过去他们曾大量出口温州茶。人们希望出口船只的增加，能够带动茶叶种植。无论如何，宁波与上海商人都认为此事值得关注。鸦片的需求依然很高，土药（不包括洋药）价格涨得很高。目前还没有人从外国进口商那里大量购进鸦片，然后再分销给下一级零售商，但人们认为这种情况不会持续

① 梅辉立（William Frederic Mayers）是英国翻译正使。参见顾廷龙、戴逸主编《李鸿章全集·31·信函三》，安徽教育出版社，2008，第 277 页。

很久。事实上，我们听说有迹象表明，已经有人准备要来做鸦片中间商生意了。

总的来看，前景日益光明。为了迎接贸易的第一缕阳光，我还会签名Spes.。(4月5日)

《北华捷报及最高法庭与领事馆杂志》，1878 年 6 月 15 日

温州

厘金征收，这件去年相当令人棘手的事情，今年已经彻底停止。所有老官吏都被替换掉了，现在的官员认识到，过高的税负只会对他们造成伤害，因为高税率只会进一步刺激走私和逃税。相反，减税政策不仅会有丰厚的回报，而且还能省掉不少麻烦。

就布匹而言，布匹厘金征收已经转变为“包税”，名义上由一个人缴纳一笔固定的钱给官府，据说这个数字是每年 2000 银圆。如果生意不好，下年就会减少这个包税额度；相反，如果生意不错，金额就会提高。从现在的情况看，温州的布匹生意不会太乐观。我说名义是一个人，是因为这笔钱背后实际是由几个人共同凑起来的。

有人试图助成由本地人掌控货物运输，以排挤外国进口商，但这种图谋很快被发现并遭到制止。我们的老道台已经走了，他的继任者（目前还只是署理）① 看起来也不是个善茬儿。他之前同外国人打过一些交道，曾在总理衙门任过职，但却未表现出对外交涉的天赋，当然老道台更加缺乏此种可贵的才能。据我所知，道台虽然被任命，但会在省城一直待到秋天，然后才会到温州上任。我很遗憾地得知，总督②似乎相当偏袒福建，他竟然同意在福建浦城设立一处厘金卡，从浙江运来的鸦片将被课以重税，运出的茶叶同样将被征收重税。这当然会对宁波和温州造成直接的打击，因为有大量的鸦片从宁波运到福建。对于温州来说，应对的方法是，只需要花时间来壮大本地茶叶贸易，以使福州的茶叶市场转移到温州。如果总督的计划实施，毫无疑问在某些地方军队的庇护下，一定会大兴走私

---

① 农历二月初九日，温忠翰补授温处道道台。参见《恭录上谕》，《申报》1878 年 3 月 20 日第 1 版。

② 闵浙总督何璟。

之风。厘金局和其他官吏转过头来会发现，他们的工作将更加困难。我认为福建官吏不太可能从浙江的同僚那里得到帮助，因为从浙江通过的货物越多，对浙江厘金局就越有利。

无论如何，设立厘卡的企图最后一定会失败，需求的压力决定，能提供最大输送能力的商埠，将赢得供应权。过去六个月以来，温州天气的确讨人喜欢——凉爽、干燥又晴朗。今天虽然下了点雨，但因为农民盼着下雨，所以我们也不会抱怨。(6月6日)

《北华捷报及最高法庭与领事馆杂志》，1878 年 7 月 13 日

温州

我们的通讯记者报道，温州在 7 月 1 日和 2 日，由英国驻温州代理领事、道台和从福州派来协助调查的候任知府三人会审，共同对被扣押的帆船进行调查，该船疑似已经失踪很久的“曼打林”号。被告方辩护说，这艘现在扣押的船只并不是“曼打林”号，而是 1875 年从福州赫奇洋行购买的一艘旧木船。随后从福州传唤来赫奇先生做证。在未来一两天内，我们将发布此次案件详情，以及有关证据的详尽报道。

《北华捷报及最高法庭与领事馆杂志》，1878 年 7 月 20 日

温州

“曼打林”号之调查

经过多次不可理解的拖延后，温州终于在 7 月 1 日和 2 日对被扣船只展开调查，这艘船被怀疑就是鸭屁股船①“曼打林”号。法庭由道台阁下、英国代理领事与从福州派来协助调查的候任知府三人组成。

这个案子，至少是按外国法律，以讲求证据的方式进行审判。中国政府的代表是何神启②先生，他是香港人，同时也是理雅各③博士的学生。何先生的英语口语和书写能力很棒，令人惊讶的是，他熟知司法程序最小

① 老闸船（lorcha），民间一般将其称为“鸭屁股船”，也被称为“花屁股船”或“福州运木船”（FooChow Pole - Junk）。关于此种船的详细介绍，可以参看旧海关出版的经典专著《扬子江上的帆船与舢板》。参见 G. R. G. Worcester, *The Junks and Sampans of the Yangtze*, Shanghai: The Statistical Department of the Inspectorate General of Customs, 1947, pp. 139 - 146。

② 何启，原名何神启。广东南海人，字迪之，号沃生。香港皇仁书院毕业。1872 年（同治十一年）留学英国，研习医学、法律。1882 年（光绪八年）回香港，做律师，连任三届议政局议员。1887 年捐款兴办雅丽氏医院，又筹设西医书院。先后发表多篇政治论文，由同学胡礼垣译成中文后编为《新政真诠》出版，宣传变法改良，对孙中山有思想影响。1895 年参与孙中山筹划的广州起义，起草对外宣言。1900 年由香港总督卜力授意，草拟《治平章程》，建议兴中会与两广总督李鸿章合作，支持两广“独立”。1913 年将所办西医书院并入香港大学。参见李华兴主编《近代中国百年史辞典》，浙江人民出版社，1987，第 347 页。

③ 英国伦敦会传教士，汉学家。1839 年受伦敦会派遣到马六甲任英华书院院长，1843 年该院迁至香港改称神学院后继续任院长，在香港从事建立教会和培养传教人员的工作达 30 余年。1876 年任牛津大学中国语言和文学讲座教授，直至去世。曾将中国“四书”“五经”译成英文，起名《中国经典》，于 1861 ~ 1886 年 （转下页注）

的细节，同时展现了被我们所认可的法律辩护风格，并能充满技巧地对我方证人提出质疑，表现出何先生对我们法庭的形式和程序非常了解。

福州方面专门派了一艘炮艇，去接何先生和上次报道提到的赫奇先生来温州。美国领事戴兰那①先生也在船上，但他并未参加这次诉讼，事实上他没有在法庭上露面。

道台决定在福州公会展开这次调查。这次调查是公开的，外国人全程都可以旁听，不过由于天气炎热，室内闷热难耐，如果改在其他地方，关注的人可能会更多。但在这样一个乏味的地方，还是有许多人会抓住任何机会，来调剂单调的生活。

中国人辩称，这艘被扣留的船只并不是“曼打林”号，而是一艘旧木船，是在1874年至1875年间从福州的赫奇洋行购得。因此法庭传唤了赫奇先生来做证，证方指出，赫奇洋行还制造了两扇门和一扇窗户，这些门窗与船只舱内框架相吻合。当时船被售卖后，门窗被从船上拆下来，并存留在福州，以备将来有必要时再拿出来生产。但似乎证据还是不够充分，还需要再找其他证据来决定船的身份。

调查之前被长期拖延，对于那些认定被扣船只就是“曼打林”号的人来说，很是不利。比如作为证人的马因先生，因为要新造或修理船只，已经离开中国去了欧洲，现在我们只能拿到马因先生手写的声明作为证据。在一般情况下，马因先生的这份手写声明已经足以做证。但从赫奇先生提供的证据可以看出，马因先生与赫奇先生提供的证据相互冲突，如果两人能够当面对质，将有助于做出判决。另外，赫奇先生已经适时且正式地向代理领事提交了一份证词或声明，内容相当可靠且慎重。这让原来对赫奇先生船只的指控变得可疑，同时也让当初扣押船只的行为更令人疑虑。赫奇先生现在说，马因先生的声明没有经过深思熟虑，也不可靠，因为这纸声明只是随意手写，没有参考任何卷宗或文件。同时赫奇还指出了马因先生现在的声明与之前的指控之间的差异。

(接上页注③)出版，至今仍被认为是优秀译本。著有《中国人的神鬼观念》《孔子的生平和学说》《孟子的生平和学说》及《中国的宗教：儒教和道教评述及其同基督教的比较》等。参见任继愈主编《宗教大辞典》，上海辞书出版社，1998，第454页。

① 美国驻福州领事。

正如我们所见，支持这艘船就是赫奇洋行旧木船的证据显示，现在这艘船的尺寸和运载能力，非常接近以前赫奇洋行拥有这艘船时的情况。

另一方面证据表明，这艘船很轻，船本身已经很大程度上被截短和改装了，一些其他船的船尾被安装到它身上。同时，纳皮尔船长认出船上有一处严重受损的地方，对此他异常肯定就是"曼打林"号的旧伤，被告方对此也没有做出充分解释。另一方面，赫奇先生非常肯定在船尾刻着一串数字，而数字随后也被找到。

上述内容也许已经足以对大多数问题表明观点，做了如此多的铺垫，我们还是必须要让证据自己说话。

此案最终判决将由北京的中外当局决定，所以在出现最终判决声明之前，我们很难打听到新的消息，也无法通过瓯江里这艘船的扣押、释放情况，来推断案情进展。无论如何，中国政府开始变得公正，愿意在衙门外面的公共建筑里进行审判，开着门欢迎任何人来旁听，这不是个坏兆头。本地人似乎最感兴趣，法庭经常人满为患。

以下是我援引的关于此案的证供。克里斯托弗·施密特宣誓证词：我是美国人，职业是引水人（pilot）。我在长江上受雇干过 2 年船长，又干过 5 年引水。在此期间我对那艘鸭屁股船"曼打林"号和它的船长很熟悉。我第一次认识船长是在 1871 年。我不知道"曼打林"号是在哪里建造的。在 1877 年 5 月 29 日那天，我看到现在被扣的船停在东门下游 4 英里的瓯江河面上。我发现它和"曼打林"号非常像，因此登船去看了看。我发现这艘船被截短了不少，但盥洗台没变，甲板室也几乎相同，只是好像矮了一些，船尾似乎被砍掉了，安上了一个中式方向舵。"曼打林"号是由松木制造，有些中式风格，也有些美式风格。"曼打林"号是长江上唯一此类风格的船只。它的舷墙①特别高，一般甲板以上改船的高度，除非切割超过 3 英尺，否则一般不会动横梁。但我发现甲板上的木材明显遭到过切割。我告诉理船厅长，这艘船看起来非常像"曼打林"号。盥洗室的地板被涂成了铅色。我带了一块木板上岸。地板的其余部分被涂成黑白相间的砖石图案。船舱与我在 1872 年底在"曼打林"号上看到的情况很像，但

---

① 沿着露天甲板边缘装设的围墙，称为舷墙。舷墙的主要作用是减少甲板上浪，保障人员安全和防止甲板上货物及物品滚到舷外。

高度明显变矮了——尺寸大约是一样的。我不知道老“曼打林”号的具体尺寸是多少。

被告律师对施密特的交叉盘问：我是因为马因船长的命令，才会登上“曼打林”号。我不记得上过几次船，但如果“曼打林”号在港内，我每天都会上船。我留意到长江上有许多鸭屁股船，和“曼打林”号很像。“曼打林”号有两个桅杆，我无法肯定扣留的这艘船就是“曼打林”号。我把木板拿给理船厅长看，并不是出于什么特别的原因，只是因为它们涂了外国油漆。

被告律师对施密特的再次交叉盘问：我不敢发誓被扣的这艘船就是“曼打林”号，尽管它的样子变了很多，但确实还是很像。

理查德·亨利·纳皮尔宣誓证词：我是皇家海军的一位舰长，目前指挥英国军舰“拿骚”号。大约是1878年4月12日这天，我应英国代理领事的要求，查看了被扣留在温州的一艘船只，我怀疑她就是“曼打林”号。在这艘船上我看到，相比第一次建造时，许多地方都进行了改装。船尾部分确实改装了。这艘船看起来曾遭受严重撞击，修补得很粗糙。另外船只明显被截短了，右舷处的破损很明显不是专业的造船公司维修造成的。我现在的证词可以被英国军舰“拿骚”号的木工证明，我已经将他带来协助做证。

被告律师对纳皮尔的交叉盘问：我曾长时间受雇于香港的英国海军船厂，对于此种中国式鸭屁股船的专业制造，相当了解。我确信，无论是哪一国的专业维修工都不会维修得那样糟糕，除非是故意的。我没有在福州造船的工作经历。

被告律师对纳皮尔的再次交叉盘问：在我看来，船尾被切掉了，原来那个船尾一定更长，但现在被一个错误的圆形船尾替换掉了。类似的，我看到船头被蒙上了铁皮，这在我看来很不寻常，或许是因为船头裂开或被切开的缘故，我不知道是哪个原因。至于切割的问题，我看到在甲板上方的上层木料顶端或船舷支柱，可能是因为断裂，或是使用锋利工具切割的缘故，已经被截断了。在我看来，这艘船是在原始构造的基础上，进行了改装。这艘船的缺陷如此明显，都让我强烈怀疑它被截短了。此外我还要说，这艘船的吃水量与它的尺寸不符。

约瑟夫·伯内特宣誓证词：我是一位美国公民，在温州担任潮汐观测员的职务。我在1868年到1869年期间接触过“曼打林”号。我第一次在长江上遇见这艘船时，正负责武穴①海关分所的事务。我曾看到这艘船往返许多次。我记不清多少次了，可能是5次，也可能是15次。我经常登船检查它的相关文件，一般都是在它装满货物的时候。我注意到扣押在温州的这艘船和“曼打林”号非常相似。我并不是因为特殊的标记才认出这艘船的，但是从这艘船的大体轮廓、船舱的建造以及地板的油漆来看，我坚定地认为这艘大家谈论的船就是原来那艘“曼打林”号。

法庭接着当场阅读了“曼打林”号船主马因先生的信。马因先生在买了这艘船后，进行过大量改造和重建，因此他对这艘船相当熟悉。马因先生去年来温州就是为了查看这艘遭扣押的嫌疑船只，在检查过后，他写了这封信。目前这封信在理论上令人信服地证明这艘船就是“曼打林”号，马因先生在信上宣称这艘船是他的“合法财产”。现在，何先生宣布将会传唤被告方证人。

托马斯·赫奇受到传唤并宣誓做证：我是福州赫奇洋行的一名商人，是美国公民。我在福州待了大约20年。自从我来到这个地方，我就拥有许多木船。在1875年的春天，我把一艘木船卖给了中国人。我不知道这艘船卖给了谁，是我嘱托船老大阿三（音译）卖出去的。现在带上来的那个人就是我说的船老大。我之前从未见过买主，直到今年才见到。我已经见到了扣押在温州的船。在1866年到1875年期间，我是这艘船的主人，因此我对这艘船很熟悉。现在扣在温州的船，就是我在1875年春天通过蒋阿三（音译）以75银圆卖掉的船。交易完成后，船被适当加高了一点儿，随后装满了木柴，我亲眼看着它顺流而下。但当时船没有现在这么高，我指的是船舷壁被抬高了。我是通过这艘船的外表认出它来的，它和普通的福建木船很像。舱室和我之前那艘旧船仍旧一模一样。右手边是盥洗室。我辨认出来，盥洗台的框架还在。对面是洗手间，洗手间的壁橱已经拆掉了，但是水管的穿孔还在。舱室的顶部是两个威尼斯人像，是用美国松木制造的。前桅杆是同样的圆木，它的顶端被截短了，有焦油涂抹过的痕迹，这是我们当时为了区分船只而做的标记。在靠近船首的位置，有一个方形的硬木，就是通过这个硬木连接上，打上铁钉，以支撑枪支。现在那里还有

① 武穴海关分所在湖北广济，是江汉关分所。

一个孔，但是里面填满了石灰。至于这艘船的舷墙支柱，在卖出的时候，我没能够给出甲板以上的准确尺寸。在舷墙支柱上面是横杆。这些舷墙支柱还在那里。我认出来船首还是一样，有一个和船头尺寸一样的大铁板，在底部位置安放着两片铁用来加固木头。船尾还和原来一样，但是似乎加了一个框架。船上还有福州海关注册编码，表明这个船尾并没有改动，这就表明了这艘船的身份，编号是27。地板涂成了黑色和白色相间的方形或菱形图案。前桅杆仍然使用甲板下面的一个铁把手固定在船上。在这艘船建造完成后，又额外建造了防擦龙骨，以增加它的抗风能力。我还留有两扇门和一扇窗户，这是在把船卖给其他人的时候从上面卸下来的，原本被留在福州，现在它们已经被我带来了，尺寸和船上的空隙是吻合的。这艘船原本是1866年的春天在福州为我建造的。我曾经用它来运输鸦片和金银，有时候也作为一艘游船。我不知道其他还有什么特殊的标记可以辨别。我已经准备好宣誓做出和之前一样的证词。在测量门和窗户的尺寸后，我们发现这些都和我从福州带来的门和窗户十分接近。但其中有一处铰链和凿孔不合。

随后到了午餐时间，暂时休庭。午餐结束后，重新召集相关人等，前往继续查看嫌疑船只，然后返回福州公会。英国代理领事随即向赫奇先生进行交叉盘问，赫奇先生回答：我在福州已经待了20年，对一般的福州木船相当熟悉。我所建造和售出的这艘船是按照福州所建的普通的船只样式建造的，就是一艘普通的福州木船。这艘船是按照我们的订单建造的，我每隔三四天都会去检查建造情况，所以对于这艘船只构造的全部细节都了如指掌。这艘船建于1866年，主要用来运鸦片和金银，有时我也会拿来作娱乐用途。这艘船1866年在海关以木船的名义注册，注册编号是27。这一点我记得很清楚，编号就在船尾。一般编号都是涂在船首，而不是船尾，但为了不破坏船的整体性美感，我们还是把编号涂在了船尾。但这并不是最原始注册的27号船，最早注册的27号船是在1861年建造的，而1865年这一艘是其替代品。我不能肯定最早1861年建造的船只，27号编号是否在船尾。我只注册过一艘木船的号码。① 我在1866年建造的那艘船

① 赫奇的意思是，他有很多艘木船，但只注册过一次，即海关编号27号。但先后有数条船共享这个注册编号。

长度介于58到60英尺之间。我无法确定具体尺寸，我没有做过记录。不过我确信它的长度不会超过60英尺。我只会发誓说它的长度就是介于58到60英尺。那艘船的船宽介于12到14英尺。我无法再确定了，因为这都是我印象中的数字。我要说，船宽更接近12英尺，而不是14英尺。我已经就这艘船的问题向美国领事做了陈述。英国代理领事指出：在他出示的这份陈述中，证人的确说过船的长度是60英尺。赫奇先生回答：我从未做过这样的陈述，我一直说的长度就是介于58到60英尺之间。如果在美国领事馆的我的证词复印件上面说，我估计船的宽度是15英尺，那是不正确的。我从未说过船宽会超过12到14英尺之间，对此我相当确信，因为我主管了这艘船只的建造。我无法准确说出这艘船的吨位。我建造那艘船是用来运输100箱鸦片。我无法给出我拥有的任何一艘船的吨位。我没有办法估算吨位。这艘船完全是雇用去运鸦片的。它几乎可以装满100箱鸦片。我说不出这等于多少吨。如果我在美国领事馆的证词上面说，这艘船只能运送100担，那是不对的。我认为我并没有说过这样的话。它可以运输300担，但是吃水会很深。我从未估计过它的运输能力，因此说不出它能运输多少担。我要说，在粗略的估算之后，你可以放200担在那艘船上。我认为粗略的计算，16担等于1吨。

英国代理领事拿出了一封信件，信件日期为1877年12月24日，由美国领事戴兰那寄给英国领事星察理，经过同意后，这封信在法庭上公开阅读。在这封信中，美国领事戴兰那写到，赫奇先生告诉他，他大约是在1874年的7月份，授权船老大蒋阿三将一艘旧木船卖出去。那艘船大约（正如他们现在讨论的）是60英尺长，船体中部约15英尺宽，可以运输30到50吨的货物。蒋阿三将那艘船以40到60美元①的价格，卖给了一位叫庆德（音译）的舢板船主。买主随后对船进行了改造，按照中式帆船样式，加高了舷墙，随后装满了木材，然后把船开往泉州。在泉州，庆德又以130银圆的价格卖给了一名李姓商人，庆德认为李姓商人把船开到了北方。

赫奇先生被要求解释目前的证词和之前证词的不同，他回答：那可能

① 按照1895年汇率计算，合76.5~114.75墨西哥银圆。参见陈诗启、孙修福《中国近代海关常用词语英汉对照宝典》，中国海关出版社，2002，第691页。

是因为戴兰那先生第一次询问我时，我身边没有参考资料和文件的缘故。在戴兰那先生问我之前，我从没听说过这起事件。至少，我印象中是这样的。戴兰那先生私下给我写信，说他从霍必澜先生那里收到一封短信，信里问到一些问题，问我是否能够提供一些信息。我认为，这是我第一次听说这件事。

法庭接着出示了一份温处道道台写给英国代理领事的信，日期为1877年12月9日，是戴兰那给星察理寄信件的15天前。证人被告知，在这份信件中，有一份他自己所写的详细证词报告，这份报告是在给美国领事的那份陈述报告之前写的，与戴兰那先生的说法吻合。法庭要求证人注意上述事实，这封写于温州的信，比福州戴兰那先生的信要早15天，这才是证人第一次做证。法庭要求证人解释为何前后矛盾，证人无法解释。赫奇先生随后继续陈述：那艘旧的木船是在1875年春天卖出去的，我一直使用那艘船直到1875年。卖掉那艘船之后，我得到75美元。我不知道它是以什么价格卖出去的。我猜蒋阿三得到的比给我的还多。他给了我75美元。我不知道蒋阿三卖的价格是多少，他说他只得到了65银圆。我看到那艘船装满木柴往下游开去了。我看到它被改装，加高了舷墙，船首也更为突出。它当时就停在福州一座桥和海关大楼之间。我走近那艘船，在甲板上看见了施工的痕迹，船被垫高了1.5到2英尺。给我的印象，施工好像是用粗糙的福州木料抬高的。自从那次我见过它后，现在舷墙又被垫高不少。我不清楚新铺的木板是横着铺，还是竖着铺。我的印象是，从船首到船尾都铺上了新木板。我不敢发誓现在的舷墙，就是我那时看到的舷墙，因为当时我只是不经意看了看。按照我的印象，现在的舷墙接近我在福州河看到她时的两倍高。我带到这里来的两扇门，是我卖掉的之前那艘船上的，是我从蒋阿三和这艘船的买主那里得到的。我不清楚在卖掉之后，这艘船的门去了哪里。它们是在我们从福州出发前的一两天，即周一或周二给我们的。甲板上的孔是安放枪支的地方，位于甲板中间偏右的位置。福州木船携带枪支并不常见，但是我们是因为运鸦片和金银才带枪的。船上就那一支枪。我不知道卖船的时候那支枪还在不在船上，但是我知道，铁栓还在，因为我记得在我们卖船的时候把它取了出来。船首下方有一块长铁片——我所有的船都有这块铁片。我不知道其他人的船有没有。我不知道原来那个舷墙的具体高度，我粗略估计，包括舷墙扶手在内大约有6.5英寸。

舷墙是嵌在扶手里面。我印象中就是这样。我确信船尾还是那个船尾——船尾可能修补过，但是形状并没有改变。我确定，船尾没有改动过，我可以向你们展示另一艘船尾几乎完全一样的船。我可以解释船长纳皮尔关于船尾进行过改动的观点，因为他不熟悉福州的中国人建造船只的风格。不过，我并未留意船长纳皮尔说的外观。我不知道是不是在福州建造的船只和中国其他地方不一样，因为我并未去过其他地方。在广州，他们大多是按照外国风格建造船只。如果看到一艘福州船上有一个外表看起来完全不属于它风格的船尾，我一定会非常惊讶。每个口岸都有其各自的造船风格。我确定，房间的地板是涂成了黑白相间的正方形或菱形。地板是在房间的前半部涂成黑色和白色，后半部涂的是铅色的雄孔雀图案。我十分确定是铅色，并且也确定是雄孔雀图案。我记得，我那艘船的前桅杆是使用一个铁箍固定。我认为，大多数的本地船只的桅杆都是用木头固定。我不知道其他的船是否使用铁箍固定。关于蒋阿三，我所记不多。现在蒋阿三不在我的记忆中了。他和我一起来到这里。他并没有在福州被拘禁——他一直都是自由之身。我是在两个星期前看到他的，但是在他登上来温州的轮船前，我并不是经常见到他。我并没有专门和他说过这件事。我曾经问过他把船卖给了谁，这艘船又是怎么来到了温州。当我听说这艘船的编号时，我突然想到我的那艘船就是这个编号。自从我来到温州，在你们问我之前，我一直都没有想起我的船上是否有一个编号，但蒋安三让我记起了这件事。在之前的任何一次调查中我都未提及那艘船有编号。关于那艘船的许多事情我都想不起来了，除非有人使我能够想起来。如果和平常一样，这个编号在船首的话，应该已经抹掉了，因为我在卖掉船的时候，都会将编号抹掉，以防中国人使用这些编号。据我了解，这艘嫌疑船只的编号还在。我不知道那艘船从我手里出去的时候，船尾还有编号。大多数船只都会将中桅削尖，但我们的船是在中桅涂上焦油，以示区别。现在这艘被扣船的中桅好像是被焦油涂过，但我没仔细看。这艘船的所有锁链、船锚和铁缆柱都被移除了。这艘船是由中国水手操纵。船桅被绳索固定住，但当初卖船的时候，绳索都被拆除了。我确定这艘船以前配备有拉线和铁滑栓，但并没有随船一起卖掉。在我印象里，船帆好像随船一起卖了，但我想不起船帆的具体种类。要么是美国钻头牌的帆，要么就是美国渡鸦牌。我想当时船帆应该是随船一起卖了，因为我又为新船买了新帆。装枪支的孔就是一般的穿孔，我说不清是圆形还是方形。我没有注意我带来的门的顶部有一个插销。（门提了上来）我看到确实有一个插销。我看到门不能从空隙里装进去。我只是测量了门和门框的尺寸。

随后法庭休庭，第二天上午10点再次开庭。

法庭上，何神启先生对赫奇先生再次进行交叉盘问，证词如下：为了让我在交叉盘问中的陈述便于大家理解，我希望提一下，我在一个月之前从未向美国领事做过详细的正式陈述或宣誓做证。我之前的陈述都是在私下里不假思索说的，并且没有参考任何资料与文件，只是为了让船夫能够摆脱在“曼打林”号案件中的串通嫌疑。一个月前的那次陈述是正式的，经过了深思熟虑（这份陈述或其副本并未交给英国代理领事，直到现在也没有提供）。证人继续说，在福州还有其他欧洲目击者，他们可以认出我通过蒋阿三卖出去的那艘船。

法庭随后传召亨利·约曼斯先生，他宣誓做证：我是英国臣民，是这个口岸的英国领事馆警察。1877年5月29日，我陪同英国代理领事，与某些中国官员一道，查看了被扣留的怀疑是“曼打林”号的船。登船之后，中国官员逮捕了2名以上与这艘船有干系的人。这艘船有两个桅杆，是一艘中式帆船。主帆是轻质的棉帆布，主桅杆上绕有绳索。关于这艘船有没有前帆，我没有特别注意。我记得主帆的情况，因为当时我拉了几下，想要看看是否有任何痕迹，如制造者的名字。我第二次看到她，船已经被开往海关大楼上游某地，我看到有人正从船上往下运盐。当它在东门外被拖走时，大约1/3的货物是盐。我注意到所有的舱口盖都被拆掉了。我每天或隔天就会去查看这艘船，这样坚持了相当长的一段时间。我在领事的命令下查看此船，船只并没有被移动。在这个过程中，所有松散的零部件不断被拆卸，直到它今天这个样子。昨天我登船时，测量了现在法庭上两扇门的尺寸。法庭上的门的尺寸与船上的门框十分接近，但靠近右舷的门板铰链，比门侧铰链垫要小0.75英寸，左舷侧的门板也有类似情况。我在门顶发现了一个插销，但门框上却没有找到对应的插销孔。我测量了门框前的两根支柱的长度，一根是7.75英寸，另一根是8英寸。支柱的顶端似乎被毁坏或敲击过。

何神启先生对约曼斯先生再次进行交叉盘问，证人回答：我不知道被逮捕的那些人与这艘船有什么关系。我指的是那些当时在船上，随后被中国官员逮捕的人。当天晚上我在领事馆看到了其中一名犯人。我无法给出他的名字。我登船是为了寻找特殊的线索，没有人给我下命令。我这样做完全出于自觉，因为我曾经是来自上海的一名警察，我认为这样做是我的职责所在。我特别注意到主帆，因为它就在舱室的顶部。在另一个场合我又看到了它，那是在当时的理船厅长的陪同下。在那些人遭到逮捕之后，我并未进行全面的搜查。

船长纳皮尔再次受到传唤，并宣誓做证：我注意到甲板上的木板间，有不规则的缝隙，甲板似乎是最近凌乱铺成的，而并不是它最原始的样子。我在甲板上找到一个依稀可见的圆形石灰痕迹，直径大约 0.75 英寸，我认为这就是提到的设置铁栓的地方。这一部分的甲板外观让我感到特别震惊，因为我听说在之前的证词中，在这里有一块方形木头，用来支撑枪架。但在我看来，从前的推测与实际情况并不符，这块甲板充满了石灰，而空洞是在方形木头的一侧，而不是在木头的正中间。

在何神启先生的要求下，赫奇先生再次做证：放置枪支的那块木头长约 3 英尺，宽 8 英寸，和甲板的材料完全不同。在我记忆中，那个孔是在横跨那艘船的中间，更靠近船尾而不是船首。原来的那个孔填满了石灰，所以才造成纳皮尔先生所说的情况。福州的木匠在这艘船上安装了一架山地榴弹炮，与外国船只安装的方式不同。和外国相比，福州木匠在安装这架榴弹炮时手艺很糙。我并不是个实干家，所以我说不出榴弹炮是怎样安装到一艘外国船只上的。

何神启先生要求潮汐测量员伯内特先生到法庭做证：那艘船在海关大楼上游的河岸停泊时，被人扣押了。扣押之后，我注意到它的船尾上有编号 27。我是在它被扣押后几天后看到的。

这就是所有的外国人提供的证据，法庭随后继续传唤中国目击者。道台亲自拿着口供进行盘问，这些口供是出庭以前证人的陈述记录。因为证人给出的口供前后有出入，为了方便起见，下面我们将证词分别列为两栏，这样一眼就能看出其中的差异（如果有差异的话）。

1877 年口供记录如下：

蒋阿三：我受雇于福州的赫奇洋行。在 1875 年 6 月，赫奇洋行有一艘旧木船停泊在河岸上，我代表洋行把这艘船以 65 银圆的价格卖给了我的朋友庆德。庆德对这艘船进行了维修，然后又转卖给了一个我不知道姓名的人。这艘船是在福州造的，是洋式风格，长60英尺，宽15英尺。

庆德：在1875年6月初，我通过蒋阿三从赫奇洋行购买了一艘旧船，支付了65银圆。我对它进行了维修，并将船抬高了1英尺，花了大约200银圆。我是用宁波产的木头和其他废船木料进行维修的。我在福州给这艘船进行了注册，船名是“庆全春”（音译）号。7月份，我把船装满木柴开到了新乡①。在第二年的5月份，因为缺钱，我就让庆治（Chin - chie，音译）把它以130银圆的价格卖给了庄广兴（音译）。后来我了解到，庄广兴又把她卖给了一位东安②的本地人，后者又把它带到了温州，外国人在温州就把船给扣下了。这艘船是按照洋式风格建造的，船体是松木，涂成了黑色。船上有两个桅杆，也是松木。

庆治：庆德是我的侄子。他在福州买了一艘船，这艘船是在福州注册的。1875年9月，他把船开到了浦沙窝（音译），因为缺钱就把船租给了另一个人。1876年6月，我替他把船卖给了庄广兴。庄广兴对船进行了维修，然后把它开到了马后（音译），在那里进行了注册，后来又把它卖给了吴阿元（音译）。

吴阿元：大家在谈论的这艘船大概是我1876年7月在新乡以160银圆买的，我在马后注册的名字是“庆明新”（音译）号。

法庭上的证词记录如下：

蒋阿三：我受雇于福州的赫奇洋行。在1875年4月，我代表洋行以75银圆的价格卖了一艘船给庆德。那艘船是在福州造的，在抬高了一点儿并维修之后，就开到了南方。我知道的就是这些。我认出来扣押在这里的这艘船就是我卖掉的那艘。

庆德：1875年4月，我从蒋阿三那里买了一艘船。那艘船长约60英尺，宽14英尺，高约4英尺。它是按照洋式风格建造，可以运载300担或更多的货物。每一担约100市斤。后来我转卖了这艘船，我把它卖了130银圆。我认出来这艘船就是我在1875年买的那艘。

庆治：这艘船是我侄子从福州买来的。至于它的尺寸和注册信息我并不清楚。在1876年7月份，我代表庆德把它卖给了庄广兴。那艘船就是目

---

① 今福州马尾区。

② 今福州长乐区。

前扣押在这里的这艘。

吴阿元：这艘船是我的老板李庆光（音译）从庄广兴那里以150银圆的价格买的。我不知道这艘船是从什么地方买到的。后来对它进行维修花了700到800银圆。然后船就去了温州。庄广兴在马后给它注册了名字“庆明新”号。1877年4月，我用它装了500担盐和60包白糖，每包大约130斤。在5月27日那天，我抵达温州，一个洋人登船后拿走了一块木板。这艘船是庄广兴注册的。我对注册情况不太清楚，我不知道登记证书的日期。从福州到这里来用的是布帆，在到了温州之后，我把它换成了毡帆。

在此阶段，法庭上的几位官员似乎很受刺激，口译员走到证人身边，不断小声对他说话，同时激烈地打着手势。县官当场告诉证人，如果他不细说的话，会把他打得皮开肉绽。法庭陷入混乱，道台下令暂时休庭吃午饭。脖子上了锁链的中国证人，被带了下去。在法庭的另一头，可以看见官员和衙役正将这群中国证人团团围住，从姿势判断，这名证人正在受到威胁，看起来他犯了大错。这名证人最后被带走，我认为证人可能受到了惩罚，但据说这与最后审判无关。至于其中原因，我并不清楚。①

再次开庭时，这名证人被再次带到堂上做证：我来这里做证之前，正在生病，头晕目眩，一片糊涂，完全不知道自己在说什么。我说的并不准确。维修这艘船的费用是70到80银圆，货物是300担的盐，正如我一年前提交给领事馆的那份诉状中写的那样。

刘仙秋（音译），之前从未有人询问过他，他受到传唤，并宣誓做证：我和我兄弟刘小川（音译）一起在造船公司上班。我记得1866年，我们为赫奇洋行建造了一艘用来运输鸦片和金银的船。那艘船长约60英尺，宽大约14英尺，大约4英尺高。它可以运载大约300担货物。是使用樟木和松木建造的，有两个桅杆。船上的舱室大约是12英尺长，7英尺高。船尾是圆的。我记不清造这艘船花了多少钱。在1875年的春天，我又为赫奇洋行建造了一艘新船替换旧船。我认出来扣押在这里的这艘船就是1866年为赫奇洋行建造的那艘旧船。

① 官员受刺激的原因，可能是吴阿元在这里突然牵扯出了后面的老板李庆光，而李庆光原本并没有受到这场官司的牵连。

证据就是这么多，在花了整整两天时间后，法庭接下来休庭。

7月3日一大早，赫奇先生就乘坐炮艇离开了温州。但是何神启先生又在这里停留了一两天协助道台处理这件案子，然后上交给北京当局。①

① 查阅《光绪朝东华录》《光绪朝朱批奏折》《宫中档光绪朝奏折》《光绪宣统两朝上谕档》《邸抄》《清代军机处随手登记档》《清代外务部中外关系档案史料丛编·中英关系卷》《中美关系史料·光绪朝》《谕折录要》《谕折汇存》，均未能找到关于此案的记载。相关内容，还有待进一步挖掘。

《北华捷报及最高法庭与领事馆杂志》，1878 年 8 月 10 日

温州

自从上次给你写信以来，这个口岸和社区又遭到一次沉重打击，怡和洋行突然宣布撤离温州。这一举动毫无疑问让温州贸易受到打击，这次挫折将再一次延缓贸易的发展，让那些刚开始不那么绝望的人，希望再次破灭。去年的这个时候，厘金局的官吏给了我们第一击，不幸的温州现在又受到二次打击，这次打击的灾难性要弱一些。温州官吏现在的心情，就如同《耶利米哀歌》里的犹太人，与去年他们给我们造成祸害时我们的感受一样。毫无疑问，新的厘金局官吏正在尽全力维护贸易，合理设定厘金税，洋商最好满足厘金局的要求，以避免缴纳条约规定的高额税率。我还是要说，虽然内地的贸易运输问题一直到不得很好的解决，但目前厘金局颁发的内地运输许可证，价格已经变得便宜也合理，但此事也许还会再添波澜，因为某些人的习性就是自私自利。

据说不止一艘鸭屁股船将会参与到温州贸易中来，我们甚至听到谣言，一些有野心的人准备买一艘小轮船参与温州贸易。可以肯定的是，无论是哪一种方案，只要能够坚持实施，必能获取厚利。你应该听说了“水中女巫”号在驶往下游时，不幸沉没的事。似乎可以确定，它现在已经成了一具残骸，现在能做的就是尽快拆除它。已经对船进行过一次检查，检查之后已经建议宣布此船报废。在英国领事的命令下，锚和部分链条已被拆除，船上几乎所有家具都被搬了出来。我们认为不久以后就会从上海传来指示，要求把这艘船卖掉，我们得到的报告显示，似乎肯定会有一些中国人参与竞争。我们社区的人数又令人遗憾地减少了，我们失去了威尔逊先生这位居民，他的离开让每个地方都感到十分惋惜。在这样一个与世隔绝的小地方，他善良友好的品格让我们感到舒适又亲切。他的去世不仅仅是一种普通意义上的厄运，无疑让所有人都倍感伤痛。祸不单行，我们昨

天接到通知，温州的邮递业务将要停止了。之前邮递业务在好博逊先生的组织下开展得非常出色，并且一直都很守时。似乎我们长久以来都很欣赏的这种守时，对于中国的承包商来说变得太令人恼怒了，中国人抓住几条航线不稳定的事实，三个邮局一起密谋，拒绝继续运营，除非每次邮递多给出一天的宽限时间。迄今为止邮政服务的费用都是由英国政府和海关承担，但我们知道在未来，海关将会独自掌控邮政业务。海关会维持必要的邮政员，并面向温州普通外国民众开展信件收寄业务。新的邮政费率目前还没有宣布，但考虑到现在温州的外国公民只有 4 个，我担心费率可能会很高，海关可能会进行额外收费。我想邮费确定下来后，上海方面就会发出通告。到目前为止，各商埠的外国社区都要感谢海关的慷慨，海关给外国社区帮了很大的忙。因此即便海关减少了给我们的恩惠，我们也没有权利去抱怨，因为这需要海关进行财政补贴。我们必须增加温州外国社区的人口，以分担这种邮政负担。

“拿骚”号正停泊在黑牛湾外，目的是调查这一地区经过的舢板。我预计它将在任何一天来温州，以继续完成瓯江水文调查，我们希望能够让它停在城外一两天。（7 月 30 日）

《北华捷报及最高法庭与领事馆杂志》，1878 年 8 月 17 日

温州

今天下午 4 点的时候刊登了出售“水中女巫”号的广告。这艘船进了港，恢复了平稳，似乎吃水更深了些。但专家说船的状况并不好，我听说中国人会把船买走。

听说轮船不再撤走，我们真是高兴坏了。贸易的前景再次变得明朗。海关已经发布了通告，将来由海关邮政收取的邮资费率如下：

信件和公文，重量在半盎司（或以下），收费 100 铜钱（即 5 便士）。

报纸，每份（不限重量），收费 50 铜钱（即 2.5 便士）。

以上是我按照英国货币做的汇率换算。可以看出，海关收取的资费相当高。但是现在只有一个社区成员，他必须承担费用（政府和海关负责其他费用），因此这个不幸的家伙只能抱怨。也许人们并不认为向那个唯一的成员征收费用有什么意义，因为海关邮政无论如何都要运营，微不足道的“大众”的小笔资费也不可能降低办公室的成本。大家可能不知道，在上海，中国人每隔一天就会和宁波之间来回运营邮政业务，往返需要花费 6~8 天。对于重半斤（即 11 盎司）的包裹，收取 100 铜钱。所以，任何希望寄送比较重的货物的人，又不太清楚运输时间差异的话，可能会发现上述信息很有用。海关邮政要用 4 天半到 5 天的时间，至今一直都在运行中。我们很想老天下点雨，但雷声大雨点小，温州最近一直很少下雨。（8 月 9 日）

《北华捷报及最高法庭与领事馆杂志》，1878 年 9 月 7 日

温州

根据我们的通讯记者报道，今天在温州为一位欧洲人举行了葬礼，葬礼让人很是悲伤。这位女士是一位传教士的夫人，感染霍乱几个小时后就过世了，留下一个只有 10 天大的婴儿。这种骇人听闻的事情让社区的所有居民都笼罩在阴郁之中。在一个如此小的社区里，大家彼此都熟悉，所以这种事情带来的冲击感格外强烈。蔡文才的夫人已经在这里住了好几年了，直到染病那一刻，她从来没有受到过当地气候的影响。她是一位热心的劳动者，受过她帮助的人都喜爱她。她也受到社区居民的尊敬。她离我们而去这一悲痛的事件，在某种程度上影响了我们所有人，这种痛苦难以言表。我们谨向最悲痛的那些人致以最深切的同情。

霍乱是在 10 天或者 2 周前开始暴发的，每天的死亡人数由 10 个增加到了大约 30 个。不过令人高兴的是，现如今霍乱疫情似乎已经得到缓解。

很奇怪，迄今为止这种疾病几乎完全局限于乞丐和最穷的人身上，很少有富裕阶层的本地人染病。20 日那天，“拿骚”号上的一名水手感染了霍乱，但是在 21 日船离开时他脱离了危险。过去的一周都在下雨，而在此之前，我们这里长期干旱，水井干涸，有时候井里面打上来的水都是浑浊的。气候变化可能导致疾病再次爆发，不过这次霍乱流行似乎并不会像去年中国爆发的疫情那么严重。（8 月 24 日）

《北华捷报及最高法庭与领事馆杂志》，1878 年 12 月 21 日

温州

自从上次写信以来，我们的生活一直都是这样的平淡无奇，所以没有机会给你写一份书信。我们拥有一艘轮船，一艘鸭屁股船，一直都在非常有规律地运营着。布匹的进口量一直都在稳定增加。厘金官员渴望鼓励贸易，所以厘金税已经降到最低限度。就目前情况而言，拿着厘金局的通行证往内地运输货物所花费的钱，要比海关子口税票便宜得多。他们声称，我们也有充分的理由相信，他们是真诚地渴望吸引外国人和外国贸易来温州。他们做出了不寻常的努力，摧毁了温州本地人模仿宁波公会建立垄断体制的企图。以目前温州所建立起来的规则和制度安排来看，对本地人来说，今后很难再有机会建立垄断性公会。温州厘金局这样的做法，自然遭到那些企图效法宁波人建立“公会体制”的温州人的怨恨。

大约 11 月 15 日，自从口岸开放以后，第一艘外国帆船抵达温州。早在德国条约正式批准之前，这位船长就已经是一位贸易老手了，他依靠曾经大量从温州出口货物的经验，决定把他的船（一艘 320 吨的三桅帆船）重新带回到温州。自这位老船长上次访问温州以来，温州城的出口贸易因为各种原因，已经被分散到温州府内的各沿海小城镇。此外，大多数情况下卖家都没什么资本，他们习惯于只向一两个人出售商品，这些买家则要么全额支付，要么支付相当可观的预付款。而买主要么是本地的帆船主，要么是由本地船陪同前往买货。运输费率相当高，因此本地船能够赚取可观的运费。为了进行竞争，勒莫特船长要面对许多困难。凭着伟大的创业精神和充沛的精力，他毫不停歇地在温州调查了七八天。他发现温州确实存在着可观的货物出口业务，但由于我所提到的原因，以及没有任何可靠的外国或本地人协助他进行调查，最后的结果很令人沮丧。经过权衡之后，他决定离开。但是当他正要往下游开去的时候，突然有人提出要用他

的船，所以他又回来了。

这次租船的价格，可能不是那么令人满意，但对于船长扩展贸易的努力来说，我们希望他能得到鼓励。无论如何，运输的货物数量将会非常可观。贸易一旦开始，未来的发展将会顺风顺水。人们只要有能力，或愿意支付小额预付款，就能雇用洋船进行运输，洋船也因此很容易得到一份不错的报酬。另外，如果货主在其他地方受过现在流行租船方式的教育，那么他们很有可能联合起来，组成一个与外地类似的小组织。温州目前中式帆船的运费很高，只有少部分中国资本家能够取得相对低廉的运费报价，货主组成一个团体，无疑能够获取更多有利的条件。和许多其他事情一样，温州人目前需要的只是略微点拨。毫无疑问，温州的贸易潜力必将达到人们长久以来所期望的高度。从这个角度来看，希望“汉斯”号的访问会给口岸带来更加持久的利益，而不是仅仅带给“汉斯”号一次运费。中国帆船抵达温州时运载着生棉和其他货物，这条信息肯定可以被外国船只利用！在温州城邻近地区，每年都会进口 10 万包棉花，中国帆船的运费比外国人要求的要高得多。我们听说，有一艘德国的三桅帆船在槟城被租来往温州运棉花。温州对海峡殖民地货物的进口无疑相当兴盛，这可能意味着温州口岸的贸易将会进入一个新时代。温州主要出口的货物有木炭、纸、药材、雨伞和竹笋等。从中国帆船的运输量以及正在等待装运的船只数量来判断，洋商似乎应该做些什么，以对目前局势加以利用。但温州目前还没有可靠的中间商代为收取运费，或从事其他相关业务，外国轮船只能对温州的情况进行猜测，我担心会出现巨大的风险。但如果船主或船长能够先行上岸，收取一笔小额预付款，利润看起来就会更有保障。

西式三桅帆船“印度”号在三四天前满载货物抵达温州，装的主要是布匹。它明天就会离开。据说它这么赶时间，是因为在上海有货物等它运。

现在的温州阳光灿烂，鸭子和鹅成群结队。我们很长时间都没有看见过一个军人，我害怕当局正在忘记我们的存在。然而我们也完全不需要军队来保护，这座口岸的本地人是如此的安静、温驯和疏远。另外，我们很高兴看到海军的朋友们能来温州。（12 月 2 日）

《北华捷报及最高法庭与领事馆杂志》，1879 年 1 月 10 日

温州

定期的轮船航班再一次带给我们希望，因此我愿意坐下来，感情洋溢地给你写这封信。

温州终于做出了明智的决定——宁波士绅组成的现在声名显赫的包租公会，通过与官府达成厘金协定，尝试进行垄断，为自己和他们的朋友牟利的企图已经遭到挫败。宁波人通过垄断，保证货物独占和优先使用中国鸭屁股船进行运输，只有货物属于公会，或能够为公会带来大量利润，才会被允许进行运输。现在宁波人巧妙的计划，已经遭到打击。正如谚语所云，早起的鸟儿有虫吃，温州人无疑总是后知后觉，现在他们也意识到必须有所改变。温州地方当局挫败包租公会的图谋后，有人告诉我，前天已经有轮船抵靠温州港。我们现在有当地最有影响力的人做后盾，并且也得到当地官吏的支持，只要能够有毅力耗下去，“永宁”号①建立起的贸易，以及港口的前景似乎是大有希望。头一两次的航程可能不会带来很多回报，扣除航运成本，利润可能相当微薄。但几乎可以肯定，只要“永宁”号能坚持航线的规律性与持久性，不久之后，航线不仅可以赚取厚利，而且轮船招商局在温州也能提前占据优势地位，以应对未来的挑战。温州货物出口与进口，都存在轮船运输的需要，同时市场唯一的要求，就是集中运输。那些一向代表中国帆船运输利益的人，现在也支持“永宁”号。“永宁”号能够保障货物集中运输，目前的局面对其极为有利。即便可能存在风险，但我还是要重申我的建议：即便三次航程都不能带来所期望的利润，但也请保持耐心，不要灰心。

① 招商局轮船。

温州最近天气应时又宜人。虽然在温州不像上海那样，能够享受歌剧与节日的欢庆，但我们还是度过了愉快的圣诞节和新年。无论如何，没什么不痛快的。毫无疑问，你必须要承认，我们的天性就是这样易于满足。(1 月 2 日)

《北华捷报及最高法庭与领事馆杂志》，1879 年 1 月 24 日

温州

据本报通讯记者报道：自从公开举行了针对“曼打林”号的案件调查以来，尽管我一直都在仔细寻找进一步的消息，但目前没有搜集到任何足够可靠的信息。

你们知道，我们的官员做事情总是习惯神神秘秘。无论如何，本次调查都有很高的价值。公开的内容已经如此之多，我们可没有期望会了解这么多。

幸运的是，为了满足公众的好奇心，中国政府不再低调，否则就会用权力施行保密措施。现在这种事情经常发生，无论是出于天朝的坦诚，还是天朝的粗心大意，外部世界总能大概探知到中国外交疑云下的秘密。

温州的“曼打林”号案件就是如此，随着案情进入新的阶段，我们将能传达更多关于“曼打林”号的情报。

另外我还要说，我确实有充分的理由保证现在传达的信息是准确的。

通过在北京的英国官员那里听来的消息判断，关于被扣留船只的身份，或者反驳这一假设的证据并不可靠，也不具有决定性，更不能令地方官吏满意。而且从现在的结果来看，也只是发出了临时停止调查行动的声明。该声明要求任何人不得拆卸船只木板，这些木板是构成船只嫌疑的证据。

但似乎吴阿元认为自己有正当理由提出赔偿，他通过闵浙总督向温处道道台提出呈请，要求英国领事强迫两个受到传唤为案件出庭做证的“英国臣民”（原文如此，下列相关姓名），向原告人支付约 4000 银圆，以补偿因扣留造成的货物、运费、船只和人身自由的损失。另外还有人告诉我，所有这些灾难，都是被告向官府提供“虚假和恶意”信息所造成的。在温州进行的调查，不容置疑地表明外国人的指控毫无根据，同时也清楚地表明被扣船只，就是从“福州赫奇洋行购买的船只”。你们也许还记得，吴阿元就是被扣的船主。现在他还在请愿书中提出声明，要求惩办证人在

法庭上做证前后矛盾。温州当地的百姓将此事看作一个大笑话，简单来说，这是对外国人的一场彻底的胜利。因为外国人总是（不知确否）公开声称，他们不仅相信，而且确定那艘船就是“曼打林”号。

无论吴阿元现在说的是真是假，但与他以前的证词、请愿书和陈述相比，现在这艘船是否就是被盗的鸭屁股船，已经成为一个问题，在我看来将会毫无疑问地引起相关人士的高度关注。

除此之外，还有一件有趣的事情是，吴阿元控诉的被告中还有一人，并不是英国臣民。他们与中国官员逮捕涉嫌船只无关，也与收集被扣船只相关情报无关。正如我前面所说的，他们只不过是证人而已。他们所做的，仅仅是在船被扣押后，护卫船只，并保证其安全。

但吴阿元似乎并不觉得亏心，他认为自己也没必要亏心。看看他如何轻易地罔顾地理事实和自然法。如果按照我们的自然法，他的控诉根本站不住脚，他与“不幸”也沾不上半点关系。

“永宁”号已经按时返回温州，虽然我担心这时候它能够接到的货物不是很多，但能见到它我们还是很高兴。中国农历新年过后，它获取运费的前景还是很令人高兴的。当地人说它每月会往返三次，但他们似乎一致认为，在头两个月，即正在将贸易吸引回旧贸易中心（温州）期间也许两次航程最合适。当然，最终决定权仍在利益所系的人手中。

为了表明温州人对“永宁”号的善意，我要提一下，某个或一些居心不良的人（据说是宁波人）到处散发关于“永宁”号不适合航运的消息。温州人对此表示强烈的反感，并且指出传单中的收费信息是虚假的，是利欲熏心的人刻意捏造的。

最后，令我们开心的是，我们终于看到了英国旗帜——英国皇家海军“雄麻鸭”号于昨日抵达温州。但天啊！只在这里待 4 天时间。我猜很长一段时间我们都不会感到这么引以为荣了。

人们告诉那些喜欢狩猎的海军官员，温州到处都是鸭子、鹅、鹬和鸻。狩猎活动令人喜爱，且常常花费不多。我想知道，我们的海军上将是不是一个“好枪手”（当然，我的意思是猎鸟方面！）。我不知道我说的这些话，是否能够让上将心软。即便不考虑我们这些被流放者，上将也该想想自己的部属的利益，他们需要一座更有吸引力、不再乏味的口岸，需要在这里建设球场、歌剧院、图书馆等设施。（1 月 15 日）

《北华捷报及最高法庭与领事馆杂志》，1879 年 3 月 28 日

来自中国新开放口岸温州的报道

梅威令医生（W. Wykeham Myers，M. B.）*

应特别要求，我们抄录了报纸《日本每周邮报》① 中关于温州的内容摘要：

商业——对于温州的商业部分，我不是很敢写，因为在这里定居之前我的职业以及经历都与商业无关。无论如何，学习总是不会太晚。获取最好的商业信息来源，需要有空闲和兴趣，而我恰好兼而有之。我还要说，即便我的论断有错，但起码事实基础是确定的。我希望即便因为我缺乏经验，无法得出正确的推论，但起码能够为读者提供正确的基础事实，让读者能够自行推断出正确的结论。

从地理位置来看，温州现在作为商埠之所以重要，是因为它是现在福州售出的大多数茶叶的天然市场。作为进口市场，它不仅与邻近的大片乡村存在着自由联系，许多口岸也会选择温州作为茶叶供应来源，而不是福州与宁波。

在这个口岸开放后的头四个月，一大批布匹和鸦片进口贸易突然涌了进来，不仅稳步增长，还表明未来丰厚利润的前景。截至目前，从温州进口的货物，已经深入到许多内陆地区，内地中国商人的订单纷至沓来。同时以前由宁波供应货物的城镇，即 250 英里远的台州和浦江，以及 100 英里远的白琳镇都已经将其采购地转移到了温州。所以大家可以看到，事情开始变得明朗。似乎过去几年的希望和预言在逐渐朝着实现那一天稳步前进。

直到温州开埠，我们都从未听说过厘金税，本地船只进口的货物到达时是不收取厘金的。厘金制度是一种全新的征税机制。这是外国人出现造

* 瓯海关医官。这篇报道，应是梅威令最早刊登在《日本周报》上，再由《北华捷报》转载。

① 日本明治时期，在横滨出版的一份日本英文报刊。

成的后果，完全是因为外国人的存在，如果这些外国人被劝说退出温州，可能会停止征收厘金税。

无论如何，头四个月还是相当美好，并没有开始征收厘金。的确，我们听到了关于要征收厘金的传言，但我们希望能够成功，希望《烟台条约》能够秉持慷慨的精神执行，希望中国会对外国人做出一些首要的让步，至少在起步阶段。如若不然，将可能拖延或阻碍温州的繁荣。然而这些令人愉快的愿景注定在 1877 年 8 月初突然破灭。因为贸易的空前兴旺，所以他们制定了厘金税，这似乎是对所有从前条约的无视。厘金税突然袭击了温州，贸易立即崩溃了。

从内地发出的订单和从这里转运到上海的订单都被取消了，定期运行的轮船立刻撤了回去，商人的户头血本无归，不再有商人造访温州，温州又恢复了往日基督教城市特有的安宁与沉闷。

温州在 1877 年开埠的时间太晚，因此没有在当年赶上茶市季节。当局也拒绝固定一个明确的厘金税率，这让未来开展茶叶贸易的所有希望（如果有外国船只运送的话）都破灭了。他们总是答复，茶叶必须按照可能通过的所有关卡支付厘金税。有人进行过一次不愉快的尝试，厘金局要求每担茶叶缴纳 3 两厘金税。茶季结束后很久，官员被劝说将厘金税率定在每担 1 两银子。但正如其他商品的厘金折扣一样，改变来得太迟了，灾难已经无法挽回。厘金税这一恐怖和令人厌恶的行径造成了严重后果，现在温州必须重新开始，而且必须受累于官府所造成的恶名。更糟糕的是，厘金局官员因为发现没有额外征税的机会，所以根据过去 4 个月已知进口货物的数量，又计算了一个厘金税总额。厘金局随后将这个总额分摊到当地的商铺里，名之曰“善后厘金”，并开始征收，征收的过程往往对商铺百般威胁。厘金局官吏都是由浙江巡抚任命，温处道道台声称没有管辖权。厘金局官员抵达温州后，就贴着海关大楼的主码头设立了厘金局。这名官员声称，他是按照条约规定建立厘金局进行管理的。厘金局完全是模仿海关大楼建立，家具和布置都一模一样。所有货物一下海关码头，立刻就会被厘金局扣押，并遭到检查，然后按照厘金局的要求征收二次进口关税。① 如果货物要运到温州以外，那么还要被进一步征收类似税款。如果按照温

---

① 指货物要受到瓯海关和温州厘金局两次征收关税。

州官员所说的条约，比如修改后的《烟台条约》，那么外国货物在缴纳海关半子口税之后，还要额外多承担两种进口税。可能几乎不需要我提醒，读者应该知道，按照原来的条约规定，如果商品只是运往“港口及港口所在城市”，那么只需要缴纳海关进口税。如果是要运往港口之外更远的地方，则需要按照常规进口税率缴纳过境费。① 同样也不需要我提醒，各位都应该知道，没有任何一份条约承认厘金税率。但如果外国人把《烟台条约》看作是一种改良商务的手段，那他就大错特错了。中国政府的态度很坚决，起码温州地方当局是这样，他们不会做任何改变。事情正好相反，所谓互惠仅仅存在于纸面上。通过《烟台条约》上的文字，尽管首先要受到条约义务和协定的约束，但每个人都白日梦般自由地设想自己可以获取最大利益。在此局面下，不幸的是《烟台条约》中某些条款的措辞似乎在某种程度上承认了厘金的征收。如果我们按照中国人的逻辑，承认中国人有权征收厘金税，那么中国人内行的做法，应该是在合法建立的厘金局机构内，迅速设立起唯一且明确的厘金税章程。温州地方官员喜欢引用条约，如果按照他们的逻辑，那么就应该这样做。因此温州厘金局制定了一系列的条例和章程，并且张贴在墙上，并以小册子的形式在店主和商人之间四处传阅。以下是对该章程的扼要翻译：

1. 凡自欧洲、日本、广州、四川、汉口与福州输入商品，无论轮船、帆船、广东三桅船、白屁股船、小艇，欲领洋货半税单照，均须依本章程在局纳税。

2. 洋行进口货物必须向本厘金局提供进口货单，其格式与海关货单类似。有关洋行在口岸进行交易时，必须依照章程规定，按照本地商人应缴之当地税款，指导买客支付厘金，本地商人缴纳厘金之后，洋行才能交货。非法交易或具有非法交易企图者，依照章程之规定，处以三倍罚款。

3. 本地转运商从洋行处购买货物转运内地，无论水陆，都要接受厘金局分卡检查。各厘金分卡负责人会要求验看厘金存票。若无存票，相关货物将被暂扣，等待汇报本局，然后决定是否处以罚款。

4. 当提供厘金存票时，相关货物要提交给本厘金局进行检查。如果包装、重量等相符，货物将被盖章放行。如果相关货物超重，则就此提出申

① 即海关半子口税。

请，并指定官员继续检查现场包裹，防止违法行径。

5. 针对土货出口，除茶叶和丝绸外，所有货物都按照海关税则的3/10征税。洋行转运土货出口免税，但（与本地人的）共谋行为一经发现，则将征收罚款。

6. 华商从洋行购买货物运往内地，必须第一时间缴纳进口厘金税，洋商才能交货。立即前往内地转运，而不是在口岸存放的货物，必须缴纳全部税额，然后由本局颁发子口税票，持有税票的货物可以分批转运，在抵达最后子口之前无须缴税。针对（华商所持）土货，目前还不能以同样方式获取子口税票进行内地转运。因此华商进行土货转运，必须按照关税征收全额厘金。在洋货中夹带舞弊，将被视为走私行为。

7. 针对存放在外国洋行的所有种类的货物，条约规定，厘金局官员可以相度机宜，随时便宜设法办理，以杜弊端。按照此条，厘金局将指派一名官员对未售出的库存货物进行月度检查和登记。（条约第46款有针对此种行为的规定）

8. 本地商人，在缴纳厘金税及获取存票后，必须认真填写此批货物将要运往的城市、街道等信息；如果货物经水路运输，还要提供水路路线的细节，以便进行全面检查，防止走私行为。

9. 如果洋行进口的货物在本口销路不畅，而需要再次出口，如果海关检查之后，证明这些货物同进口时一样完好无损，则将减免厘金税。（条约第45款有针对此种处理的规定）

10. 最近的章程指出，在外国租界内，洋货免于征收厘金税，但是超出定租界以外，将和土货一样征收厘金税。在外国租界的界限确定之前，现有厘金章程仍将继续执行。

11. 一旦外国人定居点的界限确定下来，如果发现中国商人的财产即本地商品也在租界内，将由本局进行裁定。地方当局采取此措施，是为了便于对本地商品进行管控。为了维护条约在涉及所有权方面的规定，如果本地商人和洋行共谋舞弊，或者洋行为厘金收入的诈骗行为提供保护，一经发现，将没收相关货物，并召唤洋行所在国领事，收取罚款（参见条约第48款）。

按照宁波正在实施的厘金章程，起草了上述章程，以便符合本地情况。本章程乃遵循条约规定拟成，在厘金税收总体利益之上，兼顾公平精神。（未完待续）

《北华捷报及最高法庭与领事馆杂志》，1879 年 4 月 4 日

来自中国新开放口岸温州的报道

梅威令医生（W. Wykeham Myers, M. B.）

有关鸦片的规定

1. 将按照宁波的税收系统征收温州地区的鸦片厘金税，即每箱40 两。1 箱公班土中有 40 个鸦片球，1 箱白皮土中有鸦片 100 市斤。

2. 进口鸦片，将由海关进行检查，然后在海关关栈卸货，鸦片数量将汇报至本厘金局。

一旦售出，买客须按照指示缴纳厘金，获得本厘金局提供的盖戳的放行单，此后鸦片才能交货。如有走私行为，将对走私的鸦片每担收取 1000 两的罚款。

3. 至于鸦片的厘金税，根据与洋行的协议，按照宁波的管理章程向他们收取厘金税。因此从征收的 40 两厘金中将会返还 5 两给相关的洋行中间人，1 两支付给本地牙商，其余总共 34 两上交厘金局。温州的洋行还没有按照以上描述的方式缴纳厘金，目前没有必要退还上述厘金。一旦洋行了解了这个问题，就会在适当时候进行考虑，同时也会颁布更为详细的运营控制措施。

从上述内容可以很容易地看出，不仅一般外国人，而且海关也服从于厘金局。瓯海关不仅征收海关税，而且还协助厘金局征收厘金税。温州厘金局对《烟台条约》的解释如此大胆，如果这种行径被认为是正确的，那么正如温州厘金局的章程所说，温州厘金局真的是在根据从前已有的“条约进行解释”。

15 或 18 年前，温州的（进出口）贸易很兴隆。外国货物和来自南方

港口及英国海峡殖民地①的产品大量涌入温州市场，汕头、广州和新加坡的商人纷纷在本城建立商馆，温州本地人也在很大程度上得以参与到贸易中来。这些外来资本家作为媒介，为大量本地人提供了就业机会，同时外国航运船只的数量也很是不少。

因为种种原因，许多中国商号的分号逐渐退出温州，可能是因为条约批准的口岸过多，造成温州被孤立，也有可能是因为宁波和福州拥有更好的港运条件。外地商人离开之后，虽然温州仍然拥有大量帆船，但温州人缺乏将帆船贸易聚拢在温州城的才干。造成的结果是，这些帆船纷纷到温州下游，以及出海口沿岸的无数小村镇，寻找做生意的机会。这就是温州对外国人开放时的情况，现在它正通过重新引进资本和企业，吸引贸易重回正轨。为了做到这一点，毫无疑问，首先必须在城市建立起零售业务系统，必须亲自到产茶区去游说，必须建立起炒茶和其他相关机构（可以模仿山那边的福州）。我们必须让过去因为政治危机而转移的进出口贸易商路，重新回到温州。

信心一旦建立起来，贸易就会稳步发展，一切皆有可能，很快就会吸引必要的中国资本家过来，他们将在适当的时候接管零售生意，并与先到的外国人开展规模更大的生意（因此双方的关系会更好）。毫无疑问，怀着这样的目标，东方最大和最有进取心的英国公司②之一，已经在温州开设了分行。只要公平竞争，他们的努力看起来就可以获得成功。即使因为厘金造成了混乱，他们也勇敢地坚持了下去，现在正努力恢复不景气的贸易。可惜！当温州官员终于发现自己的错误时，一切都已经太晚了，老员工们已经被解雇，现在再到茶区去做重要的商业安排已经太迟了。1878 年茶叶采摘时，这里几乎不存在商业竞争，再加上温州官吏的恶名远扬，使

---

① 故地在今东南亚。1786 年，英国东印度公司从吉打苏丹处割占槟榔屿，1800 年又在其对面的吉打海岸取得一大片土地，称威斯利省。1824 年东印度公司又获新加坡和马六甲，1826 年将其与槟榔屿合并成为海峡殖民地。华侨俗称三州府。1830 年降为孟加拉总督管辖下的驻扎官辖区，1851 年改属英印总督，1867 年升为王家直辖殖民地。后可可群岛、圣诞岛和拉布安岛并入。第二次世界大战中被日本占领。1946 年后解体。参见孙文范编著《世界历史地名辞典》，吉林文史出版社，1990，第 404 页。

② 指怡和洋行。

得被送往温州市场的茶叶数量微不足道。但依靠温州自身的优势，以及今年春天施行厘金税改后，轮船再次在温州运营，随着它们的出现，进口贸易的前景也再次变得光明。但是这种局面并未持续很久，而是再次陷入沮丧。所有希望都集中在这家洋行身上，它的存在是温州与外界保持轮船航运联系的唯一保证。也许是因为有些厌恶过去遇到的无理取闹的骚扰，这家公司突然撤出了他们在温州的机构，温州现在已没有任何洋行商业代表。在相当长的时期内，他们不得不面对巨大且非法的商业阻力，以及扩展贸易所需的巨额开支。即使是光明的前景与丰厚的回报，也不足以让他们继续在温州进行尝试，出现这样的结果并不令人惊讶。这种尝试已经为他们带来大量挫败和烦恼。但他们的离去，让温州口岸遭受到沉重一击，其严重影响可能需要长时间的努力才能消除。

上述诸多原因让美好的希望破灭了。我现在将试着列出温州真正的商业潜力，让那些对温州生意感兴趣的人，来判断温州作为贸易港口的价值，以及长久以来我们对温州的贸易期望是否正确。为此，我将引用1877年的贸易报告，并且在回顾这些报告信息的时候，努力简要地结合其他信息，以帮助理解。我需要提醒你的是，虽然这些报告的时段是1877年的前9个月，但实际上与前4个月没什么不同，因为后5个月贸易已经陷入停滞。

进口贸易几乎完全局限于布匹和少量鸦片，主要是来自上海。但也有一些船运到宁波的出口贸易。

总的货物价值达到了73600英镑。

鸦片——这里进口了39箱白皮土和10箱公班土。前者的平均价格是每担644银圆，后者是每担653银圆。

由于1877年秋季，浙江省种植罂粟歉收，印度鸦片无疑将涨到很高的价格。但不幸的是，印度似乎也发生了类似的灾难，因此未能及时填补浙江的市场空缺。1878年12月，白皮土的价格已经上涨到每担750银圆。

公班土的报价是每担670银圆，但需求并不是那么旺盛。想要将鸦片直接输入温州，有很多障碍要克服，一个是温州本地商业资本不足，需要在缺乏长期信用的情况下赊购货物。另外到目前为止，所有进口的鸦片都是从宁波经陆路运来的，当地人的公会已经具备必要的运输手段。通过这种陆路转运方式，宁波公会不仅与宁波厘金局达成了某种协议，并且看起来还可以从中合谋大量逃税。

温州自己全部的鸦片消耗量每年只有115箱左右，所以也许有人会认为可以推迟该地区的鸦片贸易，转而集中精力经营目前宁波鸦片供货范围之外的地区，以避免直接与宁波竞争。但其他地区是有可能青睐温州的，因为温州具有一定地理优势。

例如，福建的许多地区，从温州过去比宁波更容易到达，我认为这些地方一定会从温州购买鸦片，最有可能用茶交换鸦片。

福州征收的鸦片厘金税非常高，但温州厘金税与宁波相当，即每担33两或34两银子。除此之外，运输费用的差异也能带来更大的利润空间。要想了解在浙江和福建大部分地区的鸦片情况，对此我知之甚深，至少有30%到40%的人吸台浆①和白皮土的混合鸦片，其中台浆的含量要多一些。

让外国鸦片贸易量减少的最重要原因，是本省罂粟种植面积的增加，这些本地鸦片供应浙江和福建的大部分地区，还出口到台湾、上海和其他地方。台州府和温州府的总产量估计为每年约7000箱。

去年，由于各种原因，鸦片的种植量几乎不到往年的一半。在1877年8月份和9月份，起初鸦片价格达到每担约200银圆，之后起到12月一直在上涨（当时每担达到约350银圆），1878年，从2月和3月的400银圆又上涨到450银圆，随后又受到5月产量前景的进一步影响。去年因为罂粟种植歉收，本地鸦片价格保持在每担450银圆左右，要不是因为白皮土鸦片（据说白皮土是本地鸦片纯度的两倍）的价格高昂，可能早已垄断市场。总之，可以这么说（鉴于江西和福建地区的人，更偏爱印度－中国混合鸦片），应该尝试着在这座口岸输入洋药，如果想要从中获取利润，就需要消耗相当的精力与资本。如果资本不足，也可以用鸦片在产茶区进行易货，这种贸易方式被证明对外国商人格外有利。我们可以通过福州的独立中间商，进行鸦片与茶叶的易货生意。但这些本地中间商往往不太容易顺从于外国人的操纵，所以洋商最好能到当地直接与消费者接触，或者起码也该更“熟悉”这门生意。如果你能手持茶叶子口税票，当然也就能免

---

① 产自浙江台州的本地鸦片。“浙江台州产者，为台浆。象山产者，为象浆。既无厘税，又省运赀，无惑乎小民趋之若鹜也。”参见《候补同知庄淦谨拟条陈抄录》，《申报》1884年10月21日第1版。

受厘金税的骚扰。

棉布——1877 年 4 月、5 月、6 月和 7 月，即贸易取得进展的那段时期，温州进口了 35000 匹原色洋布、41900 匹洋标布和 12624 匹斜纹布。对这些洋布而言，温州是令人满意的市场。温州是该地区重要的洋布货源地，1876 年的海关记录表明了这种状况。我们可以轻易拿到棉布从宁波转运到其他地区的贸易数据，如表 1 所示。

表 1 贸易数据

单位：匹

	原色洋布	漂白洋布	洋标布	斜纹布及细斜纹布
处 州[1]	23038[2]	4650	32339	5830
温 州	39657	2337	29681	9326
衢 州	37917[3]	2905	77238	10868
泉 州	2700	—	2320	—
建 宁[4]	1380	350	2370	560
总 计	104692	10242	143948	26584

注：1）原文为"Chü - chü"，根据 1876 年宁波海关贸易报告统计，应是处州（Ch'u - chow）。

2）应为 23088，原文错录。

3）应为 39817，原文错录。

4）原文为"Chien - ming"，为"Chien - ning"错写。

资料来源：参见"Ningpo," *Returns of Trade at the Treaty Ports in China for the Year 1876*，Shang-Hai：Statistical Department of the Inspectorate General of Customs，1877，p. 183。

除此之外，宁波匹头公会发放了大量洋布厘金税照，通过该公会运出的大量洋布，海关并没有确切记录。路途上如此困难，上述地区都可以有如此大的洋布需求，如果直接从温州向这些地区供货，那么又会增加多少消费需求呢？温州不仅向上述地区开放了贸易，同时也打通了南部和东南部的贸易路线。直到温州贸易因为厘金遭到重挫之前，我们有实际证据可以表明，贸易正在向温州这条原本的新路线转移。在温州南部的平阳地区，生产一种结实耐用的土布，虽然有些出口到上海和杭州，但其中大部分都是本地消费。为了满足其生产，每年要进口 10 万包原棉，这无疑为外国航运带来有利可图的机会，当地帆船的运输经营模式十分僵化，而运输费用通常是我们的一半。

毛织品——温州刚开始进口毛织品不久，贸易就遭到了打击，因此除了说温州是一个相当有希望的市场外，没有什么可多做评论的。原本与温州已经建立紧密商贸联系的地区，现在又回到旧的宁波贸易路线。在我们这个口岸参与贸易的短时间内，实际进口量如下：羽纱 900 匹、西班牙斜纹呢 762 匹、粗斜纹呢 600 匹、厚斜纹呢 510 匹以及发光呢 1500 匹。

只有到了接近年末和寒冷季节（1876 年的这段时期，大部分时间里，温州贸易几乎陷于停滞），温州才会出现对毛织品的明显需求，如果我能给出具体数据，也许能更令人安心。以前对英国海峡殖民地的进口贸易，主要集中在温州城，贸易的大宗是藤条和红树皮。虽然现在此类进口贸易都分散到了温州下游的小城镇，但贸易毕竟仍在继续，并为对航运感兴趣的人提供了赚钱的机会。

至于金属进口方面，进口日本铜 364 担，占据第一位。铁（制钉用铁或铁丝）88 担，铅 102 担，锡 81 担；剩余未售出的 60 担钢被再次出口。煤油的需求量很大并且在不断增加。在温州所处的浙江地区，人们对糖的消费量很高，糖类贸易主要是依靠季节性的帆船运输。虽然目前该地区的糖类贸易还比较分散，但无疑将在未来汇拢于温州，因为温州对商人和船主有利。

出口——在发展对外国出口方面，温州所做不多，或者更准确地说，不仅没有为这样的尝试提供什么机会，而且还给所有公司设置了许多障碍。从微薄的利润，几乎看不到出口贸易的发展潜力。1877 年的报告显示，出口贸易总额仅为 5435 英镑。但我的目标，在于表明在贸易额如此之小的特殊情况下，我们能做什么。我将列出我能获取到的，每一项出口货物的相关信息。

温州最主要的出口商品是茶叶。虽然有上述原因，但在 1877 年仍有少量工夫茶运到温州（278 担）。我们有充分的理由相信，在 1878 年的茶季，茶农们愿意并且急于把他们的产品运过来。温州茶市的竞争并不激烈。虽然最近困难重重，但商人们会再次努力将温州变为茶叶销售市场。温州作为茶叶新市场具备一些优势，虽然从前没有向这个方向去努力，但如果商人能努力鼓励和指导茶农，那么茶叶自然会源源不断地自行涌入温州。

最好的茶叶产区与福州之间都是大片连绵的山地，交通异常困难。温州与这些茶叶产区之间有直接的水路交通，很明显，不需要太多努力，茶叶也会被吸引到温州这个天然市场来。为了更清楚地描述这条贸易路线优势的实际情况，我可以可靠地估计，相比运到福州，茶叶运到温州的运输价格每担要低2个银圆。平阳地区最近的茶区，距离温州城大约34英里。平阳每年虽然生产了大约7万担的粗茶，但每年销往国外市场的优质茶叶只有约3万担，剩下的大部分都是本地消费。

最好的茶叶一般被称之为“白毫”，准确的名称应该是“白琳”，我们正是希望未来在中国的这个地区，用此种茶叶来交换鸦片。在某种程度上说，白琳镇完全有可能成为茶叶贸易的集散地，不仅因为此地出产茶叶，而且因为它北部紧邻的地区通往外部的交通都很方便。白琳镇通往北方的路程，大约一半是由运河和河流组成。其他的茶叶产区包括温州北部的乐清、泰顺和瑞安。其中，乐清种植的绿茶品质非常好。不过，泰顺和瑞安的茶叶是通过平阳运出去的，所以往往被归为平阳茶。粗茶或未炒的生茶每年都会先运到温州，要么用于本地人的消费，要么炒过之后运往国外市场。如果外国商船能够获得茶叶运输权，那么无疑将获取重利。但不幸的是，本地常关①会额外征税，税额大概为瓯海关的一半。好博逊先生在离开之前曾提出过修改关税的问题，在他离开后的几个月里，最终准许按照发货时茶叶实际重量的八折计算，用以补贴未来因炒茶或其他原因而造成的重量损失。然而，即使有这种让步，仍不足以抵消常关与海关的高额税收。因此，茶叶将很可能继续使用中式帆船运输。有人建议，如果将征税范围扩大到温州所有出口茶叶，以及日本进口茶，并统一按价征收4%，可能就可以激活温州的茶叶轮船贸易。另一方面，人们认为这种改变可能会对一般性海关征税造成不便。毫无疑问，温州应该凭借其地理及其他优势，在茶叶贸易方面证明其重要性。但是这样做的时候，福州必将受到重大影响，目前茶叶给予福州的（包括外国人和本地人）巨大利益一定会受到极大冲击。如果考虑到这一点，那么商人所表现出的不愿意利用温州的商业机会，也就可以理解了。然而基于偏见或个人利益，以及违反自然规律的障碍，最终总会被克服，温州成为可观的茶叶市场似乎只是时间问题。

温州种植和出口的瓯柑相当有名气，瓯柑历来是出口收益的大宗。去

---

① 原文为“Native Custom”，指常关。但根据后文内容，指的应该是厘金局。可能是作者将厘金局与常关混为一谈。

年阻碍贸易的各种厄运接连不断，碰巧从上海出发的所有天津方面的轮船，竟然全都去运输水稻了，以至于没有船只运输温州的货物。最后是“欧罗巴”号将这些水果运走，这是使用外国船只进行瓯柑运输的第一次大规模尝试。但是由于提到的原因，这些货物不得不在上海折本出售，这不仅令托运人感到失望，也令所有希望通过这笔生意，向人们证明轮船运输高效性的人感到失望。众所周知，人们更看重当下的结果而不是未来的可能性。

温州地区的一般产品和工业品如表 2 所示。

表 2　一般产品和工业品

铜	木炭	雨伞
家具	铁丝	大豆
土布	薄纱	大麻
垫子	铁制品	小麦
棕	银	竹子
松木	鸦片	茶叶
靛青染料	丝绸	纸张

此外还有 17 种不同种类的药材。

所有这些产品的出口量都很大，为航运业提供了相当多的商业机会。但为了从中式帆船手中夺取航运控制权，外国船东或他们的代理商（无论如何首先必须做到）在参与竞争的过程中，必须开出与中国船主相同的货运条件。首先必须要垫付所运货物 1/3 或 1/2 的货款。对于当地人来说，他们习惯了奢侈和挥霍，只有少数例外。他们不想或不能等待商品被售出后才拿到钱，他们更愿意采用那种麻烦最少、收钱最快的处理方式。

中国船东和运货人利用这一点，往往会收取高昂的运费，这笔好投资往往能带来厚利。在船只抵达之前，开始时需要一个负责的代理商在岸上做好所有这些安排，这样处理事情的时间就会更从容。你会发现中国人的这套商业系统，相比于外国人的轮船运输系统，并不显得麻烦。毫无疑问，正如我所指出的，此种打理生意的方式，对两种运输模式都有相当助益。同时此种方法，也不仅限于航运业，同样适用于其他部门。

木炭应该成为外国商船可以运输的大宗出口商品。如果像商人和其他人所声称的那样，条约规定木炭有权在海关免费通行，那木炭无疑已经证明是航运业非常宝贵的一项收入来源。因为同样是木炭，在通过常关时，必须支付出口关税。但瓯海关却按照货价的5%征收海关出口税，另外还要再征2%的半子口税，实际税率为7%。但目前相关规定仍在审理当中，我只需要提一下，并不是在所有条约口岸都征收这种税（据说，木炭出口最多的福州就是其中之一），我们似乎可以在温州期待此种便利。过去一年冒险的结果已经给中国官员提了醒，毫无疑问，他们还受到了高层的压力，因此目前温州的厘金税比其他商埠要低。我之前提到的《温州厘金章程》已经被取消，应该已经被彻底放弃。现在的温州厘金局官吏急于与前任划清界限，着力拨乱反正，吸引外国商人与贸易到温州落脚。他们已经采取了一些措施，做出了一些安排，温州厘金包税制度（此项制度已经让宁波的外国人希望破灭，并且丧失了贸易机会）在未来已经不可能出现。厘金税照的优势在于可以通行全省，并且在将货物输往内地的过程中，厘金税照的税率比海关半子口税的要低得多。

与此同时，当地人倾向或更愿意进行易货贸易，至少在茶叶方面，这可能值得外国人促成其事。总而言之，那些商品温州能够辐射到腹地，其贸易需求巨大，外国轮船若能参与其中，可谓正当其时。

可能需要一些时间来克服外国人对温州的偏见，甚至是疑虑，有时候这些偏见是由过去人们在中国的经历所造成的。或者有人会认为，即便不包括《烟台条约》所提供的开放口岸，先前开放的口岸也已经够多了，足以吸收目前或者未来一段时间外国人所能够提供的所有企业和资本。但也有一万个理由令人相信，如果他们能利用这里的商业机会，必定能发现温州极高的贸易潜力，并获取丰厚的回报。

汇兑——1877年的平均利率为，150整洁①墨西哥银圆兑换100两海关银。1350整洁西班牙卡罗尔斯银圆兑换1170墨西哥银圆。有一段时期，温州白银出现大量出口，但在官方的压力下，白银出口很快下滑。

温州流通着许多伪造银圆，这些假币主要是在宁波、芦潮镇和台州伪造。有的几乎可以乱真，其余的价值大概为本币的52%。

在结束本文的这一部分时，我附上了一张表，列出了浙江和其他省份

① 原文为“clean”，译为“整洁”，指货币未遭磨损。

与温州进出口联系紧密的地区所出产的货物，如表3所示。

表3 浙江和其他省份与温州联系紧密地区所出产的货物

浙江省	产品
台州（Tai－chow）	鸦片、茶叶、铁、咸鱼、竹笋和薄纱
处州（Chü－chow）	茶叶、清漆、香菇以及石凳
金华（Chin－hua）	清漆、茶叶、高品质海枣、火腿和纸张
衢州（Kü－chow）	茶叶和纸张
平阳（Ping－yang）	茶叶和铁
泰顺（Tai－shun）	茶叶和铁
福建省	产品
白琳镇（Pei－lin）	茶叶
建宁（Kien－ming）	茶叶
延平（Yen－hing）	茶叶、铜和铁
邵武（Shao－wu）	茶叶和竹笋
江西省	产品
广信（Kuang－sin）	茶叶、藤条、纸张和大麻
抚州（Fu－chow）	夏布和糖
南昌（Man－chang）[1)]	茶叶和夏布
建昌（Chien－chang）	茶叶和夏布

注：1）原文是“Man－chang”，根据前后文，应是“Nan－chang”的误写。

总体上——还有一类人会造访温州，那就是传教士，他们可能会需要更多的信息。

温州对于这些先生们具有双重吸引力。从一般信徒的角度来说，温州特别易于进行传教。从世俗的角度看，传教士融入温州地方文化的不适与困难，要远远低于其他地区。为了证明此种观点，我只需要简单提到一点，温州人表现出强烈的奉献精神，他们都是狂热的偶像崇拜者，但同时也不遗余力地关心他们的宗教信仰。

除了分散在城市各地的无数寺庙外，街道上“太阳神”（Baal）的祭坛，一点儿也不比“克洛阿西娜”（Cloacina）的神龛少。并且往往这些偶像紧挨着寺庙。从温州人普遍心向宗教的情况看，可以得出一个有希望的结论。即如果能够加以适当引导，你会发现当地人非常虔诚，因此信仰的转变很令人满意。从世俗的观点看温州吸引人的地方，我认为这里的气候相当不错，并且可以获取良好与便宜的住所。有许多地方可以提供充足的用地，以建造雄伟的宅邸。如果无法建筑房屋，或者在房屋建成前需要临时住所，那么很多本地房屋，即使不加改造，也能够住得很宽敞而且舒适。并且无论房主是谁，正如我之前所述，这里的外国人很少，我们总可以慢慢将房主转化为让我们非常满意的信徒。总而言之，我可以说，只要传教士在这里定居，他的生活就不可能遭受悲惨的转折，房屋住宿和生活必需品都令人满意，我们会发现在其他地方可不是这样。

在整个城市，有几处非常宽敞的废弃商店或住宅。这些地方绝对不用花任何费用，就可以很容易地改造成礼拜堂或布道坛。正如我所展现的，温州人天生不爱惹事，因此无须庸人自扰。可以在温州周边地区进行巡回布道，完全不会遇到在其他地方与之相伴的一切艰难与困苦。在巡回布道的过程中，因为是在运河与河流上乘船航行，所以只会比家里少那么一点儿舒适。

最近10年来，中国内地会在温州常驻有两名牧师和他们的妻子。最近一年来，属于英国偕我公会的传教士在这里成立了教会。我相信，前者已经在他们的教会内吸引了40或50名信徒。罗马天主教会也已经建立了一两年，并且据说——我并不是特别确定——他们在这个地方的教会已经有多达600人皈依。

在此期间，我们被切断了与外部世界的轮船交通联系，我们不得不重新依靠海关邮政公司发送和接收邮件。好博逊先生主要负责成立的邮政系统，以最大的规律性，每周运送一次，并运行了七个月。然而不幸的是，一些本地公司因为额外摊派的费用感到生气，并拒绝继续为此付款。随后海关试图为自己组织一个特殊的邮政系统，但是后来在停摆一两个星期后，最后还是夭折了。在此情况下，我们只能使用温州本地的邮政系统，它每隔一天去宁波一次。然而，要花八天时间才能完成两地之间的旅程，但之前好博逊 - 霍必澜创立的邮政系统只需要花四天。尽管有点耽搁，我们似乎还是可以安全和正常地发送和接收邮件。（摘自《日本每周邮报》）

《北华捷报及最高法庭与领事馆杂志》，1879 年 4 月 29 日

温州

自从上次写信以来，这个口岸的贸易已经取得了极大发展。

“永宁”号和之前一样，在最有影响力的本地人支持下继续航行。每一次航行，局面都会得到改善，结果也总是更令人满意，现在似乎已经达到这样的地步：如果提供更多的支持，温州必将成为诱人的富饶之地。正如预料，定期和迅捷的运输，带动了各类货物出口的增长。

从温州运往上海的茶叶贸易，前景看起来相当不错，也许我们可以相当自信地说，今年相当数量的茶叶已经确定可以通过轮船运出去。

除此之外，一批与新成立的商贸机构有关联的宁波人，目前正在温州采购红茶。同时他们还深入茶区购买生茶，然后运回宁波进行加工。

去年，一名试图在温州卖茶的货主，由于包装上的一些缺陷，无法从温州唯一的外国买家那里获得他想要的价格。于是用他自己的船把茶叶运到上海销售，并取得了丰厚的回报。这样的结果不仅刺激了他，也刺激了他的邻居。

如果这种传言属实，那么无疑会影响到今年的茶季。你们可能会回想起，过去因为宁波的反对，想要在温州直接进口鸦片有多难。“永宁”号的第一次航行只运了一箱货，但至此开始，进口量一直在稳步增加，直到最近一次航行运来了七箱货。这种进口需求的增长，在某种程度上必须归功于厘金局官员的努力。另外可以肯定的是，温州本地的一些商人已经向厘金局提出了运输鸦片计划，如果计划能够被接受，未来厘金官员将保证每天至少有两箱鸦片运入温州。

这样的协议并非完全不可能达成，事实上这项计划被提出来本身（但这并不意味着温州厘金局会给予某种不切实际的特许权），就已经表明了温州的贸易潜力。

当然，温州大规模消费的增长，必须建立在夺取宁波经济腹地的基础上，而这些腹地与温州之间的交通联系往往更为便利。

总体说来，从上个季度的统计来看，相比于去年同期，贸易增长了将近4倍。毫无疑问，如果这种情况能够持续下去，那么前景会更让人满意。

有一名外国人已经在温州开设了一家商馆，但除此之外，温州贸易环境改善的主要获益者还是本地人。

我们从中国人那儿听到一些奇怪的消息，因为目前印度茶和中国茶的激烈竞争，决定在未来将温州建成一个重要的茶叶销售市场，温州的地理位置和其他优势，可以帮助降低价格成本。与福州相比，可以明显看出温州在运输上的优势，开辟新的市场，也有助于终止旧贸易路线上的某些"关税与勒索"①，据说福州方面已经将其合法化。

我最后还要说一点，这可能是我个人的体会，所以请读者们自行去判断我这种说法是否可信。我想说的是，目前我能感觉到，人们并不是太在意官府的渎职行为。

关于温州官吏，我要提醒你们，由于贸易的发展，目前中国人无疑是最大的获益者。中国为了吸引外国人来经商，原本给予外国人一些特权，这些特权最先仅仅是授予外国人，但现在中国人也能够享受到。并且目前为止，温州官吏还没有采取措施，以防范温州建立宁波那样的垄断组织，那样的组织对于洋商来说简直就是灾难。

工人正忙着将江心屿的一座寺庙，改造为临时领事馆。但我认为温州必须要足够重要，才值得建立领事馆。首先要选择一块地皮，建立永久性租借地。其次，才该建立英国代表的住所。

到目前为止我仍旧没有见过任何士兵，如果我们的语气表现出某种不安，那我必须要提一下，当地人对邻居一如既往地友好。当地的野鸭已经飞走，我担心现在能提供给海上朋友们的，就只剩下热忱和欢迎，每当紧急情况时他们就会出现。（4月19日）

① 指沿路厘卡。

《北华捷报及最高法庭与领事馆杂志》，1879 年 6 月 10 日

温州

我们的通讯记者说，“永宁”号的灾难在托运人之间引发了巨大的恐慌。那些在上海办货的茶商尤其惊恐，目前上海的茶市已经开市，而汉口或福州的茶市还没有开市。温州茶市，起码比福州茶市要早两个星期。有鉴于此，希望能证明这个口岸额外的吸引力。

当“永宁”号“爆炸”的致命消息刚刚传来时，我们担心会影响到本地人搭乘轮船的信心。但事实上，现在轮船的发动机由外国人操作，民众已经对轮船恢复了信心，只要工程师能够待在船上，一切就不会有问题。

将机器托付给那些只能铲煤或在轴承上涂润滑油的人，看起来实在是“贪小便宜吃大亏”。这种自信是错误的，对中国人来，他们现在可以认清这一显著的事实。

如果谣言属实，另一艘轮船也一直缺乏外国人的监督。就机器而言，这种监督对全体乘客的福祉至关重要。由于这种危害在我们的指导下已经得到纠正，我们没有理由继续多说什么。

因为要检查茶叶，海关今天异常忙碌。中国人还没有熟悉海关业务程序，将来可能会出更多岔子。

由于下雨，轮船的开船时间必须推迟，出货、检验等都集中在天气转晴的那几个小时。

“永宁”号运走了大约 1200 箱的货物，随后一艘鸭屁股船运走了 500 箱或 600 箱货物。下一次航运预计会有更多的货物，并且如果这批货能令人满意，我想出货量将比目前可能预期的更具持续性。

对温州来说，当然一切看起来都更加有希望了。毫无疑问，即便不是所有，也有许多的改善是源于轮船招商局所采取的措施。他们干得不赖，让我们祝福他们能继续保持，并繁荣昌盛。

另外，如果说我们有什么美好的愿望，我不禁要问，为什么招商局对本地人如此善解人意，对外国人却要冷酷无情呢？向外国人收取的运费往往很高。举一个例子，前几天，外国社区的某人运了六把普通的椅子，价值大约是7.5银圆，招商局竟然收取了多达5银圆的运费。我可以说，如果不是受害人不经意间提到，没有人会知晓此事。另外外国人坐船的票价，肯定要比中国人贵。

尽管这些不公平的事情，导致人们抱怨连连，但这里的外国人，都会向轮船招商局送上祝福。我们会用更加长远的眼光来看待这件事。轮船招商局来到温州，帮助我们这些孤立无援的人，并如此有效地帮助我们的港口，为恢复它应有的地位而奋斗。（5月30日）

《北华捷报及最高法庭与领事馆杂志》，1879 年 12 月 31 日

温州

最近温州发生了一件让我们感到很刺激的事情，略微改变了我们枯燥乏味的生活。在距离我们所居住的地方大概 30 里远的茶山，有人组织花会。花会是当地的一种赌博形式。此事被当地知府①发觉，于是即刻派遣永嘉知县②前往抓赌，共有大概 30 人被抓。知县在 15 日夜间，又抓捕了其他涉案的案首，其中包括一名千总应建廷（音译）。应千总的部下认为受到了侮辱，16 日这些士兵抱怨连连，17 日早上他们决心采取行动，占领并关闭了温州城的城门。到上午 11 点，温处道道台已经平息事变，士兵也允许重开城门。起码对于公众而言，“大规模兵变”已经结束。有谣言说，镇台对于民政当局没有经过他的同意，就抓捕其下属感到十分不满，目前双方已经将此事向杭州方面报告。

这里的居民生来就爱好和平，他们似乎认为问题不是很严重。事实上，他们宁可把它当成一个笑话。尽管如此，大部分店铺当天都闭门歇市，街上有成群结队的人漫无目的地闲逛，好像显示一些不寻常的事情正在酝酿。没有动乱发生，然而情况依然很糟糕。在城门被关闭期间，那些在城外有急事要入城的人，疯狂地从一个城门到另一个城门寻找入口，但这都是徒劳。

温处道道台温忠翰几个月来一直在杭州署理臬司，现在已经返回温州。而候补道梁道台③于 20 日已经乘坐“伏波”号④炮舰离开了。

这里的河流有着大量野生禽类。瑞安河离此地大约有 12 英里，据说鸭

---

① 指温州府知府张盛藻。

② 指永嘉县知县张宝琳。

③ 指梁恭辰。

④ 福建水师炮舰。

子和鹅极多，甚至连罕见的天鹅都能找到。在贸易淡季，这里在生意之余，能够提供极好的娱乐机会。

中国轮船招商局的“永宁”号现在在这个港口和上海之间定期运行，12 天一个往返。因此如果一名有活力的人造访温州，在这 12 天内，他能够有时间拜访本地商人，深入考察产茶区。这些茶园距离温州城乘船只需要三天。此外他还能有充裕的时间打野鸭和野鹅，在你回到办公桌之前，让自己的肺部充满新鲜空气吧。你的脑袋应该认识到这一点，如果不尝试深入某地的生活，你永远不可能对其有所了解。智者一言足矣。

这里的天气是令人愉快的，因为常年温暖，几乎显现不出季节性。（12 月 22 日）

《北华捷报及最高法庭与领事馆杂志》，1880 年 1 月 22 日

温州

正如我们所预料的那样，温州没有或极少有新消息。由于缺乏货物，以及中国春节的临近，最近的生意并不太好做。事实上，冬笋将会是市场上唯一的商品。然而我被告知，每两周来一次的轮船，每趟航程仍能满载货物而归。春节后春笋会上市，瓯柑也会迎来第二次收获，所以在下个月，贸易的前景令人期待。

我们的瓯柑大部分都运往天津，在 11 月中旬之前瓯柑都不是太成熟，因此只有早熟的水果可以采摘，并赶上最后一趟从上海到北方的船。其余部分，或者所谓的第二次收获的瓯柑是存储在木制地板上，并且用稻草覆盖。在这个过程中，水果被保存起来，直到白河①通船，我们才会装运货物。

我们仍然没有一个医生，似乎这种情况会持续下去。我认为在温州行医恐怕很难赚到什么钱，但是温州患病的人很多，尤其是患眼疾的病人，你几乎每天都能碰到一个这样的病人。如果有医生愿意在这里做慈善医疗②，必定能大展拳脚。

上个月的天气挺好，不太冷，但似乎即将改变。当下天空变幻无常，足以使老摩尔③自己感到困惑。(1 月 14 日)

---

① 天津白河口，即大沽口。冬天时会出现封冻。

② 指教会医疗。

③ 英国的一种年历，被称为《老摩尔年历》（*Old Moore's Almanack*）。

《北华捷报及最高法庭与领事馆杂志》，1880 年 2 月 19 日

温州

春节已经结束，这座“基督之城”的居民，已经将新衣收好，准备来年再穿。当地人平静且恪守礼仪地庆祝春节，他们会适量吃一些不洁的食物，通常也会敲锣打鼓和燃放鞭炮。但事实上，所有这些庆祝不过是在遵循“惯例”。在除夕，温州主要道路的店铺，都恰如其分地挂上了彩色灯笼。在城市和郊区，几乎所有街道也都点燃了篝火。这种危险的娱乐，竟然没有引发大火，简直是奇迹。当地所有头脑健全的人，都将这样的结果归因于玄天之主镇天大帝①，或其他什么仁慈的神。温州与中国其他地方一样，嘲讽者总能轻易找到许多腐朽之处。这场一年一度伟大的节日过后，部分当地人还提不起劲儿来开始工作，大街上曾经鲜艳的春联，现在已令人悲伤地变旧，在雨水的冲刷下渐渐失色。

在春节期间，护卫舰“超武”号②停泊在港内，这艘真正的风帆战舰挂满了旗帜，同时商船的杰出代表“永宁”号火轮也在春节间出入港口。但是，唉！现在一提到“永宁”号的名字，就让我们这些在温州的被放逐者感到辛酸。因为上海招商局提高了轮船票价，我们用辛辛苦苦挣来的墨西哥银圆，支付从温州到上海的票价，竟然与从上海到香港的票价相同。这实在很不友善，也非常不公平。尤其考虑到“永宁”号的住宿条件并不好，有时甚至还没地方给你住，由于其船长待人有礼，我们才能勉强接受这种服务。有传言说招商局会提高本地船客的票价，我们希望这只是无稽之谈。虽然这种做法对外国社区没有直接影响，但普遍认为，这对招商局

① 道经中称他为“镇天真武灵应佑圣帝君”，简称“真武帝君”，又称玄天大帝。民间认为真武大帝属水，能治水降火，解除水火之患。参见李慕南主编《信仰文化》，河南大学出版社，2005，第 58 页。

② 福建水师战舰。

而言无疑是自杀，对港口的发展前景会带来极大伤害。在此地，轮船贸易和旅客运输两项事业都还没有牢固地发展起来。同时，尽管使用外国轮船的优势开始显现，但本地商人目前还处于尝试阶段，轮船运输做的都还是些小买卖。因此人们普遍担心，货运或客运价格的上涨，会导致托运人保守情绪的回潮，迫使他们回到美好陈旧、稳扎稳打的帆船贸易，毕竟此种贸易自古以来就倍受他们祖辈的青睐。

寒冷已经离去，一同离开的还有绝大多数的野鸭和鹅。温州普遍潮湿，人们修补好雨伞和雨衣，等待春天的到来。(2 月 14 日)

《北华捷报及最高法庭与领事馆杂志》，1881 年 11 月 8 日

温州

“永宁”号轮船抵达港口的时间比预期的要晚。轮船延误是因为缺乏苦力卸货，当地的商贸全都仰赖这艘船的到来，而造成此种局面全都是因为浙江提督①抵港巡海。苦力们担心来了后会被军队拉夫，也担心给公家干活儿的报酬太低，所以都不愿意来。最近海盗消息时有所闻，所以此种指责对黄提督来讲并不公平。500 名湖北兵勇已经在台州南部海岸登陆，另有 500 人在温州北部海岸登陆。黄提督准备用这些军队以及一艘炮艇快速剿灭海盗。但据说黄提督本人负伤了，此次行动终归劳而无功。

① 时任浙江提督为黄少春。

《北华捷报及最高法庭与领事馆杂志》，1882 年 4 月 22 日

玛高温医生关于温州的医学报告*

玛高温医生在他所写的温州海关医学报告中，以美国人的视角，阐述了对温州当地健康、瘟疫、饥荒和医学地志学等主题的总体性看法。在这份医学报告中，36 页印刷得密密麻麻的纸张仍然无法将玛高温医生的所有见解和知识展示出来。因为玛高温医生在他报告的第一页上就提到，他保存的这些医学地志学知识，只是为了给下一个研究者提供参考。玛高温医生的这份医学报告详细报道了他研究过的各种不同的主题，这些主题虽然类型各不相同，并且很混乱，但是他成功地将这些内容有序地组合到一起。因此，我们应该认真研读，不要错过这份报告里的任何一个细节。在报告的开头，玛高温医生简单介绍了温州所处区域的基本情况，随后，他绘制了温州当地的气候图。他提出，温州与法国尼斯的气候类似，但没有法国南部干冷而强劲的北风或西北风。温州可以为精力旺盛的人提供猎捕老虎的机会，因为这些物种会给当地的人带来很多麻烦。但不幸的是，没有病人或者运动员愿意到温州这个港口来狩猎，因为当地无法为他们提供合适的住宿。在一年之中气候比较好的季节，温州地区呈现出的是一幅幸福而又欢声笑语的场景。但是，该地区在一年之中的某些气候恶劣的季节，将遭受山洪暴发，来自海洋的飓风以及暴雨引起的饥荒和瘟疫等自然

* 从 19 世纪 50～60 年代外国人开始接管中国海关之后，便陆续出版发行海关手册，包括各类报纸、贸易报告及数据统计。其中，季刊《海关公报》于 1868 年开始发行。它的第六部分是有关医疗方面的，称为《海关医报》，由各地海关医官负责编写。其中，有关温州的报告从 1878 年 3 月发行第一期起，到 1910 年 9 月止，共有 24 期。就温州地区的报告而言，每篇报告的篇幅长短不一，少则仅有半页，多则长达数十页。其内容大致可以分为三个部分，分别介绍温州的自然地理环境、天气降水状况以及有关当地医事方面的统计与叙述。玛高温（Macgowan）医生就是众多负责记录的医官中的一员。本文就是玛高温医生写的有关温州的医学报告。

灾害。玛高温医生在他的报告中给出了温州地区、浙江沿海区域和福州部分地区在公元291年到1858年期间发生的暴雨、洪水、干旱和饥荒的详细记录，并且在一个表格中列出了浙江省在公元95年至1864年间发生的各种流行病，同时在表格的下面对其中一些流行病进行了详细的解释。对于大众读者来说，中国人在不同时期沉迷于妄想的故事远比关于传染病、热病和天花的医学报告更有趣。但是，玛高温医生充满学术气息的研究报告中许多内容都非常有趣。例如，在他的研究报告中有关于扁鹊的记录。扁鹊是中国最早的“药王”，人们为了纪念他，专门给他修建了寺庙。公元前468到公元前440年，扁鹊有幸遇到了他的启蒙导师，这位启蒙导师建议他每天服用药物，坚持一个月。扁鹊照做了，由于坚持服用药物，扁鹊变得通灵了，并且眼光锐利，可以透视石墙，因此他可以通过自己的视角洞悉人体系统的内脏。当时大部分的医生和常人一样，无法透视石墙，而且只能靠观察病人的舌苔来了解内脏的健康情况。扁鹊因为他的天赋不仅获得了大量的物质财富，例如，他看一次病的报酬是2万亩土地，同时因为他的才能和高超的技艺，也收获了许多的荣誉。正因为如此，后来获知扁鹊被宫廷的太医暗杀而死，我们一点儿也不感到奇怪。通过引用来自江西昌州一位乐善好施的绅士在1876年的专著，玛高温医生指出，作者所在地区在1464年、1529年、1657年和1753年分别发生了一段时间的暴乱，这些暴乱也引出了关于中国人遭受巫师迫害和发生在1876年的风行中国南北的采生折割传闻的有趣报告。随后，玛高温医生介绍了道教的天师，天师是人们在被恶魔折磨的时候寻求心理解脱和帮助的对象。玛高温医生指出，中国人对“恶魔”这个词的理解和认识，并不是产生于中世纪，而是产生于古典时期。但同时我却一时想不起，在西方的古典时期，有哪些作品描述过类似的一些特性，比如辟灾、辟邪这种概念，而这些概念在很大程度上让当地的恶魔显得格外特别。以下是玛高温医生对天师的描述：

> 天师是世袭的，并且可以对恶魔行使官方的权威：遇到紧急情况时，他会发放符咒或护身符，这些东西在1862年被用来抵抗霍乱。很少有房屋的门上不挂符咒，也很少有人不在帽子或袖口上带护身符。在疾病流行的最高峰，每栋房屋的门上都能看到符咒。外国人可以由此了解到当地民众身体与精神上的不安。

通过上述大段引人入胜的描写，玛高温医生向我们描述了恶魔的本质，并抓住了其中的一个点集中描写。如果作者面面俱到，可能就不会这么通俗易懂和令人满意。玛高温医生提到一位居住在龙虎山的天师，这位道士在龙虎山过着隐居的生活，他生活的四周被密封的罐子所包围。这些密封的罐子装着的都是这位道士捕获的恶魔和小鬼。玛高温医生发现他是一个头脑简单、朴实无华的人。作者还用了大量篇幅来描写有关中国人妄想的主题，但在描写的过程中，要么是因为他自身的义愤，要么是因为受到主题的影响，在行文时语言偶尔会显得不那么专业。当作者发现温州人谣传满载外国女人的快船将要入侵温州，且这些女人长相可怕还留着红胡子，我们可以理解并且尊重这位文学大师的愤怒。玛高温医生在表达他的愤怒上做得很好，一些人也认为他在称呼这个诽谤外国女人的人为狡猾的恶棍和无赖汉上并没有很出格。但这些言论还是背离了报告中其他部分显示出的冷静哲学思维。这一点对于玛高温医生的医学报告来说是一种遗憾。如果他想从形式主义的禁锢中脱离出来，最好的解决办法就是，我们只能请作者再反复阅读自己的医学报告。如果他再读一遍自己的医学报告，会发现当地去年租界女性的死亡率很大程度上具有偶然性。对于玛高温医生报告的医学部分，我们无法擅自评论，毫无疑问，他的同行朋友会对这部分内容进行评价。但是，玛高温医生报告中关于中国人中不存在色盲这一结论，至少，我们这边的一些医生是不认同的。

《北华捷报及最高法庭与领事馆杂志》，1882 年 6 月 2 日

玛高温医生关于温州的医学报告

（本报记者报道）

致《字林西报》期刊编辑：

编辑先生：贵刊最近发表的关于玛高温医生的海关医学报告文章中，引用我的那部分关于鸦片的人均吸食量的记录有误。在发布的报告中，我提出的人均鸦片吸食量为 4. 5 钱，而杜思韦特提出的则为 3. 2 钱。实际上，这两个数字应该互换。此信背面的参考文献中杜思韦特先生所制表格中的数据，很明显能证明我的观点。我在其他刊物发表的观点也无法支撑贵刊所述如此高的平均吸食量。

德　贞

北京，5 月 24 日

《北华捷报及最高法庭与领事馆杂志》，1882 年 12 月 6 日

温州

（本报通讯记者报道）

我将会告诉你最近台州附近动乱不断——来自黄金满①的消息。黄金满共有 400 名手下，其中多为粤人②和台州人。其中粤匪有 50 名，据说这些人的枪法准到可以从 300 码以外的地方射落人衣服上的纽扣。但我认为这种说法并不可信。有了这支队伍，黄金满可以肆意抢劫台州府方圆 1 英里内的富户。朝廷派遣将领限期剿灭这伙土匪，但这名将领因为没有完成总督的命令，已经被降职处分。这名将领的军队，全都是由“勇”组成，勇军只向将领个人效忠。因此将领的解职导致军队解散，勇军们全都各自回乡了。现在这群强盗更加肆无忌惮，他们以烧杀抢掠为乐，不断实施报复行为。如果有关粤匪的传闻是真的，那么事态就变得非常严重了。我认为，朝廷在不久的将来要应付的可不是一小群强盗这么简单的势力。南方人在台州的出现让我感到震惊，政治上的重要性正在迅速升级。过去这个国家的革命史告诉我们，这样的事件，往往会在下层阶级掀起滔天巨浪。

目前，本地新闻很少，唯一可能会让你感兴趣的是：福州的一位军队将领有两位夫人，其中更年轻的那位夫人更得这位将领的恩宠。这位将军对二夫人倾尽了他所有的钱财和感情。大夫人却并不愿表现出仁慈，决定与她的竞争对手为难。她也确实这么做了，她让二夫人的生活倍感煎熬。年轻的二夫人决定逃走。她挑选了两名士兵陪同，自己也乔装打扮成军勇的模样，三人一同来到温州，住在西门附近的一个小客栈里。在这个小客

① 台州匪徒，江浙间巨盗，往往被称为“台匪黄金满”，后被浙江巡抚刘秉璋招降。参见刘体智《异辞录》，中华书局，1988，第 89 ~90 页。

② 原文为“Cantonese ”，这里指的是太平天国运动后残留下的“粤匪”，其中许多是广西人，未必全是广东人。

栈里，他们待了三天。这期间，年轻的二夫人一直不敢和陌生人讲话，因为她担心会暴露她的性别。客栈老板发现二夫人行为举止异常，推断其中必有蹊跷，于是将此事上报给本地官府。当地官吏就将包括二夫人在内的三人抓获。目前，这件事还没有完全解决，包括二夫人在内的三人还处于被监禁的状态，以等待判决。

最近天气比较坏，燥热又让人难受。但今日天气已经转凉。码头的搬运工们高兴得摩拳擦掌，因为他们预期自己可以搬运到大宗货物。

朝廷官员正在急切地询问最近出现的彗星陨落的情况，他们急于了解彗星的陨落是好兆头，还是预示着这个国家或其他国家将遭受灾难。(1882 年 11 月 28 日)

《北华捷报及最高法庭与领事馆杂志》，1883 年 2 月 28 日

1882 年中国地震

致《字林西报》编辑：

尊敬的编辑先生您好！我已经准备了一份去年在中国发生的地震的详细记录，并且附上了每次地震中伴随发生的各种现象的报告。考虑到这份地震记录表并不完整，我恳请通过你们的版面向那些观察到这些地震的人寻求帮助，希望通过他们可以完善我的这份地震记录。略去相关细节的地震记录如表 1 所示。

表 1　地震详细纪录

时　间	地震地点	信息来源
3 月 19 日	台湾	哈迪（J. N. HARDY）
5 月 27 日	台湾	《香港报》（*Honkong papers*）
6 月 3 日	福州	《福州捷报》（*Foochow Herald*）
7 月 24 日	重庆	能恩斯（Pere Dechevren）
8 月 11 日	宁波	《申报》（*Shenpau*）
9 月 12 日	温州	当地人
9 月 22 日	厦门	《厦门时报》（*Amoy Gazette*）
9 月 23 日	宁波	《申报》
10 月 7 日	福州	《福州捷报》
10 月 14 日	太原	梅斯奈将军（General Mesney）与《字林西报》（*Daily News*）
12 月 1 日	深州	上谕（Imperial Edict）
12 月 9 日	台湾和大陆地区	香港、厦门和福州的报纸，以及金斯密（T. W. Kingsmill）与领事杰美逊（Jamieson）

这份目录的大部分还存在缺陷，尤其是缺少准确的时间、方位和地震时伴随的地理现象。我特别希望这份记录能够尽早地交到朱克教授（Professor Zuck）的手上，以方便他能够及时制作地震年册。因此，我恳请您就我的请求尽早给予回复。

此致敬礼

玛高温

温州，2月17日

《北华捷报及最高法庭与领事馆杂志》，1884 年 5 月 30 日

温州

（本报通讯记者报道）

英国驻温州领事馆的一名员工，几天前从一座宝塔的顶部跌落摔死了。当时的情景是，他试图从宝塔外的一个洞里去掏一个栗鸢的窝。在掏鸟窝的过程中，他遭到了成鸟的攻击，由于栗鸢不断用翅膀和嘴进行攻击，迫使他不得不采取防卫措施。他一只手抵御栗鸢的攻击，另一只手扶着宝塔的边缘来支撑自己的身体。结果一不小心从宝塔上跌落，不久丧命。(5 月 22 日)

《北华捷报及最高法庭与领事馆杂志》，1884 年 9 月 12 日

温州

（本报通讯记者报道）

“永宁”号在进入瓯江时，发现河里有许多用草绳相连的木桩，这些木桩被插进沙子里，以防止敌船①进入港口。但这些木桩就和渔场标桩一样，毫无用处。有人建议堵塞河道，但是当官员发布告示要求每个家庭都准备一筐石头时，引发了当地民众的恐慌，目前这项提议已经被放弃。当地官府很关心外国人的安全，所以外国人目前感到安心，就如同有铁甲舰保护一样。一些流浪汉会向外国人扔东西，其他人在旁边大喊“杀，杀!”，但这些人会遭到官府鞭打的处罚。福州消息②所造成的刺激正在悄然退去。(9 月 7 日)

① 此时中法战争已经爆发。

② 指马尾海战福建水师惨败的消息。

《北华捷报及最高法庭与领事馆杂志》，1884 年 10 月 15 日

无题

最近在香港发生了骚乱①，在温州也出现了袭击外国人的事件，② 这两起事件都让人感到惊讶，因为香港作为英国殖民地有数艘战舰戍卫，而温州人通常被认为是安静的愚民。因为法国舰队侵扰中国海岸与台湾，大陆上居住的愚民很容易因此被激怒，再加上一些地位更高人士的怂恿，他们便无差别地攻击所有能接触到的外国人。在其他条约口岸，或靠近条约口岸地方的中国劳动阶级，他们的愚昧程度与上个星期袭击外国人的温州人相当。法国政府发动了对中国的战争，以一个香港苦力工人对外国人的认知，让他去区分一个外国人是法国人，还是其他国家的人，这是不太可能的事情。在未受过教育的中国人眼里，所有外国人长得都一样，并且在他们看来，所有外国人对中国都充满敌意。在外国人居住的地区，即便是受教育阶层也对外国人充满敌意，他们会利用无知的同胞来反对外国人。我们知道，对于中国乡绅、士大夫和僧侣而言，外国人的存在令他们极为厌恶。对中国各级官员来说，因为外国人往往不按他们的命令去做一些坏事，所以他们可能对外国人更感厌恶。虽然也有例外，但中国官吏阶层的基本情况即是如此。我们确信到目前为止，我们还不了解温州暴乱的具体导火索是什么，但从收集到的信息来看，这次暴乱中所有的事件都是有预谋的。这些苦力和莽夫不可能是袭击温州当地外国人的主谋，他们是肯定受到了一群地位更高人士的指使和帮助。在这些人的指挥下，这些暴徒们实施暴行的方式和世界其他地方的犯罪团伙一样，暴行的开始和实施都是计划好的。我们认为，阅读了温州暴乱事件的读者应得出结论，或者说如

---

① 指香港工人罢工事件。

② 1884 年 10 月温州发生教案，焚毁了教堂与海关。参见《教案详述》，《申报》1884 年 10 月 12 日第 1 版。

果同类事件在其他地方也不幸发生了的话，我们应该随时准备发现的是，对外国最具有敌意的正是中国的特权阶级，他们不断邀请犯罪团伙加入暴行的队伍。

通过《孖剌西报》最近的一篇文章可以判断，香港民众普遍认可的一种观点是，最近香港发生的袭击和暴乱事件是由中国一些有权势的人协助和控制的。同时，殖民地的民众也普遍认为，某些操控者，小心翼翼地躲在幕后，故意拖长袭击和暴乱的时间。另外，当地底层民众普遍指出袭击和暴乱事件之所以会结束，是因为中国的大佬们强烈要求如此。他们还指出，东华医院，或一些公会，或者两者的联合组织，首先煽动暴乱，企图篡夺政府职权。最后的指控涉及一群中国人，企图向香港殖民政府发号施令。这群人首先是谦逊地表达他们想和香港辅政司讨论这件事的愿望，当他们发现香港政府需要中国人提供想法和建议时，马上就换了副嘴脸，变得不那么恭敬了。《孖剌西报》指出，在这次会议中，一些中国人提出的建议，以及东华医院委员会过去的行为都可以证明，中国人中间一些位高权重的人渴望篡夺香港政府职权。毫无疑问这就是他们的意图。我们看到香港的广东商人们想要获得市议会的许可，将他们的伙计与亲属编练成志愿军。香港和上海的中国人都参与了专门针对外国人的暴力事件，而促使他们进行这些活动的情感因素，和前面谈到的乡绅和士大夫的情感因素可能没有区别，都来自对外国人的厌恶。我们发现，不管哪里发生暴乱，朝廷颁布的法令中有关战争中不能伤害非交战外国友人的规定和政府官员的申明，都无法为我们的安全提供保障。当暴乱发生时，当地官府毫无作为。

福州与温州官员所表现出来的漫不经心，几乎可以在所有港口的中国官员身上看到，而这些港口的外国人正在遭受攻击。这些港口的居民必须被外国军舰保护起来，直到时局恢复和平。其他地方不该重蹈温州的覆辙。外国人需要保持警惕，因为温州暴乱中有一个非常值得我们重视的问题：当犯罪团伙准备开始实施暴力活动的时候，其他人的行为举止都表现得非常正常，没有一点儿要发生暴乱的征兆，也就无法引起我们的怀疑。虽然许多中国人都知道犯罪团伙的真实意图是什么，但是没有人会提醒外国社区的居民接下来会发生什么事情。从温州暴乱中我们应该学到的一点就是，我们必须依赖自己的政府和自己的努力来保护自己。当前的局势已经明显弱化了当地官员的权威和法令的效力。随着战争的持续，骚乱的下层阶级会变得更加肆无忌惮。中国军队战胜或战败是否会将外国居民置于最危险的境地，我们还不得而知。但无论如何，外国政府一定会竭尽全力保护他们，使他们免受暴行的危害。西方列强国家去年签订的关于保护在华外国人的条约，已经赋予了他们在中国的代表足够的权利，我希望这些西方国家在中国的代表能够行使这些权利。中国的军舰在保护外国人方面是毫无用处的。以温州为例，即便这些外国人大部分都是中国政府的雇员，中国的军舰还是无法给他们提供保护。在今年年初，30 个外国居民中，有 6 个是海关的雇员。

《北华捷报及最高法庭与领事馆杂志》，1884 年 10 月 15 日

温州暴乱

从温州驶出的“永宁”号在周六抵达本港，船上的人带回了本月 4 日温州暴乱的所有细节。“永宁”号在抵达宁波港的时候，船上的人就通过电报传回了温州暴乱刚发生时的一些情况。虽然英国领事庄延龄，澳大利亚、匈牙利、德国、瑞典和挪威的领事都竭尽全力希望能够将温州暴乱的新闻从温州发送到最近的港口——宁波，但是消息未能传播出去。有人说是因为信差拒绝发送信件到宁波，也有人说是因为信息遭到了封锁。温州一直都被认为是一个比较安定的地方，当地居民给人的印象是非常愚昧的，因此他们被认为不会惹是生非。事实上，温州也被认为是中国所有开放口岸中最沉闷的一个。“永宁”号这艘外国轮船①，每隔八天会往返温州港一次。军舰很少会抵达温州的港口，而军舰的抵达对于温州这个地方来说绝对是历史上的大事件。从上次军舰抵达温州到现在已经过了很长时间，由于温州地处偏狭，加上当地居民给人留下的愚民印象，各国海军将领都会忽视这个地方，因而不会派出他们军舰中的任何一艘到此地巡航。但是，从我们记录的温州暴乱发生的情形来看，即便是军舰经常在温州港口巡视，还是无法阻止这次暴乱事件的发生。虽然，暴乱分子的后续行为让我们更倾向于相信这起暴乱事件是有计划的，但是对于温州暴乱发生的原因，还是有两种不同的观点。第一种观点认为温州暴乱事件是有预谋的，而另外一种观点则认为温州暴乱事件是当地人的一时冲动所导致的。从星期六（本月 4 日）的晚上一直到周日（本月 5 日）的早上，这伙暴徒像一群野兽，他们着了魔般的愤怒情绪随着破坏活动而不断升温。我们从几个途径获得了温州暴乱事件一些细节：一个外国居民描述了暴乱事件最

① 原文如此。

初的征兆，这个居民讲道，“当时情况的发生就像闪电一样突然”。起初一切都很平静，每个人都像往常一样工作，即使是观察能力最强的人也没有察觉到任何异样，所有人都不会想到马上会有一场暴乱发生。但是，他们都被这看似平静的一切欺骗了。星期六晚上 9 点，苏慧廉像往常一样，率领众教徒在位于城西的英国偕我公会教堂做礼拜。礼拜期间，教堂的大门都是关闭的。在一个小时之前，一群温州民众聚集在教堂的前面，一副无所事事的样子。起初他们只是在彼此攀谈，随后他们打算进入教堂。教堂向这些人出示了朝廷颁发的关于保护外国人的告示，但这群人并没有被吓退，其中一些人反而开始敲打教堂大门。与此同时，门外聚集的那群人的情绪也愈发高涨。苏慧廉听到敲门声，就派门卫去了解外面的情况。门卫一打开教堂大门，敲门的人立马就散开了。随后，这群人又开始敲门，门卫再一次对他们进行了劝诫，让他们不要敲门。如此反复了三次。苏慧廉本人实在忍不住了，立刻出门拖拉一人入室拘禁。苏慧廉的这一举动如同火上浇油，教堂外的民众重新聚集起来，他们试图营救同伴，并且决定破坏所包围的教堂建筑。在短短十分钟内他们就冲破阻碍，从后方进入到教堂内部。但是此时，教堂里的教徒们都已经逃走。在占领教堂后，他们立即放火焚烧整个教堂。短短的几分钟内，教堂就成了一片火海。在城西教堂进行报复后，他们又转往蔡文才先生的住处。蔡文才先生和中国内地会有密切的联系。他们放火焚烧了蔡文才先生的住宅。随着这些暴力活动的持续进行，住在城里的外国人也努力逃往瓯江上的一个小岛，这座小岛离温州城只有几百码的距离。住在城里的外侨包括纪默理①先生、哈密师②先生、玛高温医生、曹雅直先生、苏慧廉先生、蔡文才先生和帕卡先生，其中帕卡先生是主管罗马天主教堂的意大利神父。英国领事以及海关职员马丁先生、坎尼夫先生，领事馆的康吞先生以及他的家人都住在江心屿。而海关的沙隆霍斯特先生则住在离温州 11 英里的下游锚地。瓯海关税务司纪默理先生和海关职员哈密师先生在一起，他们从居所的后面逃了出来。他们翻过温州城墙，成功找到一艘小船，并且很快把这艘小船推入水中。幸亏他们推得够快，当他们的船刚离开岸边时，那些暴徒们发现了他们，

① 海关职员。

② 海关职员。

并且迅速跑到河岸边，对着他们愤怒地大吼大叫。如果他们落到这群暴徒手里，估计性命难保。英国领事馆就在江心屿，外国人都逃向了这里。在这些外国人逃往英国领事馆的同时，暴徒们在继续着他们的破坏活动。外国人就待在这个相对安全的地方目睹了这一切。在两座新教教堂①被烧毁后，暴徒们又转向罗马天主教堂②，浇泼煤油将其烧毁。随后，暴徒又来到了曹雅直先生的住处和他的教堂。当时曹雅直先生正好在家中。于是这些暴徒们就将他们的愤怒发泄到了曹雅直先生身上。曹雅直先生有腿疾，他在很年轻的时候就丧失了一条腿，平常走路都要依靠拐杖。因此，对他来说逃跑是件很难的事情。最后，还是在已近70岁高龄的海关医官玛高温先生的帮助下才得以逃脱。当各教堂都被暴徒烧毁后，所有人都认为这些暴徒会收手了。但是他们并没有，愤怒在不断激发他们进一步实施暴行的欲望。虽然会有片刻的间歇，但是这意味着暴徒们在积聚更大的力量，进而开展更大规模的破坏活动。在江心屿的外国人听到叫骂声越来越大，最后叫骂声变成了一声尖叫。这声尖叫貌似是攻击纪默理先生住处的信号。在这声尖叫声发出后不久，他居住的房子也成为一片火海。几分钟过后，哈密师的房子也燃烧起来。在烧毁上述的所有房屋建筑后，破坏行动也暂时告一段落。这些暴徒为了恢复体力，停止了破坏并开始休息。从疲劳中恢复过来后，他们继续前进，这次把攻击的矛头对准了瓯海关。他们把海关洗劫一空，但由于海关设在寺庙里，中国人觉得烧毁寺庙是对神灵的不敬，所以并没有放火。他们肆意破坏瓯海关的天花板和地板，把所有的家具和公文堆在一起，点起了一把火。但是，他们还是没有善罢甘休。离开海关后，他们还计划去江心屿，不过地方官员事先已将船调走，他们无船渡到江心屿。于是他们自己制造木筏，但因为风高浪急，最后还是没能到达江心屿。如果这些暴徒们当时成功登岛，后果真是不堪设想，江心屿上的外国人将毫无还手之力。当江心屿上的外国居民看到这些暴徒正在造木筏时，十分担心他们会随时登岛。所以除了英国领事外，其他人都乘船顺流而下，离开了江心屿。英国领事穿好领事制服，在江心屿等着这群暴徒的到来。城内陆地上的外国人都跑到了衙门去寻求庇护，但是意大利神父

---

① 指城西礼拜堂和花园巷基督教堂。

② 周宅祠巷天主堂。

没有去衙门避难，而是自己找地方躲了两天，两天后才露面。当外面恢复了平静后，衙门的地方官员将躲藏在衙门内的外国人护送到江心屿避难。暴徒们之所以没能找到船，是因为地方官员很早就命令船只离开右岸。前面提到的因为害怕暴徒登陆而离开江心屿的外国人，最后在中国战舰的护送下又回到了温州。

“永宁”号在周日下午抵达温州下游锚地，星期一上午抵达温州城。当暴乱停止，一切恢复平静后，“永宁”号在星期四离开了温州。当地官员认为，目前较为明智的做法是派遣士兵守卫瓯海关。

我们可以想象此次暴乱中这伙暴徒的愤怒，他们不仅破坏教堂，连外国人的宠物都不放过。他们烧死了外国人的两条狗，并且尝试去烧死玛高温医生的一匹小马。但是这匹小马成功逃脱了。这些暴徒还试图打开一个保险柜，但无论猛撬火烧，最后也没能打开。

当局因为恐惧民众的愤怒，而显得漫不经心，他们最后只成功抓获了五名暴徒。之所以抓获的人数这么少，他们给出的理由是，“无法区分哪些是良民，哪些是暴徒”。

我们从当月 12 日的《湖报》上摘录到以下细节：

> 当苏慧廉发现不能将人群驱散时，他前往地方官员所在的衙门，希望衙门官员可以协助他镇压暴徒。正在审理案件的衙门官员，看到苏慧廉前来寻求帮助，立马停止案件审理，并带领一群衙役前往现场。当他离开衙门的时候，发现教堂燃烧的烈火已经映红了天空。道台也接到了关于暴乱的报告，因为他的衙门离暴乱地点较近，所以先行抵达现场。知府、总兵、千户、团练使以及所有民政、军队官员都到达现场。由于暴乱现场人山人海，地方官员无法从人群中挤进去。另外，他们无法区分哪些是暴徒，哪些是良民，因此没有实施逮捕行动。除了安抚现场群众，让他们保持安静外，他们也无计可施。到了晚上 9 点，火熄灭了，所有的官员也回到了家中。突然，法国教堂被发现着火了，紧接着一个接一个的教堂都着火了。接连的大火使得温州的夜空犹如白昼，人群的尖叫声仿佛海浪在咆哮。幸运的是，当天晚上几乎没有风，否则教堂附近的房子可能也会着火。到了午夜，暴徒们开始了片刻的安静，但是不到半个小时，他们冲到山上海关办事

的房子并且烧毁了它。随后他们来到海关税务司位于火神庙（Temple of the God of Fire）后面的住所，他们把房子里所有的东西都搬到屋外的空地堆起来，然后放火焚烧。房子里的外国人为了保命，四处逃窜，有的跑到道台衙门寻求保护，有些则跑到知县衙门寻求保护。到了星期天的早上6点，这些纵火犯中的一些人悄悄地从西水门出城，然后直奔瓯海关。在海关，他们用与破坏海关税务司住所同样的方式进行破坏活动。他们甚至砍断了海关的旗杆并且焚烧了龙旗。当温州城军队的指挥官带领军队进到城里时，暴徒们已经将海关所有的东西都破坏完毕。由于没有船只，暴徒们没能到达位于江心屿的英国领事馆。

通过询问英国领事馆的总领事，我们没有获得导致这起暴乱发生的原因的任何信息。除了被烧毁的六个教堂，瓯海关所有被烧毁的财产，以及逃到江心屿英国领事馆的外国人外，我们没有获得其他任何的细节信息。

“健飞”号军舰①现在应该已经停泊在温州的瓯江了。我们了解到，英国驻华公使巴夏礼爵士已经致电表达了他对温州这次受暴乱影响的外国人的同情。巴夏礼先生也已经就此事面见亲王和外交大臣。亲王和大臣立即致电浙江巡抚，要求严惩肇事者。

① 英国炮舰，甲申教案后，由宁波调入温州。参见沈迦《寻找·苏慧廉》，新星出版社，2013，第49页。

《北华捷报及最高法庭与领事馆杂志》，1884 年 12 月 17 日

温州

（本报记者报道）

作为领事，施敦力先生本月 12 日从宁波返回温州。当地政府承诺赔偿此次暴乱中外国人的损失。在确保最后一笔赔偿金被支付后，庄延龄先生离开了温州。此次庄延龄对暴乱进行了成功的调解，受到伤害的外国人和当地人都对处理结果比较满意。如果将这样的结果仅仅归因于他的好运气，那么对这位才华横溢的官员来说显然不公平。正是由于他的才智，才使得这次暴乱最后以比较圆满的方式收场。

《北华捷报及最高法庭与领事馆杂志》，1885 年 3 月 18 日

中国的铁路

致《字林西报》编辑：

尊敬的先生您好，虽然上海文友辅仁会在最近的集会中，已经就中国铁路议题进行了很好的讨论，但并不妨碍我在此提供一些粗浅的意见，那些期盼这个古老（但并不衰老）国家繁荣昌盛的人可能会接受我的观点。

对于那些认为在中国修铁路太过于轻率的人来说，他们首先质疑的是，从中国的地形上来看，中国大多数的地区没有修铁路的必要。例如，在江苏和浙江北部，当地水路系统密密麻麻就像一张网一样，并且当地的人力费用非常低。因此，在当地，铁路运输是否能够完全竞争过轮船运输还是个未知数（有人认为铁路运输可能被入侵者利用，但是水路同样也可能被入侵者利用）。但是，对于一些地方来说，如果能够实现铁路运输，将带来无法估量的便利。例如，对于粮食供应非常紧缺的中国北方城市来说，如果可以实现北方与粮食生产富余的中国南方城市的铁路连通，将彻底解决中国北方城市缺粮的问题。但中国南北间还不是最需要铁路运输的地方，中国西南地区被重山险水所阻，这种阻隔更甚于大海上的狂风暴雨，使得西南孤悬于帝国其他部分之外。中国被群山阻挡的部分，主要是富庶的四川与云南两省，在地理上两省是被孤立的，使得进口货物的价格居高不下。如果可以在东西之间修建铁路（或使用马拉轨道）的话，必将让这两个地区变得更加富裕。

虽然通过火车将地理位置上相距很远的两个地方连接在一起具有非常重要的经济和社会效益，但是这些效益和军事战略意义简直没有可比性。虽然知道来自红河①的敌人正在发起进攻，但是因为路途太过遥远，中国东部军队跋山涉水，千辛万苦地赶到西边进行防御时，估计敌人早就入侵

① 越南北部河流。

并且控制了云南和四川。如同越南东京，如果入侵者在行军途中能找到大量不爱国的教民，整个中国将危在旦夕。此外，如果入侵的敌人和其他具有共同信仰的人联合起来进攻西部地区的话，整个中国也将危在旦夕。中国最脆弱的地区不在北方，而在西部。公元前 329 年，秦国将栈道修成道路，并第一次攻占蜀国。到了今天，因为发展需要以及作为帝国版图不可分割的部分，有必要在这些地区修建铁路。

玛高温

温州，1885 年 2 月 4 日

《北华捷报及最高法庭与领事馆杂志》，1886 年 12 月 22 日

温州暴乱

温州本月 9 日发生一起严重的暴乱事件。“江表”号离开温州前往上海后，一伙暴徒冲进温州轮船招商局的办公室大肆破坏。当地人不希望本地的大米被运到其他地方。虽然粮仓里的大米储备充足，但是他们担心大米运出温州城后，本地的米价会上涨。因此，他们张贴告示，示意大家不应该将大米运出温州城。

在这种形势下，招商局在温州的买办购买了 3000 袋或 4500 担大米，并准备将大米运到广东。消息一出，温州当地米价每担立刻上涨 3 元。这让当地的穷人非常不满。道台为了平复大家愤怒的情绪，向公众发布了一个公告，声称本地大米不会被运输到其他地方。后来，这名买办找到道台，并且告诉道台他之前购买了大量的大米，并且已经租借到一艘货轮来运输这些大米。如果道台不允许轮船运走这些大米，他不仅需要支付许可证的钱，同时也无法将大米脱手。随后“美福”号①轮船从上海抵达温州，以运输买办的大米，这让当地人更加愤怒。在这种情况下，道台发布了另一个告示，声称只有少量大米被运走。这个消息一出，当地穷人的愤怒情绪达到了极限。当暴徒们在集结和攻击中国轮船招商局的办公室时，大米正通过小船被运输到“美福”号货轮上。幸运的是，买办并不在办公室，而是和家人在其他地方。如果这些暴徒当时抓到了买办，可能会杀死他。当这些暴徒发现他们无法找到买办时，开始破坏办公室。办公室的底层是储藏室。除了墙壁以外，储藏室的所有东西都被他们破坏。随后，他们将办公室的屋顶掀翻，破坏了所有的书籍，并偷走了一些鸦片和钱。最后，他们还带走了办公室的一个保险柜，里面有所有文件和账本。

---

① 美国轮船。

在暴乱的过程中，知县出现在了暴乱的现场。暴徒们把所有的愤怒都发泄到知县身上。一看大事不妙，知县的轿夫为了自保，都飞奔逃命，这位官员的遭遇可想而知。暴徒将他从轿子里拖了出来，并将轿子毁成碎片。他们毫不留情地痛打这位官员，有些人甚至用石头打他的头。整个过程中，士兵们没有提供任何援助。同时，还有一些士兵加入了暴徒抢夺粮食的队伍。这些粮食一部分在货船里，还有一部分因为检查而被扣留在海关。当暴徒们准备到海关抢夺粮食时，海关的一位外国官员侥幸搭乘一条船逃到了江心屿上的英国领事馆。随后暴徒们将抢夺的粮食运回温州城，他们将粮食吊上城墙，然后拖回城内。买办目睹了整个过程，他从温州逃到宁波，并把在温州发生的一切报告给宁波政府。宁波政府立即派出“超武”号前往温州支援。但是当“超武”号抵达温州时，当地的暴乱也基本上平息了。当地的穷人走上温州的街头，宣称作为穷人也没有什么不好。因为那时有钱人都被洗劫一空，而他们却有大量的粮食。

本月 10 日，数以千计的暴徒发现一些船上装载了粮食，并且有士兵护送。他们认为这些船上的粮食是被运往“美福”号的，于是就控制住这些船。但当发现这些粮食不是被运往“美福”号后，他们允许士兵将这些粮食送到粮仓。

买办的家人害怕暴徒们对他们施暴，于是非常明智地搭乘“江表”号前往上海。买办中途在宁波也一同上了船，他们昨天已顺利抵达上海。

虽然“美福”号在本月的 14 日抵达香港，但令人感到奇怪的是，香港本地的报纸并没有关于这次暴乱的报道。

《北华捷报及最高法庭与领事馆杂志》，1887 年 4 月 6 日

赫德峰*：温州

（本报记者报道）

过路的水手、环球航海家和船长们都会注意到这座山峰。航海家们在第一次路过温州时，一定会在海图上找到这座显而易见的山峰。这座山峰之前只是经常被人提起，但是一直没有名字。最近，温州的居民为了纪念海关总税务司赫德先生在温州期间做出的突出贡献——赫德先生在任职期间，兴建了沿海港口的灯塔用于照亮海岸——就以赫德先生的名字命名了这座山峰。温州人正式将这座山峰命名为“赫德峰”是在 3 月 22 日的一次郊外野餐活动上。3 月 22 日这天正好是德国君主的生日，这一天也临近英国女王登基周年庆祝日，和美国总统克利夫兰的生日。在场所有人无不向可敬的统治者们干杯，大家热情高涨。

沿着一条铺满石头的小路，不用费很大的工夫，就可以到达位于赫德峰山顶的道观。和大多数沿海岸线的山峰一样，从赫德峰顶往下眺望，眼前是一片壮丽的美景，而最迷人的地方就是从山脚蜿蜒而上、错落有致的台阶。温州的一边是大海和岛屿，另一边则是群山，温州被包围在中间。整个温州被金色的油菜花和青绿的小麦铺满，网状的银色河道与阴沉的温州城形成鲜明对比，温州城就如同山水画中的一个污点。从山顶往下看还

---

* Hart' s Peak：赫德峰。赫德，清海关总税务司。据《温州海关记》记载，1886 年 7 月 12 日，赫德乘海关巡逻艇“凌风”号来温视察，翌日离温前往福州。那时，著名传教士苏慧廉与妻子苏路熙已在温州生活，赫德是夫妇俩的好友，彼此曾在北戴河度假时共处过，因此苏慧廉夫妇得以与他重逢。那天，赫德就坐在温州海关办公楼里听取税务司的汇报，从窗口望出去，瓯江奔腾不息，对岸青山连绵起伏。他不知道的是，在他走后，苏路熙以他的名字命名了对岸瓯北的一座山峰，叫“赫德峰”。

可以看到各种壮丽的景色，这些景观因为它们可爱的名字而显得更加有趣。这些景观的名字分别是：格蕾丝山①，珍妮山，路熙山脉，桃乐茜峰，伊芙林台阶。（4 月 1 日）

① 很明显，这些地名都是以当时温州外国人社区的女眷名字命名的，其中“格蕾丝山”是以曹雅直的夫人格蕾丝的名字命名；“路熙山脉”是以苏慧廉夫人苏路熙的名字命名。这一段内容有助于了解温州外国社区的女性社交圈。

《北华捷报及最高法庭与领事馆杂志》，1887 年 6 月 17 日

温州

（来信照登）

当我们的船驶入温州瓯江时，眼前的一切让我们感到震惊。从船上往四周望去，数英里的范围内都被洪水淹没。在这一大片水域上，零星可以看到未被淹没的农庄和墓地，还有一些小山丘，上面挤满了牛。再加上阴暗的天空，和连绵不断的群山，令人感到沮丧和伤心。我们的船开得太快，我无法详细记下一切。妇女和孩子们聚集在一起，谈论这次洪水给他们带来的巨大损失，而男人们则在他们的船里忙碌着。在某些地方，可以看到一些未被洪水冲垮的桥拱上端露出水面，在水的倒映下，呈现出海市蜃楼般的壮丽景色。肯定是一场暴雨才会引发这样大的一场水灾！当我们把目光从被淹没的城市转移到数量庞大的渔夫身上时，我们的心情才开始有所好转。这些渔夫忙碌的身影让人感觉这场水灾好像并没有对他们造成什么影响。随着洪水淹没的城市慢慢在身后消失，我们惊喜地发现，我们即将到达的地方，和我们通常见到的中国北方的城市有很大的区别，这里风景如画，美不胜收。天空也终于放晴，投射到山丘上的光影，随着云彩移动，仿佛在山丘上跳跃，跨过一座座山峰。久未出现的亮光照进若隐若现的峡谷，随处可见的溪流从高处倾泻下来，跌落在瀑布下的岩石上，激起水花万朵。所有外国船只都离开了这个港口，并且也看不到任何外国的建筑，使得这个港口看起来更具有中国本土的特色。这里的空气也很清新，让人神清气爽，和之前大雨过后那种闷热气氛带来的压迫感截然不同。

对于那些崇尚健康和自然的游客来说，在这个美丽的港口待上几天，肯定会收到大自然对他们的馈赠。这里盛产各种珍稀而美丽的蕨类植物，各个角落和缝隙里都被地衣覆盖。那些在位于城墙顶端，或者在山顶被石

柱撑起的亭台，只有领略过温州壮丽景色的人，才能表达出这座港口的美。寺庙和宝塔比比皆是。宝塔大多处于朽败的过程中，其中许多都被树木围绕，远远望去，茂盛的枝叶宛如塔顶。在港口停留的时间很短，这让我们感到十分的遗憾。当地人在我们参观每个名胜古迹时，都给予了最大的热情和无私的帮助，我们无法用语言来表达我们的感激之情。我们在老“鹦鹉螺”号、别名“江表”号上的这次旅行会驱散许多疾病。美食家也不用担心他们的饮食，因为在这个地方，他们会被招待得像在自己的甲板上一样丰富和奢华。格雷汉姆船长和他们办公室的员工对我们的照顾和关怀也是无微不至的。

《北华捷报及最高法庭与领事馆杂志》，1888 年 2 月 10 日

温州及其临近城市的旅游笔记

浙江因其繁复多样、风景如画的景观而闻名遐迩，作为古塔之都的温州就是其中一个很好的例子。温州城离瓯江河口大概 20 英里，河口十分开阔。映入眼帘的自然风光就像是一幅画卷，这幅画卷上，有高山和峡谷，有河流和海洋，还有岛屿和悬崖。江苏平原①上的清新景致最让人着迷。我们把船停泊在温州城和一个宛如仙女一般的岛屿中间。这座岛屿因为它美丽的景色和深厚的历史底蕴而闻名。之后不久，我们发现，远远看去，这个岛屿非常像一艘渡江的轮船，如果岛屿上的双子宝塔可以冒烟的话，那么看起来就会更加逼真。

和中国其他城市相比，温州城明显要干净很多，如果走在温州城的街头，你看不到什么让你觉得厌恶的东西或者闻到难闻的味道。在温州城的地下，几条沟渠作为城市的排水系统在高效有序地运作。绕着温州城的城墙漫步将是一件特别愉快和有趣的事情，而且只需要走几个小时，就能够绕城一圈。一部分城墙会跨越几座小山，在每个小山的山顶都会有一个休憩之所或亭台，站在小亭里可以将温州城以及附近农村的美景尽收眼底。其中一个小山上的亭子有点特殊，它是一个瞭望台，主要用于观察进入瓯江的轮船。这也是当地的外国人娱乐聚会最喜欢去的一个地方。因为在这个地方可以一眼就看到来自上海的轮船，而来自上海的轮船通常会让这些外国人激动不已。随处可见拆卸下来的生锈的大炮，还有各种各样生长得很茂盛的野生植物在随风摇曳。

外国居民在温州当地绝大部分时间是住在寺庙里，这些寺庙经过彻底的打扫和欧化装饰后，住起来还是比较舒服的。礼拜通常是在毗邻的房间

① 原文如此。

里进行。有人偷偷告诉我，这里唯一的台球桌，是用镶在墙里的庄严的老菩萨下面的木板做的！

瓯江下游的水禽比比皆是，在去上游之前，我们在当地花了些时间打猎。

温州当地人对上海的屋船知之甚少。但当地也有和屋船不相上下的船，这种船的规格为35×10英尺，吃水深度为8英寸。这种船可以轻易装下四个外国人，还包括仆人和船夫。由于这种船的吃水比较浅，因此特别适用于瓯江上游这种浅滩多、水流湍急的水文状况。

在一月的一个早晨，刚刚开始涨潮，我们便乘船离开了温州城。和我们一起离开港口的还有大大小小各种船只，他们去往其他地方运输木材。这些船只和我们一起航行了几个小时，在这个过程中，为了防止我们不断射杀水鸟，它们还把水鸟吓跑了。船又行驶了几英里后，水路开始变窄，并且河流的两岸开始出现陡峭的山峰，上面覆盖了各种树木和灌木丛。这种峡谷和我们一路上遇到的其他峡谷没有什么区别。到了晚上，我们抵达了一个叫作温溪的村子，这个村离温州城有90里的距离。我们已经抵达了瓯江的上游，这里的水变得清澈透明，砂石和卵石替代了泥巴和芦苇，十分美丽。又行驶了几里路，我们遇到了此次航行的第一个急流，我们的船夫决定等到天亮再尝试前进。第二天一大早，我们就开始尝试渡过这一段急流。我们在船首固定了一根杆子，杆子的两端预留了4英寸的长度，船夫利用这根杆子作为杠杆来让船体慢慢抬升，与此同时，我们和仆人则协助船夫使劲儿向前拉这根杆子。一路上我们碰到很多急流，加上本身水又比较浅，这给我们的行程带来了很大的麻烦。

有许多小木船也尝试通过急流，它们通过的方法非常聪明，让我们都很震惊。这些木船上通常只有一个人，他既是船长，又是船员，如果每艘船单独通过急流的话会花费大量的时间。因此他们采用了一种更聪明的方法，他们会一直等待，直到几艘船聚集在一起，然后众人合力将一艘船送过急流，直到所有的船都通过急流。

清晨，我们通过了一个叫青田的大城。城墙沿着河岸的方向延伸了0.25英里，并且还将一座高山的一部分圈在城墙里。露出城墙的那部分山体被杉树覆盖，和墙脚肮脏、破损严重的墙壁形成鲜明的对比。通过停靠在河边的木筏和撑杆可以判断，到这里来进行木材交易的人肯定不少。当我路过此地的时候，许多当地村民簇拥到城墙边，满是惊讶地看着我们从他们面前经过。我们在当地买了一些很棒的鱼，这些鱼看起来像鲑鱼。我们只花了50个铜钱就买了六条鱼，这个价格可真不算贵。在不远处，我们发现许多载满鸬鹚的捕鱼船。和在上海捕鱼的同胞们相比，这些使用鸬鹚来捕鱼的人，成功率明显要高出很多。

我们经过的这段河流沿途风景都很不错，由于行走的速度也比较慢，这就给了我们充足的时间来欣赏沿途的美景。在我们路过的一些地方，一个被小树林包围的寺庙坐落在沿岸的山顶上，俯视着整条河流，同时还有许多风景如画的小村庄零星地散落在有人居住的地方。坐落在青田这个地方的房子的外观要比温州以及温州附近的房子都漂亮。

在第二天的下午，我们抵达了目的地——石门洞，据说石门洞离温州有85英里远。在抵达石门洞之前，急流出现的次数已经没有之前多了，但是我们一点儿也不感到遗憾，因为不断被急流阻挡，使得我们的行程显得非常单调乏味。我们在右岸，发现群山中间有个很窄的山隙，于是决定在那个地方登陆。上岸后，我们穿过这个山隙，发现置身于一个非常美丽的幽谷当中，分岔出去的峡谷向各个方向延伸，美到无法用语言来形容。许许多多的水流从山的一侧顺流而下，重重地摔在岩石和峭壁上，激起无数的水花。从登陆的地方步行五分钟后，我们来到一座倾颓的寺院，寺院正对着一条高约200英尺的瀑布。由于正值枯水季，瀑布水量很小。在岩石下面被瀑布的水柱冲刷出的石罅里，表面已经结上一层厚厚的冰，某些地方的冰面完全可以承担起一个人的重量。瀑布所在的山峰被各种林木覆盖，山侧和山脚则是被蕨类植物覆盖，这些蕨类植物绿得有点奇怪，让人误以为现在是六月，而不是一月，因为蕨类植物的这种葱绿很少会在一月出现。

石门洞上游50里有大城，名处州，由于时间原因，我们没有能够去那里游玩。当地有大宗木材和竹子交易，然后这些木材和竹子会被庞大的竹筏队伍运送到下游城市。

我们的返程与来时不同，就像是乘着雪橇从山顶滑下一样轻松，而来程则像登山一样步履维艰。之前不断挑战我们耐心和耗费我们体力的急流，这个时候反而成了推动我们前进的动力。如果你是一个神经比较衰弱的人，就不要去挑战顺行的急流，因为它会把你弄到精神崩溃。当第一次遇到急流时，眼前的岩石好像要把你的船撕碎。你双手紧握船桨，呼吸开始变得急促。当你认为自己命中注定无法逃过这一劫，将被撞成碎片时，开始使劲挥动船桨，在船首即将触碰到岩石的一瞬间，让船重新进入到平静的水面，心跳也随之逐渐恢复到正常速率。在经历过几次急流后，你会逐渐习惯并且开始喜欢上这种刺激的体验。

在离开石门洞后的第二天下午，我们的船遇到了一阵强劲的江风，迫使我们不得不临时停靠在一个小村庄。我们上了岸，穿过这个村庄后，抵达了位于村庄旁山顶上的一个宝塔和寺院。这里，我们看到了这次旅行中所有看到的最美的风景。在返回船上的途中，一群当地的村名欢呼雀跃地欢迎我们的到来。走在人群最前面的是一个年迈的老人和一个小男孩，他们向我们递上两杯茶水，以示欢迎。这次欢迎仪式后不久，我们让大约30个小男孩赛跑，谁跑在最前面就给他现金奖励。每个地方的居民都非常的友好。第二天，我们来到一个类似农村的地方，并在那里进行了狩猎活动。在第六天的时候，我们再次抵达温州，在那里我们发现，来自上海的“海昌”① 号轮船已经停靠在岸边等候我们，船上的人也捎来了我们的信件和外面发生的各种新闻。

温州港居住的外国居民热情地接待了我们，但是我们还是得依依不舍地和他们告别，动身前往北方的城市。

---

① 轮船招商局船只。

《北华捷报及最高法庭与领事馆杂志》，1888 年 3 月 2 日

温州的春节假期

温州的外国人和当地人聚集在一起，欢度中国春节。

曹雅直夫人的女子学院和苏慧廉先生的男子学堂的结业形式就是分发礼品。之前每次结业的时候都是善良的女教师来分发礼品的，但是现在她已经回国了。这些闪闪发亮的新年树包围着的礼品对学生来说都是有用的东西，而不是一些华而不实、毫无用处的便宜货。学生非常喜欢这些礼品。

随后，代理税务司白莱寿先生表演了一个温州当地人之前从未见过的节目，这个兼具娱乐和教学的节目，白莱寿先生也从来没有表演失败过，这个节目是关于灯笼的魔术。孩子们和他们的父母在观看表演的过程中既高兴又惊讶，他们在这之前从未在这么短的时间内学会这么多东西，也从未像今天这样开心。

白莱寿先生会魔术表演的消息不胫而走，导致他不得不在内地会的小教堂重复演出，而来观看他演出的都是一些高级官员，或者他们的幕僚和一些知识分子。后来，白莱寿先生还在当地的主要衙门，给地方官员、衙役还有他们的家人表演。

道台身边的一名委员见此情景，顿生一计且窃喜，如果可以让和蔼聪明的白莱寿先生在曹雅直先生的小教堂给当地居民中的有钱人表演，并且收取他们入场的门票，那么收取的这笔钱就可以拨给黄河边受灾的百姓，帮助他们重建家园。除了要感谢博学且温文尔雅的白莱寿先生以外，还要感谢多诺芬先生改装他精美的办公室，才使得这场表演能够顺利进行。因为有了他们，这个贫瘠、沉寂的港埠的人才能受到如此大的启蒙，才能感受到外国人的友善。

温州春节假期的最后一个环节就是在当地的孤儿院派发糖果和糕点。

孤儿院里收容的失明、聋哑、智障、瘫痪和残疾的孤儿每个人都收到了一个装满糖果和糕点的小包裹，小包裹的数量有300多个，除了包裹外，他们还会收到一些瓯柑。在派发活动结束后，孤儿院的护士小姐、服务人员还有一些淘气鬼（街头流浪儿童自愿进入孤儿院）之间开展了一场有趣的抢夺大战，他们抢夺的目标就是美味可口的瓯柑。

这些慈善机构的孤儿至少在这种活动中享受到了片刻的欢愉，对这种活动的回忆和期待，会让他们暂时忘却孤儿院令人厌倦的生活，打发掉无聊的时光。

妇女不需要别人教，她们本能地知道如何在布满荆棘的人生道路上传播快乐，减轻别人的痛苦。她们将收获到无以复加的愉悦以及宝贵的心灵财富，而一旦拥有了这些东西，就很难被夺走。

《北华捷报及最高法庭与领事馆杂志》，1888 年 10 月 19 日

温州

（本报记者报道）

领事施敦力先生由于糟糕的身体状况，不得不放弃他现在的岗位。在他的接任者霍色先生从广东抵达温州后，施敦力先生将立即动身返回英国。施敦力夫妇在温州的朋友们在为他的离去感到惋惜的同时，也衷心地祝福他一路顺风。

位于瓯江入口处的永嘉场①，离温州城大约有 10 英里。本月 27 日晚间，这个村庄遭到一群强盗的袭击。村民虽然顽强抵抗，但结果反而更加悲惨，有三个村民在这次袭击事件中死亡，还有数人受重伤。这群强盗，据称是一群被遣散的军勇，不仅袭击村民，还抢劫商店。

前些天，中国内地会的一个成员在从处州到温州的路上遭到六名贼寇的袭击。虽然他乘坐的船沿着瓯江上游河岸快速行驶，但是在离温州城 60 里的地方还是遭到了袭击。在这次袭击事件中，他价值 40 银圆的衣服和书籍等物品，还有 30 银圆现款被抢。虽然没有受伤，但不幸的是，他的船也被抢了，不得不在黑灯瞎火的晚上步行走完剩下的路程。

载有王道台和他家人的中国“元凯”② 号军舰本月 5 日离开温州港口前往你所在的港口。这艘船已经在温州的一个废弃的码头停了整整一个星期了，对于当地社区的人来说俨然成了一个观光景点。

自从我们的“海昌”号商船从石浦和海门两个地方离港后，我们就没有收到和这艘商船有关的任何消息。据说这两个地方的旅客运输和珠宝出口业务收益非常可观。

---

① 永嘉场，在郡东南 30 英里。为都四，并属华盖乡。参见《永嘉县志》，光绪八年刻本，卷首。

② 福建水师木质兵轮。

罗马天主教会正在建造一座非常漂亮的教堂。这座大型建筑修好后，将成为温州城最高并且最漂亮的建筑。

从宁波出发的德国“狼”号炮艇今天抵达温州港口，并将于本月12日再次出发前往福州。上次有外国军舰抵达温州港口，还是两年之前的事情了。(10月10日)

《北华捷报及最高法庭与领事馆杂志》，1888 年 10 月 26 日

温州

（本报通讯记者报道）

我们看到一艘英国的轮船驶入瓯江，这令我们既惊讶又高兴。经过证实，这艘船名叫“福清”号，是一艘重达 77 吨的铁壳船，属于香港的霍宏德（音译）先生。让这艘货轮在福州到温州这条水路上搞运输正是这位先生的主意，目前来看，这个想法最后应该会获得成功。在当地，利用铁船进行运输还是件非常新鲜的事情。同时，外国货轮的加入势必会侵害原来在福州到温州这条水路上采用木质帆船进行运输的船主的利益，毫无疑问会引发这些船主的抱怨。据传，除了这艘外国货轮外，还将有一艘外国轮船在福州、温州、宁波和上海之间进行运输。如果这个传言成真的话，温州将马上成为一个开放的港口。

霍乱在温州当地突然流行起来，过去几天内死了很多人。德国的“狼”号炮艇在本月的 12 日离开温州，计划通过福州和汕头抵达广州。（10 月 20 日）

《北华捷报及最高法庭与领事馆杂志》，1888 年 11 月 16 日

温州

福州制造的“元凯”号炮舰从宁波满载 275 名军勇于本月 2 日抵达温州。这 275 名军勇，其中一半是特意调配到温州来的，而剩下的一半将被送到乐清县的大荆镇。在过去的一段时间里，一伙海盗给温州与台州辖区官员带来了很多麻烦。上个月，这群暴徒从玉环湾的大荆（离温州大约 200 里）抢走了两艘帆船，迫使温州的镇台不得不命令他的一艘战舰出海迎击。当战舰抵达海湾的入口时，负责指挥的官员决定就地停靠。随后，他将一部分士兵转移到一艘小帆船上作为诱饵，然后继续向海湾上游驶去。这个策略获得了成功。劫匪以为作为诱饵的这艘小帆船是一艘商船，于是迅速逼近这艘船。当他们靠近的时候，船上的士兵迅速冲到甲板上，对着这群劫匪一齐射击。拜伦曾经说过，“每一次火枪齐射都会让上千人停止呼吸”。①

但是在这次齐射后，还是有人侥幸逃脱。靠近小船的海盗发现他们落入圈套后开始反击。有三名海盗成功逃脱，但是其中一名又被抓到。被士兵控制的十名海盗中，六人在船上被斩首，另外四个则被押解到温州去执行死刑。

在上个月的早些时候我就告知过你，一群劫匪攻击了位于瓯江入口的一个村庄。从那以后，整个温州城都被恐惧所笼罩。为了防止劫匪入侵，城门一到晚上 9 点就准时关闭。

从宁波我听到当地中国人在传播各种谣言，宣称温州城这个地方如何不安全。但是这些都是夸大其词，温州当地的官员都非常清醒，整个温州城也非常安全。

“元凯”号本月 4 日离开温州前往宁波，来自福州的“庆元”号训练舰 7 日抵达温州，并于 8 日动身前往上海。(11 月 10 日)

---

① 摘自《恰尔德·哈洛尔德游记》。

《北华捷报及最高法庭与领事馆杂志》，1889 年 2 月 22 日

温州

（本报记者报道）

外国人如果想了解中国人性格里最突出的一面，最好的方法就是在中国的春节假期里拜访中国的城市。在春节里，他们毫无疑问将充分了解中国各阶层的日常生活。在中国，这些假期持续的时间通常是固定的。所有商人不需要和欠债者过多纠缠就能够成功将欠债收回，并且可以保证每次都成功。这对于这个偏僻的港口来说预示着一个好兆头。

和中国的其他城市一样，温州城也有一个收留失明和残疾儿童的收容所。我们乐善好施的玛高温医生像往年一样，给这些可怜的孩子（数量在200 个以上）分发一些蛋糕和瓯柑等食物。孩子们也会罕见地将他们的玩具赠送给玛高温医生，以回报他的善举。

在建的罗马天主教堂接近完工，这个宏伟的大型建筑将在复活节开放，到那时，浙江省的大主教赵保禄①阁下，将给这座大教堂祝圣②。

最近在当地老百姓中有一种传言，“斯美”号③或“驾时”号将依次

---

① 宁波天主堂自咸丰元年以来，历代主教中“最著威名”者当为赵保禄（Paul - Marie Reynaud，1854—1926）。他于 1884 年 3 月 7 日抵甬，其后之 42 年人生可说是倾注在了宁波。据笔者所知，在近代史上，除曾先后担任过常胜军军官，宁郡卫安勇帮带，江北巡捕房督捕、副督捕的华生少校（在甬 46 年，死于在宁波的任上）外，赵便是在甬时间第二长的外国人。

② consecrated：给……祝圣。据天主教《圣经 · 旧约》所记，“祝圣”是上帝定下的一种给人或物做上上帝标记（使人或物成为圣物或归于天主名下）或传授神权的方式，“你祝圣过的，都成了至圣之物……”。

③ Smith or Cass：“斯美”（Smith）与“驾时”（Cass）两船从英国订造，钢制船壳，各长 250 尺，深 19 尺，吃水 10 尺余，时速 15 节半，可装轻货 1000 吨，重货 500 吨，载客 600 人，分上、中和下三等客舱，都装有电灯，在当时颇为（转下页注）

驶过厦门、福州、温州和宁波，在台湾和上海两地之间进行运输。我们应该欣喜地向这条航线上的先驱“斯美”号致敬。

从上个月的早些时候开始，温州城的天气就一直处于一个不太稳定的状态。暴雨和大雪频繁光顾温州城。当地老百姓指出，这是近些年来冬天里遇到的最恶劣的天气。

上周，一场非常严重的火灾烧毁了温州城最大的当铺。和大多数火灾一样，这场火灾也是由于打翻灯油引起的。如此重要的建筑物被烧毁，给当地的官员带来了一些麻烦。为了防止愤怒的抵押者做出过激行为，当铺被迫向军队寻求保护。在永嘉县承诺全额赔偿抵押者要求的款项后，才避免了事态的进一步恶化。(2 月 7 日)

(接上页注③)先进。二船每艘造价 18 万两白银，主要航行于台湾与澎湖、上海和香港之间。

《北华捷报及最高法庭与领事馆杂志》，1891 年 7 月 3 日

温州骚乱

（本报通讯记者报道）

和其他港口一样，目前温州港的形势非常动荡。造成动荡的原因，一方面来自长江流域所发生事件的报道，另一方面则来自于一群叛乱者。叛匪驻扎在离此地几英里外的山上，他们公然对抗当地政府，官府为了平乱已经使用了各种手段。有传言称，这些已经在瓯江北岸进行大肆破坏的暴徒，试图加入温州城中愤怒的人群去攻击当地的外国人。为了方便读者了解这件事情的来龙去脉，有必要描述一下这群人在北岸的恶行。大约一个月之前，一群来自台州的强盗敲诈勒索村民，一旦没有答应他们提出的要求，他们就将这些村民无情地杀害，并且放火焚烧他们的房子。

一周或两周前，他们抵达温州，并且突袭了 20 英里外的一个村庄。他们到当地的一个富户索要钱财。对方在满足他们要求时，仅仅因为稍有拖延，这伙强盗就残忍地杀害了这户人家的主人、主人的父亲，还有他的两个妻子，同时还射杀了三个听到隔壁有动静前来询问的邻居。随后，他们将房间里的东西和毗邻的房子里的东西洗劫一空，并付之一炬。这个消息一传入温州城，当地县令立马带上所有士兵前往现场。但几天过后，带队的官员又返回了温州城，他们一无所获。带队官员称，叛乱者的数量在 200 人到 500 人之间，远在他带去的士兵的人数之上，并且这群叛乱者装备精良，使用的都是外国人的洋枪。从那以后，温州城的城门一到晚上 8 点就准时关闭，第二天早上 4 点才重新打开，同时携带武器的士兵们夜间也在城里不同地方巡逻。

本月 21 日，这伙暴徒又突袭了 30 里外的另外一个村庄。这个村庄的结局和这群歹徒袭击的上一个村庄差不多。现在城市附近的村民，只要身边还有点财物的，都舍弃了他们的房子，一窝蜂涌入温州城。据说这群强

盗已经在邻近村庄张贴告示，扬言如果这些村民不给他们送钱，就会袭击这些村庄。同时，还有传言称外国人也受到了袭击的威胁。由于士兵不敢正面对抗这群暴徒，温州城的官员都非常惊慌。据说，由于当地县令上次带领士兵抵抗失败，导致越来越多的恶人加入了叛乱的队伍，并且他们的气焰也越来越嚣张。在本月的 23 日，城里出现了一些形迹可疑的人。衙门的衙役对他们起了疑心，于是上前盘查。这群人尝试逃跑，但是其中一人还是被抓，并且从他的身上搜到一把左轮手枪和一把匕首。24 日，在地方官员对这个被抓的人进行审问时，此人气焰仍然十分嚣张。他宣称如果他被杀，他的叛乱者同伙们将马上替他报仇。据说，朝廷已经从杭州往这里调兵，同时镇台也已经去福州向总督汇报当前严峻的局势。鉴于暴徒们在瓯江北岸实施的暴行和恶徒在城内开展的破坏行动，要让这个地方马上恢复到之前的太平是不太可能的事情。同时，城里的外国居民也在不动声色地做一些准备，他们将武器擦亮，时刻准备着应对可能发生的暴乱事件。

炮艇在瓯江的出现，应该也是为了预防可能出现的暴乱而采取的防护措施。有将近一半的外国人住在温州城内，而另外一半的外国人则住在位于瓯江中心的江心屿。江心屿与两边河岸的距离均为 400 码左右。我们住的地方远离温州城，并且我们的人数也非常少。因此，我们处于更加危险的境地。（6 月 25 日）

当我还在书写上述内容的时候，英国的“金翅雀”号炮艇已经抵达我们所在的地方。只要这艘炮艇一直和我们在一起，我们就会觉得非常安全。（6 月 26 日）

《北华捷报及最高法庭与领事馆杂志》，1892 年 2 月 26 日

温州的基督徒遭遇迫害

靠近温州的一个教会发生了一些骚乱。在这次骚乱发生的前一周，当地还是一派祥和，民众对基督教的喜爱在当时还令传教士们备受鼓舞。在传教士苏慧廉先生造访该教会期间，有近 1000 人聚集到这里来聆听他传教。这些人很遵守秩序，他们在 15 分钟的时间内就安静了下来，并且井然有序。苏慧廉先生的布道持续了大概三个小时。当大部分人都离开教会后，剩下 100 个左右的询问者和基督徒，他们双膝跪地，举行了一场祷告会。虽然传教的工作在当地只开展了短短的 15 个月，但是这 100 个人中间已经有 66 个宣称自己是基督的信徒，有六人经过了检验和洗礼。这一天的工作看上去令大家都很满意，没有任何异常。

但是，到了本月 14 日，事情突然发生了变化。一些村民匆忙地来到温州城报告，说他们像往常一样开展基督教服务的时候，人群里大约有 70 个非信徒突然冲进教堂，打砸教堂里面的灯、家具和其他可以够得到的东西。他们把唱诗班的书籍和基督教的圣约书拿出教堂进行焚烧。教堂里的基督徒们也遭到攻击，其中一名教徒被暴徒们踢得很厉害，倒在地上失去了意识。

在本月 15 日的时候又陆续传出几起基督徒受迫害的事件。村里的两个头领再次带领他们的支持者出动。在这之前，只有四个基督徒受了点轻伤。但在此次暴行中，所有基督徒的房子都遭到了劫掠。房子里的居民，不管年幼的还是年长的都被赶出家门，他们的房子也被查封，只有那些宣称自己和基督教没有任何关系的家庭才得以幸免。有近 20 所房子被这群人查封后，这些房子的主人被迫离开他们的房子，无家可归。其中有一个家庭，由于大风吹开了他们的房门，这群暴徒认为是房子主人承认自己转向信奉基督教，故意打开的房门。所以他们攻击这个房子。不仅这个房子的

主人受到虐待，房子里的所有东西都被破坏得面目全非。但事实上，这个房子的主人和基督教没有任何的关系。

当英国的传教士正在给英国的领事写信说明情况的时候，转向信奉基督教的成员代表也来汇报说，在临近温州的四个村子里也发生了类似的袭击事件。在其中的一起房屋袭击事件中，由于一个基督徒在他的婚礼上拒绝祭拜佛像，暴徒们将粪秽倾倒在这位基督徒家里的米缸中，并且破坏了他们可以找到的所有东西。他们还将这位基督徒的新婚妻子打倒在地，并且恶言相向，对他们进行各种威胁。

在所有的这些基督徒受迫害事件中，暴徒们行凶的动机都是担心基督教会替代当地人信仰佛祖的传统，进而使得当地人逐渐远离佛像和寺庙。暴徒们认为，当地的繁荣和稳定都取决于寺庙中进行的各种佛像祭拜仪式，所以这些仪式才流传至今。他们害怕如果佛像和寺庙被当地人疏远，是对佛祖的大不敬，他们所在的地方必将遭受大灾。但从另外一个角度来看，基督徒遭遇迫害事件说明传教工作在当地正在不断进步和发展。

《北华捷报及最高法庭与领事馆杂志》，1892 年 12 月 30 日

来自温州的新闻

两周前席卷温州的台风给当地造成不少的灾难和人员伤亡。四艘装满圆木的帆船被大风吹翻，更多的船则被大风吹得连锚都被拉出水面，还有一些船则遭受了不同程度的损坏。除了大的帆船外，许多小型渔船的命运更加悲惨。岸边的村民非但不帮助这些受灾的船，还趁火打劫，表现得十分野蛮。他们没有任何援助的意思，而是忙着捡拾被大风吹上岸的船只的残骸。更有甚者，强行从失事的船上抢走装载的圆木。这些被台风弄得筋疲力尽的船长也毫无办法，只能眼睁睁看着这些毫无同情心的人哄抢圆木。由于温州城出现了不同以往的寒冷天气，贫穷的老百姓，特别是生活不稳定的老百姓没有足够的衣物，只能在寒冬里瑟瑟发抖。

《北华捷报及最高法庭与领事馆杂志》，1893 年 7 月 21 日

玛高温医生逝世

玛高温医生，这位在上海时间最长的外国居民，一位被广大中国人所熟知的绅士，昨天早上，在他位于文监师路的家中安详地去世，享年 79 岁。玛高温出生于马萨诸塞州的福尔里弗。50 年前，他作为传教医生，第一次来到宁波。美国南北战争爆发后，他回到美国，在北方军队中当军医，并受到华盛顿当局的嘉奖。美国战争结束后，他于 1865 年重返中国。返回中国时，他的身份是一家大企业①的代表。这家企业提议通过白令海峡修一条直达中国的电报线。也就是从那时起，他将自己的办公室设在上海。玛高温医生的妻子和玛高温医生一样，在中国也非常受欢迎。玛高温医生的妻子于 1878 年去世，之后玛高温医生就像换了个人似的。玛高温医生只有一个女儿，是阿查立爵士②的妻子。阿查立先生于 1879 年在海关给玛高温医生设了一个职位，他同时供职于上海和温州。在温州，他可以全方位地去研究民俗学和自然历史。他是一个热衷于收集各领域各类型信息的人，同时也乐于讲述他收集到的信息并传给他人。他很早就为我们的报纸专栏做出了许多贡献，此外他对传教工作、科学以及文学出版工作也做出了许多贡献。他是一个和蔼且心地善良的人，不管是在家里还是在公司，他常常会给我们讲一些新鲜的趣闻。他在追求真理时往往充满无穷的精力。他能将令人厌烦的生活过得丰富多彩，他最近这趟西伯利亚漫长而艰难的旅行就是个很好的例子。上周六，从北京和天津回来后，玛高温医生就一直处于生病的状态，但是他拒绝向医生寻求帮助。他一直在盼望李鸿章总督给他回复关于美国新任公使的介绍信，这位新任公使就是杨儒③，

① 指美国东印度电报公司。

② 英国外交官，曾担任驻华大使。

③ 杨儒时任温处道道台，可能因此与玛高温结交。

最后李鸿章总督推荐他为华盛顿公使馆的顾问。星期二的时候玛高温医生开始卧床不起，哲玛森医生被派往玛高温的住所给他看病。但是，周三的时候，玛高温医生又穿戴整齐地出了门。他被人劝说重新躺回床上，早上10点半，当家人正准备给他递牛奶时，发现他已经在睡梦中安详地去世了。玛高温医生死后，他远在英国的女儿阿查立夫人马上收到了关于父亲去世的电报。玛高温医生的葬礼将于今天下午5点30在新公墓进行。

《北华捷报及最高法庭与领事馆杂志》，1893 年 12 月 15 日

温州附近的海盗

虽然最近闽浙海岸线加派了战舰巡逻，以防止海盗的出没，但是福建和台州的海盗还是和以前一样多，并且和之前一样凶残。装满大米和其他杂货的商船在从宁波前往福州的途中，被埋伏在温州附近的几个海盗袭击。这些海盗登上商船，抢夺了一切值钱的东西，还攻击船上的人，造成 25 人死亡和重伤。总督已经下令捉拿这些海盗，并且派出了由众多战舰组成的舰队前往追凶。但是在大多数人看来，这次出征可能仍以失败告终。

《北华捷报及最高法庭与领事馆杂志》，1894 年 7 月 13 日

温州

（本报特约记者报道）

台 风

6 月 25 日，周五。台风从离温州港口特别近的距离肆虐而过。从早上 5 点开始，气压计度数就开始不断下降，直到下午 5 点才开始逐渐上升。下午 5 点是气压最低的时候，气压计的指针指向 28.95。这个过程中，一直吹的是西北风。其他的气压计观察员也是在下午 5 点的时候注意到气压计的读数降到了最低。星期五一整天，每个人都是在焦急中度过，他们一直在为“泰安”号轮船的安危而担忧。“泰安”号轮船在周三清早离开温州港，船上的乘客有满思礼领事和瓯海关税务司那威勇①。

意识到“泰安”号轮船已经安全

所有人都希望“泰安”号轮船能在台风来临之前，提前进入安全的避风港。直到昨天（7 月 2 日，星期一）晚些时候，满思礼和那威勇先生出现在我们的社交圈中，大家才开始忘却这场台风。

乘客的故事

随后，满思礼和那威勇先生给我们讲述了他们在船上的遭遇。“泰安”号轮船星期三早上离开温州港口后才航行了 35 英里，发动机就出现了故障。于是，轮船被迫停泊在位于鹿栖山和爿山屿中间一个比较糟糕的锚地。星期五的时候，台风从这个锚地经过，轮船感受到了台风巨大的威力，沉在水底的三个锚在风力的作用下，被拖拉着朝爿山屿下的暗礁方向

① 后者前往上海休假，前者则前往福州任职。

移动了2英里。幸运的是，最后锚还是找到了可以固定的地方，无助的船员也得以幸免于难。气压计的最低读数为28.31。星期天，来自温州的中国“超武”号炮艇出现在人们的视野中，“泰安”号马上向对方发出求救信号，希望对方可以将他们拖到较安全的避风港。这艘船的指挥官态度非常傲慢，十分不情愿地做了一次无效的尝试，随后敷衍地说了句“拖不动”，就匆匆离开，朝着宁波的方向驶去。随后，大海恢复了之前的平静，台风也消失得不见踪影。“泰安”号轮船上的维修师卖力地尝试去修复在台风中损坏的引擎和转舵装置。到了周日晚些时候，“泰安”号已经可以缓慢地朝另一个非常安全的锚地——青菱屿行进。

一位人道的官员

星期一，一艘名为“元凯”号的中国炮艇进入“泰安”号的视线。同样，“泰安”号发出信号向对方求救。这艘船和“超武”号一样，乘客当中也有官员。事后了解到，这位官员是温州的镇台。这位官员的善心无人可及，他不仅指挥“元凯”号上的船员将“泰安”号急需的转舵等装置借给他们，并且还将“泰安”号上的所有中外乘客转移到“元凯”号轮船上，将他们送回温州。当“元凯”号轮船离开的时候，“泰安”号轮船也以2节的速度慢慢地向上海行进。

受害者

船上的部分茶叶和其他货物都因为浸水而受损严重。为了减轻整条船的负重，所有乘客的行李都被要求扔出船外，因此，所有的中国乘客都丢掉了他们的行李。虽然这些乘客买了全额的船票，但他们只能住在甲板上，因为他们票价里1/4的钱是用来运输他们的货物的。他们希望轮船招商局能够赔偿他们的损失，但是估计对方给他们的补偿会比较少。自从“泰安”号在这条航线航行以来，大家都知道这艘船的发动机有缺陷，并且动力不足。“泰安”号轮船上没有蒸汽起锚机，并且没有足够的水手来投掷锚。当它离开温州的时候，不得不雇用岸上的苦力来起锚。在星期天这天，当台风离开之后，船上所有的船员和一些乘客不得不共同出力起锚。船上的舵机非常简陋，转舵和舵轮之间通过绳子连接，而不是采用铁杆连接。连接驾驶舱和发动机室的电线在台风中被损坏，因此驾驶舱给发动机室下达的命令必须靠一名水手口头传达。英国贸易委员会将如何看待这样的一艘轮船在海上航行呢?

毫无疑问，整个社区都为满思礼先生和那威勇先生奇迹般的逃生而感到高兴。从他们谈论这件事情的情况来看，这将注定是他们难忘的一段经历。

赞美之词

满思礼先生和那威勇先生都高度赞扬了福瑞格斯特船长以及他的船员和工程师。虽然“泰安”号失去动力被迫停靠在一个破旧的锚地，并且已经无计可施，但是福瑞格斯特船长还是尽到了他最大的努力试图让这艘船走出困境。如果不是因为“泰安”号轮船的锚最终找到了可以固定的地方，它早就撞上了爿山屿上的岩石。由于害怕轮船撞到岩石，船长曾两次将满思礼先生和那威勇先生召集到甲板准备弃船。

天　气

现在，这里的天气很热。我们盼望轮船的出现，因为它会给我们带来外面发生的各种新闻大事。

台风带来的后果

台风对温州城当地的老百姓造成的损失非常小，甚至连“麦克维的房子”都没有受到台风的任何影响。(7 月 3 日)

《北华捷报及最高法庭与领事馆杂志》，1894 年 12 月 28 日

温州

（本报记者报道）

之前，“普济”（*Universal Benefactor*）号轮船每次离开都不会打破我们这个寂静的山谷日常的宁静。但自从“普济”号上次离开温州港口后，当地社区中的两位尊贵女士的危险遭遇成了许多人茶余饭后的谈资。星期三的晚上，这两位女士去位于温州郊区的一个村庄，她们准备在当地基督徒的家里留宿，并且参加上晚上进行的礼拜活动。礼拜活动后，她们因为疲惫准备上床休息，此时没有察觉到有任何的异常。直到午夜时分，当发现屋子里出现十几个带着枪和长矛、举着火炬且面带凶相的人时，她们才察觉到危险。这群强盗将女人们的手镯和耳环全部扯下来，屋子里充满了女人的尖叫声。这两位女士努力尝试去护住她们身上盖的东西，但还是被强盗粗暴地从床上拖下来。不仅如此，这群强盗还用竹片去抽打她们。她们所有的东西，包括寝具、衣服等都被强盗夺走了。如果不是当地的一位勇敢的女宣教士从强盗群中奋力挤出一条路来到这两位女士的身旁，并把她们从隔壁的房间拖回来的话，这两位女士很可能会被这群强盗带走并作为索要赎金的人质。事实上，她们光着脚快步走到一个小山坡的半山腰。半山腰上夜风阵阵，非常阴冷，她们身上也只是穿了一件很薄的睡衣。由于跑得太快，加上没有穿鞋，她们的脚也受伤了，不仅青肿，还流着血。她们一直瑟瑟发抖地坐在半山腰，直到枪声停止，强盗们的火炬光亮渐渐远去。当她们重新返回村庄的时候，发现不仅是她们，当地村民所有可以搬得动的家私都被洗劫一空。除了财物外，强盗还带走了三个男人，其中就包括这两位女士的仆人。第二天，这两位女士艰难地返回温州城，并且向领事报告了这件事。

被抓获的强盗

村民在上次的袭击事件中抓获了三名强盗，但其中两个强盗侥幸逃脱了。没有逃脱的那个强盗现在被关押在地方官员所在的衙门里。村民知道这三个强盗的名字，他们到其中一个强盗的家里去，地方官员也假装前去调查这件事情。但实际上，他并没有亲自去，而是派了几个跑腿的前往。这几个跑腿的衙役非但不关心这个案件，反而向已经一贫如洗的当地村民强行索要他们的差旅费。

担惊受怕的官员

官员们看上去似乎不太了解他们手里的权力有多大，事实上，他们知道自己的权力，只是害怕去执行。官员的胆怯懦弱，以及士兵从对抗日本人的区域撤退，使得邻近这个区域的老百姓遭了殃。一群强盗集结在一起，大肆掠夺他们同胞的财物。

领事奇怪的声明

领事已经派出一个代表去道台那里。但是据我们了解，派去的代表向道台转达的意思是，这两位女士的护照已经被撤回了，一旦她们出游超出温州的边界，士兵就会将她们带回温州。

《北华捷报及最高法庭与领事馆杂志》，1895 年 2 月 22 日

温州

（本报通讯记者报道）

谣言和谣言

中国人普遍存在的一种习惯是：坚信那些可能事实上并不是真的事情；从来不会去思考那些可能是真实的事情；对已经发生的事实毫无概念。当你告诉一个生活在长江南部的当地人山东、旅顺沦陷了，他的表情是眼睛和嘴巴张得老大，一脸惊愕状，嘴里不自觉地说出一句“啊?”。他们根本都不知道还存在一个叫旅顺的地方。你告诉他登州目前正在开发和投资，他完全不明白你说的地方在哪儿，也不明白你说的这件事有什么意义。英国的轮船恰巧到舟山群岛进行观光；一个月或两个月后，这艘船开往烟台，都忘记了舟山群岛这码子事。虽然这只是一件寻常事，但传到中国人这里就变成了各种谣言。其中一种说法是，日本人在舟山群岛挥舞着英国的国旗，并且他们非常确信，日本人去舟山是为了纪念斯洛克姆。

《北华捷报及最高法庭与领事馆杂志》，1895 年 3 月 1 日

温州

（本报记者报道）

一起社会事件

本月 11 日，在税务司那威勇先生家的餐厅举办了一场盛大的音乐会。虽然观众人数不多，但大多是具有一定音乐鉴赏能力的嘉宾。由于之前指定的主持人感冒或者担心任务繁重而无法胜任这个工作，所以缺席了这次音乐会。在这种情况下，劳里（Lowry）医生接替了主持人的工作。我们更愿意相信之前的主持人是因为生病而无法担任主持人这个工作，因为温州这段时间的天气一直都非常糟糕。但在温州，被喊去担任音乐会的主持人，不管从哪方面来讲都是一件让人心烦的事情。附上的节目单里给出了一个菜单。来自温州港的林顿先生①的精彩演出让所有的观众都入了迷，特别是“pot boiler”这一幕，在短短四分钟的时间里呈现出了绿树、高山和河流等场景，美不胜收。“普济”号弗洛伯格船长的小提琴独奏同样引人入胜，观众听得是如痴如醉。因为节目太精彩，台下观众都意犹未尽，“再来一遍”的呼声不绝于耳。这场音乐会的开始部分看起来更像是一场葬礼活动，直到海和德②先生朗诵马克・吐温的作品《奥里莉亚的倒运未婚夫》。海和德先生绘声绘色的表演引起了在场所有观众的共鸣。这种重

① 全名为 Albert Linton，19 世纪 90 年代活跃于上海，擅长油画，长期在上海中央饭店（Central Hotel）举办画展，并绘有大量以温州为题材的油画作品。林顿关于温州的油画作品目前在何处，还有待进一步发掘。

② 海和德（James W. Heywood，1867—?），英格兰普雷斯顿（Preston）人，偕我公会（循道公会前身）传教士。光绪十七年（1891）来温州协助苏慧廉工作，1896 年第转赴宁波。1912 年又回温出任温州教区负责人，直至 1929 年回国。引用自沈迦《一条开往中国的船：赴华传教士的家国回忆》，新星出版社，2016，第 153 页。

要的社交活动在温州几十年内都不太可能出现第二次，必将载入温州的史册。以下是这场音乐会的节目单：

第一部分

1. 开场序曲：《无言之歌》－小提琴，演奏者：霍厚福先生和海和德先生

2. 歌曲：《轻骑兵的冲锋》，演唱者：劳里医生

3. 歌曲：《誓死捍卫真理》，演唱者：拉蒙德先生

4. 钢琴曲：《卡门》，弹奏者：林顿先生

5. 歌曲：《圣城颂》，演唱者：苏慧廉夫人

6. 宣读：《奥里莉亚的倒运未婚夫》，宣读人：海和德先生

7. 小提琴独奏：苏格兰咏叹调《逝去已久的日子》，演奏者：弗洛伯格船长

8. 朗诵：《一位水手母亲的祈祷》，朗诵者：永勒夫先生

9. 歌曲：《贝都因人爱歌》，演唱者：苏慧廉先生

10. 宣读：《关于幽默的讨论》，宣读者：霍厚福先生

第二部分

1. 开场序曲：小提琴，演奏者：霍厚福先生和海和德先生

2. 歌曲：……《毛笔之歌》，演唱者：林顿先生

3. 歌曲：演唱者：拉蒙德先生

4. 歌曲：《好伙伴》，演唱者：苏慧廉夫人

5. 小提琴独奏：《贡多拉船夫》，演奏者：霍厚福先生

6. 宣读：《纽扣》，宣读人：苏慧廉先生

7. 钢琴曲：《米卡多》，弹奏者：林顿先生

8. 歌曲：《见风使舵》，演唱者：海和德先生

9. 小提琴独奏：《蓝色多瑙河》，演奏者：弗洛伯格船长

10. 歌曲：《四个快乐的铁匠》，演唱者：拉蒙德先生

最后乐章：小提琴和钢琴协奏曲

《马赛曲》

《天佑女王》

一场流行病

一场严重的流行病——天花（没有影响到音乐会的举办，音乐会也没有导致天花传染）已经折磨这个地区长达数月的时间。受这场流行病的影响，有数千人丢掉了性命，而死亡的人当中，大多是儿童。事实上，这种流行病最大的一个特征是它主要在儿童和青年人中间传播。在乐清市，有超过1000人死于天花，而在邻近这个市的一个大村庄里也有200人死于天花。这些都是温州辖区内一些因天花而死亡的情况。随着时间的推移，这种流行病的影响在逐渐减弱，就算是最近感染上这种病的人也很容易康复。

防御行动

目前"龙湾山"① 已经有士兵布防。这群士兵目前也在忙着构筑防御工事。他们将地基填高，并尝试在上面架设大炮。另外，温州的所有城门也有士兵把守。只要日本人胆敢进犯，必将遭遇这些士兵的迎头痛击。

风　水

温州城内的人还是比较文明的，我们走在路上也不用担心会遭到袭击。但是，由于新领事馆事件，城内的外国人还是可以感觉到当地的老百姓对他们充满了敌意。欧洲人认为新领事馆的修建可能会对当地的美景造成小范围的破坏，但是仅此而已。但温州当地人却不这么认为，他们坚信，新领事馆的修建破坏了当地的风水。在省会城市的上一次科举考试中，来自温州府的考生没一个考上。这种令人感到蒙羞的事情在温州已经好多年都没发生过了。到底是什么原因导致这种情况的发生呢？是因为这些参加考试的学生缺乏热情，还是他们在考试的时候开小差、磨洋工？两者都不是。主要的原因在于，这座神圣小岛上的土壤遭到了西方野蛮人的破坏，风水受到了影响。去年，一位当地的老者站在这座新的领事馆的对岸，用尽全身的力气对着领事馆进行叫骂，并且号召当地人联合起来，将

① 龙湾山，也叫云亭山。参见《宗湘文观察督办海防》，《申报》，1895年4月4日，第2版。

这座建筑夷为平地。最近，当地人向英国政府提出严正的抗议，要求对方将这座领事馆拆掉。但是，尽管当地人不断抱怨，英国政府也不为所动，领事馆上的米字旗依旧安然无恙地随风飘扬。

官员阻挠

战争激起了当地人对本地基督徒的仇恨，这也影响了当地的传教活动。这些基督徒因为接受英国传教士的指导，因此，他们被当地人称为野蛮人。上周末一群暴徒破坏了在乡下举行的一场礼拜活动，参加这次礼拜的基督徒多达100人。这群暴徒将所有与圣经、圣歌有关的书籍堆在一起，一把火全部烧毁。女人们身上的衣服全被撕扯下来，她们的首饰也全被抢走，男人则遭到这群暴徒的殴打。县令来到现场，宣称要严肃处理这件事情，但最后他什么都没有做。这起事件只是最近发生的众多基督徒受迫害事件的一个缩影。一个礼拜堂觉得有必要扩大房屋的面积，于是就购买了邻近的一个院子。道台下令让县令去传唤这个院子的房主和负责这起房屋交易的文书。因为私自将土地出售给外国人，而且事先没有通知县令，这些人受到县令的大声辱骂，并且威胁要剥夺房产交易局的登记资格。此外，县令还下达命令，今后如果外国人购置房屋，打算出售房屋的主人首先必须得告知县令，并征得所有邻居的同意，且房屋必须是独栋。这种事情以前在当地从未发生过，如果县令真的按他下达的命令执行的话，外国人在当地购买房屋将成为不可能的事情，因为中国人都不敢出售他们的房屋。在这个开放的港口，似乎我们又要经历旧时代官员的淫威和干涉了。在动荡不安的时期，向地方官员寻求帮助是很自然的事情。但是，当你发现你要寻求帮助的正是和你作对的人的时候，还是会感到相当吃惊。由此来看，大清帝国已经时日无多①。

---

① 原文是“Mene, mene, takel, upharsin”，是源自《圣经》的俗语，有人在巴比伦的城墙上写下这些字句，暗指王国时日无多。

《北华捷报及最高法庭与领事馆杂志》，1895 年 3 月 8 日

温州

（本报通讯记者报道）

平静时刻

在温州，我们已经掌握了生存之道，那就是，要么靠追忆逝去的美好事物而活着，或者靠对未来的坚定信念而活着。但是，对我们其中的一些人来说，每天的日常工作就像是要敲碎一颗坚硬的坚果一样辛苦，我们随时准备带着疲惫的身躯大喊“我们的休息时间都去哪儿了！”。尽管如此疲惫，尽管像所有的先知一样，在这些工作完成之前，我们无法预知未来，但是我们还是对未来充满信心。

“普济”号轮船

由于一路上都是大雾天气，“普济”号轮船花了三天时间才抵达温州，并且这趟航行也是糟糕透顶。“普济”号带回来的新闻和我们之前获得的一样，充满了各种不确定性。停战协议目前还没有正式宣布，李鸿章也没有前往日本。我们还需要耐心等待两周甚至三周时间，因为在“普济”号抵达之前，我们自己的轮船也已经动身前往天津。虽然我们现在处于未知的黑暗当中，但在同情和惋惜的同时，我们也告诉船上的朋友们，现在平原上到处盛开着芬芳的油菜花，明媚的阳光和凉爽的微风正在向他们召唤。

军事准备

我们为数不多的健身活动现在也不能开展了。士兵们在当地外国人非常喜欢去游玩的山上聚集，他们对待绅士们的态度是嬉皮笑脸，而对独居的妇女则十分粗暴。山上有一处外观十分亮眼的观景台，这个观景台四周

现在被土方工事所包围。在白天，这个观景台是无法进入的。一些据说是从未被使用过的枪械被放置在观景台的四周。虽然有人提出，开枪的人所面临的风险可能要比站在枪前面的人更大，但是这些枪最终还是留在了那里。道台将四周的土全都堆到了观景台上，而且还开了两扇门。虽然很难解释为什么要在观景台上立两扇门，但是可以确定的是，如果不进口一大批火炮回来，这些工事将毫无用处。

强　盗

我们听说一群强盗在城里出现，县令前几天已在河两岸增派士兵把守。这天清晨，一群强盗袭击了离温州城 150 里的一个村庄。村庄的村民利用他们自制的枪械武装自己，进行了英勇的抵抗。战斗持续了一整天。到晚上的时候，这群强盗被迫撤退。战斗造成一名强盗和两位村民死亡。县令带了一群士兵前往村庄进行调查，但是最终他们还是和以前一样，无功而返。返回后，他们又恢复到之前游手好闲的状态。知情人士将这起非法的暴力事件归因于穷困。

《北华捷报及最高法庭与领事馆杂志》，1895 年 3 月 29 日

温州

（本报通讯记者报道）

寒　流

即便是这个港口城市，也无法躲过暴风雪的天气。在当地一些老人的印象里，温州在二月份已经有几十年没有遇到过这种奇怪的天气了，先是狂风暴雨，紧接着是一场大雪。大家不仅担心当地早季的水果会受到影响，还担心这种早春天气会影响茶叶的产量。但瓯柑的花苞还没开放，产量应该不会受到很大的影响。

我们的新道台

前几天，我们的新道台和镇台一起去视察了炮台和军队，以准备应付臬司（顶替巡抚）的到访。我们听说，这位新上任的道台向军队的官员施加了很大的压力，要求他们尽快将劫匪和海盗消灭干净。有报道称马上就要进行电报调查，但是调查者需要四处去借相关的仪器设备。因此电报调查是否能够成功进行，我们拭目以待。据说温州马上就要架设电报，但测绘员还在四处借调设备，结果如何让我们拭目以待。

对战争的无知

如果不是因为所处的环境蒙蔽了他们的眼睛，那么听到当地老百姓对战争无知的评论时，我们肯定会觉得非常可笑。前几天我们听到他们这样评论，“外国人在进行叛乱”，另一伙人回答说，“但外国人肯定只是说说而已，不是真的要叛乱”。

借　钱

我们听说一则要求百姓借钱给皇帝的告示已经张贴了出来，告示中提到，只要愿意借钱给皇帝，每年可以获得 7% 的利息。虽然我们没有见过这种公告，

但是已经可以听到有人略带嘲讽地在议论这件事情了：“皇帝什么时候穷成这个样子了呢，需要乞求老百姓借钱给他？谁会借给他钱啊?”最近，衙门里的人都在议论这件事。就在上周，一个男人来到了镇台的衙门，随后在桌上留下一封信，并且称这封信是提台①让他送过来的。镇台衙门的人放走这名男人后打开了这封信，发现这封信确实来自提督。信中写道，皇上无法维持整个宫廷的正常运行，想放弃他的皇位。同时，他还恳请各级官员选出一名更加适合的人来掌管整个朝廷。这封信在整个衙门和整个地区都引起不小的骚动。

让人们感到害怕

受特殊公告的影响，今年禁止举办和复活节相关的各种活动。由于在国外，大家都非常看重这个节日。因此，这个节日被禁止后，大家都感到非常不满。其中有一个外国男人，带着链条，假扮成上帝使者的模样，威胁大家说，上帝因为复活节被禁这件事情非常生气。

条约，一纸空文

在著名的《万国公报》② 里提到，总理衙门下令，在当地官员未调查清楚该房屋的出售是否会破坏邻居的风水之前，任何的土地都不能出售给外国人。现在，这则通告里提到的内容已经从抽象的东西变成了现实。超过 100 份的通知已经下发到各地土地登记员和地保等人的手里，告知他们不能将土地转移到欧洲人手里，除非房屋的租借人已经征求了当地官员的同意。这些通知带来的最大影响是，当地的土地拥有者都不敢进行土地交易。因为一旦他们进行土地交易，衙门的那些寄生虫就会黏到他们身上，吸光他们的血，让他们家破人亡。当地的外国人向英国领事馆代表提出强烈的抗议。虽然领事馆也向总理衙门提出了抗议，但是并没有任何效果。这些东方人还是我行我素。对于英国的居民来说，之前签订的条约就是一纸空文。令人感到遗憾的是，北京方面对这些公然排外的命令无动于衷。现在，这些命令第一次在温州付诸行动，其目的是阻止当地人将土地租售给外国人。中国人在英国购买土地不会遭到禁止。但是在温州这个条约港口，虽然当地人

---

① 提督的尊称。

② 《万国公报》的英文为 *Wan Kwoh Kung Pao*，但《字林西报》在引用时，一般称其为“*Missionary Circular*”。

都急切地想出售他们的土地，但是当地的官员仗着总理衙门的命令从中百般阻挠。当地人如果敢出售土地给外国人，他们就会被带到县令或者道台那里，在公开审理中遭到恐吓，并且受到这些官员下属的敲诈。因此，当地人再也不敢将土地出售给外国人，当地的土地交易也明显受阻。

两件趣事中的第一件

在“普济”号离开的这段时间里，这里发生了两件有趣的事情。本月12日，是中国内地会曹雅直夫人的50岁生日，也是她到中国25周年的纪念日。对于其他大多数在华的外国人来说，很少会有曹雅直夫人的这种特殊经历。为了纪念这一特殊的日子，苏慧廉代表温州的所有传教士，向曹雅直夫人赠送了一块金表。有大约300名中国客人也应邀参加了曹雅直夫人的寿宴和教会活动。他们为了庆祝曹雅直夫人的生日和特殊的纪念日，向她赠送了大量精美的绸缎（价值70美元）和一些书法卷轴、画卷和烛台。由于事先并不知道大家精心准备了这么多礼物，所以当收到这些礼物时，曹雅直夫人感到非常的意外和惊喜。此时的教堂里人声鼎沸，举行的教会活动也给到场的各位留下了深刻的印象。

两件趣事中的第二件

本月18日，为了庆祝另外一名传教士的生日，也举办了一场类似的宴会。和曹雅直夫人的宴会相比，这次宴会的氛围更轻松和欢快一些。我们这位亲切的医生，肯定会记住这个光荣、虔诚和不朽的圣帕特里克节。劳里夫人为了这次庆祝活动精心准备了节目和晚宴。一场关于“妇女权利”的辩论赛拉开这场庆祝活动的序幕。霍厚福医生是这场辩论赛的正方，而苏慧廉先生则是辩论赛的反方。这之后还举行了唱诗、音乐会、交换电话号码、清谈等活动，这些活动一直持续到午夜才结束。

更换领事

听说我们的领事，法磊斯先生已经收到消息，他离开温州的时间可能比预期的要早。因为法磊斯先生在温州工作的时间早已逾期，能够提前离开温州，这种“解脱”在他看来实在是件令人高兴的事情。大家都在猜测法磊斯先生的接任者是谁，一个名叫艾伦①的先生很有可能接替他的工作。

① 英国驻华领事先后有多人名叫 Allens，这里不知道是哪一个。

《北华捷报及最高法庭与领事馆杂志》，1895 年 4 月 11 日

温州

（本报记者报道）

确认澎湖列岛被占领

来自厦门的“北京”号①轮船本月 29 日（周五）抵达温州港口。船员宣称，由于日本人已经占领了澎湖列岛和台湾海峡，所以“北京”号最终没能去台湾。此外，“北京”号轮船还带来了李鸿章遭到预谋袭击的消息。现在这个话题已经成为大家茶余饭后的谈资，并且在当地引起不小的轰动。如果这位勇敢的老人可以从伤势中恢复过来，这起袭击事件对他来说反而是件有利的事情。一方面，可以增加他在国民当中的威望。另一方面，也可以打破人们对他的偏见。因为他一直主张通过和平谈话来解决争端，导致国民都认为他是胆小懦弱而不敢派兵迎战。

“北京”号轮船着火

“北京”号从厦门到温州的途中不幸遭到炮火的袭击。结果，船员不得不将船上装载的石油丢弃掉。由于船上的官员反应迅速，采取的措施得当，大火很快被控制了下来，并没有对船体造成太大的损坏。

强盗的诡计

匪徒们又开始忙碌起来。一周前，120 个手握枪支和其他武器、打扮成抚台士兵模样的匪徒从楠溪出发。其中一个匪徒双手被铁链捆绑，假装成一个犯人，而船长则坐在椅子上伪装成地方官员。他们装作朝廷官员押解犯人赴杭州的样子。穿过一座大山，他们抵达了一个离青田城很远的大

① 招商局船只。

路村，并且在晚上的时候袭击了这个村庄。虽然村民英勇抵抗，但还是徒劳。整个村庄被洗劫一空，凡是能够被带走的都被这群匪徒抢走了。偕我公会位于大路村的传教点也未能幸免于难，幸运的是只丢失了一些不太值钱的文件。土匪没有从原路返回，而是选择了另外一条路。在返回的途中，他们又袭击了位于石溪的孙岔村（音译）。他们的人数从最开始的 120 人减少到 94 人。减少的这些人可能是为了将抢到的东西运回老窝而提前离开了。

饥饿的匪徒

我们被告知，匪徒中的六个人袭击了山上一座孤零零的房子。在这所房子里，匪徒们捉获了房子的男主人，并把他绑到了树上。而房子里其他的人则被他们控制一个狭小的空间里。这群麻木不仁的匪徒宰杀了这户人家养的猪，并将可食用的内脏煮来吃掉。饲养的猪被杀对男主人来说简直是晴天霹雳。因为，对于在家务农的小户人家来说，饲养的猪和家里的马一样重要。这件事情发生后，石溪和楠溪当地的富人受到了惊吓。由于害怕受到匪徒的袭击，他们让全副武装的家仆整晚守卫在门外。其他的村民则只能靠加固房门、墙壁和购买火枪自卫。农村用来生产火药的材料都是违禁品，所以大家不禁要问，当地人和匪徒手中的火药到底是从哪里来的？

一个典型的案例

前几天，社区的一位居民在北边一座高达 1500 英尺的山上碰到了县令。当时县令正急着赶路，因为他要去另外一个地方给一具中国人的尸体验尸。村庄里几户比较富有的人家被指控为凶手。我们听到的关于这起死亡事件的可靠消息是这样的：去年秋天，这位死者偶然得知他舅舅埋藏 184 银圆的地点。于是，他把这个消息告诉了另外一个住在比较远的村子里的男人。两人计划将这笔钱偷过来然后平分。正如计划的那样，他们之间的这笔交易非常成功。但是，还是有人看到了他们偷钱的过程。于是，这位死者逃跑了。他的妻子被带到县令的面前进行审问。县令试图从他妻子的嘴里问出一些线索，但最后一无所获，于是就放弃了审问。这位死者的妻子被衙役囚禁在牢房里。但是这位死者花了 80 银圆贿赂牢房里的衙役，成功将他的妻子从牢房里救了出来。他的妻子从牢房出来后，揭露了自己的丈夫犯罪的真相。这位死者的舅舅这边一打听，发现他妻子所说句句属实。按照中国的习俗，出卖自己的亲人是大逆的行为。于是，他的舅舅就带着一群人冲到他的家里，打砸他的房屋和财产。这样一来，周围的人都知道了这位死者的一家都不是什么好东西。两个月后这位死者就病倒了，不久就去世了。于是，这位死者的亲戚就指控他的舅舅和当地一些富户为凶手。因为这些被指控的都是一些富贵人家，于是处理这起案件的衙役就起了贪念。毫无疑问，在这些衙役的煽动下，县令也起了贪念。他提出去游玩两天，在游玩的过程中，县令出动了 10 台轿子和 60 个随从，要求这些富户好生伺候这些随从，并支付轿夫的所有费用。衙役们对这种出游都非常满意。但这样做的结果是，不仅破坏了节俭美德，而且也毫无公平正义可言。

《北华捷报及最高法庭与领事馆杂志》，1895 年 4 月 19 日

温州

（本报通讯记者报道）

恐 慌

日本人正在向温州城逼近，恐慌正在蔓延。那些把家里的“财宝”①看得很重的人，现在都在认真思考是否要搬迁到更远的地方去。对中国人来说，“财宝”这个词指的是财物，而不是守护神。对于这些人来说，最大的障碍来自他们的犹豫不决，他们担心自己的财宝躲过了敌人的子弹和大炮，最后却落到了匪徒和不可靠的亲戚手里。这种犹豫就像在拉岩石礁和卡律布狄斯大漩涡之间行舟一样，真是左也不是，右也不是。同时，当地官员在日本人可能进入温州的各个入口处设下了难以逾越的障碍。敌人的船首先要面临被鱼雷炸飞的危险，即便是侥幸逃脱，也没有机会安全经过沿岸修建的炮台。一小部分幸存下来的破烂不堪的船经过这些炮台时，将被炮台上的新大炮和明代或更早朝代遗留下来但经过修复的旧大炮炸成碎片。这些古老且珍贵的大炮世世代代保卫着温州城，它们的炮筒里塞满了中国人历代祖先永不屈服的精神。这些老家伙可不像那些现代大炮，现代大炮不过是些暴发户，无法吹嘘自己的纯正血统，也无法吹嘘自己身上几英寸的铁锈。除了有时因为纪念 50 名墨西哥人会想到这些古老的大炮外，大多数时候它们都是被人遗忘的，只有上面的野草长出来又枯萎，枯萎了又长出来，日复一日，年复一年。但是，现在这些古老的大炮被拉到税务司的操场上，点燃木炭，进行焙烧。一方面可以烧去上面的铁锈，另一方面，可以将先辈们的精神融入大炮的钢铁之躯中。然后这些大炮又被运回炮台，重新安装在炮架上。那些躲过了其他危险的日本船只最后路过

① 原意是古罗马时期家中的两位守护神，被引申为财物。

这里的时候，一旦进入这些大炮的射程，整条日本船将哀号声不断。“敌人的鲜血可以告诉你这些大炮的威力!”但是也有人曾经指出，因为年久失修，这些大炮是否安全是个未知数，那些使用这些大炮的人在未对敌人造成伤害之前可能先伤到自己。

艺 术

所有的这些战前筹备工作，看上去并没有给外国的居民在精神上留下什么深刻的印象。今天，来自你们港口的林顿先生在“普济”号轮船的甲板上举办了一场他个人的油画作品展（所有的油画作品都是林顿先生待在温州的时候画的），这对我们来说也是一次愉快的消遣。其中他的两幅作品，一副名为《天门山的瀑布》，另一副名为《飞流的瀑布》，受到观展人的极度推崇。他的第三幅作品《河流上的日落》也吸引了很多人驻足观赏。其中有些人甚至认为这是所有展出作品中最好的一副。《寺庙内部》这部作品同样令人印象深刻。任何一位拥有这幅作品的人在看到它时，都会联想到他在中国的那段难忘经历。除了上面的作品外，这次展览还展出了林顿先生的人物画像。虽然大多数的人数画像都是还没有画完的素描，但是，凭借着林顿先生的勤奋和他众所周知的才华，这些画像一旦完工都将成为非常优秀的作品。林顿先生对当地人承诺，一定让温州变得声名鹊起，并且增加来访游客的数量，不管他们是否带着颜料板和画架。

《北华捷报及最高法庭与领事馆杂志》，1895 年 5 月 10 日

温州

（本报通讯记者报道）

土地问题

我刚收到你寄给我的这一期带有苏兹贝格（Sultzberger）先生书信的报纸。我非常高兴地发现，除了一些老人外，温州当地人都非常喜欢阅读温州本地的报纸。我也非常感谢苏兹贝格先生给我的提醒。但是，他信中的内容也只是进一步证实了我之前提出的“中国人现在可以在欧洲购买土地而不会遭到反对”这一言论，因为现在是 1895 年，而不是 1872 年。我还想重复强调的是，温州不是一个内陆城市，但是那些没有在这里生活过，或者在这里生活过，却因为“普济”号离开这个港口后再也没有返回的人，会认为这个城市看起来更像一个内陆城市，而不是一个商埠。温州是一个开放的口岸城市，因此评价它为一个野蛮和封闭的城市并不合适。虽然中国在很长一段时间内都将自己放在这样一个位置上，并且到了现在为了强调治外法权，还是会提出这种说法，却仍然无法改变温州是一个开放口岸的现实。按照签订的条约规定，不管政府官员是同意还是反对，温州城都应该给予英国臣民租借土地的权利。温州城唯一能做的就是遵守这份条约，直到它可以签署一份新的条约。如果新的合约可以签订的话，中国的臣民不仅可以租借土地，还可以在英国或者其他更加发达的大陆国家全额购买土地。但是，已经签订的这份条约不管是在温州当地还是中国的其他地方，都是一纸空文。除非在签订契约前已向县令提出请求，并且征得县令的同意，否则没有哪位负责房屋登记的官员敢向英国臣民发放许可证明。任何人，只要你在中国的经历不局限于上海，并且你了解中国政府对欧洲人的态度，就很容易明白这件事情背后的隐情是什么。除非你提出保证说可以承担在衙门的各种开销，否则没有租借人愿意在转让协议上签

字画押。很明显，欧洲的公使们都不接受总理各国事务衙门提出的附加条款，但是他们也只能心照不宣地默认这些条款。

休　战

对于知道内情的人来说，“休战”这个词对于这个地方就是一种羞辱。但是休战的消息传播的速度远没有丢掉澎湖湾和台湾岛的消息那么快。对于当地的普通老百姓来说，两亿白银的军事赔偿款对他们来说非常难以理解。他们唯一能做的就是叹息，也可能想说“这种事情太常见”，但又不敢说出口。

关于防御

考虑到日本人已经逼近台湾地区，为了做好温州城的防御，民兵组织被征召守卫整个温州城。他们打扮成消防兵的样子，穿着醒目的服装，手持借来的矛和三叉戟，负责夜间的巡逻。来自各行各业的商人也加入民兵组织中，以补充整支民兵队伍的实力。这些商人每隔三天负责一次夜间巡逻。可能休战的消息一传来，这支民兵组织就会被迅速解散。一方面，他们多巡视一天，官员们就要多付给他们一天的钱；另一方面，和守夜相比，商人们也更愿意待在家里。

几个海盗

数日前几个海盗在这里被斩首。一位在瓯江口海盗袭击事件中受枪伤的男人在偕我公会医院接受了治疗。劳里医生在霍厚福医生不在的情况下对他进行外科手术，并取出了子弹。霍厚福医生在三个月前也实施了一例类似的手术，当时也是一位当地人因为海盗袭击中枪，子弹嵌入了该男子头部左边太阳穴的位置。经过手术，这位伤者侥幸生还。我这里要说到的另外一件事情，比上面提到的还要恐怖。上个星期天，也就是 4 月 21 日，一艘载满游客的轮船在刚离开东门码头不远，就被一阵狂风给吹翻。船上 26 名乘客中只有 7 名乘客获救，其他全部淹死。在淹死的这群人中，有两位是中国内地会的基督徒，他们刚从结束的礼拜活动中返回。

第一季茶

“普济”号轮船满载一船的货物（其中包括 3000 担茶叶和其他商品）驶离温州港。

《北华捷报及最高法庭与领事馆杂志》，1895 年 6 月 7 日

温州

（本报通讯记者报道）

酷 刑

我们的道台这次因为镇压海盗的事情又出名了，并且赢得了当地人的钦佩。除了海盗外，没人有会反对这一点。但是这之后发生的事情还是让我们非常惊讶。因为和海盗的残忍手段比起来，道台在审判海盗过程中所使用的酷刑要残忍得多。据我们了解，在他儿子的帮助下，道台每天都要对之前没有被砍头的几个海盗进行审问。鉴于后面所要遭受的经历，可能当初直接被砍头对于他们来说是件更幸运的事情。昨天，我们在大街上看到这几个可怜的海盗头上戴着枷锁，被人拖拉着往前面走。这一幕也促使我们把这件事情背后的一些细节传达给我们的读者，以让他们可以了解事情的真相。通常，审问犯人都是在县令的衙门里进行。但是这位道台显然是担心县令不会把所有的精力放到审问犯人身上。所以，他派人到县令的衙门把审问犯人的刑具拿到了自己所在的衙门。在道台的衙门里，两个可怜的海盗每天跪在铁链上，脚踝的位置被两块木板夹住，不能动弹。他们的背直直地靠在一个十字形竖起的木板上，辫子从木板上的洞里穿过去，以便将他们的头固定，从而保证他们的背是直直地贴在木板上。他们胳膊中间的位置被绳子绑在十字架横向的长杆上，他们的手指头被长杆两头顶端垂下的绳子绑着。只要审问他们的人一动这个刑具，他们的四肢就会感到极度的疼痛。不一会儿他们就因为过于疼痛而昏迷过去。为了让他们从昏迷中恢复意识，行刑者用长竹鞭抽打他们，再用冷水浇他们，使其保持清醒。经过一天的严刑拷问后，海盗被扔进了令人感到厌恶的地牢。第二天他们又会被拉出来进行审问，继续遭受和昨天一样的酷刑。黑暗的日子仍然没有过去。中国的这种严刑逼供，与西班牙宗教裁判所别无二致。

洪 水

上周，瓯江发了一场大的洪水。这场洪水中，棺材、水牛和家具全部随着洪流被冲到了大海里。由于水势太猛，在相当长的时间内瓯江都是无法渡过的。在洪水的巨大冲击下，停靠在西门码头的一艘帆船的船锚离开了固定的位置。为了重新让船锚固定下来，船员不得不将绑在船上的一个竹筏解掉。竹筏一离开船体，便随着洪流迅速冲往下游。不幸的是，竹筏撞上了两艘台州的帆船，这两艘船被撞翻后迅速沉入水底，船上的11位可怜的乘客也不幸葬身在洪流当中。

一次事故

上周，我们社区的两位成员在经过一条小河时，被一位军官和他的手下拦了下来。他们想了解有什么快捷有效的方法可以将六小时前不幸被河水吞没的同伴从水里打捞出来。通过和他们的交流，社区的两位成员了解到，这位军官和他的手下是下午步行到这里的。当他们到达这里的时候，发现渡船在河的对岸，并且船上也没看到有船夫。于是，他们当中一位年轻的士兵，一个河南人，脱光了衣服跳进河中准备游到对岸的渡船上去。但是，当他游到一半的时候，“河水下面就像有一个恶魔抓住了他的腿，一下就把他拖到水下去了”。这位沮丧的军官和他的手下整个下午都在用一头绑有石头的麻绳在水下打捞这位年轻士兵的尸体，但是一无所获。

这是懒惰吗？

在两周或更早以前你的一篇通讯文章中，对日本人和中国人进行了比较。你在文中提到，和日本人比起来，中国人要懒惰得多。这让包括我在内的一些在温州的外国人都感到很惊讶。非常碰巧的是，那天我在读你的这篇文章的时候，我们的船受潮水的影响，被迫停在了河的上游。迫不得已，我们只得从船上下来雇请轿夫抬着我们继续前行。抬我们的这些中国男人凌晨2点就要起床，然后一直工作到太阳下山。下午4点我们雇用他们之前，他们一直忙着插秧或者给稻田抽水。他们在雨中抬着我们行进了30里才抵达温州城。把我们送到目的地后，收到了我们的钱，简单吃了几口饭，又得步行30里回家。他们到家的时间已经是晚上的11点。匆匆忙忙睡几个小时后，第二天凌晨2点，他们又要起床开始新一天的工作。在中国所有的南方城市，在这个时节里，每个人都要从破晓工作到日落，并且干的都是非常辛苦的农活。我们附近正在搭建一座新的建筑。在这个工地上干活的石匠和木匠6点吃完早餐后就开始工作。他们11点之前吃午饭。下午1点前又开始工作，4点吃完晚饭后继续工作到下午6点半才结束这一天的工作。这就是当地工人日常工作的情况。而在商店里工作的人，他们工作的时间更长。商店在早上6点到7点间的某个时间开门，直到下午7点才关门。有些商店晚上也要营业，工作时间更长。商店里的工人很少有在晚上8点或9点就结束工作的。学校早上7点就开门了，学生很晚才会离开学校。每天清早你都能听到这些学生在令人讨厌地大声读书。从我们目前的经历来看，我无法判断上海的男孩子是懒惰还是勤奋。但是如果一定要说他们懒惰，那肯定是他们老师的责任。你可以说他行动缓慢或迟钝，但是绝对算不上懒惰。

《北华捷报及最高法庭与领事馆杂志》，1895 年 6 月 14 日

温州

（本报通讯记者报道）

在严刑逼供下认罪

我们听说上回提到的两个因为从事海盗活动而被道台严刑逼供的可怜男人最后还是认罪了。另外一个被抓的海盗目睹了这两人被严刑拷打的整个经过，坦言宁愿死都不愿意接受这种痛苦，所以他马上就认了罪。我们应当说这个人还是很明智的。因为摆在他面前的只有两个选择：一个是被严刑拷打后认罪，然后再被处以死刑；另一个是认罪而不经过严刑拷打，直接被处死。认罪意味着死亡，而拒绝认罪则意味着一直遭受严刑拷打，直到你认罪为止。

狗急跳墙

最近城里发生了另外一件让大家都非常感兴趣的事情。一个商人（下文中的商人 1 号，编者注）的房子临近一条小运河。另外一个商人（下文中的商人 2 号，编者注）的商铺则建在运河之上。几年前，由于许多人都在温州运河沿岸大兴土木，当地政府就发布通告，严禁在运河上新建或改建房屋。我们上面提到的商人 1 号一门心思想把商人 2 号从当地赶走，这样一来他房屋四周的空间就将变大。于是他就到当地衙门去告状，控告商人 2 号私自在公用的运河上改建房屋。虽然县令驳回了他的诉状，但是道台这里最终还是通过了他的请求。于是在没有得到任何赔偿的情况下，商人 2 号在运河上的商店就被拆除了。在告状中尝到甜头的商人 1 号又把目标对准了住在街对面的另外一个男人。这个男人家里很穷，主要靠在运河上一个很小的蛋糕店烘焙和售卖蛋糕来维持生计。这一次，商人 1 号又得逞了。在他的强迫下，这位可怜的男人不得不拆除了他的蛋糕店，取而代

之的是建了一个凉棚来维持他的蛋糕生意。虽然这位可怜的男人再三恳请，希望不要拆除他的凉棚，给他和他的家人留口饭吃，但是最后他的凉棚也被强制拆除了。这天，这个被拆蛋糕店的男人在路上恰巧碰到了迫害他的商人 1 号，之前所受的各种压迫和欺辱让这个男人怒火中烧，他用强劲的手臂一把将商人 1 号揽住，不停推搡，直到把他推倒在一片堇菜地里。这名商人自觉受到平生未有之侮辱，非常生气并决心打官司，而这名男人觉得自己没钱，打官司肯定打不过那名商人，于是就逃跑了。我们都不禁希望这个男人永远都不要再出现了。

两面派

虽然总理衙门最近发布了关于废除之前提出的土地转让给外国人必须征得当地官员同意这一规定的通知，但是当地的官员在几周前就寄出几百份通知，要求负责房屋登记的职员还是按旧的规定来执行。为了给新规定在一些区域的实施制造障碍，这些官员发给下面职员的通知被公开张贴出来。我们精力充沛的领事先生很快就注意到了这件事情。他立即与当地政府取得联系，质问他们是否意识到新的通告里面已经废除了之前要求的土地转让给外国人必须征得当地官员同意这一规定。领事先生从当地衙门得到的答复是，他们是在向下属发出内部通知之后才收到新的上级指示，之前他们并不知道有新的规定。领事法磊斯先生向当地政府提出，既然这些“内部”的通知已经被公开张贴，并且已经在人群中产生了不小的影响，那么有关废除之前要求的新规定也应该公开张贴出来。我们相信，他肯定会成功。因为，当地政府考虑到欧洲各国的利益和英国大臣的威名，应该会满足法磊斯先生的要求。

一起被报道的灾难

据说，在最近发生的那场洪灾中，有两个村庄被洪流冲毁，有超过 200 名村民丧命。但到目前为止，我们仍然无法完全确认这起报道的真实性。(5 月 5 日)

《北华捷报及最高法庭与领事馆杂志》，1895 年 6 月 21 日

温州

（本报记者报道）

领事的离开

我们的领事，法磊斯先生因为休假而暂时离开了温州。离家七年的他身体状况一直不是很好，所以对他本人来说这次休假也是弥足珍贵。他离开后，办公室的同事肯定会非常怀念他，因为他在当地的威望无人可以代替。由于精通中文写作，并且可以说一口流利的中文，他深谙中国官员的本性。在温州任职这段时期，他遇到的两位中国官员都让他感到非常棘手和头痛。即便如此，在工作中，他始终保持着充沛的精力。他努力工作的唯一目标就是希望可以推动中国的文明进程，而不是原地踏步。

一位典型的中国高级官员

在最近一次与他的继任者的谈话中，法磊斯先生觉得有必要把他对中国官员的了解告诉他的这位继任者。在前面我已经给你讲过，道台给县令下达命令，要求当地老百姓在未获得当地官员许可的情况不得将土地出售给外国人。道台给县令下达的这些通告在农村被公开张贴出来，虽然这些通告没有在城内被公开张贴，但还是在百姓当中产生了不小的议论。由于道台的这种做法违反了条约的规定，法磊斯先生提出强烈抗议，并且指出总理衙门已经发布了新的通告，新通告中外国人从当地购买土地不再需要经过当地官员的批准。我们听说，在法磊斯先生抗议过后，道台承认已经收到了新的命令，但是仍然拒绝将已经公开张贴出来的通知撤掉。因为他坚信总理衙门的真实意图是不希望公众知道新的命令中提到的具体内容。我们还了解到，道台

援引了四川总督反洋①（也是最近各种暴乱的发动者）的观点来支持自己的态度。据我们了解，目前这件事情已经上报到浙江巡抚和北京以等候进一步的裁决。通过这次裁决，我们希望总理衙门的新命令可以尽快落实下去，同时也希望这次裁决可以让中国官吏不再以折磨犯人为乐，而是明辨是非。尽管中国在最近的战争中失利，但某些中国高级官员仍故意找外国人的麻烦，对于满洲皇帝来说，这可能意味着在未来遭到羞辱。“高卢全境被分为三个部分，其中一部分……”② 中国的这些官员，可能会将这句形容高卢的话，在不是高卢的地方使之成真。(6 月 17 日)

① 这里说的是 1895 年的“成都教案”，导致四川总督刘秉璋被开缺。

② 原文为拉丁文，引自恺撒的《高卢战记》。作者在此处有恐吓与轻侮清政府的意思，也可以看出甲午战败后，中国的国际地位一落千丈。

《北华捷报及最高法庭与领事馆杂志》，1895 年 7 月 12 日

温州

（本报记者报道）

另一起暴乱

由于战争已经结束，当地人也不用继续在城墙上警戒敌人的入侵，然后决定是否要披上外国人的披肩打扮成洋人的模样，以躲过敌人的追杀。他们采用各种暴乱的手段来舒缓自己紧张的情绪，同时以此为乐。四川教案的消息已经传到了这里，加上另外一起被夸大的平阳县（中国内地会一所传教点所在地）教案事件，使得当地的局势动荡不安。不用多说，这里的局势已经糟糕透顶。

所谓的起因

两周之前，在一次龙舟节上，离平阳 30 里远的两个村庄分别派出一条龙舟进行了一场比赛。结果其中一个村庄输掉了比赛。比赛有输赢这很正常。但是输了的这个村庄想弄清楚，到底是什么原因导致了他们的失败。于是，他们找来了一个道士。这个道士说他发现了一座没有眼睛的佛像，他认为这就是他们输掉比赛的原因。因为佛像在当地是神圣的象征，没有人敢动它。所以，如果不是基督徒将佛像的眼睛挖掉的话，那还会有谁呢？因此，他们断定这件事就是基督徒干的。村里的一群人于是就到当地一位非常重要的基督徒的家里并且威胁他，如果他们的龙舟在下次比赛中再输了的话，就把他的房子烧掉。这一天，正好是 6 月 27 日，星期三。由于受到了威胁，这位基督徒就把这件事情通知了县令。等到周六的时候，这群人就开始了他们的破坏活动。他们的第一个目标是一个刚建立的教堂。很快，这个教堂就被夷为平地。一个历来主张反洋，并且怂恿村民进行破坏活动的士绅感觉事情要闹大，也开始害怕起来。他跪在暴民面前，

恳求他们不要再进行破坏活动，但是为时已晚。这些村名已经烧红了眼，他们的血液已经沸腾起来，停下来已经是一件不可能的事情。他们从这一家破坏到那一家，直到所有基督徒的房子都被他们烧光才停手。房间里的东西也全部被他们翻出来，一把火烧个精光。除了基督徒的房子外，和他们毗邻的房子也未能幸免。无家可归的基督徒只得逃到平阳，向当地传教士寻求帮助。第二天，暴民们继续在其他村庄搜寻基督徒的身影。

破坏工作

星期一，县令和温处道台的幕僚恰好在平阳。于是他们就和士兵一同前往暴乱现场。在去往现场的路上，他们需要越过一条河。数以千计的人等在河的对岸，并且控制了渡船。晚些时候，这两位官员让其他士兵在原地等待，他们自己则乘另外一艘船去对岸。到了对岸后，他们发现局势难以控制，于是象征性地发布一些命令后就放弃了，乘船返回到河的这边。

威胁扩大破坏的范围

但混乱的秩序并没有恢复，破坏活动还在继续进行。周一、周二、周三，更多的房屋遭受了破坏。周六和周日，破坏房屋的活动仍在继续。基督徒们沿江的房子正在遭受破坏，并且暴徒们也在不断聚集。20 所房子消失了，20 户被迫离开他们的家，51 个无家可归的人现在住在传教士的家里寻求帮助。现在，暴徒们威胁要过江，攻击那些住得较远的基督徒。我们的领事傅夏礼（Fox）① 先生向温州道台提出强烈的抗议。于是，道台在周六的早上派出 400 名官兵赶往平阳暴乱现场。虽然平阳离温州城只有 12 小时的路程，但是这群官兵在周日的晚上仍然没有抵达现场。据称，他们在行进的途中休息了一段时间。还有一种说法是，他们在经过久安河时受到了阻拦，从而影响了行程。

---

① 傅夏礼（Harry Halton Fox，1872—1936），英国人，1890～1892 年任英国驻华使馆翻译学生。1895～1896 年任英国驻温州领事，1905 年任英国驻宜昌领事，1913～1917 年任英国驻成都总领事，其中 1914～1915 年曾代理汉口总领事。1917～1929 年在北京任使馆商务参赞。引用自李盛平主编《中国近现代人名大辞典》，中国国际广播出版社，1989，第 806 页。

榜样的力量

温州城和邻近城市的百姓都在大肆吹捧平阳人，称赞他们敢于大胆地攻击外国人和他们的宗教。在过去的一周里，不管是年轻人还是老人，他们态度都发生了比较大的变化，对每一个看到的外国人，都坚决表现出反感和厌恶。和以前相比，年轻人叫嚣得更加厉害，而他们的长辈则更加大胆，脏话也更加难听。如果不想让这种情绪继续蔓延，必须马上采取有效的措施进行控制。有些人怀疑，这种现象背后的真相可能不仅仅是对外国人的偏见那么简单，而有更深层次的原因。

同　情

最近，玛高温医生的亲人去世了，社区的每一位居民都为这位备受尊敬的先生和他可怜的小女儿感到深深的惋惜和同情。(7 月 8 日)

《北华捷报及最高法庭与领事馆杂志》，1895 年 7 月 26 日

温州

（本报记者报道）

事情往好的方向发展

平阳暴乱事件的影响没有进一步扩散，这让我们感到很高兴。但是也不能高兴得太早，整个地区仍是干柴烈火，任何一个小火花都能重新将暴民心中的怒火点燃。如果是那样的话，住在附近的数以千计的基督徒都将陷入一片哀号。我们的领事傅夏礼先生是一位勇敢的领袖。即便是道台，也开始承认傅夏礼先生是位非常勇敢的人。因为在这样的局势下，他还坚守在他的领事馆里，领事馆的旗帜也一直高高飘扬。另外一件让人感到高兴的事情是，欧格讷①爵士已经从总理衙门那里获得了许可，撤去之前张贴的关于土地买卖的通告。这道之前由道台下发给县令，之后又被公开贴出的通告中提到，在未征得当地官员许可的情况下，当地人不能擅自将土地出售给外国人。我们相信，撤掉之前的通告，同时用新的但是内容完全相反（即当地人向外国人出售土地，不需要征得当地官员的同意）的通告来代替它，一定可以让新的规定得到很好的实施。你能想象这样的一个场景吗？一边是恐怖的暴乱事件，而在另外一边，当地的最高官员却在威胁当地人，称如果未征得当地官员的同意私自将土地出售给外国人，他们将遭受严厉的惩罚。除了威胁当地人以外，这位官员还威胁衙门的职员，称如果他们准许土地交易的发生，将遭受免职等惩罚。这位官员放任人命关天的大事不管，却抓着土地交易这种小事不放，简直让人匪夷所思。

建议的补救方法

在暴乱中被破坏的房子目前已经开始重建，并且当地政府也给予承

① 英国驻华公使。

诺，所有的房子都应该被修复好。虽然房屋重建工作看起来进展得非常顺利，但是中间还是出现了一些小插曲。当地的一些游手好闲的乡绅不希望因为修建房屋而停止他们嬉戏和玩闹的生活，同时，村庄里的年轻人也非常享受这一点，他们知道他们不会因为罢工而承担任何的责任，因此不愿意按照村里长官的指示来办事。每次暴乱后造成的这些损失，会明显减少暴乱发生的频次。平阳的县令最近公开审理了一起案件。虽然这位县令之前承诺过在逮捕基督徒之前要征得教会的同意，但是他把自己的承诺完全抛诸脑后，派出他的手下，在光天化日之下，将一位基督徒从数里外的乡村拖到了城里。一路上，这位基督徒受尽了沿途老百姓的各种嘲笑和揶揄。这位基督徒被带到衙门后，衙门马上被围得水泄不通。当地一位牧师想要从人群中挤进去都没有成功。这位可怜的基督徒在众目睽睽之下，接受了县令的审问。县令指控他将佛像的眼珠子和佛像腹中的神脏掏了出来①，但是并没有传唤证人来当面对质。很明显，在平阳暴乱发生后的第二天，当地的地保②去这个基督徒的家里，指着一个祖先传下来的香炉对他说：“既然你是基督徒，你用这个干什么？”随后，这位地保拿起他手里的香，将香的末端插到香炉里，然后把香炉打翻到地方。地板上有之前来祭拜的人留下的纸钱，里面卷着佛像腹中的绳线。这位地保指着这些东西质问道：“这些都是什么？”“这到底是为什么？你肯定是一个反对崇拜圣像的人！”很显然，对这位基督徒的指控完全是陷害。基督徒否认了这位地保对他的指控。但是这位地保还是对他进行了诽谤性的控告。以上就是平阳暴乱后的一些最新的进展情况。与此同时，我们之前提到的51个被暴徒赶出家门的基督徒仍然无家可归，他们的食物和日常必需品都得靠他们的基督徒同伴、当地人和外国人提供。早稻已经到了可以收割的时节，但是他们不能去收割。之前有观点认为，对于一个中国人来说，要想成为基督徒是件很容易的事情。这个观点完全是错误的。所有的中国基督徒或多

---

① 佛眼和神脏：民教冲突的发端来自寺庙里供奉的菩萨“佛眼”被剜，“神脏”被盗。为何“盗神脏”？因旧时菩萨腹部填充的五色线绳中夹有一些银线，窃贼“盗神脏”为了“偷取菩萨腹中线钱”；为何“剜佛眼”？可能是窃贼“自欺欺神”心理作祟，以为没了眼睛的菩萨就看不见是谁冒犯的。

② 地保：在地方为官府办差的人。

或少都要遭到流放，许多中国基督徒因为他们的身份丢掉了工作，还有一些基督徒在家中或者村庄里遭到了迫害，其他一些中国基督徒则遭遇过目前四川和平阳的基督徒正在遭遇的事情。但是，让人感到震惊是，即便有这么多难堪的经历，他们还是表现出了惊人的坚忍。

涌入的士兵

周日，“元凯”号轮船载着500名士兵抵达温州城，使得当地的守军数量出现了明显的增加。我们现在也在等待进一步的消息，以了解守军人数突然增加的原因。（7月18日）

《北华捷报及最高法庭与领事馆杂志》，1895 年 8 月 2 日

温州

（本报记者报道）

一份及时的公告

两天或三天之前，我们的道台发布了一份及时的公告。鉴于你们中的一些读者可能会对这份公告感兴趣，以下是这份公告的译文：

余以道台①辖温处两府，尊奉浙省巡抚②之令，布告如下：

浙江巡抚，遵兵部下达之严令宣布，总理衙门奉皇帝上谕，令所有地方官员召集下属，秘密监察并细致审理，以查明是否存在针对洋人之冤假错案。若其事属实，从速办理，所涉官员必要重惩，以防患于未然，以免教徒再受伤害。又需在礼拜堂审理，并将公告贴出，以儆效尤，使其知畏惧，借生事端者，必严惩不贷。若未能防患于未然，涉事地方官员，无论文武，无论府道，一律开缺，定不宽恕。

此令接自巡抚，深望地方从速解决事端，安抚百姓，执行朝廷严令。目下平阳教案与礼拜堂有关。本官偕同镇台，率兵三十赴平阳，以维治安。据本官所知，此次教案并无士绅参与，地方愿赔付平阳教案遭受损失之洋人。瑞安县有暴徒肆意散布谣言，本官已派兵前往搜捕。温州自上次教案（1884 年）以来，当地各界皆深知其害，另受害之洋人皆

---

① 宗道台：宗源瀚（？—1897），字湘元，江苏上元人，行政长官俗称“道台”。温处道辖温州、处州两府，治所温州。

② 廖巡抚：廖寿丰（1836—1901），字谷似，又字阁斋，晚号止斋，江苏嘉定（今属上海）人。咸丰八年（1858）、同治十年（1871）进士，改庶吉士，为国史馆编修。清光绪七年（1881），任浙江粮储道。光绪十三年，为贵州按察使，次年调浙江。光绪十六年，任福建布政使。旋至河南，任布政使与护理巡抚。光绪十九年，为浙江巡抚。

已获赔付。目下温州百姓与洋教徒，生活甚为融洽。以巡抚此项严令观之，余以道台之任，责在预防。是以本官刊布此告示，深望尔等，无论乡绅学子，无论城里城外，皆需牢记。其一，洋教本意在劝人向善，如若不愿信教，亦无人相逼。其次，纵使华人入教，亦我朝赤子，无论其行善行恶，赏罚在我。本官赏罚皆依行公正，据其行迹，与入教与否无关。汝等当以平日智识，劝诫愚民，太平即康乐，天下太平，衅事自化为小事，不足道也。使小民各安其业，各守太平。另有目无法纪者，惯滋事端，借口‘官府不惩办洋人，吾辈自办之’。此等皆贼也，必惩之。道府县官吏之责，何其重也，吾等必当依法重惩，如若不然，必追悔莫及。（6 月 4 日）

容易轻信别人的中国人

这是目前我见过的所有告示里最好的一篇，我们相信此项告示一定可以让当地百姓暂时平静下来。这段时间发生的各种教案（平阳教案、四川教案和冒犯台湾日本人的事件）带来的各种谣言已经把他们弄得心神不宁。在最后一起事件中，也就是台湾的事件中，大家普遍得知，40 艘炮艇，包括 38 艘日本炮艇和 2 艘英国炮艇被黑旗军一举击沉。据我们了解，刘永福①的手下在燃油上覆盖谷壳，在夜间偷运到军舰附近，并且派人潜入水底将日本人炮艇的螺旋桨固定死。这样一来，日本人的炮艇就失去了动力，黑旗军的鱼雷轻而易举地将他们一网打尽。日本人的 40 艘炮艇全部被击沉，成千上万的日本人死亡。我们还了解到，刘永福在这次行动中还抓获了日本天皇的嗣子，于是他以这位王子作为人质，向日本方面索要 3 亿两白银作为赎金。以这起事件为原型的彩色连环画（里面涉及日本总督和其他高级官员被审判和处决、日本军舰被击沉和他们的军队被打败等细节）在当地非常畅销，这放在以前是不太可能的事情，因为当地百姓对连环画一点儿都不感兴趣。（7 月 27 日）

---

① 刘永福（1837～1917），字渊亭，汉族客家人，广西钦州（今属广西防城古森洞小峰乡）人，祖籍博白东平，清末民初军事人物，原是反清的黑旗军将领，1883 年率黑旗军参加中法战争，屡次大败法军。甲午战争期间，奉命赴台抗日，但最终失败。1895 年 5 月 25 日台湾割让后，拥立巡抚唐景嵩为台湾民主国总统，自称大将军。

《北华捷报及最高法庭与领事馆杂志》，1895 年 8 月 16 日

温州

（本报记者报道）

当地人的态度

当地的人的态度一点儿都不友善，自从 1884 年的温州教案发生后，当地人就再也没有对外国人友善过。但是，他们对外国人的态度还是发生了一些变化。之前他们都是在外国人的身后对外国人说一些难听的脏话，现在他们变得更加好斗。如果刘永福捕获了几艘日本运米货轮，最后能够被谣传成 40 艘战舰（其中还包括两艘英制战舰）的话，那么在温州这个愚昧的地方，600 名日军在桃园被伏击会被谣传成什么样子？我们不敢去想。当地人态度的这种转变多半要归功于数以千计的在当地出售的彩色连环画。这些连环画里展示了刘永福斩首日本高级军官、日本船沉没和日本军队溃败等各种场景。此外城里每座房子的墙壁上几乎都贴着这种连环画。因此，整个城市都被一种好战的情绪所笼罩。一位英国人在路过离温州 20 英里的一个城市时，当地人愤怒地朝他投掷石头。同时，离温州仅 2 英里的一个城市，教会活动也被当地人成功阻止。虽然几天前道台曾严重警告过当地人，让他们不要威胁和阻止教会活动的正常进行，但他们还是我行我素。

事情变得更加糟糕

一周前，虽然礼拜堂里的人提前六天向道台请示，希望对方可以为布道所提供安全保护，但一个重要的礼拜堂还是遭到了袭击。现在，之前住在礼拜堂的 70 个家庭变得无家可归，礼拜堂地板上的每一块瓷砖都被撬开，任何值钱的东西都被洗劫一空。英国领事馆的领事向道台提出强烈的抗议，但是道台只派出了非常少的军官前往调查。除了军官外，道台还派

出了六名衙役，但是只有两名衙役到了现场。到现场后，除了张贴告示外，他们什么都没做。这起暴乱的发起人在当地被众人所熟知，他们也公开宣扬这起暴乱事件和他有关。此外，这些人的名单一早就被送到了道台那里，但是他没有采取任何行动。在短短的几天内，由于没有任何的阻碍，这起暴乱事件很快就扩散到温州府全境。导致这场暴乱发生的原因有三个：第一，禁止出售土地给外国人的公告在道台的要求下被公开张贴出来；第二，发生在平阳的暴乱事件让当地局势变得更加动荡；第三，前面说到的连环画对当地人的影响。

怪　事

两天前，一位自称是卖棉花的小商贩在一所教会的门梁上吊自杀。幸运的是，他被人及时发现并救了下来。但是，由于他的脖子被用来上吊自杀的绳子勒得太紧，流了大量的鼻血。经过了解，他之所以自杀，是因为他早上卖棉花时，他所有的货物都被一个陌生男子抢走了。他的故事可能是真的，但是让我们感到奇怪的是，在当前局势这么动荡的情况下竟然会发生上吊自杀事件，这种事情之前在这里从未发生过。另外一件之前也从未在这里发生过的奇怪的事情就是，一个仆人死在了他欧洲主人的家里。据说这位仆人接连吃了3个5~6斤的大西瓜，吃完西瓜后他又喝了大量的茶，这之后就躺在外面一块平坦的大石头上睡着了。不久就下起了瓢泼大雨，但是大雨并没有把他淋醒。直到感觉到寒意，他才从睡梦中惊醒。之后他就染上了痢疾，不久就去世了。他的父亲，并没有因为儿子的去世而过分悲伤，而是因为他的另一个儿子分到的遗产比他还要多而心怀不满，于是就前往外国雇主的家里指责对方毒死了他的儿子。但是，在地保到来之前，经过深思熟虑后，这位老人家又从外国人的房子里离开了。

气　候

因为大旱，土地龟裂。稻田里的早稻也因为干旱而枯萎，这让当地的农民感到非常悲伤。（8月5日）

《北华捷报及最高法庭与领事馆杂志》，1895 年 8 月 23 日

温州

（本报通讯记者报道）

古田教案[①]

来自厦门的“广济”号轮船[②]带来在福建附近的古田发生的一起屠杀教徒事件的消息，但是并没有具体细节。到目前为止我们都不敢相信这是真的。我们一直在等待，不停地在祈祷，希望这一切都不是真的。唉！但是这一切看起来都是那么真实，我们一遍又一遍地问我们自己，心中充满了无限的恐惧和悲伤。

谁将是下一个受害者？

当然，这些外形看起来像人的恶魔，他们屠杀教徒的手段无比邪恶！毫不夸张地说，他们玷污了他们所站的那片土地！他们毫无人性！即便是我们当中最温和的人，也希望这群恶魔能尽快地自食其果，停止污染他们脚下的土地。

公　愤

凯斯琳·史荦伯只有 12 岁。一想到这种噩梦般的遭遇，让她堕入无尽的黑暗，会一直牵绊她前进的脚步，我们的心就开始滴血。我们社区的每

① 古田教案：光绪二十一年六月十一日（1895 年 8 月 1 日）发生于福建省古田县的一场教案。当天，古田斋教教徒袭击了其时正于古田华山上避暑的英国传教士史荦伯（Robert Warren Stewart）及其妻儿和随行的其他女性教士，死难 11 人，焚毁房屋两栋。英文将“古田”拼作 Kucheng，是根据古田当地的读音，福州话也是这么读的。

② “广济”号轮船 1887 年在上海建造，轻载 313 吨，重载 550 吨，船价 2 万两。

一位成员都为这起空前的、丧尽天良的罪恶行径感到惊恐和憎恨，也对在古田山上发生的惨案中幸存下来的人表示无比的同情。

正确的途径

我们认为，尽我们最大的努力给我们所在国家的政府施压，让他们阻止这些暴行不再发生，是我们每个在中国生活的英国公民的责任。我们已经给几家报纸写了亲笔信，同时还给我们认识的国会成员捎去了亲笔信，希望通过这种方式能够引起公众对这起暴行的关注。

白莲教

如果白莲教是古田教案的策划者和实施者的话，那么我们身边有许多白莲教的人。整个城市和邻近地区都有白莲教信徒。

平阳乙未教案

平阳乙未教案已经平息下来，并且政府将支付4000银圆用于赔偿当地的外国人和本地人在这次暴乱中蒙受的损失。这比当初要求赔偿的金额少了1200银圆。枫林教案①目前还没有赔偿结果。

① 1895年8月间，在温州府永嘉县楠溪枫林一带，发生教案。参见《瓯东零拾》，《申报》1895年8月23日第2版。

《北华捷报及最高法庭与领事馆杂志》，1895 年 9 月 6 日

温州

（本报通讯记者报道）

远　景

英国皇家海军“彩虹”号应在这个时候抵达温州港口，但我们社区所有人连它的影子都没有看到。“彩虹”号停泊在离温州城 30 英里远的青菱屿附近。“彩虹”号从锚地派出一艘舰载艇前去观察附近是否有暴乱正在发生。这艘舰载艇在去往瓯江上游的中途撞上了暗礁，船底破了一个大洞，河水瞬间涌入船内，导致船体沉入江底，船员不得不游到岸边去。快到岸时，岸边“友善的”当地人发现了他们，于是向他们投掷石块。当地人发现水兵投掷的石块又直又准，觉得吃了亏，于是转身逃跑。将当地人赶跑后，水兵们随后找到一艘小船，其中一位水手乘着这艘小船回到“彩虹”号报告消息。当“彩虹”号派出一支全副武装的队伍来支援时，水手们才松了一口气。这支队伍一直守卫在他们身边，直到沉没的舰载艇被打捞出水面并且维修好为止。这个过程持续了两到三天，其间“彩虹”号仍然停泊在青菱屿附近，没有人看到它的身影，直到它最后离开此地。因此，“彩虹”号被我们称为“远景”。

道台的行径

道台的行为令人非常不快，这多少让人觉得有点遗憾。例如，就在“福尔费”号轮船离开这儿不久，他就下令逮捕了“福尔费”号的引水员。正是在这位引水员的引导下，“福尔费”号才能进入到下游锚地。领事私下向道台递交了照会，告知他本人他的这种做法违背了条约的规定。于是道台就将这位引水员释放了。可想而知，这位引水员在被释放前肯定被衙役们狠狠敲诈了一笔，并且使用的手法肯定是威胁这位引水员，如果他不

愿意出钱，他们将把更多的引水员抓进衙门。“福尔费”号轮船离开了，“彩虹”号又来了。但是幸运的是，“彩虹”号拒绝进入瓯江，尽管当时瓯江的水位比较适合“彩虹”号停靠。当地所有人都知道在瓯江的入口处停了一艘英国巡航舰，我们都惊讶于他们是通过何种方式知晓此事的。当然，他们本能的推断是，道台不会允许这艘船进入瓯江。因为大家对道台的处理方式了解得非常透彻，在没有征得他同意的情况下，他不会允许任何一艘外国轮船进入瓯江。“彩虹”号没有进入瓯江，看上去好像是在配合道台的工作似的，这让道台觉得非常有面子。直到今天我们才了解到，道台在平阳教案彻底结案前，拒绝进行赔付。到现在为止，没有一个暴民被捕，所有基督徒想要重建房屋的请求也被拒绝。在另外几起损害英国人利益的重大事件中，道台的态度也发生了一八十度的转弯。但是，在这之前，我们都非常期望这些事情能够往好的方向发展。道台的这种做法让我们感到非常气愤。

一件非同寻常的事情

本月 26 日发生了一件非同寻常的事情。一支由八个英国人组成的军队进入温州城。他们当中的一员这一天正走在街上，手里拿着一卷纸，突然遭到了一个中国人的袭击。这名中国人一把拽住了英国人的脚，想把他掀翻在地。没有得逞后，他一把将英国人手里的纸抢走，然后逃走了。毫无疑问，那位英国人追了上去，并且在不远的一个房子里将躲在床下的这名中国人抓了出来（整个过程都不太容易）。随后，这名中国人被关进了县衙门，到现在都没有被放出来。有报道称这个中国人精神有问题。让人感到奇怪的是，类似这样的事在和平时期从来没有发生过。

大　雨

一场大雨连续下了 48 个小时，这场大雨对于当地的农民来说简直是雪中送炭。因为当地已经干旱太久了，如果再照之前那样干旱下去，他们肯定要闹饥荒。最近霍乱和痢疾在我们当中频繁发生，导致当地的死亡率不断上升。（8 月 27 日）

《北华捷报及最高法庭与领事馆杂志》，1895 年 9 月 20 日

温州

（本报记者报道）

关于瑞安

瑞安市位于平阳县和温州市的中间位置，是一座非常重要的县级城市。平阳的传教士们数年来每次路过这里都要遭到瑞安人的辱骂和石头攻击。如果从温州到平阳还有其他路可以选择的话，传教士们肯定会很高兴地避开这条路。但遗憾的是，从温州到平阳必须得经过瑞安。

英国领事遭到石头攻击

由于平阳教案让当地局势变得更加动荡，英国领事馆的傅夏礼先生觉得非常有必要前往现场进行察看。虽然收到了来自各方的警告，示意他不要去现场，但他还是愉快地出发了。因为他们的船一早就抵达了平阳，而此时，当地人由于前一天晚上吸食了鸦片，还没有从吗啡的镇静作用中清醒过来，所以一切看上去都很平静，和平常的出行没有两样。但是，到了第二天，当傅夏礼先生等一行人准备乘船离开平阳时，他们发现已经有上千人等在那里。平阳当地的衙役悄悄地将傅夏礼先生送到船上，并且将船护送到城郊后就离开了。衙役离开后不到五分钟，当傅夏礼先生还在思考传教士是不是没有必要这么容易激动时，他乘坐的船突然遭到一阵又一阵石头雨的攻击。作为一名英国人，与生俱来的那种勇气使得傅夏礼先生马上冲了出去，想要和攻击他的人当面对峙，但是在随从的恳求下，他又迅速返回了舱内，以求自保。这次袭击给傅夏礼先生的船和他船上的瓷器带来了巨大的损失。但是，弥补这种损失的方法只有一种。这种损失也不应该只是单方面的。要想阻止这种恶作剧的再次发生，必须对投掷石头的人实施一个月的枷刑。

枫林教案仍然没有解决。但是这中间发生了一件有趣的事情。几周前，我们要求派一名县令去枫林暴乱的现场做一个调查。我们收到的答复是，县令因为担心去往枫林的路况太差，无法通过，所以他从来没有去过枫林。换句话说，他们就是在无故推脱，这也是中国人对外交涉时惯用的伎俩。

故意撒谎

巧合的是，就在县令答复我们说他从来没去过枫林后的不久。比去枫林的路程上还要远一天的地方发生了一起谋杀案，县令必须得去案发现场。县令经过枫林到达了那里，关于这起案件的调查也正在进行中。之前县令说他从来没有去过枫林，现在他却从枫林路过到达了更远的案发现场，很明显，县令是在故意撒谎。从枫林教案发生后我们要求县令去暴乱现场到现在，已经过去了六周的时间。

让人感到愉快的评论

这位县令还是传唤了一些枫林当地的乡绅来和他会面。他不经意间听到这些乡绅在背地里说的一些贬低他的话，例如，“让我们把这个野蛮人扔进井里”，等等。这些话伤害到了这位县令的自尊心，他非常愤怒，就向枫林当地的官员抱怨这件事情。但是对方的回复和之前回复枫林教案中的暴行时一样：“他们都只是些孩子。”这让他感到非常愤怒，他评论到，如果这些人对待自己的父母官都是这种态度的话，对待基督徒的手段，肯定就像基督徒们描述的那样残忍和粗暴。如果这位县令之后真的按他说的来做，枫林教案还有解决的希望。但问题是，他真会这样做吗?

对上海当局的呼吁

不知道你们这些来自模范租界的神父们是怎么想的，竟然会允许让这种明显会挑起暴乱、抢劫和谋杀的宣传手册和书籍从上海这个大都市散播出去。如果真的像这些连环画、小册子和新闻报上说的那样，中国的所有南方城市在不久的将来将成为一片火海。我手里有两本小册子。这两本小册子一看就是在上海印刷的，并且采用的是铅字印刷的方法。下面的内容是我从这本小册子里随手翻到的一段话：“日本人为了保命四处逃窜，但也是徒劳的。没有在大火中被烧死的这些日本人最后也被淹死了。因此，到中午的时候，日本军队已经失去了20条军舰和2万多条人命。除了日本军队外，其他国家也损失了不少的军舰。”难道你们真的想要袖手旁观吗？难道你们真的不打算阻止这些明显会挑起事端的刊物的出版和传播吗？随信附上两本我前面提到的小册子。(9月9日)

《北华捷报及最高法庭与领事馆杂志》，1895 年 9 月 27 日

温州

（本报记者报道）

枫林教案

自从上次我提到枫林教案到现在，在案件审理过程中发生了明目张胆的扭曲正义的事情。在枫林教案中受到迫害的四位基督徒被关进了监狱，并且遭到了严刑拷打。但是，枫林教案的元凶却被无罪释放，他们高高兴兴地回了家。不仅如此，审理此案的官员还鼓励他们继续进行破坏活动。我给你简单讲述一下枫林教案的经过。一周以前，就有人发出警告，说有些人正在酝酿制造一起事端。傅夏礼先生于是立即通知道台，希望道台可以采取一些预防措施。但是道台什么也没有做。不久就发生了袭击事件，基督徒被暴民从家中赶了出来，他们的房屋被破坏，家中的财物也被洗劫一空。

官员搪塞

我们的领事先生想让道台派出一名值得信赖的官员前去处理此案。但是道台拒绝派出县令前往，并且声称，县令之前从没到过枫林这个地方。道台明显是在说谎。因为除了温州城外，枫林是他所管辖的区域内最大的一个乡镇。一个月后，县令必须去往比枫林在路程上还要远一天的地方。在返回的途中，他去道台那里汇报枫林的情况（之前道台对县令下达的命令），他汇报的情况是枫林当地没有遭受任何的损失。但是，真实的情况是，枫林教案中遭受损坏的财物的价值高达 300 银圆。

局面恶化

在抚台的命令下，道台最后还是下令让他的一名亲信对枫林教案进行

了审理。于是，在上周五，也就是本月的13日。开始了对这起案件的审理。在长达五小时的审问过程中，当事官员采取了最暴力的方式对四名基督徒进行恐吓和威胁。整个审问过程中，这四名基督徒都是跪在坚硬的石砖上，官员拒绝了教徒要求把手撑在地上以缓解膝盖疼痛的请求。要知道，在这之前，即便是犯下滔天大罪的罪犯，衙役也会允许他们下跪时用手支撑身体。这名委员发现不能在没有借口的情况下，继续拷打或将教徒送进监狱时，他要求负责记录的文员当着大家的面写下这些基督徒已经承认了对当地乡绅的诬陷，并且他们已经收到了他们之前被抢走的所有东西。此外，还要求教徒承诺以后将不会在枫林这个地方举办教会活动。这些内容被记录下来后，官员首先要求被指控的暴民先签字画押。这些暴民当然乐意了，他们一边签字一边对这种明显有失公平的判决拍手叫好。暴民签完字后，四位基督徒也被要求在这份记录上签字画押。但是他们四个人坚决不同意这样做。见此情形，当事的官员暴跳如雷，数次命令手下鞭打这四位基督徒。到最后，见这四位基督徒还是不肯签字画押，于是停止了对他们的鞭打，反而开始对他们提各种问题：“是洋教教你们吸食毒品的吗”，“不，洋教禁止任何和毒品有关的东西”；“是洋教教你们赌博的吗”，“当然不是”；是洋教教你们酗酒的吗”，“仅仅是适量”；“是洋教给你们偿还债务吗”，“当然”。“那么你们就是欠朝廷的土地税，把他们关进牢里”。这四个可怜的基督徒，他们已经失去了一切，但最后还是逃不掉坐牢的厄运。在牢房里，狱卒将他们绑了起来。每个人的脖子上都被一根铁链缠绕，铁链的一端往下从手铐的中间穿过，和手铐绑在一起。于是，每个基督徒都是脸朝天花板的姿势。这四个基督徒一直保持这种姿势在牢房里站立了八个小时。当时，领事恰好因为周末离开了，他们做梦也没有想到事情会发展到这种地步。这些基督徒不停地向狱卒和县令求情，但是没有任何作用。到了午夜，他们用钱贿赂狱卒，狱卒才同意帮他们把脖子上的链条稍微松一松。这个时候，他们才可以像正常人一样站直。就这样，他们以这种姿势一直站到第二天中午。在这个过程中，他们仍然在一遍又一遍地向狱卒求情。

不久，有人把四名基督徒被捕入狱的消息告知了领事，领事以最快的速度赶了回来。在返回的途中，潮水将他乘坐的船挡在了瓯江上游。但领事并没有在原地等待退潮，而是采用步行的方式继续赶路。步行了10英里路后，领事在周日的晚上抵达了道台的住所。但是，即便是领事亲自去求情，也是徒劳的。道台还是拒绝释放那四名基督徒。因此，这四名基督徒目前仍继续被关押在监狱里。第一位基督徒被指控的罪名是没有缴纳地税，领事提出补上地税或保释，但都遭到拒绝。事实上，这位基督徒没有欠朝廷任何的地税。其他三位基督徒虽然欠了地税，但数额也非常低。第二天当领事再次要求道台放人时，道台同意在补齐地税后可以释放三名基督徒，但第四名基督徒因为诬陷当地的乡绅，仍然不能被释放。

需要采取坚决的行动

整起事件都是由道台一手策划的，后面的所有事实也会证明这一点。去年，这四位基督徒的庄稼受到当地人的破坏。但是，直到法磊斯先生和道台大吵了一架后，他们才获得了不到损失的1/3的赔偿。这次争吵也让法磊斯先生和道台两人关系交恶。道台也一直耿耿于怀。之后不久，一位英国居民想在当地购买土地，道台想尽一切办法搅黄此事。随后，他在枫林的各个角落都贴满了告示，禁止当地人将土地出售给外国人。当要求他下令将告示撤掉时，他拒绝撤掉针对英国人的告示。但他在私下里下令撤掉了禁止出售土地给法国人的告示。在枫林教案发生的前一周，领事要求道台采取一些措施缓解当地紧张的局势，也遭到了道台的无视。而在这起暴乱发生之后，道台也没有采取任何措施进行控制。有充分的证据表明，基督徒被捕入狱的整起事件都是在道台的衙门里密谋进行的。那位不幸的县令只是道台的一颗棋子，他做的每一件事情都要受到道台的监控，并且征得道台的同意。审理这起案件的当事官员也是道台的亲信。每天的审问工作他都要征求道台的意见。最早发现这起暴乱并且报告严重损失的衙役们，在早上开庭审理的时候被县令要求重新写下他们提出的证据。同时，县令还质问他们，为什么胆子这么大。在县令汇报暴乱情况的时候，他们汇报的情况和县令反映的情况恰好相反。

这里还会再次发生暴乱吗？

我们都在想，这座城市是否正在酝酿其他暴乱事件？如果接下来我们没有任何的暴乱事件可以报道，那将会是一个奇迹。与此同时，傅夏礼先生也正在尽全力维护领事馆的荣誉。如果当时“彩虹”号没有停在瓯江

口，而是进入到瓯江的话，估计将是另外一种情景。自2月以来，就再也没有炮艇进入过瓯江。(9月18日)

三个男人被释放

附录：我们了解到，道台已经同意让四位基督徒补上他们之前欠的地税。四位基督徒中的三位已经被释放出来。但是第四位因为诬陷乡绅的指控，目前仍然被关押在牢房里。让人感到担心的是，这几位基督徒签字画押的记录里，可能有一些他们本人不知情的内容，这些内容有可能违背了他们的真实意愿。

《北华捷报及最高法庭与领事馆杂志》，1895 年 10 月 18 日

温州

（本报通讯记者报道）

悲伤的一周

温州刚刚经历了黑暗的一周。我们从来没有经历过这样一连串流行病爆发的情形。首先是中国内地会的成员染上了霍乱。梅启文夫妇的儿子是第一个感染上霍乱的。霍乱是从平阳那边传过来的，目前也急需医疗援助。紧接着被传染的是学校的三个女学生。梅启文先生匆忙地给他的儿子举行了葬礼，但不幸的是，仅仅四天后他也成了霍乱这场天灾的受害者。伍德曼先生在周六的晚上也被霍乱给击垮了，他的那口气一直都没有咽下去，直到周三晚上去世。他挚爱的妻子（了解她的人都为她的人格魅力所折服）在他的床前日夜守护和照顾他，直到她自己也被这种疾病所感染。虽然知道自己将不久于人世，但是伍德曼夫人还是将所有事情都安排得井井有条，并且将教堂和学校的所有事情都交代给了其他人。之后伍德曼夫妇以一种非常平和的心态静候死神的降临。伍德曼夫人在周三的早上去世，她的先生在这天的晚上跟随了夫人的脚步。伍德曼夫妇被葬在我们坟场的同一块墓地里。虽然我们想了各种办法，采取了各种医疗手段，但还是没能挽救伍德曼夫人的生命。除了偕我公会的霍厚福医生和海关的劳里医生以外，英国皇家海军“火炬”号的彭尼医生也给我们提供了热情的帮助，因此每一位病人的身边都有医生看护。

运输事故

这周发生的第二起不幸的事故就是“广济”号在运输的途中沉船。我们相信你们肯定也已经知晓此事。在本月 5 日的晚上 8 点，“广济”号轮

船在檀头山（Montagu）①附近撞上了一个未做任何标记的暗礁。当时的海面上正是暗流涌动，一个接一个的海浪不断撞击着“广济”号轮船。看上去“广济”号是在两个海浪的夹击下撞上了礁石，因为船身突然被抬高，但好在损伤并不严重。但铆钉的松动导致海水进入到这艘蒸汽船的锅炉房，并且眼看就要逼近锅炉口。“广济”号上的官员果断采取行动，他们穿过一条陌生且危险的航线抵达了一个相对安全的地方，船也相对安全地下锚。与此同时，虽然底层锅炉已经被海水淹没，但是船上的工程师阿岱先生和船上唯一的司炉工在海水没过他们腰部位置的情况下，仍然英勇地坚守在一线。他们用尽全力，希望让上层锅炉里的火保持燃烧，从而为整艘船提供动力。但是没过几分钟的时间，上层锅炉也被海水浇灭，整艘船最终也沉入了海底。虽然遭遇了不幸，但是船上官员和工程师们敏捷的反应和英勇的行为仍然值得我们称赞。我们还听说，“广济”号的船长当时也在船上。我们对他的遭遇深表同情。因为他是一名能力非常强的航海人，在各种条件错综复杂的海域进行航行一直都是他的长项。

大 火

这周发生的第三起不幸的事故就是，城内发生了一起近年来最大的一起火灾。城里主要街道上沿道路两旁的房子都被大火烧毁。超过1000人一夜之间无家可归。偕我公会的房子也差点着了火，好在发现及时，还没烧到这里就被控制住了。这就是我们遭遇到的黑暗的一周，也是我们再也不想碰到的一周。

“火炬”号抵达

“火炬”号已经在这里停留了七天。在没有征得道台许可的情况下，它就驶入瓯江。这让道台非常反感。舰队司令就道台的无礼行为提出了强烈抗议，这可能会让道台有所收敛。

基督徒遭受迫害

蒙受各种羞辱并且被监禁的第四名基督徒现在仍然被关押在牢里。听

① 位于浙海关宁海县。

说，道台已经数次许诺释放这名基督徒，但是每次执行的时候，道台就要求这名基督徒另外再写几份声明，要求他在声明中做伪证，承认整起事件都是由他一手捏造。这名基督徒宁愿继续被监禁，也不愿意写这种明显带有侮辱性的文字。这件事情最新的进展是，道台同意在不需要写其他声明的情况下将这名基督徒释放。但这是不是道台的又一次敷衍，还有待明天见分晓。

运动会

由于恐怖的霍乱使得我们社区的每个人精神面临崩溃，因此，对于“火炬”号的来访，我们也没有表现出很高兴的样子。但是，“火炬”号上的船员在周六这天举办了一场音乐会。为了表示对他们的感谢，社区所有人尽力在今天举办了一场趣味运动会。我们的领事在他家的运动场主持了这场运动会。这场运动会的项目非常丰富，包含了100码无障碍赛跑、障碍赛跑、拳击、击剑和拔河，等等。欢乐的时光总是特别短暂，感谢“火炬”号轮船上的船员给我们这些住在温州的人带来的这些美好而又珍贵的回忆。

离　别

今天，我们社区里非常重要的一名成员——劳里医生，离开了我们，他和他的小女儿目前正在去往英国的途中。他是我们这里的万金油，不管是欧洲人还是当地人，只要有用得到他特长的地方，他都乐意效劳。不管是当地人的教会还是欧洲人的教会，他都给予了非常多的帮助。教徒们都对他心怀感激。只要是和社区福祉有关的事情，他都非常感兴趣。因此，社区的人很快就会察觉到他的离开。如果劳里医生还有机会回到这里的话，我相信这里的人一定会满心欢喜地迎接他。（10月14日）

《北华捷报及最高法庭与领事馆杂志》，1895 年 11 月 1 日

温州

（本报通讯记者报道）

针对评论的评论

你们报纸的评论员非常友善地对我援引自一个月前我寄给你的书籍里的内容进行了更正。但是他的更正很容易让读者忽略我要表达的真实意思，因此我觉得有必要针对他的更正做一个解释。当然，他更正的那个“误”字我现在已经深深地印在了脑海里。但事实上，如果我的评论中缺少了这个字的话，评论员无法了解我隐藏在这些文字背后的真实意图。我真实的目的是希望引起大家对当前正在发生的这件事情的关注和重视。这件事情就是，从上海那边传出来的印刷精美的刊物里面，对刘永福在台湾的传奇故事进行了肆意的夸大和捏造，这些纯属捏造的内容将生活在中国南方的外国人置于非常危险的境地。

我援引的书籍中是这样描述刘永福的传奇故事的。刘永福首先命令手下用绳子将日本军舰的螺旋桨捆住，然后下令让着火的竹筏去撞击日本军舰。日本军舰努力尝试去避开这些着火的竹筏，但是为时已晚，因为他们发现他们的船已经无法移动。结果，日本军舰遭到了来自四面八方的炮火的攻击。深陷这种既无法前进也无法撤退的困境中，日本军队成了任人宰割的羔羊，军舰上所有的士兵不是被大火烧死，就是跳进海里被淹死。在这次战役中，日本军队的 20 艘军舰全部被摧毁，死亡的人数达到了 2 万人，并且一些其他国家的军舰也意外地受到了损坏。让我感到很意外的是，“意外”这个词在我的来信中被评论员删掉了。但是真实的情况是，没有一艘日本军舰，没有一名日本军人，没有任何一艘其他国家的军舰遭遇任何不幸。人们可能不会知道，“意外”这个词从我的信中被去掉将对我真实意思的表达产生多大的影响。我无法指出我在信中用到的具体词

汇，但是我知道我的真实意图是希望引起大家的关注，让大家了解到，有关刘永福破坏日本军舰的报告会点燃当地人好战的情绪，因为上海一些公司发布的这些出版物里令人感到愤怒的谎言会让当地已经非常动荡不安的局势变得更加危机重重。对于中国人来说，日本人和我们没有两样，都是外国人。中国人对地理的无知俨然已经成为一个笑柄。如果当地人被这些出版物误导，认为刘永福正在对日本人赶尽杀绝的话，那么所有中国南方的城市对于外国居民来说都不安全。就在上周，我发现很多人围在考场附近的一个货摊旁边。这个货摊上摆满了各种生动形象的连环画和小册子（我前面提到的从上海流出的刊物）。所有这些内容不仅将侵害在华外国人的利益和安全，还将点燃那些受不平等条约影响的中国人好战的情绪。

官员的策略

枫林教案中的第四名基督徒最终还是被释放了，但是从释放的过程来看，道台是多么的卑鄙和无耻。上周六，这名基督徒被带到他的折磨者面前。这位道台的亲信对他进行了各种恐吓和威胁，还用特制的竹片鞭打他。在这位亲信的命令下，这名基督徒被鞭打了1000多下。但是他宁死不屈，并且大喊“就算你们鞭打我一万次，我也绝不会在你们要求的文件上签字画押”。在前面我们已经讲过，文件上的内容主要是要求这名基督徒承认他对当地乡绅的所有指控都是捏造的。于是，折磨者停止了对这名基督徒的鞭打。但在道台亲信的命令下，衙役们押解着这名基督徒，让他双膝跪地。随后几个衙役拉着他的左手，使劲地往左边拉，还有一些衙役拉着他的右手，使劲地往右边拉，还有一名衙役控制住他的手，另一名衙役则用东西撬开了他紧握的拳头，用墨水在他的手上涂抹后，强压着他的手按在文件上。就这样，他被迫在这份违背他真实意愿的文件上签了字。这就是所谓的中国官员口中的公平正义。要知道他们接到的命令是保护这些受威胁的人，而不是去恐吓和威胁这些人。每次我们的领事向中国官员提出抗议和请求，他们都以发布声明作为回应。但是仅仅停留在发布声明上，他们并不会去执行这些声明中提到的内容。与此同时，道台殷勤地提出建议，想和英国领事协商一下这起案件，但这次协商是否能够成功，我们拭目以待。

邀　请

“普济”号轮船又重新恢复了温州航线的航行。我们也希望它能够一直在这条线路上航行下去。如果你是一名上海人，并且你想暂时换个环境出来散散心，我们邀请你过来旅行，感受一下这条航线。从上海到温州的这条航线，一定是中国海岸最美丽、最便利的航线。

《北华捷报及最高法庭与领事馆杂志》，1895 年 11 月 22 日

温州

（本报通讯记者报道）

可怕的谋杀事件

几天前温州城内发生了一起可怕的命案。这起命案发生的时候，无人察觉。因此，目前还没有获得任何和行凶者相关的线索。直到昨天早上，被害者的尸体漂浮到水渠上，大家才发现有人被杀了。死者的头和身体几乎完全分离，并且有一部分肠子和内脏露在尸体的外面。尸体是全裸，因此无法从他身上获得任何有用的东西来确认他的身份。另外，大家认为死者有可能不是本地人，而是山东或者广州人，因此他的身份就更加难以确认了。当听到发现尸体的消息后，除了少数女人外，当地数以千计的老百姓蜂拥而至。这从某种程度上体现了当下这些中国民众是多么的麻木不仁。

更多的迫害

在道台的命令下，枫林的这位基督徒再一次被捕，并且被关押进了牢房。三周前，这位基督徒从牢房被释放出来。回到家后，在他家里进行的礼拜活动又重新开始。当地人并不反对这种礼拜活动，而且在第二个周日后，他们看上去似乎已经接受了基督教。因此，当衙役出现在礼拜活动的现场并将发起这次教会活动的基督教负责人带走的时候，大家还是感到非常惊讶。道台的幕僚和县令将这位基督徒之前被迫签字画押的文书放到他的面前，质问他为什么要重新开始教会活动。这位基督徒的回答是，他只是把他的房子借给了教会，这次活动是教会举行的，和他无关。当两位官员提出让他撤回之前准许其他基督徒在他的住所进行教会活动的承诺时，他非常坚决地拒绝了两位官员的要求。因此，他再一次被关押进了牢房。

在牢房里，他要和暴徒、小偷、谋杀犯和其他各种恶人共处一室。

违背条约

领事已经向道台提出了强烈的抗议，要求释放基督徒，但还是徒劳。道台拒绝释放基督徒，并且提出只有这位基督徒承诺不再于枫林进行类似的教会活动，才能将他释放。道台的这种做法是对条约和公义的公然藐视！除了在家里举行教会活动外，这位基督徒并没有触犯其他任何法律。为了给这位基督徒扣上罪犯这顶帽子，道台也是处心积虑。他将这位基督徒的两位邻居传唤到衙门，承诺给他们一定的好处费（每天 10 文钱），让他们做伪证，说这位基督徒举行的礼拜活动扰民，已经影响到他们的正常生活。但是，这两位邻居曾经私下里说过，他们其实并不反教。他们在袭击事件中主动去保护这些基督徒就是一个很好的证明。他们其实很想回家，但是又不敢违抗道台的命令，所以才不得已做伪证。由于要补偿袭击事件中遭受的损失，抑或是暴徒还没有被抓捕归案，因此这位基督徒的案子就一直维持目前这样一个现状，他本人也一直被关押在牢房里。我们可以很清楚地看到，道台从来没有为他所做的任何事情感到羞愧过。温州当地和中国其他地方的领事记录文书中提供的大量证据可以让我们坚信，中国当下的官员和几十年前的官员相比，更加傲慢和无礼，并且更加仇视外国人。（11 月 13 日）

《北华捷报及最高法庭与领事馆杂志》，1895 年 12 月 13 日

温州

（本报通讯记者报道）

收　成

今年晚稻农作物的收成还远远达不到让人满意的地步，并且在一些地区的晚稻几乎颗粒无收。虽然大米的价格很有可能上涨，但是温州府内并不担心会出现粮荒。受大米价格上涨影响最严重的往往是底层的老百姓。对于一个三口之家来说，一品脱米的价格上涨五钱，他们的食物供应量将减少 1/4。

台州海盗

据说，台州府靠近南部的地区目前的情况比较糟糕。大米已经运往那个地方，以赚取一个好的价钱。因此，台州沿岸的居民非常担心在接下来的这个冬天里，海上抢劫的事情将更加频繁。这些海盗都是台州本地人。如果台州的官员能够顾及大米运输的安全，如果我们的道台不是一味地迫害基督徒，而是将他多余的精力用在武装船只和派出船只在乐清沿岸巡逻上的话，可能只需要花很少的钱就可以收获相当多的民意支持。

迫　害

照现状来看，道台目前还是将枫林基督徒扣押在牢房里，而且这位基督徒目前病得非常厉害。除了允许基督徒的礼拜活动在自己的住所进行外，这位基督徒并没有触犯任何一条法律。即便是道台也没有对他进行其他指控，并且提出只要他承诺停止在其住所进行教会活动，就可以马上将他释放。这种公然违反条约的行为，可以证明朝廷、总督和其他部门张贴出的表面看起来慷慨的公告只是逢场作戏，主要目的就是暂时平息外国人

对这件事情的不满情绪。要求释放被扣押基督徒的请愿再次被送往北京和杭州。大家都希望这位在迫害事件中表现得非常勇敢的基督徒可以尽快被释放，同时也希望枫林基督徒迫害事件中遭受的严重损失可以得到赔偿。

一次徒劳的尝试

上周日，在温州城河对岸的一个村庄里，中国内地会成员竭尽全力想在当地一位基督徒的家里开展一次礼拜活动。尽管道台之前承诺要为这次活动提供安全保障，但是这次活动还是以失败告终，并且这位基督徒的房子也遭到严重破坏。中国内地会成员发现，从这个村庄逃到另一个村庄去开展礼拜活动也是徒劳的，他们最后还是被赶了出来。尽管这个村庄之前举办过多次礼拜活动，但是他们提出的理由是，“如果其他村庄可以把你们赶出去，那我们也可以”。

道台和法国“里昂”号炮艇

法国“里昂”号炮艇 11 月 26 日抵达温州港口，它在港口停留了一天两夜后于当月 28 日离开港口。道台之前将为数不多的几门火炮架在城墙上。他听说“里昂”号每到日落时分就会发一炮，于是他下达命令，要求手下的士兵在对方发射炮弹后的一小时或约一小时后发射一枚炮弹进行还击。没有人知道他这样做的目的是什么。双方的这种交火只发生在“里昂”号停靠在港口时的两个晚上。（12 月 3 日）

第二部分

英文文献

r junks cruising after pirates abo
n-Chê sea coast, it seems that th
of Fukien and T'aichow are sti
merous and as savage as ever.
nd its consort bound from Ningpo t
w laden with rice and sundries wer
y attacked near Wênchow by a co
pirates, who boarded the merchant
aving ransacked everything of valu
he latter, left them with twenty-fiv
nd seriously wounded. Stric
have been issued by the Governo
al, T'an, for the capture of the pirate
ute a large fleet of war junks is no
at it seems to be the universal opinio

nchow as its Consul on the 12th inst.,
Parker taking leave on a new de-
ure, having first secured the last instal-
t of the indemnity that the authorities
ed to pay for losses sustained by
gners in the recent disturbances. To
be Mr. E H. Parker's success in giving
ral satisfaction to foreigners and native
orities in regard to the questions raised
e riot to good luck, would be unjust to
accomplished officer. It was tact that
ted an amicable settlement

bitants of the so-called "C
ave put away their store-cl
ar. The rejoicings were co
uietness and decorum, the
of nastiness was eaten,
ount of tomtomming and f
ulged in; in fact, everyth
accordance with "olo c
Year's Eve most of the
ncipal thoroughfares were
ted with coloured lamps,
re lighted in nearly all th
ty and suburbs. That this
sement did not result in
onflagration is simply miraculous,
mmunity is by all right-thinking
ttributed to the special interve
ien Tien Ta Ti, the great Lord o
Heaven, or some other benevole
hough here, as elsewhere, scoffers
ound who point to the saturated co
verything or to some other such

cal Report
American
xpression, spread himself out over the
whole subject of the health, pestilence
amines, and topography of the place
Thirty-six closely printed pages have
not sufficed to relieve him of his whole
burden of knowledge, for at the begin
ning of his paper he says that he reserves
he medical
ccasion; but
f which he h
ully have th
hat we sho
uch a trifle
He begins
listrict in wh
nd passing

ung-kong, running as she n
rt of the most influential
fter trip with improved
esults, seems now to have
o that point where if more
of necessity become m
g superfluity. As has bee
the impetus given by
y means of shipment has
nt export of al
spects for tea

t the s
way th
rejoic
nd de
iness
tomton
; in fa
nce wi
Eve m
orough
colour
d in m
uburbs.
did no
imply
all rig
e spec
the gr
e other
elsewhere,
to the saturated condition
some other such commo

NEWS FROM WÊNCHOW.

During a fierce gale which raged at Wen
chow about a fortnight ago, several seriou
disasters occurred, attended in many case
with lost of life. Four large junks, lade
with poles, were upset and many other
dragged anchor or sustained other injuries
whilst a great number of small fishing craf
suffered a worse fate. The villagers on th
coast showed great barbarism. Instead o
affording succour, they busied themselve
with picking up wreckage thrown ashore
In the worst cases they even wrested th
poles away from the shipwrecked people
who in their exhausted state were made t
yield the logs to the merciless people
Owing to the unusually cold weather a
Wenchow there is considerable sufferin
amongst the poorer classes, who are no
provided with extensive wardrobes, an
especially amongst those who have a pre

To the Editor of the
NORTH-CHINA DAILY NEWS.

SIR,—Although the subject of
China was ably discussed at a lat
of the Shanghai Literary and D
iety the question was not so exh
reated as to preclude me from
nall contribution, assuming that
be unacceptable to those who
ary (but no
ically, it
think th
emature, th
where it
needed;
northern C
courses, an
is doubtfu
cessfully
It was ur
oyed by an
of China

(COMMUNICATED.)

vastation that met ou
e river of Wênchow wa
les and miles the countr
vast expanse of wate
steads and graves, an
nds crowded with cattle
frowning background
a most depressing an
We passed too quickl
by the pen. Women an
roups, doubtless talkin
sses, while the men we
in their boats. In some places wher
he bridges were still standing only th
pper portion of their arches was visibl
ooking like mirages—water above, belo
nd around them! Great indeed mus
ave been the downpour to have caused suc
n inundation. It was a comforting chang
o turn one's gaze from the immense
ountry to the numberless fishermen pu
uing their calling as if no such thing
some troubles existed. The flooded cou

be sent to Ta-c
Yo-ching-hsien
f pirate-robbers
aused considera
ties of both this
chow. Some tim
adoes plundered two
n the Yu H'uan Bay
ere) which caused the
y to order one of his
d against them. On
ce of the bay the office
n-vessel decided to an
rred a party of soldier

(FROM A CORRESP

Notice to mariners, also
ad to feminine sphere.
emarkable Peak on the
avigators see on their
Wênchow, having only
nd never named, has no
he denizens of Wênchо
Hart's Peak," in recogn
ices which the Inspecto
mperial Maritime Custo
y illuminating the coa
ormal recognition of the
y the Wênchowese, in pic-nic assembled
n the 22nd March, and that being th
irthday of the Emperor of Germany, nea
o the celebration of the Queen's Jubile
nd within measurable distance of th
atal day of President Cleveland, th
ealth of those estimable rulers was drun

OUR OWN CORRE

ing, on ent
d some strag
strawropes, t
that were
ent the enem
ing. Had they resisted
would have been as usele
A proposition that was m
channel has been abandon
a panic was created by a
quiring every family to b
darins a basket of stones.
as secure as if they had
protection; the authoriti
solicitous for their safety.
threw missiles, and others

RIOT AT WÊNCHOW.

The *Yungning*, from Wênc
ived here on Saturday, b
ticulars of a riot which had
nchow on the night of the
e first intimation of this ri
phed up from Ningpo from informatio
pplied by the *Yungning* on arrival a
t port, though efforts had been made b

Macgowa
ow recen
put down
sumption
Southwaite
ld be tra
, which a reference to Mr. Dou
's table on the opposite page rend
ent. My views elsewhere publis

The North – China Herald and Supreme Court & Consular Gazette, October 26, 1876

Islands off the Wenchow River, Wenchow River and Wenchow

ISLANDS OFF THE WEN-CHOW RIVER.

Ten miles N.E. from Wên-chow Point lies Taou Island, the largest of all the islands to the Eastward; it is well cultivated, and has a number of small villages on its shores, the largest being 開門 Ke-mong, on the S.E. point of the island. There is good anchorage off this village, and good shelter from N.W. to N.E. Formerly, when the convoy business on the coast of the Chê-kiang and Fu-kien provinces was in the hands of foreigners, there were several foreigners living in this village, where they had a station, and many were the depredations committed by them. But the Cantonese proving too strong for them, they were at last compelled to leave for the northward. The inhabitants of this island are nearly all Fu-kien fishermen, whose junks may always be seen cruising around the island.

Islands off the Wen-chow River

Ten miles N.E. from Wen-chow Point lies Taou Island, the largest of all the islands to the eastward; it is well cultivated, and has a number of villages on its shores, the largest being 開門 Ke-mong, on the S. E. point of the island. There is good anchorage off this village, and good shelter from N. W. to N. E. Formerly, when the convoy business on the coast of Che-kiang and Fu-kien provinces was in the hands of foreigners, there were several foreigners living in this village, where they had a station, and many were the depredations committed by them. But the Cantonese proving too strong for them, they were at last compelled to leave for the northward. The inhabitants of this island are nearly all Fu-kien fishermen, whose junks may always be seen cruising around the island.

Four and half miles east from the mouth of the river lie the islands of 虎豆山 Hu-tao and 九麂山, and E. by No. two miles from these Quang-ta island, with several small islets to the Eastward, and the "Cliff Rocks" to the Northward. All these islands are well cultivated, inhabited by Fu-kien fishermen, and have numerous small villages on their shores. S. E. from these islands lies a large group known as 山穴, the largest of which are 洞豆山, 尾岙山, 半邊山, 狀元山, and several other smaller ones. This is a line of group islands, well cultivated and numerously populated. On the S. W. side of 洞豆山 is a good anchorage known as Bullock's harbour. Here water may be procured, and bullocks of the best description. The harbour may be known by a remarkable conical island called Coin Island, with several small rocks lying N. ½ W. from it. Formerly this group was infested by Cantonese pirates, and very few convoys passed this without having a brush with them. At present, there are not many pirates amongst these islands; and were Wen-chow opened to foreign trade, piracy in these waters would receive its death-blow.

There are a great many approaches to the river, but, with the exception of one, they are of no use to navigation, owing to shoalness of water and sandbanks. I will therefore only describe the channel that foreign vessels will be obliged to use in approaching the river.

This channel lies nearly East and West between 虎豆山 and 狀元岙; is little more than half a mile broad; the only dangers in the channel are a sandbank with only 1½ fathoms water on it at low water, and the "White Rock" of Hutao Island; but this rock is always out of water, and therefore easily avoided. There is also a rock off the South point of Hutao Island, about half a cable from the shore, which, however, is easily avoided by giving the point a clear berth.

If a small lighthonse similar to the one on Square Island were erected on the largest of the Cliff Rocks, and a Buoymoored on the sandbank, vessels would have no difficulty in making this channel at night. With reference to Buoys and Beacons, I would advise the use of wooden Buoys and Beacons on account of the cheapness of the materials at this place; and, as expensive iron Buoys and Beacons would offer an inducement to the natives at first going off to purloin them; whereas, the comparative want of value of the other materials would insure their safety.

Wen-chow River

Fives miles W.N.W. from Hu-tao Island 虎豆山 (*Hu-tau*) lies Wen-chow Point, the entrance to the river; and W.S.W. from this point lies Wenchow Island 靈冠山 (*Wan-chu*), the first and largest of all the numerous islands in this river. A large sandbank runs from it in a S.E. direction for over six miles, and the shoals from this bank extend across to 尾岙山 Niaow. On the west point of this island are three small round hummocks, the rest of the island being all low land with several villages over it. The north shore of the river from Wenchow Point to a small projecting hill of the Walled City 磐石城 is low land, with several fine villages along the bank of the river. The river in this part of the river varies from three to fourteen fathoms. The next islands, after passing the Walled City on the north shore, are four in number; one lying close under the north shore, and the other nearly in the middle of the river off Jar Point anchorage, forming the north shore of this reach.

We next arrive at the reach in the River shown on the small chart, where, should the port be opened to foreign trade, the shipping will be compelled to anchor.

From the small fort east of Jar Point to the Broken Jetty in this reach, there are several small villages, the names of which are marked down, together with their positions, on the chart. There is a very fine ancestral hall in one of these villages, which would answer well for a Custom House; it having near it two well built stone jetties, one of them 240 feet long by 15 feet broad; the other 120 long by 10 feet broad. The water here varies from two to fourteen fathoms at low water; the anchorage extending over a mile from E. to W. along the south shore; the tide at springs runs from 3 to 5 knots per hour, and has a rise and fall of 17 feet. The above mentioned island which forms the north shore of the anchorage, is a low, swampy mud flat, with but few houses on it, and offers fine facilities for docks. The northern shore of the river, from the Walled City 磐石城 to a large canal abreast of Wen-chow-fu, consists of a chain of lofty hills running down to the banks of the river, and, being uncultivated, looks very desolate. The next group of islands in this river are six in number, and are by the natives designated mud islands. They are situated to the northward of Fort Hill, and a small channel runs up inside of them to Wen-chow city. Numerous sandbanks extend from these islands in all directions, and at low water they have the appearance of being one large island.

The north shore of the river from Fort Hill to Wen-chow city is a low, well cultivated plain, with numerous small hamlets scattered over it. This portion of the river is very shallow, and at low water is closed by a sandbank running northward from one of the above mentioned islands. Wen-chow-fu 温州府 is situated on the south shore of the river, and its walls run down to the river's bank. There are several small islets lying to the northward of it, one of which in particular is worthy of notice. It is about a quarter of a mile long, running E. and W., has a magnificent joss-house on it, and two very old pagodas.

The river above the city takes a westerly direction, with several small islets in it, and the scenery of this portion of it is very picturesque; the high ranges of mountains on both shores running down to the river's edge.

Abreast the city is a branch of the river running to the northward for about 100 li, to a wild mountainous district called Nan-chi.

Wen-chow

The department of Wen-chow 温州, in the south-east corner of Che-kiang province, is bounded on the north and west by the departments of Tai-chow 台州 and Ch'u-chow 處州, on the south by the province of Fu-chien, and on the east by the sea. Its total area cannot be much under 3,500 square miles, with a population of about 3,000,000.

Wen-chow-fu 温州府 in Yung-chia-hsien, is situated on the south bank of the Wen-ch'i 温溪 river, 20 miles from its mouth. The city is built on a well cultivated plain encircled by high hills, at the distance of about ten miles. Its walls were first erected during the fourth century, and enlarged and rebuilt by the Emperor Hung-Wu, in 1385. They are formed of stone, diagonally laid, and measure about six miles in circumference. The streets are wide, straight, well paved and clean. The Custom House outside the East gate, the Yamen of the Taotai in the south-west corner of the city, and the Founding Hospital 育婴堂 near the centre, are among the principal public buildings. The last named, built in 1748, contains one hundred apartments. It is supported by the interest of invested subscriptions, and the rental of alluvial lands presented to it by the Government. The number of foundings on the establishment's books at one time, varies from two to three hundred. When of suitable age the boys are either articled to tradesmen, or adopted; the girls are betrothed as wives, or employed as house servants. There is also a Beggar's Asylum 養濟院 outside the south-west gate. It was built during the 14th century, and is supported by the state. The monthly allowance for each recipient is one tael and a half; but the treatment received from the keepers is so brutal that few, unless really starving, will avail themselves of its alms.

Two pagodas on an island abreast of the city are objects of some curiosity, on account of their age, and for having been for a short time the retreat of Ti-ping, the last Emperor of the Sungs, when making his escape from the Mongols under Kublai Khan, the founder of the Yuen dynasty.

Previous to the year 1861, this was the only port in the department at which Tea was allowed to be exported, which, in a measure, made it the market for the trade of the surrounding country. The city was then in a flourishing condition. But in order to prevent the Teas from falling into the hands of the T'ai-p'ing rebels, who over-ran the whole district during that year, this regulation was exchanged for the one now in force, which authorizes the exportation of Tea at any of the Custom stations along the coast; consequently the enormous trade formerly concentrating here now finds its way to all the minor ports on the seaboard.

The principal business the place at present possesses is the export of wood and bamboos, brought down the river in rafts from Ch'u-chow. The annual value of this trade is estimated to be not less than $2,000,000. The shops and yards engaged in it are situated in the west suburb, where immense quantities of bamboo and poles are kept on hand.

There is also a slight import trade done in sugar and opium; the latter being nearly all brought overland from Foochow by Fu-chien merchants residing in the city.

Many of the leading firms have their houses most conveniently situated on the banks of the numerous canals surrounding the city; by this means their good are conveyed from the ship's side to the godown without the expense or annoyance of coolies.

The people are anxiously waiting for the port to be opened to foreign commerce. They have none of the ridiculous notions usually met with at the open ports, respecting foreigners. When Europeans pass along the streets there is no exhibition of terror among the women and children, or scurrilous remarks heard from the men; even the opprobrious terms of "Fan-kwei," "Yang-kwei-tsi," and "Hung-ma-jen," are here exchanged for the more respectable one of 番人 "Fan-jen".

The Wen-ch'i river is not of sufficient depth to allow vessels of more than nine feet draught to ascend higher than Chwang-yun-ch'iao 狀元橋, a small village on its south bank, ten miles below the city. From the entrance to this village it is wide and deep, with few obstructions, and by the assistance of a few buoys to mark out the channel, vessels of any size would find no difficulty in navigating it. The steepness of the river bank, the great rise and fall of tides, and the low price of iron and wood at Chwang-yun-ch'iao, make it one of the most desirable positions on the coast for the erection of dockyards and arsenals; while its spacious anchorage, and facilities for landing goods, and shipping them to the interior by the different canals, are strong arguments in favour of its being the site of the future foreign Settlement.

The North - China Herald and Supreme Court & Consular Gazette, April 5, 1877

Wenchow

Wenchow

COMMISSIONERS of Customs have been appointed and taken their stations at the several newly-opened ports, but although the officers who are to open English Consulates have been nominated, we have not yet any announcement of their having hoisted their flags. The date announced for the formal opening however, has passed; and we shall, we presume, soon see the Coast and Yangtze steamers advertised to call at Wenchow and Wuhu on their way to Foochow and to Hankow. It is worth while, in the meantime, to see what prospects there are for trade at these places, the opening of which has been so long talked of. And curiously enough, now that the moment has arrived, the natives at least at these two ports seem more anxious than foreigners for the consummation. The people of Wenchow especially are described as more friendly disposed than any with whom their visitors have yet come in contact, and as looking forward to commercial intercourse with foreigners with eager anticipation. Situated about eighteen miles from the sea, on the banks of a river which drains one of the most fertile districts of Che-keang, Wenchow should be a place of considerable trade; and so, in a quiet way, it seems to be. It is a question what degree of impulse will be given by the facilities for communication which the frequent passage of steamers will afford. The import of shirtings is at present said to reach a value of about $1,000,000 yearly, and that of opium some 3,000 to 4,000 chests. Considerable quantities of cotton are imported from Shanghai and Ningpo, and of sugar from Chinchew and Formosa; most of which will presumably furnish cargo for steamers when these enter upon the trade. This year, there has been a large import of rice, owing to the injury done by floods to the local crops, but that was a reversal of the ordinary course,

Editorial Selections.

WENCHOW.

COMMISSIONERS of Customs have been appointed and taken their stations at the several newly-opened ports, but although the officers who are to open English Consulates have been nominated, we have not yet any announcement of their having hoisted their flags. The date announced for the formal opening however, has passed; and we shall, we presume, soon see the Coast and Yangtze steamers advertised to call at Wênchow and Wuhu on their way to Foochow and to Hankow. It is worth while, in the meantime, to see what prospects there are for trade at these places, the opening of which has been so long talked of. And curiously enough, now that the moment has arrived, the natives at least at these two ports seem more anxious than foreigners for the consummation. The people of Wênchow especially are described as more friendly

Wenchow being generally a considerable exporter of the grain. The principal export is likely to be tea; and it is an interesting question how far this new outlet will affect the trade of Foochow. About 100,000 piculs are at present said to go to Shanghai and Foochow from the Ping-yang district; and the produce of Peh-ling (Pak-lum) district, which now finds its way overland to Foochow, is tolerably certain to come by water to Wenchow instead, now the port is opened. Some 200,000 piculs are predicted from this neighbourhood, besides smaller quantities from other sources of supply. Silk is a feature of local industry, but of a coarse kind and used only for Chinese consumption; some is grown in the neighbourhood, but more is imported to supply the requirements of the local manufacturers; and the export of silk goods is said to reach about three quarters of a million taels. Native opium, alum, timber, and paper, are exported in considerable quantities; and iron is spoken of as a possible article of future commerce. The natives say it exists in large quantities in the districts of Chingtien and Taishan, and hope that the mines will be allowed to be worked after the opening of the port.—As we have mentioned on a former occasion, there is ample water for coasting steamers to come up to the city; and a site for the English Settlement has accordingly been selected in close proximity, outside the north-east angle of the wall. The river near the shore is too shallow for steamers to approach; and whether the business will be sufficient to justify the construction of wharves and pontoons, or whether it will be constructed by means of lighters, is for the future to decide. Earlier reports on the river had fixed on a place ten miles below the city as the proper site for a Settlement, under the impression apparently that steamers could not find anchorage nearer the city; but his has been shown to be a mistake, and the advantage of approaching as closely as possible to the business quarters of the Chinese, is evident. Wenchow was one place fortunate enough to escape capture by the Taepings, and is therefore in exceptionally good condition. It is clean and well-paved, and the people are prosperous. Their good disposition towards foreigners has been always remarked on; and the courtesy shown by the gentry to the official visitors who have lately been prospecting in their neighbourhood, has been as marked as the ill-will evinced by the same class at Ichang. Let us hope that the results from the opening of their port will be as satisfactory as they anticipate.

The North - China Herald and Supreme Court & Consular Gazette, April 5, 1877

Wenchow

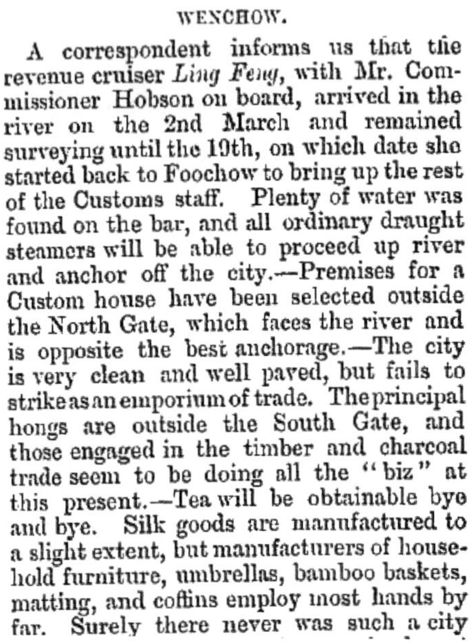

WENCHOW.

A correspondent informs us that the revenue cruiser *Ling Feng*, with Mr. Commissioner Hobson on board, arrived in the river on the 2nd March and remained surveying until the 19th, on which date she started back to Foochow to bring up the rest of the Customs staff. Plenty of water was found on the bar, and all ordinary draught steamers will be able to proceed up river and anchor off the city.—Premises for a Custom house have been selected outside the North Gate, which faces the river and is opposite the best anchorage.—The city is very clean and well paved, but fails to strike as an emporium of trade. The principal hongs are outside the South Gate, and those engaged in the timber and charcoal trade seem to be doing all the "biz" at this present.—Tea will be obtainable bye and bye. Silk goods are manufactured to a slight extent, but manufacturers of household furniture, umbrellas, bamboo baskets, matting, and coffins employ most hands by far. Surely there never was such a city

Wenchow

A correspondent informs us that the revenue cruiser *Ling Feng*, with Mr. Commissioner Hobson on board, arrived in the river on the 2nd March and remained surveying until the 19th, on which date she started back to Foochow to bring up the rest of the Customs staff. Plenty of water was found on the bar, and all ordinary draught steamers will be able to proceed up river and anchor off the city.—Premises for a Custom house have been selected outside the North Gate, which faces the river and is opposite the best anchorage.—The city is very clean and well paved, but fails to strike as an emporium of trade. The principal hongs are outside the South Gate, and those engaged in the timber and charcoal trade seem to be doing all the "biz" at this present.—Tea will be obtainable bye and bye. Silk goods are manufactured to a slight extent, but manufacturers of household furniture, umbrellas, bamboo baskets, matting, and coffins employ most hands by far. Surely there never was such a city for joss houses, and but few are in decent repair.

The U.S.S *Palos*, with Mr. Consul Lord on board, arrived from Ningpo on the 21st. Mr. Lord is reported to have selected a concession lot adjoin that measured over by Mr. Davenport. Junks are high and dry off this position at low water, but whether intending settlers will take any note of the fact remains to be told.

The North - China Herald and Supreme Court & Consular Gazette, April 28, 1877

Wenchow

Wenchow

Up to the 11th, the community consisted of the long resident missionaries—Messrs. Stott and Jackson, and the members of the Customs' staff. On the 11th, the *Mosquito* arrived with reinforcements in the shape of Mr. Consul Alabaster. He has seen the officials, I believe, and employed himself in hunting for premises to serve as a Consulate. Not having seen the British ensign floating in the breeze on shore, I take it that to date the search has been unsuccessful. In the city people seem perfectly indifferent, either to the presence of foreigners or to the fact that steamers are now at liberty to visit the port. They don't seem to want anything unless it is a small cargo of rice. Native opium is plentiful, and piece goods come overland from Ningpo. Kerosine lamps are used in the principal shops, and matches are cheap. As to tea, a contract might be made for some raw leaf from the Ping-yang district, but the season is now well advanced. No foreign merchant has established to date, nor has a merchant vessel put in an appearance. (18th April)

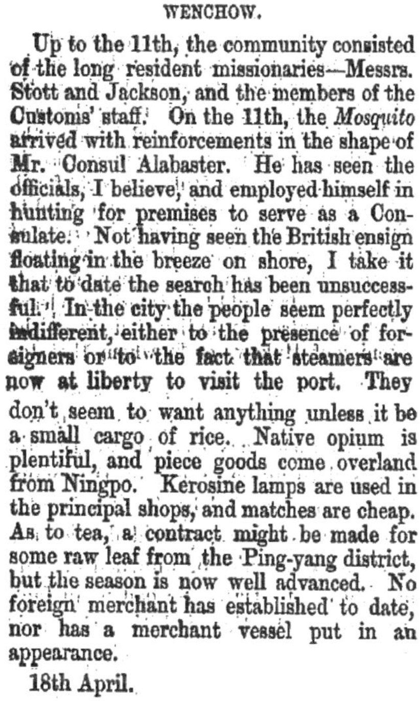

WENCHOW.

Up to the 11th, the community consisted of the long resident missionaries—Messrs. Stott and Jackson, and the members of the Customs' staff. On the 11th, the *Mosquito* arrived with reinforcements in the shape of Mr. Consul Alabaster. He has seen the officials, I believe, and employed himself in hunting for premises to serve as a Consulate. Not having seen the British ensign floating in the breeze on shore, I take it that to date the search has been unsuccessful. In the city the people seem perfectly indifferent, either to the presence of foreigners or to the fact that steamers are now at liberty to visit the port. They don't seem to want anything unless it be a small cargo of rice. Native opium is plentiful, and piece goods come overland from Ningpo. Kerosine lamps are used in the principal shops, and matches are cheap. As to tea, a contract might be made for some raw leaf from the Ping-yang district, but the season is now well advanced. No foreign merchant has established to date, nor has a merchant vessel put in an appearance.

18th April.

The North - China Herald and Supreme Court & Consular Gazette, May 5, 1877

Wenchow

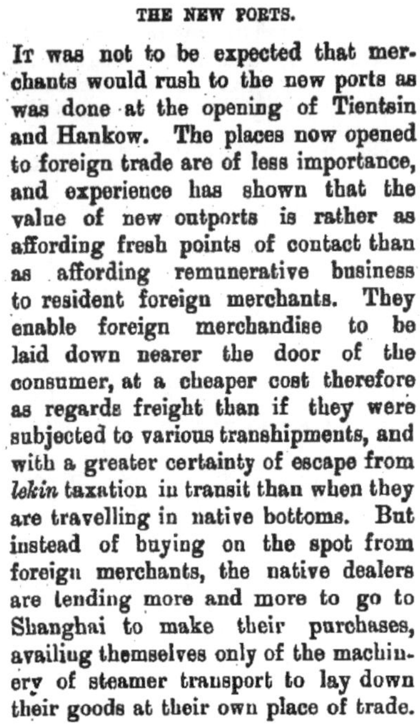
THE NEW PORTS.

It was not to be expected that merchants would rush to the new ports as was done at the opening of Tientsin and Hankow. The places now opened to foreign trade are of less importance, and experience has shown that the value of new outports is rather as affording fresh points of contact than as affording remunerative business to resident foreign merchants. They enable foreign merchandise to be laid down nearer the door of the consumer, at a cheaper cost therefore as regards freight than if they were subjected to various transhipments, and with a greater certainty of escape from *lekin* taxation in transit than when they are travelling in native bottoms. But instead of buying on the spot from foreign merchants, the native dealers are tending more and more to go to Shanghai to make their purchases, availing themselves only of the machinery of steamer transport to lay down their goods at their own place of trade.

The New Ports

It was not to be expected that merchants wonld rush to the new ports as was done at the opening of Tientsin and Hankow. The places now opened to foreign trade are of less importance, and experience has shown that the value of new ontports is rather as affording fresh points of contact than as affording remunerative business to resident foreign merchants. They enable foreign merchandise to be laid down nearer the door of the consumer, at a cheaper cost therefore as regards freight than if they were subjected to various transhipments, and with a greater certainty of escape from *lekin* taxation in transit than when they are travelling in native bottoms. But instead of buying on the spot from foreign merchants, the native dealers are lending more and more to go to Slanghai to make their purchases, availing themselves only of the machinery of steamer transport to lay down their goods at their own place of trade. Obviously tle resident foreign merchant, then, has little opportunity; except at apecial seasons—at Hankow and Foochow, during the tea season, for instance—there is little occupation except for a few commission houses; the great bulk of the business is done at Shanghai;which tends more and more to become a commercial emporium whither produce is brought, and whence foreign goods are sent out, from and to the whole of the Yangtze and Nortlern ports. But even takiug all these circumstances into consideration, it must be admitted that the opening of tle new ports has fallen remarkably fat. It might bave been expected that two or tlree foreign houses would have been at once established, at each of the three new ports in which Shanglai is interested; but Wenchow seems, as yet, to be the only place at which the experitent has been made. Of Ichang we know as yet very little; its chief value lies probably in its being the head—so far at least as the present class of steamers is concerned—of the navigation of the Yangtze. Shase, a little lower down tle stream, wlich is made only a port of call, seems to be the chief place of trade. But we may take it for granted that steamer agencies will shortly be establisbed at Ichang; and we shall gradually learn more about its capabilities. Wenchow and Wuhu, however, seem to be the natural outlets for fertile and well-watered districts; and might become places of considerable trade if foreign energy and capital were brouglt to bear upon their development. Clearly they are not places where foreigners can expect to go and pick up a business ready-made. They are not places where those who have been uufortunate elsewhere can hope to rapidly retrieve their fortunes. They are sites of a considerable native trade; but if this trade is to be developed so as to be of value to foreigners, capital and energy are required, to collect produce which used to permeate through other channels. Both are natural outlets for tea-producing districts; but such teas as now find their way to foreign markets do so through other channels, to Foochow, Ningpo, and Chinkeang. For the present year these teas have been already contracted for, and will follow their old routes. If foreign capital is employed next year, they can probably be collected at the new emporia; and will presumably be laid down there at a cheaper price in view of the shorter distance to be travelled. It is as advantageous to a merchant to buy produce as near as possible to the place of production, as it is to land his goods as near as posible to the place of sale; and herein is one object of opening new ports—multiplying points of contact. Even if foreign merchants do not attempt to develop a local business, the providing of greater facility of carriage will no doubt lead the native dealers to collect produce at the nearer port, instead of sending it overland to the dearer one. Before the Taeping Rebellion, Wenchow seems in fact to have been the emporium of a considerable tea trade—the port where the produce of all the neighbouring districts was collected; but this concentration was only an element of temptation to the Taepings, so the producers elected to disperse their trade through the neighbouring minor ports, and it has since continued in tle fresh grooves. The opening of the port to foreign trade will probably have the effect of again attracting business to its old centre.

The North-China Herald and Supreme Court & Consular Gazette, June 9, 1877

Wenchow

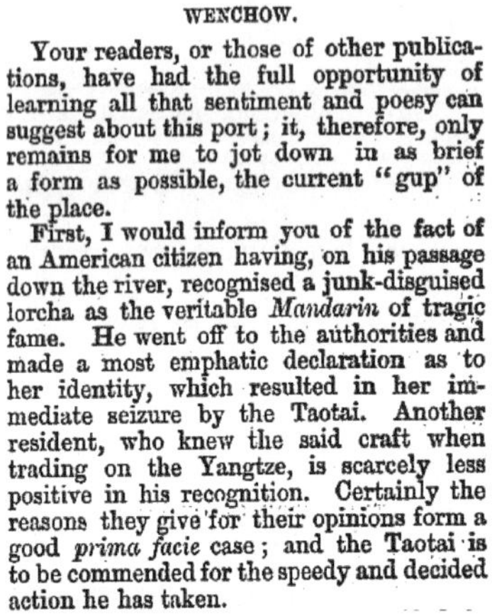
WENCHOW.

Your readers, or those of other publications, have had the full opportunity of learning all that sentiment and poesy can suggest about this port; it, therefore, only remains for me to jot down in as brief a form as possible, the current "gup" of the place.

First, I would inform you of the fact of an American citizen having, on his passage down the river, recognised a junk-disguised lorcha as the veritable *Mandarin* of tragic fame. He went off to the authorities and made a most emphatic declaration as to her identity, which resulted in her immediate seizure by the Taotai. Another resident, who knew the said craft when trading on the Yangtze, is scarcely less positive in his recognition. Certainly the reasons they give for their opinions form a good *prima facie* case; and the Taotai is to be commended for the speedy and decided action he has taken.

Wenchow

Your readers, or those of other publications, have had the full opportunity of learning all that sentiment and poesy can suggest about this port; it, therefore, only remains for me to jot down in as brief a form as possible, the current “gup” of the place.

First, I would inform you of the fact of an American citizen having, on his passage down the river, recognised a junk-disguised lorcha as the veritable *Mandarin* of tragic fame. He went off to the authorities and made a most emphatic declaration as to her identity, which resulted in her immediate seizure by the Taotai. Another resident, who knew the said craft when trading on the Yangtze, is scarcely less positive in his recognition. Certainly the reasons they give for their opinions form a good *prima facie* case; and the Taotai is to be commended for the speedy and decided action he has taken.

Speaking generally, I feel justified in reporting that commercial prospects are decidedly hopeful; although, the port having been opened at so late a period of the season, it can scarcely be expected that much will be done this year in tea. Even for this, however, there is good promise for the future. Piece goods undoubtedly will take; and should merchants of standing and worth care to follow the good example set them, I fancy they may not be disappointed in their expectations. Opium at present is scarcely to be thought of; the facilities for smuggling which import through Ningpo affords are a formidable obstacle to the sale of the drug when brought here and subjected to *lekin*.

This is undoubtedly the cleanest and (as far as sanitary precautions and advantages can secure), the healthiest city in China. So far, the weather has been cool and delightful. It appears that the native opium crop has failed this year to the extent of about 5% of the usual yield. This may cause an increase of the import of the Indian drug.

The North - China Herald and Supreme Court & Consular Gazette, June 30, 1877

Wenchow

Wenchow

Since I last wrote we have been visited by ten days of incessant and heavy rain, with the consequent freshets. The river rose considerably, and the current on certain days attained a speed of seven knots; but in no instance have we heard of any loss of life or even damage, although in some cases the force of the stream caused one or two junks to drag for some distance. The mud is so soft that under influences such as those now described, the anchors have but feeble hold, and even in the case of H.I.G.M.S. *Cyclop* gave way, without however causing more trouble than that involved by a berth further from the position that was at first taken up.

WENCHOW.

Since I last wrote we have been visited by ten days of incessant and heavy rain, with the consequent freshets. The river rose considerably, and the current on certain days attained a speed of seven knots; but in no instance have we heard of any loss of life or even damage, although in some cases the force of the stream caused one or two junks to drag for some distance. The mud is so soft that under influences such as those now described, the anchors have but feeble hold, and even in the case of H.I.G.M.S. *Cyclop* gave way, without however causing more trouble than that involved by a berth further from the position that was at first taken up.

Apropos of the mud, a curious fact was noted by the Naval officers whilst surveying the Upper Anchorage. One of the boats happened to ground on a bank formed just below an island lying about three-quarters of the way across the river; and, although the tide was running *strong ebb* and the men pulling, still the boat remained fast in the mud, and with it moved visibly up stream and against the rowers. This phenomenon, with others, is thought to indicate great uncertainty as to the permanency of any channel that may now be laid down in the new charts.

Apropos of the mud, a curious fact was noted by the Naval officers whilst surveying the Upper Anchorage. One of the boats happened to ground on a bank formed just below an island lying about three-quarters of the way across the river; and, although the tide was running strong ebb and the men pulling, still the boat remained fast in the mud, and with it moved visibly up stream and against the rowers. This phenomenon, with others, is thought to indicate great uncertainty as to the permanency of any channel that may now be laid down in the new charts.

The Captain and officers of the German gunboat, however, continue indefatigable in surveying from daylight to dark, and have nearly finished that portion of the river comprehended between the Upper limit of the port and Jar Point (lower anchorage). We understand that the *Cyclop* will go on surveying until all the work has been completed, or she receives orders to proceed elsewhere.

Mr. Main arrived by the *Conquest* and has, we believe, no hesitation in identifying the suspected lorcha as the *Mandarin*. This makes the third European who expresses himself confident as to her identity, which, with the strong circumstantial evidence afforded by the absence of any trustworthy papers, or even plausible account of how she came into her present owner's possession, and the suspiciously marked trouble that has been taken to disguise her, would appear to put the question beyond a doubt. Meantime, the matter has been reported and referred to Peking by both H.B.M. Consul and the Taotai. It will be interesting to note how, in the event of her being undoubtedly proved to be the Mandarin, the Chinese Government will get out of the new phase set up by the utter absence of "due diligence" indisputably proved by the fact of her trading so long on their coast after the murder; the numerous reports that have from time to time been made to them of her having been seen by various foreigners; and finally that as soon as foreigners get access to the port she has been always assumed to be trading to, she is at once recognized, and on H.B.M. Consul's representations seized. The complication will not be simplified by the strenuous denials hitherto given by the Chinese to the foreign assertions, or the fact that her comings and goings, so patent to even chance passers-by on the high seas, must have been, or certainly ought to have been, equally well-known to them.

The vessel is now scarcely worth the trouble of breaking up; the causes that have led to this great depreciation will no doubt have weight in deciding the question as to right for indemnity, and be not the less effective in rebutting any plea that may now be set up as to the "non-responsibility of a Government for the acts of individuals, *beyond using due diligence in the apprehension of offenders, making sincere efforts to restore as much of the stolen property as possible,* and to take such steps as may seem necessary for preventing such crimes in future."

Trade is much as before. We notice the *Conquest* takes about $59,000 away with her, it is to be presumed to be laid out in the purchase of goods or to pay for that already imported. As it all goes to Ningpo, it looks as though the Chinese, with characteristic conservatism, continue to buy their merchandise through Ningpo, merely substituting steamer for junk transport. This is a piece of obstinacy, however, which is likely to speedily remedy itself by appeal to that most sensitive part of the Celestial merchant, his pocket.

Upwards of 200½ chests of tea go up to the Shanghai market. The Teamen here are asking the most ridiculous prices, and what is more they somewhat firmly believe that they have only to go North to get them. This again may possibly correct itself.

The North - China Herald and Supreme Court & Consular Gazette, September 1, 1877

Lekin Regulations for the Wenchow District

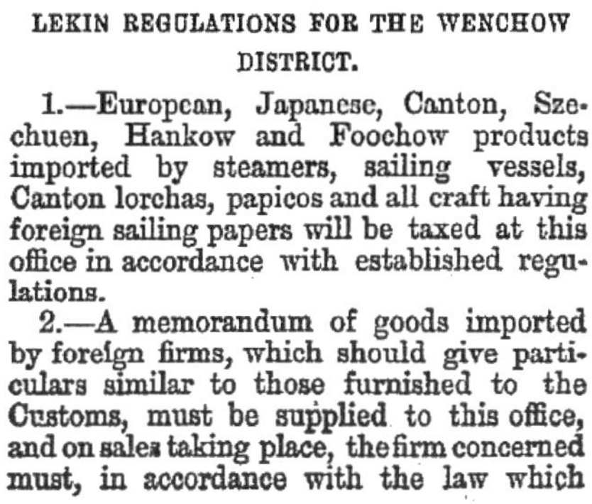
LEKIN REGULATIONS FOR THE WENCHOW DISTRICT.

1.—European, Japanese, Canton, Szechuen, Hankow and Foochow products imported by steamers, sailing vessels, Canton lorchas, papicos and all craft having foreign sailing papers will be taxed at this office in accordance with established regulations.

2.—A memorandum of goods imported by foreign firms, which should give particulars similar to those furnished to the Customs, must be supplied to this office, and on sales taking place, the firm concerned must, in accordance with the law which

Lekin Regulations for the Wenchow District

1.—European, Japanese, Canton, Szechuen, Hankow and Foochow products imported by steamers, sailing vessels, Canton lorchas, papicos and all craft having foreign sailing papers will be taxed at this office in accordance with established regulations.

2.—A memorandum of goods imported by foreign firms, which should give particulars similar to those furnished to the Customs, must be supplied to this office, and on sales taking place, the firm concerned must, in accordance with the law which prescribes payment of local dues by native merchants, direct the purchasers to proceed and pay *lekin*, after which the produce may be delivered. Should underhand dealings, or attempts will result in a fine,—already defined by regulation, of treble the amount of *lekin* leviable.

3.—Goods purchased from foreign firms by native brokers for transport inland, either by land or water route, will be examined by all branch *lekin* offices, the persons in charge of which will call for, and examine *lekin* receipts issued by this office. Should no receipts be forthcoming, the goods concerned will be detained pending report to this office and decision as to the fine to be inflicted.

4.—When proferring payment of *lekin*, the goods concerned should be submitted for examination, and if packages, weight, &c., agree, the goods will be stamped and released. Should the goods concerned be numerous or bulky, on application to that effect being made, an officer will be deputed to proceed and examine the parcels on the spot, to the prevention of underhand doings.

5.—In the case of exports—excepting tea and silk which will be dealt with separately—all goods will be taxed to the extent of three-tenths of the (Customs) tariff rate. Goods owned by foreign hongs are exempt from impost, but acts of collusion (with natives) will, on detection, result in the infliction of a fine.

6.—Native merchants purchasing goods from foreign firms for transport to the interior, must, in the first instance, tender payment of import *lekin*, after which they may take delivery. On goods destined for the interior under transit pass, and not for storage in the port, all local dues must be paid in full, on which this office will issue passes under which the goods may be forwarded in instalments, and without liability at the last barrier reached. As to (Chinese owned) native produce, it has not, to date, been permissible to convey the same under transit pass; therefore, *lekin*, as per tariff, is payable thereon. Attempted frauds in connection with this produce will be treated as acts of smuggling.

7.—As to the goods of all description stored in foreign hongs, it is provided by treaty that the *lekin* officials may, at convenience, devise measures for the prevention of smuggling and other malpractices; with this intent, therefore, this office will appoint an officer to make monthly inspections and take note of unsold stock. (This action is provided for by Art. 46 of the Treaty.)

8.—Native merchants, when paying *lekin*, and obtaining passes, must make careful note as to the city, street, &c., for which the goods are destined; also furnish particulars of the water route to be traversed in the event of the goods being forwarded by water, in order that full inspection may be made, and acts of smuggling be prevented.

9.—If it be sought to re-export goods imported by foreign firms on the scope of their being unsuited to the market; *lekin* thereon will be remitted if on examination at the Customs it is proved that they remain as intact as when imported. (Art. 45, of the Treaty provides for this treatment.)

10.—Recent regulations provide that within foreign Settlements foreign products are exempt from *lekin*, but that beyond Settlement limits *lekin* is leviable on foreign and native produce alike. Pending the fixing of Settlement boundaries, the regulations hitherto in force affecting *lekin* levies will be enforced.

11.—The Settlement boundaries once determined on, this office will take cognizance of native produce, the property of Chinese merchants found therein, this measure constituting a simple control over native merchandise by the local authorities. Should there be connivance with foreign firms in respect to ownership, or should the latter extend protection with a view to frauds on the *lekin* revenue, detection will result in the confiscation of the goods concerned, and the Consul to which the foreign firms is amenable being called on to levy a fine, to the end that treaty stipulations be upheld, (Vide Art. 48 of Treaty.)

The above rules, based on those in force at Ningpo, have been drawn up to meet the circumstances of the occasion; they are in accord with, and in a measure explanatory of Treaty stipulations, and are put forth in a spirit of equity in the general interest of the *lekin* revenue.

Regulations Respecting Opium

1.—*Lekin* on opium in the Wenchow district will be collected in accordance with the Ningpo system, viz., at the rate of Tls.40 per chest, 40 balls constituting a chest of Patna, and 100 catties one of Malwa.

2.—On opium being imported it will be examined by the Customs and deposited in foreign godowns under bond, report of the amount arriving being made to this office. On sales being made, the purchaser is to be directed to pay *lekin* and obtain the stamped release slips supplied by this office, after which the drug may be delivered. Cases of smuggling will be visited by a fine of Tls.1,000 for each picul smuggled.

3.—As regards to the Opium *lekin*, it is customary at Ningpo—owing to a mutual agreement existing amongst foreign firms—for them to pay the *lekin*, hence, from the levy of Tls.40, the sum of Tls.5 is refunded to the compradore of the firm concerned, and Tl.1 is paid to the native broker, a sum of Tls.34 accruing to the *lekin* office.

Foreign firms in Wenchow not having arranged for making payments in the manner just described, there is no necessity, at present, for making the refunds mentioned.

So soon as foreign firms have come to an understanding on the question, the allowance will be made in due course, and, at the same time, more detailed measures for exercising control over operations will be promulgated.

The North - China Herald and Supreme Court & Consular Gazette, September 1, 1877

Wenchow

Wenchow

Trade here received a rude shock the other day by reason of the high *lekin* tariff which was suddenly sprung on us. A set of "rules," ludicrous in the extreme, accompanied the table of rates; and in it all the clauses in the Treaty alluding to the Customs were twisted round and made to bear on the subject of proclamation. For instance, one rule stated that by Treaty (sic) foreigners as well as natives were subject to *lekin*. Again, another notified that twice a month the *lekin* officers would inspect foreign godowns, "and by checking the contents with the Customs statement the difference would show what goods ought to have paid *lekin*," &c., &c. This was stated to be an exact copy of the regulations in force at Ningpo. Extraordinary precautions were taken at first to prevent the circulating documents, containing the rules, falling into foreign hands; but in spite of all it was not long before our authorities were in possession of them. The Chinese immediately combined to resist the extortion, with the result of quite stagnating trade. Orders were sent to Shanghai to stop shipments. This last has had the effect of depriving us of our usual and solitary steamer. The native merchants further threatened to close their places, and in the end so intimidated the Taotai that the proclamations were withdrawn and modifications promised. The merchants are not quite satisfied yet; but in escaping this Seylla I fear foreigners are threatened with a Charybdis. The "Ningpo *lekin* guild" have, of course, suffered severely by the opening of this port, and they are afraid that they not realize even the comparatively small amount they pay for farming the tax.

They are, therefore, making great efforts to persuade one or two of the leading merchants here to join them in farming the *lekin* at Wenchow. Now it will be remembered that at Ningpo they were quietly allowed to do this. They acquired the right to levy for a comparatively small payment,

WENCHOW.

Trade here received a rude shock the other day by reason of the high *lekin* tariff which was suddenly sprung on us. A set of "rules," ludicrous in the extreme, accompanied the table of rates; and in it all the clauses in the Treaty alluding to the Customs were twisted round and made to bear on the subject of proclamation. For instance, one rule stated that by Treaty (sic) foreigners as well as natives were subject to *lekin*. Again, another notified that twice a month the *lekin* officers would inspect foreign godowns, "and by checking the contents with the Customs statement the difference would show what goods ought to have paid *lekin*," &c., &c. This was stated to be an exact copy of the regulations in force at Ningpo. Extraordinary precautions were taken at first to prevent the circulating documents, containing the rules, falling into foreign hands; but in spite of all it was not long before our authorities were in possession of them. The Chinese immediately combined to resist the extortion, with the result of quite stagnating trade. Orders were sent to Shanghai to stop shipments. This last has had the effect of depriving us of our usual and solitary steamer. The native merchants further threatened to and forming a guild of all the native importers, the amount was readily made up by the imposition of a very low rate.

But the moment an unhappy foreigner dared to import a bale, he was taxed by these conspirators to the *full* theoretical amount, and not one step could his goods go until this was paid. This cannot be! Will explain those learned in treaty rights; but, alas, it is too true, as amny a man reduced from comparative affluence to the verge of ruin can testify. Strange to say, also, so great was the lethargy exhibited at the outset by those deeply concerned, that no struggle was made, not even an official protest filed. When too late, and the daring fraud had got a firm footing, there arose lamentations and whines; but even then, when urged to make an effort, the reply came sobbingly but decidedly: "No, the trade has passed into native hands, their guild is too strong, it is not worth while trying now." Well! This is what the Ningpo men (and, it is said, at the head, the *lekin* official himself one of them) are trying to effect here. Thanks to unusually favourable circumstances, peculiar experience, and much energetic ability, sanguine hopes are entertained that the schemers will be foiled and our port, (hitherto week by week showing fairer commercial prospects), saved from the utter ruin our crafty neighbours intended for it and us.

It is freely circulated as an inducement (of course amongst natives) that by this means the foreigner will be driven out; and Ningpo is brought forward as the all-convincing proof.

For the first time in our experience, Britishers have now to place all their hopes in interference foreign to their Government, and many longing eyes are cast towards the German and other Ministers who are said to be so strenuously fighting to neutralize the retrograde and disgracefully disastrous effects of the boasted Chefoo Convention.

The above is all the "news" our port affords at present, beyond the fact of our being stricken with rage and disappointment at the withdrawal of the *Conquest*, owing to *lekin* misdoings. Oh Sir Thomas! Sir Thomas! If we could only see how far the bad effects of our impetuosity and obtruseness may penetrate, how even comparatively minor concerns are disastrously affected, what care we could take and what foolish acts would we be saved from!! (SPES.)

The North-China Herald and Supreme Court & Consular Gazette, September 8, 1877

The Lekin Regulations at Wenchow

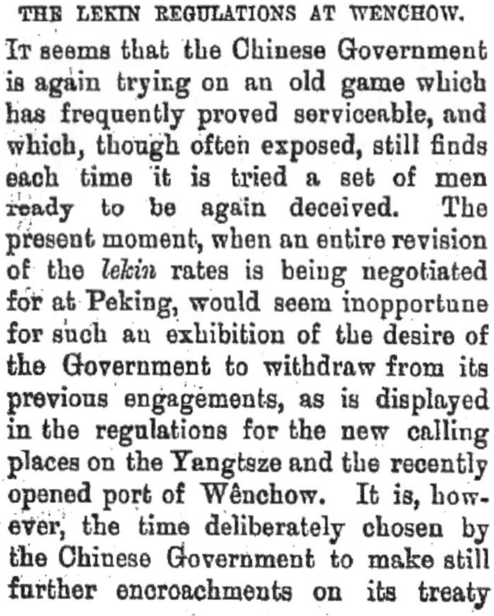
THE LEKIN REGULATIONS AT WENCHOW.

IT seems that the Chinese Government is again trying on an old game which has frequently proved serviceable, and which, though often exposed, still finds each time it is tried a set of men ready to be again deceived. The present moment, when an entire revision of the *lekin* rates is being negotiated for at Peking, would seem inopportune for such an exhibition of the desire of the Government to withdraw from its previous engagements, as is displayed in the regulations for the new calling places on the Yangtsze and the recently opened port of Wênchow. It is, however, the time deliberately chosen by the Chinese Government to make still further encroachments on its treaty

The Lekin Regulations at Wenchow

IT seems that the Chinese Government is again trying on an old game which has frequently proved serviceable, and which, though often exposed, still finds each time it is tried a set of men ready to be again deceived. The present moment, when an entire revision of the *lekin* rates is being negotiated for at Peking, would seem inopportune for such an exhibition of the desire of the Government to withdraw from its previous engagements, as is displayed in the regulations for the new calling places on the Yangtze and the recently opened port of Wenchow. It is, however, the time deliberately chosen by the Chinese Government to make still further encroachments on its treaty stipulations. We are all familiar with the history of previous difficulties with China. Little by little exactions were heaped up and obstructions placed in the way of intercourse, till at last trade became impossible; and some further step, insignificant in itself, became the occasion of actual quarrel. Finding, however, that war was a difficult game to play, the Chinese Government has tried the more congenial method of diplomacy, and has succeeded in getting back much that it lost by former ruder methods. ——It was evident, however, that there must be something plausible to give up in the approaching struggle with the German Minister, in order to avoid some still more unbearable concession. Were the game to be played out on ground occupied prior to the convention at Chefoo, it was evident that something of importance must be pushed up to meet the extra pressure placed upon the Government. There were, unfortunately, indications of weakness in that instrument. It wanted that precision of expression which a Minister entirely in earnest would not have failed to have made use of; and one or two ambiguous words, capable, like the swords of the gate-keepers of Paradise, of being turned every way, were permitted to be inserted. This weakness and ambiguity in the instrument has been skilfully taken advantage of to the utmost, not so much in the hope of ultimate success, as with the object of the prior occupation of a position from which the skilful diplomatist may gracefully retire. The matter has been reduced to a simple question. The German Minister presses the Chinese Government for a certain amount of concession; that Government in the most liberal spirit accepts the position, and agrees that at a certain time it will be ready to proceed with the game. Meanwhile, it wilfully increases the mass of obstructiveness, so that there may be the greater ability to concede, and apparently the greater praise due for its ready acquiescence. It is something like an old trick with a too complaisant tailor. A. has an old score which the tradesman presses him to reduce. A. willingly accedes and names a time when he will settle the amount he can pay up; meanwhile, as he wants clothes, he goes to the tradesman and orders several new suits; when the time comes for payment he offers half the price of the latter towards a reduction of his debt. He has palpably done two good things. He has got his clothes at half their price; and has besides, by his readiness in meeting the views of the tradesman, effected a temporary release from the pressure which the latter was bringing to bear on him. He has kept his promise to the letter, and what could the latter expect more? It was certainly the tailor's fault if he allowed himself to be "sold" by such as simple device, and A could not be blamed by any reasonable man. So the Chinese Government, finding that something must be yielded, makes new aggressions in the hope that when the time comes for payment of the next instalment, a too affable Minister may permit the last move to remain unquestioned, and proceed from it in his demands, rather than from the *status ante quo*.

The North - China Herald and Supreme Court & Consular Gazette, September 22, 1877

Wenchow

Wenchow

Matters are pretty well in *status quo*, the officials mildly demanding *lekin* at whatever rates they can get, and taking promises to pay in lieu of money. In some instances, (where the victim is supposed to be insignificant), a show of forcing the tax is made. Demands are also freely made for a payment of back *lekin*, *i.e.*, that *due on goods imported since the opening of the port*. It is important to note that only a vey nominal rate of *lekin* was levied in a *few* instances *prior to* the arrival of foreigners; and in a great many cases none at all. All this zeal in imposing the "military tax," and the sudden discovery of the necessity for it, has sprung into existence contemporaneously with foreign advent. The officials, however, seem to have been a little scared—thanks to the energy of our Consul—and have called in all the pamphlets previously circulated, torn out those precious rules, and now simply content themselves with issuing the bare tariff. An original book cannot be got at present for love or money, and I have no doubt but that even the condensed translation, which appeared in you late issue, caused much timorous regret in the official breast. A foreigner who sold some goods to a native the other day, finding that the purchaser was thought to belong to the class available for pressure, volunteered to pay the *lekin* himself, and include it in the price, but he was most anxiously and repeatedly informed by the officials that they "would on no account take a single cent from a foreigner until the power to enforce payment arrived from Peking." They eventually squeezed the buyer, however.

Meantime we are without steamers. Why, we know not; the Chinese here declare that they have no end of cargo in Shanghai waiting for conveyance. The U.S.S. *Palos* came in to-day and

WENCHOW.

Matters are pretty well in *statu quo*, the officials mildly demanding *lekin* at whatever rates they can get, and taking promises to pay in lieu of money. In some instances, (where the victim is supposed to be insignificant), a show of forcing the tax is made. Demands are also freely made for a payment of back *lekin*, *i.e.*, that due *on goods imported since the opening of the port*. It is important to note that only a very nominal rate of *lekin* was levied in a *few* instances *prior* to the arrival of foreigners; and in a great many cases none at all. All this zeal in imposing the "military tax," and the sudden discovery of the necessity for it, has sprung into existence contemporaneously with foreign advent. The officials, however, seem to have been a little scared—thanks to the energy of our Consul—and have called in all the pamphlets previously circulated, torn out those precious rules, and now simply content themselves with issuing the bare tariff. An original book cannot be got at present for love or money, and I have no doubt but that even the condensed translation, which appeared in you late issue, caused much timorous regret in the official breast. A foreigner who sold some brought us some news of the outer world; when we shall next hear, goodness or rather badness only knows.—Cholera has appeared to a limited extent, but the sanitary advantages of this place—its perfect drainage and unusual cleanliness—lead us to hope that this dread diease may not become epidemic. We have had incessant rain for the last ten days, and the natives say we may expect a continuation of the same pleasant condition until the end of the month. I am obliged now to fall back on the usual feminine excuse for concluding an uninteresting letter, by stating (what in this case is a fact) that "we positively have no news, it is quite too awfully dull;" so looking for better luck next time I will at present sign myself SPES.

The North - China Herald and Supreme Court & Consular Gazette, October 4, 1877

Wenchow

WENCHOW.

Cholera has unfortunately made its appearance here, and is now admitted by the natives to be epidemic. The daily mortality is given at 35, but it is said to be steadily decreasing. Happily no foreigner has been attacked yet, and our Consul, with his usual energy, has got the Taotai to issue a proclamation calling on the people to observe certain sanitary rules which have been suggested by Mr. Warren. To-morrow a Joss is to be paraded, and the officials speak most hopefully of the speedily beneficial effect this is sure to have. When a man is once attacked, the Chinese—beyond in a few cases applying local acupuncture—do absolutely nothing, hence the high death rate, nearly every case proving fatal. From the description given, I should not think the type of disease the most malignant; and can't help believing that treatment would tend to promote recovery in at least an appreciable number.

Wenchow

Cholera has unfortunately made its appearance here, and is now admitted by the natives to be epidemic. The daily mortality is given at 35, but it is said to be steadily decreasing. Happily no foreigner has been attacked yet, and our Consul, with his usual energy, has got the Taotai to issue a proclamation calling on the people to observe certain sanitary rules which have been suggested by Mr. Warren. Tomorrow a Joss is to be paraded, and the officials speak most hopefully of the speedily beneficial effect this is sure to have. When a man is once attacked, the Chinese—beyond in a few cases applying local acupuncture—do absolutely nothing, hence the high death rate, nearly every case proving fatal. From the description given, I should not think they type of disease the most malignant; and can't help believing that treatment would tend to promote recovery in at least an appreciable number.

Touching *lekin*, the officials are in a great state of perturbation. They have now reduced the rate on piece goods to 96 cash per piece, but even at this can get no payments. Opium, nominally taxed at Tls.40 per picul, will be gladly passed for Tls.32, but alas! The people are not to be propitiated. “This high tax is extortionate and unprecedented, and why because foreigners come and trade here should we be taxed extra, we did not bring them!” Such is the burden of reply to the collector; and really the officials seem to have no power to enforce their demands. The other day a foreigner, wishing to forward some goods inland, was sending them from his godown to the Custom House to be examined, when the bearers were stopped by someone stating he was a *lekin* official, and payment demanded. On the coolies refusing to accede, and further telling the self-styled official where the goods were going and for what purpose, the latter set on them and beat them, whereupon they dropped the goods and rushed back to their master. Chase was given and the offender was caught. Failing to give a proper account of himself, he was detained until the authorities could be communicated with. This was about nine o'clock in the morning; at six o'clock p.m. it was discovered that he really had some connection with the *lekin* people; but no one could be got to own him. He was, therefore, released. This foreigner sends out with all his goods a slip, stating to whom they belong and where they are going. He has informed the *lekin* officials that of course if they stop his property he is at present powerless to prevent them, and will leave the goods in their hands until steps can be taken elsewhere to protect him, meantime holding them responsible for all loss by detention or otherwise. Hitherto no action has been taken by the *lekin* men, and although several have been seen going about with an umbrella in one hand and a drawn sword in the other, they bolt with extraordinary speed the instant a foreigner comes in sight. —I have been going over the trade returns issued by the Customs for the April-June quarter, and our port by no means makes a bad show. We are ahead of Wuhu as far as piece goods are concerned, and this in spite of the great disadvantage we labour under when compared with that port as regards regular communication. Of course a package can always be dropped by some passing river steamer; but for this place intending shippers must preserve alike their patience and their goods until a chance offers.

Again, the analysis seems to prove that a new field for Shirtings and T-Cloths has been opened up, and not, as was prophesied, simply a transference of trade from Ningpo brought about. Anything that we do in that last way will be so much more to the good, and quite irrespective of our inherent capacity. Thus it will be seen that in the quarter under notice 60,705 pieces of Shirtings and T-Cloths came here direct; whilst to Ningpo there were imported during the same time 306,849 pieces against 298,553 for same quarter last year, being an increase of 8,296 pieces on 1877. We have reason to believe that during the short time subsequent to June, when left untrammeled, it will be found that this favourable and promising condition of affairs became more and more satisfactory, but now!—*horresco referens*—*lekin* has stepped in and spoilt all; and a *lekin* that was not levied before we came.

Rain continues to fall heavily. We fear the *Palos* will take back but poor accounts of our port, but if it is any comfort to you and to them, learn that this is a "most unusual year" and that for a better condition of things we are all living in a sanguine state of SPES.

For the last eight days we have had very bad weather; day by day rain, and as the atmosphere is getting cold now, I am afraid the paddy, which is still green, will suffer very much.

The shooting season is setting in, but till now our sportsmen have only killed a few snipe; it is said that down at the "Lower Anchorage" there is any amount of game during the season, viz., wild geese, ducks, pheasants, deer, and even wild boar.

Several foreign residents are living in the city and a long way from the Customhouse. It is very disagreeable and tiresome to walk through the streets in Chinese cities, especially when it is rainy and dirty weather; and as chair coolies are very bad here, one foreigner ordered a jinricksha from Shanghai; but the coolies here did not understand how to manage the thing; another member of our community, however, was struck by the idea to have a donkey for drawing the jinricksha. I am quite sure that many readers of your journal will heartily laugh, imagining such a vehicle, but I can assure you that it is quite a comfortable conveyance, and recommend the Shanghai residents and others who keep a jinricksha to employ instead of the coolie a donkey, the latter having certainly many advantages over to the former.

U.S.S. *Palos* arrive here on the 14th from Shanghai, and will leave on the 20th for Ningpo; besides this steamer we have not seen a European vessel in port since the departure of the s.s. *Europe*, which left this for Foochow on the 2nd inst.; but I hope that as soon as the Northern ports are closed, we will have a regular steamer here, perhaps twice a month. (18th September)

The North – China Herald and Supreme Court & Consular Gazette, October 11, 1877

Wenchow

Wenchow

The officials have found it convenient to intimate that 40 percent will be deducted from the total number of pieces, bales, catties, &c. in estimating the *lekin* tax to be paid. This brings the tax nearly to its old standing. The traders seem somewhat propitiated, and it is rumoured that orders will be sent to Shanghai, as before, and trade resumed. As the Calvinists would say, "The Lord grant it may be so, and all of contrary opinion consigned to perdition." The head *lekin* official has been recalled, but whether this means submission or stronger fight we can't say. *Lekin* is probably doomed, thanks to German and other national efforts, but I fancy a struggle will be made *in articulo mortis*.

Cholera did not stay long with us, and has now disappeared entirely. The maximum mortality was 35 per diem and this only for two days. Had any sort of treatment been adopted, I fancy our deaths would have been fewer by a good deal.

The *Conquest* leaves us, swearing she won't return for three months. This I hope is exaggeration, as the oranges will be ready for shipment in three or four weeks, and then the freight is likely to be good for a steamer; but it is necessary that one should be "on hand" so as to divert the trade from the old junk system. We hear on all sides hopes expressed that some steamer or the other will be here to take the fruit. Since *lekin* has been so oppressive, all the merchandise (e.g. rattans, dates, &c., &c.,) have been shipped from Shanghai and Ningpo by junk, as this taxation is either evaded by that course or so much modified as to amount to the same thing. It seems foreign contact is the grand excuse for *lekin*, and the moment this can be avoided the necessity for the imposition of the tax subsides. If there is diplomatist in China who thinks, or who believes in past Treaties, one would surmise that this fact might set up much reflection.

WENCHOW.

The officials have found it convenient to intimate that 40 per cent will be deducted from the total number of pieces, bales, catties, &c., &c., in estimating the *lekin* tax to be paid. This brings the tax nearly to its old standing. The traders seem somewhat propitiated, and it is rumoured that orders will be sent to Shanghai, as before, and trade resumed. As the Calvinists would say, "The Lord grant it may be so, and all of contrary opinion consigned to perdition." The head *lekin* official has been recalled, but whether this means submission or stronger fight we can't say. *Lekin* is probably doomed, thanks to German and other national efforts, but I fancy a struggle will be made *in articulo mortis*.

Cholera did not stay long with us, and has now disappeared entirely. The maxmium mortality was 35 per diem and this only for two days. Had any sort of treatment been adopted, I fancy our deaths would have been fewer by a good deal.

This, however, must be essentially a tea port, and confident hopes are entertained that next season good tea will come here, either for sale or shipment for Shanghai. The tea growers are willing to take piece goods and opium in barter, and as these will go up under transit pass, and the tea come down under the same, *lekin* will not be able to interfere. It is said that foreign advent is likely to stimulate tea cultivation in this neighbourhood. Nous verrons.

The withdrawal of the regular steamer seems to have been inopportune, and to have aided the rebound from the healthy state of trade which she was gradually forming; but, of course, if immediate returns are possible, it is unnatural to expect merchants to pass them by and look to future contingencies, however energetic they may have been whilst these temptations were absent. I trust, however, that some steamer will be here to take the fruit exports.

As before, we are very dull in the way of news, and I feel constrained, in trustful expectation of better times, to sign myself as before SPES. (4th October)

The North – China Herald and Supreme Court & Consular Gazette, October 25, 1877

Wenchow

WENCHOW.

The only news of interest since my last is that the *lekin* on tea has at last been fixed at 25 tael cents per chest less than the Customs' transit dues. This will of course cause the inland duty to flow directly into the pockets of the local authorities, and beyond the reach of the Imperial treasury.

I say "at last," for you can have no idea of the work and solicitations that were necessary before the desired information could be obtained. The Taotai is always ill, and apparently quite unfit for duty. There is a rumour that he is going on leave. Well, we can't get a worse, even if a more obstructive one; as the latter will at least have to assume a position of active hostility, a condition much more tangible than the opposite state. The native teamen seem to be looking with rather a longing eye towards our port, and there seems to be no doubt but that, if only a little capital comes here, the best "Foochow" teas will be on hand, and probably, at least at first, obtainable at lower prices than in the market from which their generic appellation is got. At any rate, a considerably quantity is likely to come here for shipment either to Shanghai or even Foochow; as in the

Wenchow

The only news of interest since my last is that the *lekin* on tea has at last been fixed at 25 tael cents per chest less than the Customs' transit dues. This will of course cause the inland duty to flow directly into the pockets of the local authorities, and beyond the reach of the Imperial treasury.

I say "at last," for you can have no idea of the work and solicitations that were necessary before the desired information could be obtained. The Taotai is always ill, and apparently quite unfit for duty. There is a rumour that he is going on leave. Well, we can't get a worse, even if a more obstructive one; as the latter will at least have to assume a position of active hostility, a condition much more tangible than the opposite state. The native teamen seem to be looking with rather a longing eye towards our port, and there seems to be no doubt but that, if only a little capital comes here, the best "Foochow" teas will be on hand, and probably, at least at first, obtainable at lower prices than in the market from which their generic appellation is got. At any rate, a considerably quantity is likely to come here for shipment either to Shanghai or even Foochow; as in the latter case there seem to be some official obstacles in the way of an overland transit, which do not exist in Chekiang province, and so prefecture will be given to the sea route.

Besides this, and I am glad to tell it as I dare say you will be to hear it, there is some jealous struggle going on between the Fohkien and Chekiang authorities, as the former, when theirs was the only port or market, increased the tax on teas coming from our province; and the latter, now that opportunity has arisen, encourage smuggling across the Fohkien borders for transit to Wenchow.

The facilities for shipment here are immeasurably superior to those at Foochow. The anchorage is extensive, and with a clear run out to sea. Water deep, even at a low state of tide; and the city within easy reach either by the river itself or the large canal which runs directly to it.

Of course the vested interest question in Foochow will act as a deterrent at first; but trade convenience may in the end overcome this.

Our sportsmen are getting ready for the season, and we hope to be able to report large bags before the winter is over. The oranges are coming on, and will I trust soon prove sufficient inducement for some steamer to come and take them.

Waiting for the coming steamer, and looking for the festive “*Cha-ze*,” I continue to sign myself, SPES. (18th October)

The North - China Herald and Supreme Court & Consular Gazette, November 29, 1877

Wenchow

Wenchow

Availing myself of the privilege usually accorded to persons undergoing penal servitude, I elect to address this periodical communication with the outer world to your care. As prisons go, the routine here is perhaps not so bad, although for certain geographical reasons solitary confinement is perhaps enforced to a greater extent than a very good-hearted Pentonville warder might think absolutely necessary. Considering that this isolation is entirely due to the official sins of omission and commission, for which we are not responsible, we certainly thought it pressing severity to an undue length when H.M.S. *Curlew* arrived without any letters, not to mention papers. We were informed that her departure had been duly notified, but no postal announcement appeared, and, therefore, no mails were sent. Of course, we know that good nature and sympathy with suffering humanity is all that gives us a right to hope that the information would be passed on to the proper postal quarter. We also remember that the time when the *Curlew* left Shanghai was an exceptional one, for the Races were pending and the up-country trips fitting out. Still, we cannot help hoping that when it is known how entirely dependant we are on the charitable efforts of those in a position to aid us, by stretch of Christian kindliness one spare second may be seized to perform a benevolent act fraught with so much happiness to the residents of Wenchow. For six weary weeks we have not seen a Shanghai paper and have received but one mail. We have sent couriers away regularly every second Saturday and contracted with them to make the return trip—but alas! They have not brought letters back. Playing the role of Bathsheba's child to our David, it appears, so to speak, that though we may go to you, you cannot

WENCHOW.

Availing myself of the privilege usually accorded to persons undergoing penal servitude, I elect to address this periodical communication with the outer world to your care. As prisons go, the routine here is perhaps not so bad, although for certain geographical reasons solitary confinement is perhaps enforced to a greater extent than a very good-hearted Pentonville warder might think absolutely necessary. Considering that this isolation is entirely due to official sins of omission and commission, for which we are not responsible, we certainly thought it pressing severity to an undue length when H.M.S. *Curlew* arrived without any letters, not to mention papers. We were informed that her departure had been duly notified, but no postal announcement appeared, and, therefore, no mails were sent. Of course, we know that good nature and sympathy with suffering humanity is all come to us. However, to quote from another obituary record, “Friends kindly accept this intimation.” A special courier leaves Ningpo for Wenchow on or about every Friday, letters to be addressed to the care of the Customs at the former place. L.P.O. please note.

So much for the particular, now let us go to the general, and probably more interesting. The last excitement has been a direct open attempt at intimidation and coercion of a Chinaman, who had sold some wood to a foreign merchant for shipment in a foreign vessel. *Mirabile dictum*! The informant was the unhappy native himself, who with his wife and belongings fled in terror of his life to the hong of the merchant to whom he had sold the wood. First, I must inform you that several of the officials here own or are interested in junks, shops, and trade generally. To take two instances. The Chentai is a large junk owner and has also several shops in the city. One of the Sub-Prefects is similarly engaged in commerce. To continue:—A cry was raised that if foreigners were allowed to buy wood, &c., and ship in foreign vessels, the junk trade would be ruined, and with it these influential persons. Hence, soon after the sale before mentioned had been effected, and a portion of the wood shipped, a petty mandarin proceeded to the house of the vendor and threatened him with everything, from imprisonment up to decapitation, if he dared to sell another stick or had any further dealings with foreigners. That portion of the wood unshipped was peremptorily stopped, and the vessel had to proceed without it. I should mention that *lekin* was duly paid for the lot shipped, but not accepted when tendered for that stopped.

After all, we may have to be grateful to Wenchow for bringing into prominent view so early in the day, the intentions of the Chinese as to carrying out and interpreting the Chefoo Convention. We see the *lekin* office boldly placed alongside the Custom House; we find unprecedented rates levied on all cargo, immediately on landing, and whether intended for sale in the “port or city” or beyond; then (MARK WELL), should the goods go further they have AGAIN to pay a similar tax. That is to say, the first imposition is as an ADDITIONAL IMPORT DUTY *merely*, and exceeds in amount that paid to the legitimate Customs; should the merchandise be going further, then a similar sum as *transit due* must be paid. Thus, before goods can reach the country consumer, they must have paid two import duties and one transit impost. The Custom House and its adjoining *lekin* office are at the head of the only jetty or landing place, just outside the North-Gate, so that the extra import duty can be and is readily levied simultaneously with the Customs. Undoubtedly the fear of foreign competition has alarmed the official traders, and to this fact must we in part ascribe the grand energy and audacity with which the only apparent lever at hand for warding off the danger has been used. Great was the joy when the Conquest was "driven off," and general the triumph amongst the junk owners. I believe arrangements are nearly completed for farming the tax. The Chinese tendency is to utilize this acquisition, so that those who really or nominally purchase the right to levy *lekin* will pay scarcely anything, whilst foreigners and those whom it may please the monopolists to look on as hostile, must pay the full amount set down in the published tariff. Whether this will be managed here as successfully as at Ningpo, remains to be seen. I rather fancy that, thanks to certain influences and experience which foreigners are fortunate enough to be able to count on, should merchants bestir themselves as they ought, the attempt (if made) will be in the long run frustrated. The official commercial interest in the exclusion of foreigners, however, will increase the temptation to try on the old tricks, as it will also render the right to levy farmable at minimum outlay. Of course, should the Chefoo Convention be ratified, resistance would be useless; those that care to remain, must then try to make themselves as happy as possible in the restricted area, or, (rejecting the modern euphuism "Settlement," use the old term) "factory," in which they will be confined, whilst the cordon of *lekin* collectors, reveling in the majesty of British protection, will find their task an easy one, and necessarily infinitely simpler than it used to be under the Treaties. In such an event, well may the Celestial victors glory in the knowledge that, by their exquisite "diplomacy," they have been able to convert what purported to be an humble and sincere amend for horrible outrage, into a triumph of exclusivism such as the most brilliant campaign could scarcely have accomplished, and which our military successes before Canton and Tientsin had done so much to prevent.

In anticipation of the Fu-tai's arrival, most of the laboring classes in city and suburbs have had to don the military garb, as apparently there are no end of what used, in the old days of naval pursers, to be called "widow's men"; and of course these ideal warriors must assume material form during the great man's stay. One sees the uniform everywhere, in the fields, carrying loads, and at all sorts of work. They have to go for instruction during a certain part of the day, and afterwards return to their respective avocations. By the way, a great portion of the urgently needed military tax yclept *lekin* goes to pay these same "widow's men." In keeping, however, with his ready aptitude for excuse, if the virtuous Chinaman was asked for an explanation, he would at once reply that these dummies were instituted as an economical plan for keeping up the military respectability of the country on paper, and were so many more proofs of the urgent need there was for the increase of a palpably inadequate *lekin*.

It is not the least of the many remarkable anomalies in diplomatic intercourse with China, that whereas in treating with other nations the knowledge of the existence of gross immorality rather strengthens the hands of him against whom it is arrayed, and in direct ratio to its extent aids in overcoming resistance, at Peking the contrary would seem to be the case; for it appears that diplomatists have to spend much of their time in devising means for so ignoring the glaring frauds and falsehoods, that the burlesque of treating a people with whom dishonesty is a merit on the same footing as powers holding very different views, might be rendered as little apparent as possible.

All the large canal boats have been impressed for weeks past, in case His Excellency should arrive unexpectedly and require their services. This, of course, is a great hardship, as the unhappy owners can earn nothing, and are paid little if anything.

As though we had not been afflicted sufficiently, our little community has met with a truly great loss in the removal of Mr. H. E. Hobson to Takow. If we have had one blessing vouchsafed to us, it has taken the form of the two leading officials sent to open this port—both of them able, energetic, and universally liked. Were it not that we have now to mourn the loss of one, it would be invidious to make special reference to either. It is those coming hereafter who will have most cause to praise the discretion, foresight, and firmness displayed by the two officials on whom has developed the responsibility of arranging and guarding the innumerable and important details attendant on the opening of Wenchow. Certain I am that Mr. Hobson's name will be held in as affectionate and grateful recollection in the future of this port as it has long been in the past of the old ones; and I feel sure that I only write that which is the hearty desire of all my fellow residents, when in their name I wish much happiness and long life to our late able, kindly, and popular Commissioner.

In saying farewell to Mr. Hobson, we do not forget to welcome his successor, a man whose long experience in China and in his service is likely to be of no less use to him than to the port whose destinies he will now take part in watching.

As you will doubtless say: what with growling, Chinese iniquity, and mourning, this is a somewhat lugubrious letter; but when affairs reach their worst they are apt to mend; though "slow grinds the mill," let us trust it may crush "exceeding sure;" and therefore, giving comforting play to my naturally sanguine disposition, I will, in spite of all, continue to believe (and wish you to do the same) that there may yet be for us all in China—SPES.

The North – China Herald and Supreme Court & Consular Gazette, January 10, 1878

Wenchow

WENCHOW.

Winter, after a severe struggle and considerable rain flow, seems to have gained the ascendency, and in consequence fires become more than luxuries. Of stirring incidents, we have nothing new to report. The "wood case" referred to in my last communication, has (on account of the unwillingness of the native officials to enter on a matter likely to be compromising) been remitted to the German Consul at Shanghai, for any further action that he may now think necessary.

We may mention that attempts have been made to get at the native witness, even to the extent of sending a posse of police to take him out of the foreign hong in which he has taken refuge; but on the foreigner declining to give him up except in obedience to a warrant, backed as by treaty provided, the constables withdrew. I understand that counter-charges have been drawn up against the unhappy individual. Report fixes the number of these at seven. From the same source

Wenchow

Winter, after a severe struggle and considerable rain flow, seems to have gained the ascendency, and in consequence fires becomes more than luxuries. Of stirring incidents, we have nothing new to report. The "wood case" referred to in my last communication, has (on account of the unwillingness of the native officials to enter on a matter likely to be compromising) been remitted to the German Consul at Shanghai, for any further action that he may now think necessary.

We may mention that attempts have been made to get at the native witness, even to the extent of sending a posse of police to take him out of the foreign hong in which he has taken refuge; but on the foreigner declining to give him up except in obedience to a warrant, backed as by treaty provided, the constables withdrew. I understand that counter-charges have been drawn up against the unhappy individual. Report fixes the number of these at seven. From the same source we hear that the charges are now said to comprehend offences unconnected with the wood affair, and not relating to foreigners. As, however, the first accusations were (we have every reason for believing) to the effect that after selling this wood to a foreigner, he had attempted to smuggle it on the purchaser's behalf, and that this charge was only allowed to drop on the discovery that perhaps the difficulty of proving a man guilty of smuggling that for which no duty was leviable might be great, I am inclined to think it possible that the after-thought indictment may, in spite of assertions to the contrary, have some relation to the point at issue with foreigners.

However, the man still remains in the hong, and if only a third of the threats made against him are capable of being carried out, I should strongly advise his continuing to do so.

Something in the same line, though not so tangible, occurred the other day, when the *lekin* officers went to a native merchant's shop in the city, and overhauling his books discovered that he had made some purchases of a foreigner. Upon which they quietly observed that, as these goods had been obtained from a foreign source, it was probable they had evaded the vigilance of the *lekin* officers, and thereupon inflicted and obtained an exceedingly heavy fine.

This has occasioned a little stir in the Chinese mercantile breast, and there is serious talk of their forming themselves into a guild; for, as they somewhat significantly remark, direct intercourse with foreigners seems to rouse prejudices in the minds of the Wenchow officials against individuals so engaging; that as in most things "union is strength," so the guild thus formed would present a body more capable of resisting the forces which can be so effectively brought to bear against solitary persons. Nor do they scruple to openly state as a further inducement, the probability that in a year or so, under the guise of farming, some arrangement may be made between themselves and the *lekin* officials which, though certainly not likely to be of any benefit to the revenue, may be adjusted in a way to suit the interests and even prejudices of the contracting parties. Brought in immediate contact as we are with these working of the Chinese mind, the memorial to Lord Derby in favour of the Chefoo Convention, and the letter of the Secretary of the Anti-Opium Alliance to the newspapers, struck us as being somewhat peculiar, and we might even say scarcely warranted by the facts.

Far be it from me to insinuate that any of the respected and respectable signatories to either document would wilfully lend themselves to that which they knew to be untrue, or aid in propagating a false impression; still, it must be admitted that both memorial and letter may be charged with presenting the *suggestio falsi* and exhibiting instances of *suppressio veri*. The great point attempted to be established in the memorial is the assertion that the duty levied by the Chinese on foreign produce is a just and reasonable one, and by no means exceeding or perhaps equalling that imposed by other nations. Now, from the general tenour of the remarks, it would seem that the Customs tariff has been brought forward as the basis for the statement, and, except as bearing on opium, *lekin* almost entirely kept in the background. This last would appear to point to the same influences as promoting both appeals.

Now, I fancy no one does or would say that the Customs imposts, as a whole, are other than may be fairly demanded. That they are equitably levied through one of the most perfectly organized systems to be met with anywhere, I assume most people in China will readily admit; and, whilst doing so, most heartily wish that the transit dues were——as provided by treaty—— solely collected through the same medium. Writing in China, and from Wenchow, it is unnecessary to point out how very different a thing "*lekin*" is, how very opposite its purposes, and how markedly the corruption surrounding its collection stands out, when compared to the almost perfect system that has been degraded into covering the iniquity against which foreigners cry out. The one, governed with unimpeachable integrity and guided by prominent intellect, really adding to the revenues of the country and to some extent benefitting the nation; the other ruled by dishonesty and purely personal interests, is worked by lowest cunning and bigotted spite, and though only adding to the incomes of a comparative few, presses sorely on the general public. It may no doubt be convenient to dwell on the excellence of the one whilst seeking to hide the vices of the other; but knowing as we in China do the true state of affairs, the analogy certainly seems inappropriate and very likely to mislead those not similarly informed. Who can say what *lekin* is levied, or fix the amount beyond which it never goes? We know that in certain places and under certain officials it averages from 7 to 10 per cent *ad valorem*; but we also know that as there is no limit to the amount facility of imposition, secresy of personal appropriation, and a gratification of spleen or bigotry may inflict; so also are we aware that all these conditions, though subservient to the will or ability of the person or persons engaged, and therefore interested, in the collection, are capable of fulfilment and are fulfilled in a way doubtless unknown either to the memorialists or the secretary of the A.–O. Alliance. It is absurd to quote any published tariffs; audacious as these are, they may be either exceeded or reduced as the object to be served and the power to enforce permits. This last is often secured by a union with a select number of commercial participants, the numerical strength of whom is not sufficient to materially diminish the individual share of the plunder, whilst it is all potent in bringing about the desired end, to the disastrous exclusion of those not comprehended in the "ring." Equally ridiculous is it to speak of protest or action before the tribunals appointed. Suppose, in a rare instance, as the one lately met with here, you did occasionally get a native willing to sacrifice his future prospects, and "it will be" his life——the well known resources of collusion, perjury, and subornation would so complicate the matter that, unless the legal form was abandoned, but little else than vexation of mind would be the result. The foreign plaintiff is too heavily weighted. If he were wicked enough (and perhaps there may be a comparative few who would not hesitate to adopt reciprocatory measures) he would be easily detected; whereas in the mass of Chinese and from the depths of China the effort to detect the sinning native would indeed be hopeless, to say nothing of the higher influences which would aid in sheltering him. The two systems of judicial investigation are so diametrically opposed, and based on such opposite foundations, that any attempt at an alliance, or, as they are technically termed, mixture, is impracticable where the interests of those under whose arbitrary direction the one system is worked, are in any way involved. The process that assumes truth until lying is proved, and innocence where guilt is not established, assorts ill with that where the very converse obtains; and the forms of the one only offer facilities for the corrupt displays of the other.

When accusing foreigners of being hard on the Chinese, it would seem as though an attempt had been made to play on a very old string without consideration as to whether the reality warranted the hypothesis. The good folks at home, in the plenitude of their truly British benevolence and Christian feeling, which boisterously expends itself on any other than their fellow countrymen, whether heathen or savage, and with more zest as it affords opportunity for depreciating their nationals, would appear to ignore the fact that the natives of China, no less morally then politically, may be divided into two classes—the one comprehending the officials, the other the governed. Now this distinction is of some importance, especially as most of the public information obtained in England regarding the Chinese comes from person brought solely in contact with the non-official class. I fancy no impartial person will deny to the latter very many excellent qualities and a very remarkable freedom from intuitive vice. I mean of course in their relationship to one another; for they have been so deceived and excited by their rulers as to foreigners, that it would be scarcely fair to quote those peculiarities sometimes to be observed in their intercourse with us as being common to the native character. In reading that interesting little work, "China and the Chinese," I was struck by the expression that, on conversion, the Chinese are not overcome by conscious guilt, "not feeling that they are sinners to the same extent and degree as we do, *simply because they are not*." Now, without entering into the connexion which has called forth the remarks from the Rev. writer, I submit that this accords with our knowledge of the Chinaman's general moral standing, and that they do on the whole compare favourably with Westerns. Heinous crime is very rare; thieving is not common, and they exercise benevolence one to another to an extent that is certainly remarkable. They certainly, however, do not regard lying in the same light that we do, but amongst themselves this is so well understood that many of its worst effects are warded off or rendered least harmful. We only permit a similar disregard to truth, and are perfectly understood to do so, in minor conventional matters such as making statements as to our joy at hearting of the birth of some one's cousin, our grief at the death of his grandmother, our benevolent submission to loss in trade for the benefit of the purchaser, &c., &c. All this is known to have a certain meaning, and, therefore, does in fact bear that interpretation. The Chinese greatly extend this habit, and in fact in most things consider politeness and expediency rather than accuracy of statement; but then, they too have their points of honour, and very strong ones, e.g., after conclusion of a bargain, though only verbal, a Chinaman is seldom known to break his agreement, and many other instances could be quoted in amelioration of the gravest failing shown by Celestials. They are docile, hospitable, and, when free from official promptings and deceptions, kindly and generous; no hedge bristles with blunderbusses, and no wife is roasted or kicked to death. But if this be true of the people, what shall we say of the officials? All that is bad in other nations, all the evil lacking in the governed classes here appears to have been concentrated in the rulers and their offices. Their very existence depends on the grossest tyranny and unlimited unscrupulousness. Every person or thing that is likely to affect their despotic supremacy, that, by ameliorating the condition of the people, or opening their eyes, is likely to put an end to the monopoly of corruption—I say, all that is good or beneficial, because it is hostile to all that is bad and detrimental, is an object of hatred to them. It may be asked how, if the people are so good, do the officials, drawn from amongst them, become so bad? The reply is simple; no one can become an official until he has specially studied and proved himself to have studied the code of iniquity which governs yamen life, and on the strict observance of which the very essence of that life depends. Brought into contact with the people, we find them anxious and delighted to deal with us. We see our connexion resulting in a general and immediate increase of prosperity in the neighbourhood visited by foreigners; but, then, how soon does the official element step in and mar this; how directly can every untoward occurrence, every interruption to the harmony of intercourse, be traced to official jealousy, bigotry, and arrogance. Could the people as a body be allowed free expression of their ideas as to the rules which should govern them in their relationship to foreigners, I fancy there is not a man who has been a year in China would decline to submit to their judgment. Their interests and ours are too closely allied: the official greed for power and cravings for spoil are too opposed to civilization for us ever to be other than benefited by popular will, or impeded, and, if possible, crushed by official inclination. The central authorities being brought into forced contact with other Powers, and also possessed of certain personal qualities, may be and perhaps are more enlightened, and, therefore, less open to the censure applicable to the officers in other parts of the Empire. It is even possible that the will to improve and progress is great at Peking; but the power is palpably lacking, and must ever wanting so long as the relationship with the tributary dependencies is somewhat similar to that, though not possessed of quite as much power, existing between a large commercial firm and its independent agencies.

Touching the opium question, I do not suppose the amount of *lekin* imposed on the drug has ever caused very much outcry, or at any rate this particular form of tax has not appeared to have received the same notice, nor is it really of the same importance as that levied on other foreign articles of import. The direct opium trade is nowadays confined, in China at least, to but on or two; and although no just or even accurately sentimental reason has been given as yet for the suppression of the trade, still, if with a return of the great magnanimity which the Chinese profess to expect, they were to throw open the country and thus give a *quid pro quo* for what they ask of us, I am inclined to think that in a short time the general British trade would be benifited, and even those few individuals directly affected might find other openings equally remunerative for developing their capital and enterprise.

But the Indian Government will have most to say about this matter, and I do not think they are likely to treat it lightly. It is charmingly entertaining to read the arguments in favour of the suppression. I cannot believe that a person professing to be so well posted as the Secretary of the Anti-Opium Alliance can be ignorant of the amount of native drug cultivated in China; but there is one thing of which that he possibly may be ignorant, and once more foreigners shall draw their enlightenment from Wenchow. Hear and ponder, then, Oh! Ye humanitarians, and believers in the Chinese wish to get rid of Opium. On arrival at Wenchow—mind you, a new port, previously however in free communication with Ningpo, where large quantities of foreign Opium are imported—we found the native drug cultivated all round and down the province to the eastward of this river. But what think you? The drug grown here is specially good and the cultivators especially expert. It therefore competes most favourably with the foreign article, and has hitherto succeeded in almost excluding it. The growth of the poppy is to be diligently pursued, so say the natives, until the rest of the province has been brought under cultivation; and then, Mr. Secretary, rejoice and be glad, for Ningpo will probably import much less noxious Malwa. The cultivation of the poppy in China does not seem to interfere with the other crops, and is certainly a very great ornament to them. Then, seeing that the return is so enormous, the wily husbandman is not unwilling to spare the little ground on which the plants stand. And can it be seriously believed that the Government of China, if willing, could prevent, or is really willing to put down, the growth of the soporific plant? Oh, surely not. Surely everyone knows that nominally the growth has been for long prohibited; but that it affords too great an opportunity for the local officials to raise occasional drafts, and, therefore, is as carefully winked at. Doubtless another proclamation would be issued from Peking; equally surely would it be posted as directed; and joyfully certain is it that the Mandarins throughout the land would thus have a righteous excuse for increasing their squeezes. If the Anti-Opium Alliance be successful in driving out the foreign drug, they will certainly deserve official gratitude also. The people, officials and others, will have opium, they will die as readily in resisting its suppression as they are now willing sacrifices to its use. The Central Government is utterly, entirely, powerless, and will never make any real attempt against it. In matters likely to rouse the masses, no Government is more tender than that of Peking.

The German lorcha *Chang An* arrived here the other day, bringing on our heavy mails. She leaves on or about New-Year’s day, taking with her some Customs officers.

The North – China Herald and Supreme Court & Consular Gazette, January 17, 1878

Wenchow

Wenchow

The Taotai has declined to allow the export of copper cash intended for another Chinese port. A foreign merchant desiring to forward a remittance in this coin by a foreign vessel then on the berth for Ningpo, sent in his bond in the ordinary way to be stamped; this the Taotai refused to do, thus prohibiting the shipment. We have reason to believe that H.E is acting in opposition to advice coming from a source one would have thought likely to influence him simply replying that the supply of other articles of export may always be adjusted to suit external wants without interfering with or stinting the local requirements, whereas this is not the case with copper cash, which, once sent away, never returns (sic), and cannot be reacquired in any other way, he entirely pooh-poohs any allusion to the treaty which, it would seem, he assumes is completely set aside by the arguments he has advanced. In this instance, the foreign loss is two-fold, as the vessel loses her freight and has to take ballast in lieu, and of course the merchant is foiled in his commercial attempt. We understand that protest and claim for loss has been duly noted, and that this matter has followed the preceding ones to the proper quarters.

It is snowing here today, and the weather is altogether unpleasant. If asked, in future, as to the meteorological attributes of Wenchow, we shall, with the little Greenock boy, be able to refute the assertion as to constant rain, by the statement that "it whiles snaws."

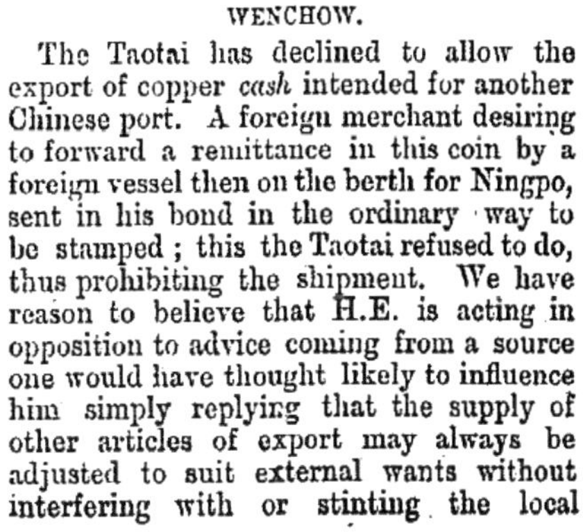

WENCHOW.

The Taotai has declined to allow the export of copper *cash* intended for another Chinese port. A foreign merchant desiring to forward a remittance in this coin by a foreign vessel then on the berth for Ningpo, sent in his bond in the ordinary way to be stamped; this the Taotai refused to do, thus prohibiting the shipment. We have reason to believe that H.E. is acting in opposition to advice coming from a source one would have thought likely to influence him simply replying that the supply of other articles of export may always be adjusted to suit external wants without interfering with or stinting the local

The North – China Herald and Supreme Court & Consular Gazette, March 14, 1878

Wenchow

WENCHOW.

Our only present news is that in the heart of the city a tremendous fire has taken place, burning a great number of houses; indeed, but for the intervention of the high prison wall, it threatened to destroy the whole quarter. It occurred late at night, and by daylight was over; a man, a boy and a girl burned fortunately represent the only loss of life. The locality is brilliant with yellow and red posters declaring the gratitude of the occupants of houses adjoining the area of destruction, to "Heaven's God," for sparing their property, and trusting he will be pleased to forbid or prevent any future fiery display.

1st March.

Wenchow

Our only present news is that in the heart of the city a tremendous fire has taken place, burning a great number of houses; indeed, but for the intervention of the high prison wall, it threatened to destroy the whole quarter. It occurred late at night, and by daylight was over; a man, a boy and a girl burned fortunately represent the only loss of life. The locality is brilliant with yellow and red posters declaring the gratitude of the occupants of houses adjoining the area of destruction, to "Heaven's God," for sparing their property, and trusting he will be pleased to forbid or prevent any future fiery display. (1st March)

The North - China Herald and Supreme Court & Consular Gazette, March 28, 1878

Wenchow

Wenchow

There is an extraordinary demand at present for foreign opium. The Chinese have abstained from getting any via Ningpo, under the fear of steamers arriving and bringing the drug direct. The result is that there is none to be had, and the native stock (by reason of the bad crop) is small, and commanding unprecedented prices. Great hopes were entertained as to the supply the *Europe* would bring; but there have been disappointed, in as much as no opium was on board. As may be supposed, the high prices, &c., have cut off or diminished to a great degree the daily luxury, and in proportion to the craving is the willingness, at present, to pay anything for the sacrifice.—How is it steamers cannot get freights to tempt them calling here en route South? Junks are arriving every day laden with oil, which commodity commands most remunerative sales, and for which there is still great demand. In a short time the cotton will be coming. Large quantities are yearly consumed in the adjoining districts. Surely steamers could cut out the junks in a trade they are admittedly incompetent to take part in. every steamer that comes here now will increase the trade of the place; and that the Chinese themselves fear this is proved by the energetic action they are taking in Ningpo and Fohkien to favour a continuance of the old method of supply.—The *Nassau* is outside busy surveying. The *Moorhen* left on Monday for Foochow.（23rd March）

WENCHOW.

There is an extraordinary demand at present for foreign opium. The Chinese have abstained from getting any viâ Ningpo, under the fear of steamers arriving and bringing the drug direct. The result is that there is none to be had, and the native stock (by reason of the bad crop) is small, and commanding unprecedented prices. Great hopes were entertained as to the supply the *Europe* would bring; but these have been disappointed, inasmuch as no opium was on board. As may be supposed, the high prices, &c., have cut off or diminished to a great degree the daily luxury, and in proportion to the craving is the willingness, at present, to pay anything for the sacrifice.—How is it steamers cannot get freights to tempt them calling here en route South? Junks are arriving every day laden with oil, which commodity commands most remunerative sales, and for which there is still great demand. In a short time the cotton will be coming. Large quantities are yearly consumed in the adjoining districts. Surely steamers could cut out the junks in a trade they are admittedly incompetent to take part in. Every steamer that comes here now will increase the trade of the place; and that the Chinese themselves fear this is proved by the energetic action they are taking in Ningpo and Fohkien to favour a continuance of the old method of supply.—The *Nassau* is outside busy surveying. The *Moorhen* left on Monday for Foochow.
23rd March.

The North - China Herald and Supreme Court & Consular Gazette, April 20, 1878

Wenchow

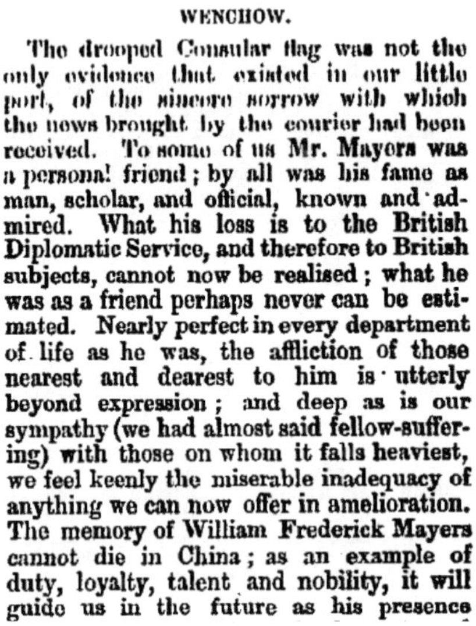
WENCHOW.

The drooped Consular flag was not the only evidence that existed in our little port, of the sincere sorrow with which the news brought by the courier had been received. To some of us Mr. Mayers was a personal friend; by all was his fame as man, scholar, and official, known and admired. What his loss is to the British Diplomatic Service, and therefore to British subjects, cannot now be realised; what he was as a friend perhaps never can be estimated. Nearly perfect in every department of life as he was, the affliction of those nearest and dearest to him is utterly beyond expression; and deep as is our sympathy (we had almost said fellow-suffering) with those on whom it falls heaviest, we feel keenly the miserable inadequacy of anything we can now offer in amelioration. The memory of William Frederick Mayers cannot die in China; as an example of duty, loyalty, talent and nobility, it will guide us in the future as his presence

Wenchow

The drooped Consular flag was not the only evidence that existed in our little port, of the sincere sorrow with which the news brought by the courier had been received. To some of us Mr. Mayers was a personal friend; by all was his fame as man, scholar, and official, known and admired. What his loss is to the British Diplomatic Service, and therefore to British subjects, cannot now be realized; what he was as a friend perhaps never can be estimated. Nearly perfect in every department of life he was, the affliction of those nearest and dearest to him is utterly beyond expression; and deep as is our sympathy (we had almost said fellow-suffering) with those on whom it falls heaviest, we feel keenly the miserable inadequacy of anything we can now offer in amelioration. The memory of William Frederic Mayers cannot die in China; as an example of duty, loyalty, talent and nobility, it will guide us in the future as his presence helped to aid and direct us in the past; and this fact will no doubt, when time has to some extent modified the despair of recent grief, form a very precious solace to sorrow that must in any case be, to many, of lifelong endurance.

We were delighted yesterday at seeing two notices put up, announcing the advent of a steamer from Shanghai and one from Foochow. There is no doubt greater activity this year than last, amongst the natives; and even the most despondent begin to speak hopefully. Some outside natives have arrived, with the intention they say of seeing what the opportunities for a tea trade look like; whilst there are others who have come here with special reference to the native tea, which has in past years been exported in considerable quantities from Wenchow as it best could be. It is hoped that increased facilities for export may cause increased cultivation; at any rate, the

Ningpo and Shanghai men seem to think matters worthy their notice. Opium is of course much desired, and the native drug (there is no foreign) is commanding high prices. There are as yet no people here to buy wholesale from the foreign importer and sell in smaller quantities to sub-retailers; but it is thought that this condition of affairs will not continue long. Indeed, we hear there are already signs of establishments being started for doing the necessary intermediary peddling.

Altogether things may be said to be looking a little brighter; and, in welcome of the first gleam of sunshine, I will once more sign myself SPES. (5th April)

The North – China Herald and Supreme Court & Consular Gazette, June 15, 1878

Wenchow

Wenchow

Lekin, that bugbear of last year, seems to have completely subsided. All the old officials have been superseded, and the present ones recognize the fact that an excessive tax only injured themselves, whereas the contrary policy would not only be remunerative but the means of saving an infinity of trouble by reason of the increased incentive to smuggling and evasion generally which the high rate gave rise to.

WENCHOW.

Lekin, that bugbear of last year, seems to have completely subsided. All the old officials have been superseded, and the present ones recognise the fact that an excessive tax only injured themselves, whereas the contrary policy would not only be remunerative but the means of saving an infinity of trouble by reason of the increased incentive to smuggling and evasion generally which the high rate gave rise to.

As far as piece goods are concerned, the tax has been "farmed," nominally, to one man for a fixed sum, said to be $2,000 per annum, to be lowered next year should the speculation be unsuccessful, or raised if the results are such as to warrant this being done. It would appear that the former is certainly the most probable issue. I say nominally to one man, for there are undoubtedly others who contribute to the funds.

As far as piece goods are concerned, the tax has been “farmed,” nominally, to one man for a fixed sum, said to be $2,000 per annum, to be lowered next year should the speculation be unsuccessful, or raised if the results are such as to warrant this being done. It would appear that the former is certainly the most probable issue. I say nominally to one man, for there are undoubtedly others who contribute to the funds.

An attempt was made to favour cargo passing through native hands, as against that imported by foreigners; but this was quickly discovered and most effectively put down.—Our old Taotai has gone and his successor (himself, however, only a *locum tenens*) does not seem to be much of an improvement on the antiquated fossil he relieved. He has had slight previous experience of foreigners, that is to say he has been an underling in the Tsung-li Yamen; but up to this he has not shown himself superlatively gifted with common sense, a commodity which the other lacked only in a more marked degree. The Taotai regularly appointed to this place has, I understand, stayed for a time at the provincial capital, and will not come on here until the Autumn.—I regret to learn that the Viceroy seems to be showing undue partiality towards Fohkien, and has permitted the erection of a prohibitive barrier at Poo-cheng in that province, at which opium coming in from Chekiang is very heavily taxed, and tea going out subjected to the same penal imposition. This is, of course, a direct hit at Ningpo and Wenchow, as from the former place a very great deal of drug found its way to Fohkien; and to the latter only time is wanted to develop a tea trade which must detract considerably from that at present existing at Foochow. Should the plan be carried into effect, a system of smuggling, supported by armed force, will undoubtedly arise, and the *lekin* and other officials probably find their work cut out for them. It is not probable, I should think, that the latter will get much aid from their colleagues in Chekiang, as, of course, the more of either articles that passes through their stations the better for them.

However, these attempts must in the end be defeated, and the pressure of demand direct the supply into channels offering the greatest facilities for accommodating it. Our weather for the past six months has been simply delightful—cool, dry and bright. Today rain has fallen; but as this was somewhat desired by the farmers, we cannot complain. (6th June)

The North – China Herald and Supreme Court & Consular Gazette, July 13, 1878

Wenchow

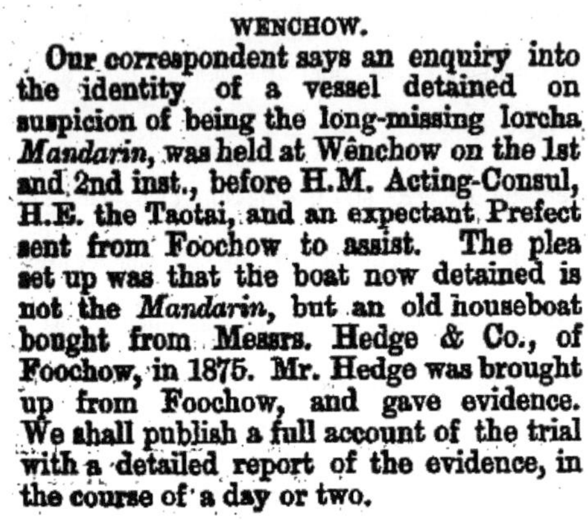
WENCHOW.

Our correspondent says an enquiry into the identity of a vessel detained on suspicion of being the long-missing lorcha *Mandarin*, was held at Wênchow on the 1st and 2nd inst., before H.M. Acting-Consul, H.E. the Taotai, and an expectant Prefect sent from Foochow to assist. The plea set up was that the boat now detained is not the *Mandarin*, but an old houseboat bought from Messrs. Hedge & Co., of Foochow, in 1875. Mr. Hedge was brought up from Foochow, and gave evidence. We shall publish a full account of the trial with a detailed report of the evidence, in the course of a day or two.

Wenchow

Our correspondent says an enquiry into the identity of a vessel detained on suspicion of being the long-missing lorcha *Mandarin*, was held at Wenchow on the 1st and 2nd inst., before H. M. Acting-Consul, H. E. the Taotai, and an expectant Prefect sent from Foochow to assist. The plea set up was that the boat now detained is not the *Mandarin*, but an old houseboat bought from Messrs. Hedge & Co., of Foochow, in 1875. Mr. Hedge was brought up from Foochow, and gave evidence. We shall publish a full account of the trial with a detailed report of the evidence, in the course of a day or two.

The North – China Herald and Supreme Court & Consular Gazette, July 20, 1878

Wenchow

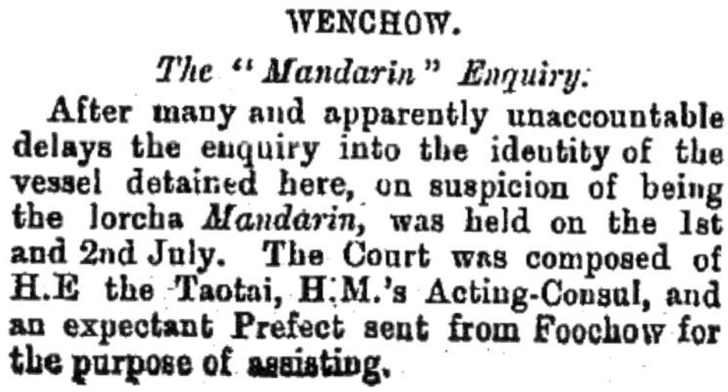
WENCHOW.

The "Mandarin" Enquiry:

After many and apparently unaccountable delays the enquiry into the identity of the vessel detained here, on suspicion of being the lorcha *Mandarin*, was held on the 1st and 2nd July. The Court was composed of H.E the Taotai, H.M.'s Acting-Consul, and an expectant Prefect sent from Foochow for the purpose of assisting.

Wenchow

The "Mandarin" Enquiry

After many and apparently unaccountable delays the enquiry into the identity of the vessel detained here, on suspicion of being the lorcha Mandarin, was held on the 1st and 2nd July. The Court was composed of H.E the Taotai, H.M.'s Acting-Consul, and an expectant Prefect sent from Foochow for the purpose of assisting.

The case, at least as far as the foreign evidence went, was conducted on behalf of the Chinese Government by Mr. Ho-shen-chih, a native of Hongkong and pupil of Dr. Legge. Mr. Ho speaks and writes English perfectly, and showed a surprisingly intimate knowledge of the forms and routine of our Courts, from the minutest detail of judicial procedure to the skillful worrying of a witness after the most approved legal style.

The official mentioned above, Mr. Ho, and Mr. Hedge, came up from Foochow in a gunboat specially detailed to convey them. Mr. Delano, the American Consul, was also on board, but he took no part in the proceedings, and indeed did not appear in Court.

The Taotai elected to hold the enquiry in the Foochow Guild. The investigation was therefore an open one; foreigners coming and going during the whole time, which, taken in conjunction with the general heat, intensified in its effects as it was by the stifling condition of the room, would have seemed remarkable elsewhere; but in this generally dull place anything is gladly seized on to vary or relieve the monotony.

The plea set up by the Chinese is that the vessel under detention is not the *Mandarin*, but an old houseboat, purchased in 1874 or 1875 from Messrs. Hedge and Co., of Foochow. Mr. Hedge was called to prove this; and he or they also produced two doors and a window, which they stated would be found to correspond with a frame pointed out in the cabin; and which said doors and window had been removed from the houseboat after her sale and kept in Foochow until this necessity arose from producing them. It would appear, however, that other evidence must be looked to for deciding the question of identity.

The long delay that has taken place before holding the investigation, is to a certain extent unfavourable for those holding that this is the very *Mandarin* herself, as Mr. Main, the owner and rebuilder or repairer of the lorcha, has had to leave for Europe; and as will be seen there is only his written declaration as to her identity to fall back on. This would, under most circumstances, he sufficiently conclusive; but it will be seen from the nature of Mr. Hedge's evidence that the power to confront the two conflicting and best informed witnesses on each side would have tended much to facilitate a prompt decision in the matter. Again, Mr. Hedge appears to have made previous depositions or statements which have been duly and officially forwarded to the Acting Consul as being reliable and deliberate. These would certainly seem to throw great doubt on the allegation as to this being Mr. Hedge's houseboat and undoubtedly have tended to increase in great part the suspicions which led to her original seizure and prolonged detention. Mr. Hedge now says, however, that these were not deliberate or reliable statements, as they were made off-hand and without reference to books or papers; and gives this as the probable explanation of any discrepancies that may appear between his present evidence and that he was officially alleged to have given before.

As will be seen, the evidence from the side of the upholders of the houseboat theory, necessitates the boat being now, as to dimensions and carrying capacity, very nearly the same as she was when in Hedge and Co.'s possession.

On the other side, it is strongly urged and supported by evidence that cannot be looked on as being other than of a very weighty character, that this boat has been largely cut down and altered and a stern of some other craft grafted on her. Again, Captain Napier is very strong as to the marks of serious injury, to which no explanation appears to have been offered. On the other hand, Mr. Hedge speaks very strongly about the number; and a number was undoubtedly found on the stern of this boat.

But perhaps the foregoing will serve sufficiently to indicate the points which would seem to admit of most question, and with these prefatory remarks, the evidence must be left to speak for itself.

The ultimate judgment in the case now rests with the authorities, foreign and native, at Peking; and so of course nothing further can be heard until the bare statement of the conclusion come to is made, or its nature inferred from the release or detention of the vessel lying under embargo in the river. Still it is not an unfavourable sign of a desire on the part of the Chinese authorities to appear impartial, that they have not confined this inquiry to the impenetrable limits of their Yamen; but by holding it in a public building and with open doors enabled anyone who chose to listen, to do so. The natives seemed most interested, and the Court was often oppressively crowded.

The following was the evidence adduced:—CHRISTOPHER SCHMIDT deposed—I am an American citizen, and pilot. I was formerly employed in the Yangtze for two years commanding a lorcha, and five years as pilot; and during part of that time was intimately acquainted with the lorcha *Mandarin* and her captain. I first made his acquaintance in 1871. I do not know where the *Mandarin* was built. On the 29th of May, 1877, I saw the vessel detained now in the Wenchow river about four *li* below the east gate. I saw that she resembled the *Mandarin* very much, and went on board to look. I found her apparently much cut down, but the washstand was the same, the house very nearly the same, but appeared to have been lowered, and the stern seemed to have been cut off and fitted with a Chinese rudder. The *Mandarin* was built of pine wood, some Chinese, some American. The *Mandarin* was the only vessel of that particular build on the Yangtsze. She was excessively wall-sided and razeeing would not alter the beam unless more than three feet were cut off. The timbers were showing above the deck, and had evidently been cut off. I told the Harbour-master that she looked pretty much like the *Mandarin*. The flooring in the washroom was painted lead color. I took a board ashore. The other part of the flooring was painted in black and white diamonds. The cabin was very much the same as in the *Mandarin* when I saw her in the latter end of 1872, but had apparently been lowered—the size was about the same. I do not know the dimensions of the old *Mandarin*.

Cross-examined—I have been on board the *Mandarin* whilst commanded by Captain Main. I don't know how often, but every day when in port together. I have noticed many boats of lorcha build, like the *Mandarin*, whilst on the Yangtsze. The *Mandarin* had two masts; cannot say positively that the vessel detained is the *Mandarin*. I had no particular reason for showing the Harbour-master the boards, except that they were painted with foreign paint.

Re-examined—I cannot swear that the vessel detained here is the *Mandarin*, but she resembles her although she is very much disfigured.

RICHARD HENRY NAPIER deposed—I am a Captain in the Royal Navy, at present commanding H.M.S. *Nassau*. About the 12th of April, 1878, I visited a vessel detained at

Wenchow, on suspicion of being the lorcha *Mandarin*, at the request of H.M. Acting Consul. In the vessel I visited large alterations had been made since she was first built. The vessel had been decidedly altered at the stern. She had also received a severe blow, which had been awkwardly patched up. She had been both shortened and cut down. The repair to the injury on her starboard side was evidently not the work of a professional shipwright. In this opinion, and in the evidence I now give, I am borne out by the carpenter of H.M.S. *Nassau*, whom I brought with me to assist.

Cross-examined—I have the experience only of such Chinese professional shipwrights as are employed at the British Naval Dockyard at Hongkong, and from long acquaintance with that class of work. I feel certain that no professional hand, no matter of what nation, could have so badly executed the repair in question, unless purposely. I have had no experience of Foochow shipwrights.

Re-examined—The butts of the planking have in my opinion been cut and a false rounded stern substituted for the original one, which must have been much longer. Likewise I saw an iron plate, or stem iron, which appeared to me unusual and placed there in consequence of a split or rent, I cannot say which. As regards cutting down, I saw above her deck the heads of the upper timbers or bulwarks stanchions, which were shortened both by fracture and sawing or cutting through with a sharp instrument. These, in my opinion, had the vessel been as originally constructed, would have been found capped by a rail. This not being so, and their evident shortcoming, causes the strongest presumption that she has been cut down. I would add, the vessel appears unreasonably shallow for her size.

JOSEPH H. BURNETT deposed—I am an American citizen employed as acting Tide-Surveyor at Wenchow. My acquaintance with the *Mandarin* dates from about 1868-69. I first saw her while I was in charge of the Customs barrier at Wu-shueh, on the Yangtze. I saw the vessel pass backwards and forwards a number of times. I don't know how many times. Might have been five or might have been fifteen. I often went on board to examine her papers, generally when she was loaded. I notice a great similarity between the vessel detained here and the *Mandarin*. I have no special or particular marks by which I could positively recognize her, but from the general outline of the vessel, construction of the cabin, and painting of the flooring, I am strongly of opinion that the vessel in question is the original *Mandarin*.

A letter from Mr. Main, the owner of the lorcha *Mandarin*, was here put in and read. He had considerably altered and rebuilt the vessel after purchasing her, and was of course intimately acquainted with her build and appearance. He came to Wenchow last year for the purpose of examining the vessel detained on suspicion, and after his inspection he wrote the letter, now handed in, officially, and positively identifying this boat as the *Mandarin*, and claiming her as his "lawful property." Mr. Hoh now said he would call his witness, and

THOMAS HEDGE was called and deposed—I am a merchant at Foochow in Messrs. Hedge and Co., and am an American citizen. I have been about twenty years in Foochow. I have owned houseboats ever since I have been in the place. I sold a houseboat to Chinese in the Spring of 1875. I do not know to whom the boat was sold; it was sold through the head boatman, Ah-san, by my orders. The man now brought forward is the said boatman. I never saw the man who bought the boat until the present year, that I am aware of. I have seen the boat detained at Wenchow. I have had previous knowledge of this boat, as her owner, from 1866 to 1875. She is the same boat as I sold through Chiang Ah-san for $75, in the spring of 1875. After I sold her she was raised a little, loaded with firewood, and I saw her go down the river. She was not raised as much as present. By raising, I mean the balwarks have been raised. I recognize her by her general appearance, her resemblance to the ordinary Foochow houseboats. The house is the same as in my old boat. On the right hand side was the washroom. The frame of the washstand is still there, which I identify. On the opposite side was the W.C., the closet of which has been removed, but the hole through which the pipe led has been stopped up. There are now two venetians on the upper end of the house, made of American pinewood from old boxes. The foremast is the same spar, the upper end of which is cut smaller and shows signs of having been coal-tarred, which was a distinguishing mark of our boats at that time. Near the bow of the boat there is a square piece of hardwood put in where the boat was built, through which an iron pin passed on which the gun was pivoted. The hole is there now, but filled up with chunam. As to her bulwark-stanchions, when sold, I am unable to give the exact measurements above the deck. On them was a rail. Those stanchions are still left there. The bow I recognize as the same, with a large iron plate the whole length of it and near the bottom were two pieces of iron put on to strengthen the wood. The stern remains the same, but has been added to by a framework over all. The Foochow Customhouse registered number is still on the boat, showing that the stern has not been altered and showing the identity of the boat.

The number is 27. The flooring was painted in black and white squares or diamonds. The foremast is still fastened on the boat by an iron band under her deck. After the boat was built, a false keel was added to enable her to lay closer to the wind. I have with me a pair of doors and a window, taken away when the boat was sold by the man who bought her, they have been in Foochow until now, when they were given over to me to bring up, and the measurements agree with the spaces on the boat. The boat was built for me at Foochow in the spring of 1866. I used to carry opium and treasure, and sometimes used her as a pleasure boat. I don't know of any further special marks by which to recognize her. I am prepared to make the same statement on oath as the foregoing. Measured the doorway and the window and found that they corresponded very nearly to the doors and window I brought with me from Foochow. One hinge did not correspond with its cutting.

The court now adjourned for tiffin. On reassembling, they proceeded to inspect the suspected vessel, and on their return to the Guild, Mr. HEDGE was cross-examined by H.M.'s Acting-Consul, and stated——I have been in Foochow twenty years, and am well acquainted with the ordinary Foochow houseboat. The boat I built and sold was built in accordance with the regular form of vessel built at Foochow, and is a regular Foochow houseboat. This boat was built at our order, and I inspected the building every three or four days, and am fully acquainted with the whole details of her building. She was built in 1866, and employed in carrying opium and treasure and for pleasure purposes. She was registered at the Customs as a houseboat, in 1866, as No. 27. This I know of my own knowledge, and I know that she had this number on her stern. It is not usual to place the number on the stern, but we put it on this boat in order to preserve its appearance. As a rule the numbers are painted on the bow or house. This boat was not the one registered as 27, but a substitute for one which was so registered in 1861, the license passing on. I cannot tell if she, the original boat, was numbered 27 on the stern. I had only one houseboat registered. The length of the boat I built in 1866 was between 58 to 60 feet. I cannot tell for certain which. I have no record. I am certain she was not over 60 feet. I won't swear further than that she was between 58 to 60 feet. Her beam was between 12 to 14 feet. I cannot speak more certainly, as I am speaking from memory. I should say she was nearer 12 than 14 feet. I have made a statement in regard to this boat to the American Consul.（Statement produced, and witness shown that by this statement he is reported to have said positively that the length of the boat was 60 feet.）Witness replied—I never made any such statement, but have always given the length as being from 58 to 60 feet. If the copy of my deposition at the American Consulate states that I estimated the beam as being 15 feet, it is incorrect. I never said more than from 12 to 14 feet, and I cannot speak more positively, notwithstanding the fact of my having superintended the building of the boat. I cannot give you the tonnage. The boat was built to carry 100 chests of opium. I cannot tell the tonnage of a single boat I have. I have no means of estimating the tonnage. The boat was altogether employed in carrying opium. With close stowing she could carry 100 chests. I cannot say what the equivalent in tons would be. If the copy of my deposition at the American Consulate makes me say that the boat could carry only 100 piculs, it is incorrect. I don't think I could have said so. She could carry, but would be very deep in the water, 300 piculs. I have never gone into the estimation of her carrying capacity, and cannot say how much over 100 piculs she could carry. I should say after rough calculation, that you might put 200 piculs into her. Roughly, I should reckon 16 2/3 piculs to a ton. (Letter dated December 24th, 1877, from Consul Delano to Consul Sinclair, read and put in by consent. In this letter Mr. Delano reports Mr. Hedge as stating that about July, 1874, he authorized his head boatman, Chiang Ah-san, to sell an old houseboat, that the boat was as nearly (as they can now say) about 60 feet long and 15 feet beam amidships, and would carry over 30 to 50 tons. Chiang Ah-san sold it to a sampan man there named Ching-te for some 40 to 60 dollars. The purchaser altered her by raising her in the style of a junk, loaded her with firewood, and sent her to Chin-chieu, where she was again sold to a man named Li, for $130.00. Ching-te thinks that Li took her north.)

Witness was asked to explain the discrepancies between this then statements and his present, and replied—It may be when Mr. Delano first applied to me I made statements off-hand without reference to books or papers. I never heard anything officially about his matter until Mr. Delano applied to me; at least this is my impression. Mr. Delano wrote me privately, stating he had note from Mr. Warren asking for information, and asking if I could give any. This was, I think, the first I heard of the affair.

A despatch from the Taotai, dated December 9th, 1877, to H.M. Acting-Consul, written here fifteen days before Mr. Delano's letter was sent to Mr. Sinclair, was then produced, and it was pointed out to witness that in this despatch a detailed report of a deposition alleged to be made by him before the American Consul was given, and that it agreed in effect with Mr. Delano's statements. Witness' attention was also called to the fact that it was written fifteen days earlier (and in Wenchow), than the date of Mr. Delano's letter in Foochow, which he (witness) had stated was about the time he had first been applied to. On being asked to explain this inconsistency, witness replied he could not, and then proceeded—The old houseboat was sold in the spring of 1875, and I had been using her up to that time. I got 75 dollars for her. I don't know what she was sold for. I expect Chiang Ah-san got more than he gave me. He gave me 75 dollars. I don't know anything about what Chiang Ah-san got for her, or his statement that he only got $65. I saw the boat dropping down the river loaded with firewood. I saw she was raised and had those protruding bows. She was between the bridge and the Custom-house. I was pulling by her and could see the moulding of her deck, and that she was raised from 1½ to 2 feet. My impression is she was rasied with rough Foochow wood. The present bulwarks have been raised since I then saw her. I can't tell whether the new planks ran horizontally or vertically. My impression is they ran fore and aft. I can't swear that these are the same bulwarks I then saw, as I got only a passing glance. My impression is that the present bulwarks are nearly double as high as they were when I saw her in Foochow river. The two doors I brought up here, as belonging to the boat before I sold her, I got from Chiang Ah-san and the purchaser of the boat. I have no knowledge where these doors have been since the boat was sold. They were given to me on Monday or Tuesday last, a day or two before we started. The hole in the deck through which the gun-pivot ran was right in the center of the piece of wood placed on the deck to receive it. It is not usual to carry a gun in Foochow houseboats, but we carried it because we carried a good deal of treasure and opium. The boat had only that gun. I don't know if it was there when the boat was sold, but I know the iron pin was, for I remember taking it out when we sold the boat. Down the stem of the boat was a long iron stem-piece—all my boats have this. I don't know if others have. I cannot give an idea of the height of the original bulwark stanchions; roughly estimated I should say they were about six inches and a half, including the rail. The stanchions were let into the rail; that is my impression. I am certain it is the same stern—it may have been patched up or repaired, but the shape has not been altered. I am positive the stern has not been altered, and I can show another boat in Foochow with an exactly similar stern. I account for Captain Napier's opinion as to the stern being altered from the fact of his not being acquainted with the Foochow Chinese manner of building. I do not notice the appearance spoken to by Captain Napier, however. I don't know whether they build boats differently in Foochow from other parts of China, as I have no experience of other places. In

Canton they build more after the foreign fashion. I should be surprised to see a Foochow boat with a stern which has all the appearance of not belonging to her, but of having been stuck on. Every port has its own manner of building boats. I am certain that the floor of the house was painted in black and white squares or diamonds. I am sure they were black and white. The floor was painted black and white in the fore part of the house. The after part was painted with Peacock's lead colored composition. I am quite certain it was lead color, and also that it was Peacock's composition. I know that the foremast in my boat was fastened with an iron band. I think most of the native boats' masts are fitted in with wood. I don't know whether other boats are or are not fitted with iron bands. Chiang Ah-san is not in my memory now. He has come here with me. He has not been confined in Foochow—he has been at liberty. I have seen him within the last fortnight, but until he came on board the steamer to come here, I have not seen him frequently. I have not talked the case over with him particularly. I have asked him who he sold the boat to and how she came to come to Wenchow. When I heard this boat was numbered, it occurred to me mine had been registered. I did not think of it until I was asked since my arrival here in Wenchow, whether there was a number on my boat; but then I recollected it. I have not at any previous examination mentioned the fact of her being numbered. There are many things about the boat which I would not think of until they were recalled to me. Had this number been, as is usual, on the bows, it would have been removed, as when I sell a boat the numbers are removed to prevent the Chinese using them. To the best of my belief and knowledge, the numbers in this case were not removed. I do not know that when the boat left my hands she had the number on her stern. I know that when I had the boat, her numbers were made of copper and nailed on. Most houseboats would have their masts tapered to represent topmasts. Our boats have their mast-heads tarred, as a distinguishing mark. The mast-head of this boat appears to have been coal-tarred, but I have not inspected it closely. All her chains, anchors and ironbitts were taken out. She was Chinese rigged. Her masts were wire stayed, by the wire rope was all removed when she was sold. I don't know whether the sails were sold with her. I am certain she had wire stays and iron blocks, but these did not go with her. I am under the impression her sails went with her, but I cannot tell what they were. They were either American drill or American ravensduck. I think they went with her, because I got a new suit of sails for the new boat. The hole the iron-rod for the gun pivot went through was a regular perforation, I can't say whether round or square. I did not notice that on the top of one of the doors I brought, there was a bolt. (Door produced.) I see there is a bolt. I have not seen the doors fitted into their spaces. I simply measured the doors and also the spaces intended for them.

The Court then adjourned until ten o'clock next morning.

On the Court re-assembling, Mr. HEDGE was re-examined by Mr. Ho-shen-chih and deposed as follows:—In order to make my statements on cross-examination understood, I would wish to mention that I have made no detailed official statement or deposition to the American Consul until about a month ago. The statements made before have been made privately and offhand, and without reference to books or papers, and with a view of clearing the boatmen from any complicity in the case of the lorcha *Mandarin*. The statement made a month ago was an official and deliberate one. (No report or copy of this statement has been made or sent to the Acting-Consul, nor was it produced or tendered now.) Witness proceeded—There are other European witnesses in Foochow, who could recognize the boat which was sold by my order through Chiang Ah-san.

The court then called Mr. HENRY YEOMANS, who deposed—I am a British subject, and H.M.'s Consular Constable at his port. I went down in attendance on H.M.'s Acting Consul for Wenchow on the 29th May, 1877, accompanied by some Chinese officials, for the purpose of seizing a boat supposed to be the lorcha *Mandarin*. We went on board and the Chinese officials arrested more than two persons connected with the vessel. The boat was a two masted one, Chinese rigged. The mainsail was light cotton canvas, the mainmast was stayed with wire rope. I did not particularly notice whether she had any sail forward. I remember the mainsail, for I pulled it over several times to see if there were any marks such as maker's name on it. The next time I saw her was after she had been brought to a place above the Custom-house. At that time there were several people taking salt out of her. She had about ⅓ cargo of salt when she was hauled up the creek outside the east gate. I noticed that all the hatches had been taken away. I used to visit her after this about every day or every other day, for some considerable time. I visited her by the Consul's orders, to see that she was not moved. All the loose things were being taken away one after the other until she was left as she now is. I was on board her yesterday, and I measured the two doors now in Court. They fitted very nearly except that the hinges of the starboard side were ¾ of an inch smaller than the bed on the doorjamb, and the same was the case on the port side. I saw there was a bolt on the top of the door, but there was no socket to receive it on the corresponding part of the door frame. I measured the stanchions forward, that is, two of them; one was 7 ¾inches and the other 8 inches. They appeared as though the top had been broken or knocked off.

Cross-examined by Mr. Ho SHEN-CHIH—I did not know that the men arrested were connected with the vessel. I mean those found on board the vessel and arrested by Chinese officials. I saw one of the prisoners again at the Consulate the same night. I cannot give you his name. I was not told when I went on board the vessel to notice anything particularly. I did so of my own accord, being an ex-policeman from Shanghai, and I thought it was my duty to do so. I happened to notice the mainsail particularly, because it was on top of the house. I noticed it on another occasion, when in company with the then Harbor Master. I did not make a thorough search after the men were arrested.

Captain NAPIER, R.N., recalled and deposed—I noticed that there was a certain space in the deck of very irregular form, that appeared to have been filled in at a more recent date than when the vessel was decked. The material appeared to be chunam. There was a light circle of chunam perhaps about 3/4 of an inch in diameter, which I took to be the place where the iron pin spoken of was represented to have passed. I was particularly struck with the appearance of the deck at this part, because I heard it stated in evidence that a square piece of wood had been placed to support a pivoting gun. The space filled with chunam was totally at variance in my opinion with such a supposition, bearing up resemblance to a square, and the position of the supposed hole being quite at one side instead of in the centre.

Mr. HEDGE recalled at request of Mr. Ho Shen-chih—The piece of wood that was let into the boat was about 3 ft. long by 8 inches wide and of different material entirely from the deck. The hole, to the best of my recollection, is in the centre going athwartship, but fore and aft a little nearer the stern than the bow. The original hole would be fitted with chunam, making the irregular piece to which Captain Napier referred at the end of his evidence. A mountain howitzer, fitted in such a boat by Foochow carpenters, would not be fitted in similar manner to that observed in foreign vessels. Foochow carpenters fit a mountain howitzer in a rough way, as compared with foreigners. Not being a practical man, I cannot say how howitzers are fitted on board a foreign vessel.

Mr. BURNETT recalled by Court at request of Mr. Hoh—After the seizure of the boat, when she lay on the bank above the Custom House, I noticed the number 27 on her stern. I saw it within a few days of her seizure.

This concluded the foreign evidence, and the court then proceeded to call the Chinese witnesses. The Taotai examined them himself from slips which it would appear were records of their statements given before coming into Court. As the consistency of evidence now led with that given on previous occasions by the same witnesses was challenged on several occasions, for the sake of convenience the two depositions are given in parallel columns so that the difference (if any) may be seen at glance—

Deposition taken in 1877: —

CHIANG AH-SAN—I was in Hedge & Co.'s employ at Foochow. In June, 1875, Hedge & Co., had an old houseboat laid up on the river bank which I sold on their behalf to my friend Chin-te for $65. The latter repaired and sold her to some one whose name do not know. The boat was built at Foochow. She was foreign built and 60 feet long by 15 feet wide.

CHIN-TE—In June, 1875, early in the month, I bought an old boat from Hedge & Co., through Chiang Ah-san, and paid &65. I repaired her and raised her a foot; and spent about $200. I repaired her with Ningpo wood and wreckage. I registered her at Foochow, as the Chin-chuan-chun. In July I took her to Shinchiang with a cargo of firewood. In the May following, being short of money, Chin-chie at my request sold her to Chung-kung-shing for $130. I learnt afterwards that the latter sold her to a native of Tung-an, who took her to Wenchow, where she was seized by foreigners. The vessel was foreign build, her hull of pine, painted black. She had two masts, also of pine.

CHIN-CHIE—Chin-te is my nephew. He purchased a boat at Foochow, which was registered there. In September, 1875, he took the boat to Poo-sha-ow and being short of money chartered her to another man. In June, 1876, I sold her for him to Chung-kung-shing. The latter repaired her and took her to Ma-hau, where she registered her, afterwards selling her to Woo Ah-yuan.

Woo AH-YUAN—I bought the vessel in question about July, 1876, at Sin-chiang, for $160, and I registered her at Ma-hau as the Chin-ming-shin.

Depositions made in Court, and taken down at time: —

CHIANG AH-SAN—I have been in the employ of Hedge & Co. at Foochow. In April, 1875, I sold a boat on behalf of the firm to Chin-te for $75. The boat was built at Foochow, and after being raised a little and repaired she was sent south. I know no more of her. I identify the boat detained here as the one I sold.

CHIN-TE—In April, 1875, I bought a boat from Chiang Ah-san. The boat was about 60 feet long and 14 feet beam and about 4 feet deep. She was of foreign build and could carry 300 piculs or more; each picul being 100 catties. I sold her for $130. I identify this boat as the one I bought in 1875.

CHIN-CHIE—This boat was bought by my nephew at Foochcow. As to her certificates of dimensions and register I know nothing. In July, 1876, I sold her to Chung kung-shing, on behalf of Chin-te. That vessel is the one at present detained here.

Woo AH-YUAN—This vessel was bought by my owner, Li-chin-kung, from Ching-kung-sing, for $150. I don't know where the vessel was bought. Afterwards $700 or $800 were expended in repairing her. She then came to Wenchow. She is registered as the Chin-ming-shin by Chung-kung-shing at Ma-han. In April, 1877, I loaded her with 500 piculs of salt and 60 bags of white sugar, each bag containing of 130 catties. On the 27th May, I reached Wenchow, and a foreigner came on board and took away a plank. It was Chung-kung-shing who registered the vessel. I know nothing about it, nor do I know the date of the certificate of registry. The sails when she came from Foochow were cloth. On arrival at Wenchow, I changed them for mats.

At this stage, the several officials in Court appeared to be excited and the Interpreter crossed over to the witness and kept whispering to him, gesticulating violently at the same time. The *Hsien* now informed witness that if he was not careful he would beat every bit of skin off his body. In the midst of the confusion, the Taotai gave the signal for adjournment for tiffin. The witness had a chain put round his neck and he was dragged away. In another part of the building he was surrounded by officials and underlings, and judging by the gesticulations and threats he must have offended in some serious way. He was last seen being led away, it was understood for punishment; but it is said that this was not eventually resorted to. What the cause of this display was did not appear.

On re-assembling, the witness was again brought forward and stated:—When I was here before I was ill, dizzy, and confused, and did not know what I was saying. What I said then was inaccurate. The money expended in repairing the vessel was from 70 to 80 dollars, and the cargo consisted of 300 piculs of salt, as stated in my petition presented at the Consulate a year previously.

LIEU SHIEN-CHIU, who had never been examined before, was then called and deposed.—I and my brother Liu Seao-chuan are in business together at shipwrights. I remember in 1866 we built a boat for Hedge and Co. to carry opium and treasure. The boat was 60 feet long, about 14 feet in beam, and about 4 feet deep. She could carry about 300 piculs. She was built of camphor wood and pine, and had two masts. The house was 12 feet long and 7 feet high. Her stern was round. I don't remember what she cost. In the spring of 1875, I built a new boat for Hedge & Co., to take the old one's place. I recognize the vessel detained here as the one we built in 1866, for Hedge & Co.

This concluded the evidence, and the Court then rose after having sat for two full days.

The gunboat with Mr. Hedge on board left early on the morning of the 3rd; but Mr. Ho-shen-chih remains here for a day or two to assist the Taotai in getting the case in form for submission to the authorities at Peking.

The North – China Herald and Supreme Court & Consular Gazette, August 10, 1878

Wenchow

WENCHOW.

Since writing you last, the port and community have sustained another severe blow in the somewhat sudden withdrawal of Messrs. Jardine, Matheson & Co. By this act trade has undoubtedly received a shock which will once more tend to throw it back, and cause a still longer postponement of hopes which had begun to seem perhaps slightly less desperate. About this time last year the conduct of the *lekin* officials inflicted the first deadening stroke, and now unfortunate Wênchow seems as though she was again hit in a way only less disastrous. On this occasion the officials are as loud and probably as sincere in their lamentations at the turn matters have taken, as we were when they were the offenders. There can be no doubt that the new *lekin* staff have done and are doing all that in them lies to favour trade, and by a wise arrangement of their tariff have so managed that in consulting one's own interests it would be better to pay their demands than incur the higher rate enforced by treaty. Again, whereas it has more than

Wenchow

Since writing you last, the port and community have sustained another severe blow in the somewhat sudden withdrawal of Messrs. Jardine, Matheson & Co. By this act trade has undoubtedly received a shock which will once more tend to throw it back, and cause a still longer postponement of hopes which had begun to seem perhaps slightly less desperate. About this time last year the conduct of *lekin* officials inflicted the first deadening stroke, and now unfortunate Wenchow seems as though she was again hit in a way only less disastrous. On this occasion the officials are as loud and probably as sincere in their lamentations at the turn matters have taken, as we were when they were the offenders. There can be no doubt that the new *lekin* staff have done and are doing all that in them lies to favour trade, and by a wise arrangement of their tariff have so managed that in consulting one's own interests it would be better to pay their demands than incur the higher rate enforced by treaty. Again, whereas it has more than once happened that the ordinary transit pass has been treated with scant consideration up-country, there can be no doubt but that the cheaper permit now issued by the *lekin* office will by reason of its source meet with on obstruction from those whose habit it is to concern themselves with these matters.

Lorchas are, it is said, once more to take up the carrying trade, and we have even heard it rumoured that some enterprising individual intends to put a small steamer on this line. There can be no doubt but that if either plan be adopted, and *regularity* attended to, in the end the return will be remunerative. You have of course heard of the unfortunate disaster which befell the hulk *Waterwitch* on her way down the river. It would seem almost certain that she must be looked on as a total wreck, and all efforts now directed towards her speedy demolition. A survey has been held on her, and as the result of the examination her condemnation is recommended. Under the orders of H.M. Consul, the anchors and part of her chains have been removed, and nearly, if not all, of the furniture on board has been got out. It is assumed that directions will shortly arrive from Shanghai for her sale, and report seems to promise some competition amongst the Chinese. Our community is now sadly reduced, and in Mr. Wilson we lose a resident whose absence would be anywhere regretted; but in a small and isolated place like this, where a kindly and genial disposition such as his helped so much to keep up the social comfort and good fellowship, his loss partakes more of a general misfortune, and is certainly the cause of universal regret. As though calamities enough had not fallen on us, we were informed yesterday that the courier service which had been so ably organized by Mr. H. E. Hobson, and which up to this has worked so well and regularly, would cease. It appears that the regularity which we have so long appreciated has become too galling to the Chinese contractors, and seizing as a plea the fact of a few fines having been inflicted for slight irregularities, the three postal offices have conspired together, refusing to run any longer unless a day more be allowed for each trip. The expense of the service has hitherto been borne by H.M. Government and the Customs; but we understand that in future the latter will undertake it entirely themselves, keeping the necessary staff of couriers and charging postage for all letters and papers sent by and coming to the general public of Wenchow. The rates have not been announced yet; but as the said public consists only about four persons, I fear it will necessarily be a high one if any important portion of the cost is sought to be obtained from sources outside the Customs. I suppose when the postage is fixed, the decision will be notified in Shanghai for the information of intending correspondents, although hitherto there, as at many other places, the residents have been indebted to the generosity of the Customs for that which has proved one of the greatest possible boons to the community. Of course we have no right to complain if the favour conferred is only reduced by a demand for pecuniary compensation; and we must hope that increase of our numbers may by-and-bye lighten what may just now appear somewhat of a burden.

The *Nassau* is out at Bullock Harbour surveying the “Sampan pass,” but she is expected to come in any day for the purpose of completing the river, and we hope to have her for a day or two off the city. (30th July)

The North - China Herald and Supreme Court & Consular Gazette, August 17, 1878

Wenchow

Wenchow

The *Waterwitch* is advertised for sale at 4 p.m. today. She has made a dock for herself, and, having righted more, seems as though she were sunk deeper. This, however, experts say is not the case; and I hear Chinese speak of getting her off.

We were truly delighted to hear that steamers are not to be withdrawn after all. This may yet bring things right. The Customs have issued their circular as to the rates of postage to be charged in future by their Courier, as follows:—

WENCHOW.

The *Waterwitch* is advertised for sale at 4 p.m. to-day. She has made a dock for herself, and, having righted more, seems as though she were sunk deeper. This, however, experts say is not the case; and I hear Chinese speak of getting her off.

We were truly delighted to hear that steamers are not to be withdrawn after all. This may yet bring things right. The Customs have issued their circular as to the rates of postage to be charged in future by their Courier, as follows :—
Letters and despatches,
for each ½ oz. or under...100 *cash* (say 5d.)
Newspapers, each, with-
out regard to weight... 50 *cash* (say 2½d.)
The approximate calculations into sterling are mine. As will be seen, this is a very high rate; but as there is now only one member of the community who will have to bear the expense (Government and Customs franking the rest), none but this unfortunate need complain. Perhaps, as the Customs'

Letters and despatches, for each ½ oz. or under …100 *cash* (say 5d.)

Newspapers, each without regard to weight… 50 *cash* (say 2½d.)

The appropriate calculations into sterling are mine. As will be seen, this is a very high rate; but as there is now only one member of the community who will have to bear the expense (Government and Customs franking the rest), none but this unfortunate need complain. Perhaps, as the Customs' courier, it would appear, has to run at any rate, and the small contributions of the minute "Public" cannot go far towards reducing the cost to the office, it may not be thought worth while inflicting the tax on the solitary representation of that great body. It may not be known in Shanghai that the Chinese run couriers every alternate day between this and Ningpo and *vice versa*, doing the trip in from six to eight days. The charge is one hundred (100) *cash* for a packet weighing ½ a catty (say 11 oz.) So that anyone wishing to send heavy matter, where the difference of time in transit is not of importance, may perhaps find the above information of use. The Customs' courier takes from 4½ to 5 days, and has hitherto run most regularly.—We are in great want of rain, which threatens for a while, but seldom comes. (9th August)

The North – China Herald and Supreme Court & Consular Gazette, September 7, 1878

Wenchow

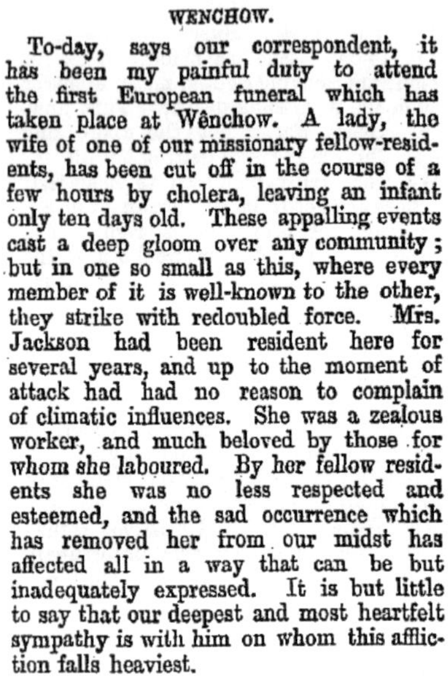

WENCHOW.

To-day, says our correspondent, it has been my painful duty to attend the first European funeral which has taken place at Wênchow. A lady, the wife of one of our missionary fellow-residents, has been cut off in the course of a few hours by cholera, leaving an infant only ten days old. These appalling events cast a deep gloom over any community; but in one so small as this, where every member of it is well-known to the other, they strike with redoubled force. Mrs. Jackson had been resident here for several years, and up to the moment of attack had had no reason to complain of climatic influences. She was a zealous worker, and much beloved by those for whom she laboured. By her fellow residents she was no less respected and esteemed, and the sad occurrence which has removed her from our midst has affected all in a way that can be but inadequately expressed. It is but little to say that our deepest and most heartfelt sympathy is with him on whom this affliction falls heaviest.

Wenchow

Today, says our correspondent, it has been my painful duty to attend the first European funeral which has taken place at Wenchow. A lady, the wife of one of our missionary fellow-residents, has been cut off in the course of a few hours by cholera, leaving an infant only ten days old. These appalling events cast a deep gloom over any community; but in one so small as this, where every member of it is known to the other, they strike with redoubled force. Mrs. Jackson had been resident here for several years, and up to the moment of attack had had no reason to complain of climatic influences. She was a zealous worker, and much beloved by those for whom she labored. By her fellow residents she was no less respected and esteemed, and the sad occurrence which has removed her from our midst has affected all in a way that can be but inadequately expressed. It is but little to say that our deepest and most heartfelt sympathy is with him on whom this affliction falls heaviest.

The outbreak of cholera began about ten days or a fortnight ago, the mortality running up from ten to about thirty per diem, but happily it now appears to be on the wane.

Strange to say, the disease has hitherto confined itself almost entirely to the beggars and very poorest people, scarcely any of the better class natives having suffered. On the 20th, a seaman belonging to the Nassau was seized, but when the ship left on the 21st he appeared to be out of danger. Prior to the rains, which have fallen for the last week, we had been suffering from prolonged drought, and thus the wells had become dried up or what little water collected in them seemed to be impure. This, coupled with certain atmospheric changes, may have led to a reappearance of the disease, which however does not seem to exist to the same extent, or be of equal malignity, with that which visited China last year. (24th August)

The North – China Herald and Supreme Court & Consular Gazette, December 21, 1878

Wenchow

Wenchow

Since last writing, the even tenour of our life has been such as to offer no opportunity for drawing up a communication. We have had one steamer, and a lorcha has been running pretty regularly. The import of piece goods has been and is steadily increasing. The *lekin* officials, in their desire to encourage trade, have arranged a most favourable tariff. As it at present stands, goods sent up country under their pass are charged considerably less than would be the case if a Customs transit pass was taken out. They profess to be, and we have good reason for believing are, sincerely anxious to attract foreigners or foreign trade to the place. They have made great and unusual efforts to suppress certain attempts to establish the Ningpo system of guild monopoly, and looking at the regulations and arrangements which have now been established, it will be difficult for natives to institute such a system here in future. In doing this they were influenced to some extent by the resentment shown by the Wenchow people towards those Ningpo men who sought to establish the “guild process.”

WENCHOW.

Since last writing, the even tenour of our life has been such as to offer no opportunity for drawing up a communication. We have had one steamer, and a lorcha has been running pretty regularly. The import of piece goods has been and is steadily increasing. The *lekin* officials, in their desire to encourage trade, have arranged a most favourable tariff. As it at present stands, goods sent up country under their pass are charged considerably less than would be the case if a Customs transit pass was taken out. They profess to be, and we have good reason for believing are, sincerely anxious to attract foreigners or foreign trade to the place. They have made great and unusual efforts to suppress certain attempts to establish the Ningpo system of guild monopoly, and looking at the regulations and arrangements which have now been established, it will be difficult for natives to institute such a system here in future. In doing this they were influenced to some extent by the resentment shown by the Wênchow people towards those Ningpo men who sought to establish the "guild process."

The first foreign sailing ship that has come to the port since its opening, arrived about 15th Nov. The captain had been an old trader in the days before the ratification of the German treaty, and reliant on this experience of the amount of export cargo that used in those days to be shipped from Wenchow, he determined upon bringing his vessel (a 320 ton barque) up to the city. From a variety of causes the export trade that used to be concentrated here at the time of his last visit, had got considerably diffused over the small riverine ports between the city and the sea; besides which the owners of cargo, being in most cases persons without capital, are in the habit of selling their produce to one or two individuals, who either pay them in full or make considerable advances towards the same, these latter being either junk owners resident here, or those who have accompanied their vessels to the place. Notwithstanding very high rates, native craft are thus able to collect considerable amounts of freight, and in his competition against them, Capt. Le Moult had much to contend with. With great enterprise and no less energy, he diligently canvassed the whole place for seven or eight days. He found that his idea as to the presence of export cargo was not erroneous, but for the reasons I have given, and the absence of any reliable agent, foreign or native, to assist him in his research, at the end of this time the result being disheartening he determined on leaving, and had actually weighed and was proceeding down the river when an offer was made that caused him once more to return.

This charter is, perhaps, not a very brilliant one, still we hope that it has somewhat rewarded his plucky efforts to open the trade; and at any rate it seems pretty reliably ascertained that cargo is to be got, and in considerable quantities; and, further, that the trade once started, its development will be easier in the future. With any one able or willing to make small advances against the cargo, there can be no doubt but that ships would readily find employment at remunerative rates. Again, many of the holders of cargo, if once educated as to the manner of chartering in vogue at other places, will, it seems very probable, by joining together, institute a similar system here, and by so doing undoubtedly acquire much more favourable conditions for the sale of their produce than the present high rate of junk freight and comparative low prices which the few capitalists are able to enforce, renders possible. In this as in many other things, the people of Wenchow only require instruction, and there can be no doubt but that the capacities of the place will be found to come up to the expectations that have been long held about it. In this view it is to be hoped that the visit of the *Hans* will prove of more lasting benefit to the port than the actual amount of her freight would at first sight seem to promise. Junks are arriving with raw cotton and other cargo; surely this might be got hold of by foreign ships! In the district immediately adjoining this, 100,000 bales of cottons are imported annually, and at rates of freight which are very much higher than would probably be demanded by foreigners. We hear that a German barque has been chartered in Penang for this; and as there is no doubt a brisk import of Straits produce, another epoch in the advance of the port may have been marked. The chief articles of export are charcoal, paper, medicine, umbrellas, bamboo shoots, &c., &c.; and judging by the quantities going away in junks, and those stored up awaiting shipment, it would seem as though something ought to be done to get hold of them. In the absence of some responsible agent to collect freight, and otherwise work up the business, I fear, however, it would be too risky for a steamer, with the necessarily short time at her disposal, to come in on mere speculation; but should a sailing vessel arrive with an owner or captain on board, ready and willing to make comparatively small advances, it would seem likely that profitable returns might be looked for.

The *Hindu* (lorcha) arrived three or four days ago with a very full cargo, chiefly piece goods; she clears again tomorrow. The rapidity of her movements are said to be due to freight awaiting her at Shanghai.

Weather just now is splendid; duck and geese swarming. We have not had a man of war for a tremendous time. I fear even the authorities are becoming forgetful of our existence; however, as far as protection goes, there is no call for any with so quiet, docile and apathetic a people as the natives of this port. Still we shall be glad to see our naval friends when they can come. (2nd December)

The North - China Herald and Supreme Court & Consular Gazette, January 10, 1879

Wenchow

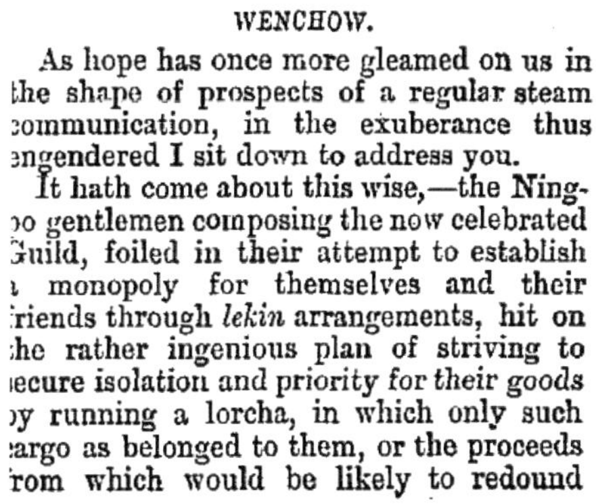

WENCHOW.

As hope has once more gleamed on us in the shape of prospects of a regular steam communication, in the exuberance thus engendered I sit down to address you.

It hath come about this wise,—the Ningpo gentlemen composing the now celebrated Guild, foiled in their attempt to establish a monopoly for themselves and their friends through *lekin* arrangements, hit on the rather ingenious plan of striving to secure isolation and priority for their goods by running a lorcha, in which only such cargo as belonged to them, or the proceeds from which would be likely to redound

Wenchow

As hope has once more gleamed on us in the shape of prospects of a regular steam communication, in the exuberance thus engendered I sit down to address you.

It hath come about this wise,—the Ningpo gentlemen composing the now celebrated Guild, foiled in their attempt to establish a monopoly for themselves and their friends through *lekin* arrangements, hit on the rather ingenious plan of striving to secure isolation and priority for their goods by running a lorcha, in which only such cargo as belonged to them, or the proceeds from which would be likely to redound to their profit, was permitted to be carried. The Wenchow people are no doubt slow and difficult to rouse, but after a while, like the proverbial worm, they thought it expedient to turn; and the result is, I am told, the starting of the steamer which arrived here the day before yesterday. Backed by the most influential natives of the place, not unfavourably looked on by the officials, if only a little perseverance is expended, the prospects for the *Yungning* establishing a trade and advancing the prosperity of this port seem very hopeful. She may not for one or two trips show any very large returns; indeed it is possible she will do little more than pay her way; but it seems almost certain that if the time is kept up with regularity and persistence, a comparatively short time will elapse ere not only a profitable return for her efforts will be acquired but it also seems highly probable that she will establish a position which future opposition will find very hard to assail. The cargo, both export and import exist; and only requires to be centralized. Supported as this steamer is by those who have hitherto been prominent in promoting its diffusion on behalf of their junks, it would seem that she sails under the most favourable auspices for securing the required concentration. Even at the risk of being tedious, I will once more venture to repeat the advice to those interested: Have patience, and be not disheartened because one, two, or even three trips do not show such profits as a too sanguine disposition might expect at the outset.

The weather is charming and seasonable, although in the absence of those operatic and other festive attractions which Shanghai offers, we have perhaps not had quite so gay a Christmas and New Year as has been vouchsafed to you, still we have not been unhappy; this doubtless you will admit shows a contented disposition. (2nd January)

The North - China Herald and Supreme Court & Consular Gazette, January 24, 1879

Wenchow

Wenchow

Our correspondent writes:—Since the time when the *Mandarin* enquiry was publicly held, though I have carefully sought for further information I have been unable to collect any of a sufficiently reliable nature to report.

You know the mystery that proverbially shrouds everything with which our officials have to do; still, seeing that great interest is felt in this investigation, and that so much has already become public, perhaps our wish for less reserve than has been, and is, maintained, may not be quite unwarranted.

WENCHOW.

Our correspondent writes:—Since the time when the *Mandarin* enquiry was publicly held, though I have carefully sought for further information I have been unable to collect any of a sufficiently reliable nature to report.

You know the mystery that proverbially shrouds everything with which our officials have to do; still, seeing that great interest is felt in this investigation, and that so much has already become public, perhaps our wish for less reserve than has been, and is, maintained, may not be quite unwarranted.

Fortunately, however, for the gratification of public curiosity, the Chinese are either less reticent or are wanting in power to command a similar amount of secrecy; and it therefore frequently happens that, whether through celestial frankness or indiscretion, the outside world manage to get an inkling of what is going on beneath the clouds of diplomacy.

Fortunately, however, for the gratification of public curiosity, the Chinese are either less reticent or are wanting in power to command a similar amount of secrecy; and it therefore frequently happens that, whether through celestial frankness or indiscretion, the outside world manage to get an inkling of what is going on beneath the clouds of diplomacy.

Such an opportunity has turned up here; and this, together with the nature of the new phase assumed by the case, enables me to impart some further intelligence *re the Mandarin.*

I may add, however, that I feel fully justified in assuring you of the accuracy of what I now communicate.

Judging from what I hear, the decision come to in Peking by our authorities, as to the identity of the vessel detained with the missing lorcha, or the trustworthiness of the evidence brought to rebut this supposition, is by no means conclusive or satisfactory to the native officials; and indeed from what I can gather would simply seem to amount to a declaration of temporary cessation of action, in as far as is comprehended by desistance from further attempts to gain possession of the few rotten planks which are all that now constitute the suspected craft.

It appears, however, that Woo Ah-yuan has thought himself justified in filing a petition through the viceroy in Foochow to the Taotai here, praying that our authorities be moved to compel two "British subjects" (sic.) (named), who appeared in response to official summons as witnesses in the case, to pay to the plaintiff a sum amounting to about $4,000 for detention, loss of cargo, freight, vessel, and personal liberty; adding, I am informed, that all these disasters were consequent on the "false and malicious" information laid by the defendants before the authorities. The groundlessness of these statements was conclusively shown at the enquiry held here, and that at the same time the lorcha under detention was clearly proved to be "the one purchased by the petitioner from Messrs. Hedge & Co., of Foochow." Woo Ah-yuan, it will perhaps be recollected, is the same individual who on previous occasions stated that he was merely the master of the lorcha; besides which there are other statements, said to be set forth in the petition, that would seem to be inconsistent with those made by the plaintiff when a witness before the Court at Wenchow. The native public here look on the whole matter as a great joke, the chief point of which consists in the belief that this is only a continuance of the victory which has been gained over foreigners all through, as the former have (rightly or wrongly) always most openly asserted, not merely their belief, but their certain knowledge as to this boat being the very *Mandarin* herself.

Whether or not any of Woo's present assertions when contrasted with his past depositions, petitions, and affirmations, materially strengthen the case of those who contend that this is the stolen lorcha, is a question which will, I have no doubt, prove of high interest to all immediately concerned.

Be this as it may, it is perhaps not uninteresting to point out that one of the defendants named is not a British subject; and that neither had anything whatever to do with giving or collecting the information on which the Chinese officials acted when arresting the implicated vessel. As I have said before, they were merely witnesses, appealed to after the lorcha had been safely hauled up and put under guard.

This does not seem to disconcert Woo Ah-yuan, however, nor need it do so, seeing how easily he gets over certain geographical facts and natural laws, which notoriously oppose his opening assertions about the defendants and their connection with "his misfortunes."

The *Yung-ning* has duly returned, and we are of course glad to see her, although I fear she cannot hope for very much cargo at this time. The prospects of her getting good freights after the

Chinese New Year are cheering. The natives say she is to make three trips per month; but they all seem to unite in thinking that for the first two months—namely while the trade is being coaxed back to its old centre—perhaps two voyages will be found most convenient. This, however, is a matter which rests entirely with those whose interest it is to specially weigh such considerations.

Apropos of the steamer, and in proof of the goodwill entertained towards her by the Wenchowites (natives), I may mention that some evil-disposed person or persons (said to belong to Ningpo) diligently circulated reports reflecting on the sea-worthiness of the *Yung-ning*. This has been strongly resented by the Wenchow people, and pains taken to show the falsity of charges which have palpably arisen from interested motives.

We are at last favoured with a sight of the flag—H.M.S. *Sheldrake* arrived yesterday; but alas! Only for a four days' stay. I suppose we shall not be similarly honoured for a very long time.

Naval officers who care for shooting are informed that ducks, geese, curlew and plover abound; and good sport can always we had at little expense. I wonder if the Admiral is a "gunist" (of course I mean fowlingly!), and whether the above statement will soften his heart, if not on behalf of the Wenchow exiles, at least in the interest of the members of his service who ought to have some relaxation allowed them after the balls, operas, paper hunts, &c., of the more attractive ports, have become monotonous. (15th Jan)

The North - China Herald and Supreme Court & Consular Gazette, March 28, 1879

Some Account of Wenchow, the Newly - Opened Port in China

W. Wykeham Myers, M. B.

SOME ACCOUNT OF WENCHOW, THE NEWLY-OPENED PORT IN CHINA.

BY W. WYKEHAM MYERS, M.B.

By particular request, we copy the following extract from the above-named paper, from the *Japan Weekly Mail* :—

Commercial.—It is with no little diffidence that I commence this portion of my paper, as neither my profession, nor experience, prior to settling here, is of a nature to have brought me much in contact with matters mercantile; still it is never too late to learn, and if leisure and the enjoyment of reference to the best and highest sources of information can help me, I have certainly had both. I will therefore only add that if wrong in my deductions, I am at least sure of the authenticity of my facts, and I would fain hope that supposing the former consequence of my inexperience be apparent, that I shall at least have placed my readers in possession of such undeniable premises as to render it no difficult task to draw accurate conclusions.

Some Account of Wenchow, the Newly-Opened Port in China

W. Wykeham Myers, M.B.

By particular request, we copy the following extract from the above-named paper, from the *Japan Weekly Mail*: —

Commercial. — It is with no little diffidence that I commence this portion of my paper, as neither my profession, nor experience, prior to settling here, is of a nature to have brought me much in contact with matters mercantile; still it is never too late to learn, and if leisure and the enjoyment of reference to the best and highest sources of information can help me. I have certainly had both. I will therefore only add that if wrong in my deductions, I am at least sure of the authenticity of my facts, and I would fain hope that supposing the former consequence of my inexperience be apparent, that I shall at least have placed my readers in possession of such undeniable premises as to render it no difficult task to draw accurate conclusions.

From its position Wenchow would at present seem to owe its anticipated importance as a seat of trade to the fact of its being the natural outlet for most of the teas now sold at Foochow. As a market for imports it has free connection not only with a large tract of country in the neighbourhood, but also with many districts which would no doubt choose this port as a source of supply in preference to Foochow and Ningpo.

During the first four months after the opening of the port, a vigorous import trade in piece goods and opium sprang into existence, steadily increasing and promising to prove remunerative; by the end of this time the Wenchow imports had reached a considerable distance into the interior, orders were coming down from many Chinese merchants at various inland places, and the following city and towns, previously supplied by Ningpo, namely, Tai-chow, Poo-ching, 250 miles away, and Pei-ling, 100 miles off, were already transferring their purchases to the Wenchow market. Thus it will be seen things began to look bright; and it almost seemed as though the hopes and prophecies of past years were making steady progress towards realization.

It would appear that up to the time of Wenchow being opened, *lekin* was unknown, the imports arriving in native craft being in this respect untaxed. On the contrary, it was given out on the institution of the new levy that it was a consequence of foreign advent due solely to the presence of foreigners and might cease if they were induced or constrained to withdraw.

At any rate, the absence of this tax was one of the happy concomitants cheering that prospects of the first four months; true, we heard rumours of what was coming, yet the strength of our wishes created, and the extent of our success fostered, hopes that, perhaps after all, the Chefoo Convention was to be carried out in a spirit of generosity, and that one of its chief concessions to foreigners would be nurtured, at least in its infancy, by an absence of all those controllable influences likely to impede or retard its prosperity. These pleasant visions, however, were in the early part of August, 1877, fated to be abruptly dispelled, for at this time a *lekin* establishment, as unparalleled in the exorbitance of its demands, as it seemed disregardful of all previous treaties, swooped down with scorching blight, and trade immediately collapsed.

Orders sent from the interior and those forwarded from this to Shanghai, were cancelled, the steamer that had been running regularly was at once withdrawn, accounts were closed, and Wenchow, speedily deprived of its trading visitors, resumed the quiet and apathy peculiar to the ecclesiastical city it is.

Opened too late in the season to divert the earlier teas here, all hopes of later crops being attracted (supposing there had been foreign vessels to ship them in) were utterly destroyed by the refusal of the authorities to fix even a definite rate of *lekin*, their replies always being that tea must pay whatever was demanded at the various barriers through which it might pass. One unhappy lot that tried the experiment was taxed at the rate of Tls. 3 per picul. Long afterwards, when the season was over, the officials were induced to fix the rate at Tl. 1 per picul; but this, in common with other reductions, as will be seen further on, came too late to neutralize, or even modify, the disastrous effects of prior occurrences. Wenchow had now to make a new start and outlive the baneful consequences of the terror and evil repute which had been inspired. To make things worse, the *lekin* officials, finding no opportunity for fresh imposition of tax, drew up a calculation based on the known amount of goods imported during the past four months, distributed the total as they thought proper amongst the shops of the place, and commenced to levy what they called "back-lekin," accompanying their demands by threats of various kinds. The head official appointed by the Governor of Chekiang, and over whom the then Taotai professed to have no jurisdiction, came in great state, setting up his office at the head of the chief jetty, next door to the Customs, the treaty provisions for the existence and governance of which he asserted were those authorizing and regulating his establishment. The very fittings and arrangements of his office were got up in as close imitation of his neighbours as the original similarity of the two buildings admitted. All packages of goods landed on the jetty were immediately seized on and examined by the underlings; and a levy according to a published tariff imposed as a second import duty. Should the goods be going beyond the "city of the port," then a further and similar impost was inflicted, thus according to this officer's rendering of the treaty, somewhat modified as he said by the Chefoo Convention, foreign goods in future would be subjected to two import duties over and above transit dues. I need, perhaps, scarcely remind my readers, that according to the original treaties, the foreign Customs import duty covered foreign goods for the "port and the city of that port," and if going further a regular transit rate is duly provided. It is also perhaps, unnecessary to mention that such a tax as *lekin* is unrecognized by any of the treaties. It would appear, however, that foreigners in looking on the Chefoo Convention as a reparative measure were mistaken; at any rate, so hold the Chinese, for their authorities asserted most strenuously, at least they did here, that it was nothing of the kind; but on the contrary a reciprocal arrangement, the parties to which, governed solely by regard for the strict and literal meaning of the words as written, were at full liberty (former obligations and agreements notwithstanding) to deduce the utmost benefit to themselves which each might think the language permitted. In this state of matters it seemed unfortunate that the phraseology of certain clauses of the Convention should seem to extend some recognition towards the levy of *lekin*. If we admit the soundness of the Chinese reasoning and hold with them that they were justified in locking on *lekin* as recognized, then it certainly does not appear so strange that they should appeal to the only agreements which specify rules and regulations for the governance of imposts on trade, and apply them to the establishment which had now come into legitimate existence. At least this would seem to be the line of argument the native officials must have followed when referring to the Treaty as their authority for acting as they did. They drew up a set of rules and regulations which they posted over the walls and freely circulated in pamphlet form amongst the shop-keepers and merchants. The following is a condensed translation of the said rules: —

1.—European, Japanese, Canton, Szechuen, Hankow, and Foochow products, imported by all classes of foreign vessels, will be taxed at this office in accordance with regulation.

2.—A detailed memorandum similar to that furnished to the Customs, of all goods imported by foreign firms, must be supplied to this office; and, on sales occurring, the firm concerned must in accordance with the law enforcing payment of local dues by native merchants, direct the purchaser to pay his *lekin* prior to delivery of goods. Any attempts at evasion or smuggling will result in a fine amounting to treble *lekin* leviable.

3.—Goods *en route* inland will be examined at various places and the receipts from this office inspected. Should the latter not be forthcoming, the goods will be detained until, after reference to this office, the fine to be inflicted has been decided on.

4.—when offering payment of *lekin*, the goods will be examined; and if found to agree with the details of the application the goods will be passed. If the latter are bulky, an officer will proceed to the spot (godown or landing place) and there examine them on application being made to this effect.

5.—Exports. Excepting tea and silk to be dealt with separately, all goods will be taxed to the extent of 3/10ths of the Customs' tariff. Goods owned by foreign hongs are exempt from import, but acts of collusion (with natives) will result in the infliction of a fine.

6.—Native merchants purchasing foreign goods for transport inland, must tender payment of *lekin* before taking delivery. On goods destined for interior, under transit pass, and not for storage in port, all local dues must be paid in full, on which this office will issue passes permitting use of the transit pass and obviating liability at the last barrier. (Chinese owned) native produce has not up to date been permitted to go inland under transit pass; on this, therefore, *lekin* must be paid as per tariff. Attempted frauds in connection with this produce will be looked on as smuggling.

7.—It is provided by treaty that *lekin* officials may at their convenience devise measures for preventing smuggling and other malpractices with goods of all descriptions stored in foreign hongs. With this intent, therefore, an officer will be appointed to make monthly inspection and notes of unsold stock. (This is provided for by Art. 46 of the Treaty.)

8.—All passes to contain a careful note setting forth the city and street to which the goods they cover are destined; and also to furnish particulars of the water route to be traversed (if going by water) in order that inspection may be facilitated and smuggling prevented.

9.—Foreign firms re-exporting goods as unsuitable to the market may have the *lekin* thereon remitted, if examination at the Customs proves the to be in same condition (as intact) as when imported. Art. 45 of Treaty provides for this.

10.—Recent regulations (Chefoo Convention) provide that foreign goods within foreign settlement boundaries are exempt from *lekin*; but that beyond these limits *lekin* is leviable on foreign and native products alike. Pending the fixing of said boundaries, the regulations hitherto in force affecting *lekin* levies will be enforced.

11.—Settlement boundaries being fixed, native produce, the property of Chinese merchants found therein will come under cognizance of this office, thus constituting a simple control over native merchants by the local authorities. Should there be connivance with foreign firms in respect to ownership, or should the latter extend protection with a view to fraud on the *lekin* revenue, on detection the goods will be confiscated and the foreigner implicated handed over to his Consul for punishment by fine, to the end that treaty stipulations may be upheld. (See Art. 48 of Treaty.)

The above rules, based on those in force in Ningpo, have been drawn up to meet the exigencies of the occasion. They are in accord with, and in a measure explanatory of, treaty stipulations, and are put forth in a spirit of equity in the general interest of the *lekin* revenue. *(To be continued.)*

The North – China Herald and Supreme Court & Consular Gazette, April 4, 1879

Some Account of Wenchow, The Newly – Opened Port in China

W. Wykeham Myers, M. B. (Concluded, from "Japan Mail")

Some Account of Wenchow, The Newly-Opened Port in China

W. Wykeham Myers, M.B.

(Concluded, from "Japan Mail")

Regulations Respecting Opium

1.—*Lekin* on opium in Wenchow district will be collected in accordance with the Ningpo system, viz., at the rate of Taels 40 per chest, 40 balls constituting a chest of Patua, and 100 catties one of Malwa.

2. — Opium on importation will be examined by the Customs and deposited in foreign godowns under bond, report of the arrival being made to this office.

On sale the purchaser is to be directed to pay *lekin*, and on the production of the stamped release slips only, may delivery be granted. Smuggling to be punished by fine of Taels 1,000 for each picul smuggled.

3.—By mutual agreement existing amongst foreign firms, it is customary for them at Ningpo to pay the *lekin*; and in return from the levy of Taels 40, five taels are returned to the compradore of the firm concerned, and Tael one is paid to the native broker, leaving 34 taels as the sum accruing to the *lekin* office. No such arrangements having been made as yet in Wenchow for payments as above described, there is no occasion for granting the refunds mentioned, but as soon as such an understanding is come to, a similar allowance will be granted and at the same time more detailed measures for controlling operations promulgated.

From the foregoing it will readily be seen how completely subservient not only foreigners generally, but the Customs, were to be to the *lekin* office, not merely as payers but also as assistants in enforcing and collecting the tax. The interpretation put on the Chefoo Convention is

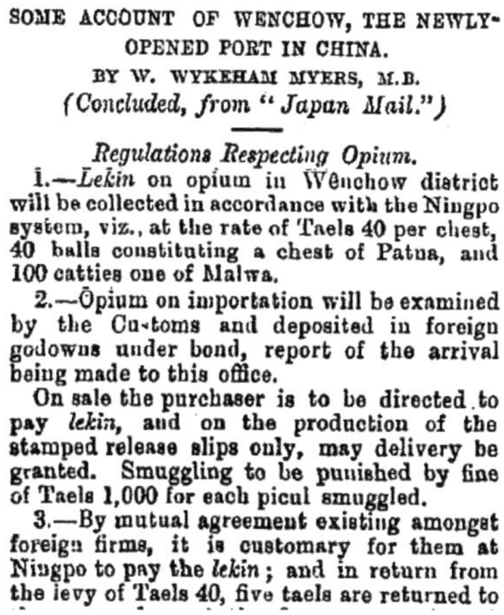
SOME ACCOUNT OF WENCHOW, THE NEWLY-OPENED PORT IN CHINA.
BY W. WYKEHAM MYERS, M.B.
(Concluded, from "Japan Mail.")

Regulations Respecting Opium.

1.—*Lekin* on opium in Wenchow district will be collected in accordance with the Ningpo system, viz., at the rate of Taels 40 per chest, 40 balls constituting a chest of Patua, and 100 catties one of Malwa.

2.—Opium on importation will be examined by the Customs and deposited in foreign godowns under bond, report of the arrival being made to this office.

On sale the purchaser is to be directed to pay *lekin*, and on the production of the stamped release slips only, may delivery be granted. Smuggling to be punished by fine of Taels 1,000 for each picul smuggled.

3.—By mutual agreement existing amongst foreign firms, it is customary for them at Ningpo to pay the *lekin*; and in return from the levy of Taels 40, five taels are returned to no less clearly than boldly set forth, and if this rendering is correct it is certainly, as the proclamation puts it, “explanatory of the Treaties” previously in existence.

Fifteen or eighteen years ago there was a brisk trade (import and export) carried on at Wenchow. Foreign goods and produce from the Southern ports and Straits Settlements were in considerable demand, several Swatow, Canton, and Singapore houses were established in the city, and although the inhabitants of Wenchow proper do not seem to have engaged very largely in trade, still through the medium of these outside capitalists employment was provided for a large number of natives and a not inconsiderable amount of foreign shipping.

From a variety of causes the branches of native houses established here gradually withdrew, probably in consequence of the isolation which a more general ratification of treaties conferred on the port, and the greater facilities Ningpo and Foochow were enabled to offer. Left to themselves, the Wenchow people lacked the energy to carry on or encourage the concentration of trade with junks, which had hitherto existed at the city; and as a result of this, these vessels sought contact with the consuming districts at the numerous small towns and villages lower down the river and those on the sea coast adjoining its mouth. This was the condition of affairs when Wenchow was opened to foreigners and it now behoved the latter by a re-introduction of capital and enterprise to tempt back the trade to its former state of concentration. In order to do this there is no doubt but that at first almost a system of retail business would have to be established in the city, the tea-districts must be personally canvassed, establishments for firing and otherwise preparing the tea (such as exist on the Foochow side of the mountains) set up, and other means taken for diverting the trade both export and import from the paths which it had been constrained by political exigencies to follow in the past.

Confidence once established and trade firmly set going, there seems every probability that the necessary intermediary native capitalists would soon be attracted, and would in due course take over the peddling portion of the business, carrying on the larger (and therefore to foreigners more congenial) transactions with those who had preceded them. No doubt with some such object in view, one of the largest and most enterprising British firms in the East opened an agency at Wenchow, and as long as they had fair play their efforts seemed likely to be crowned with the success they merited. Even after the *lekin* emeute had taken place they bravely held on, now and again making efforts to revive the blighted trade; but alas! By the time the officials were brought to see the error of their ways, and the old staff dismissed, it was too late to commence those all essential arrangements at the tea-districts. The depressed state of affairs which had existed here up to this time had doubtless deterred other firms from starting, and when the crops of 1878 came to be gathered, the absence of any kind of competition, coupled with the ominous official repute which the port had acquired, prevented any but an insignificant quantity of tea being sent to this market. Taking advantage, however, of the improved *lekin* arrangements, in the spring of this year steamers once more began running, and, with their advent, prospects for import trade again brightened; but this was not to be for long, as naturally disheartened, and perhaps somewhat disgusted with the vexatious interference they had met with in the past, the firm in whom all hope were centered and whose presence was the sole guarantee for the continuance of steam communication, suddenly withdrew their agency, and Wenchow as left without a single representative of foreign commerce. Considering that for so long they had had to face single handed the force of unparalleled and illegitimate obstruction, that in the primary efforts to start and nurture trade great expense must have been incurred, it is not a matter for surprise that even dawning prospects of brighter days and return for their efforts should have failed to induce persistence in attempts which had previously resulted in so much disaster and annoyance; but be this as it may, by their departure the port of Wenchow received a blow, the severity of which may take long years of struggle to efface.

So much then for the causes which led to the destruction of apparently well grounded hopes. I will now try to show what the capacities of the place really are, leaving it to those interested in the question to decide whether the expectations hitherto entertained as to its value as a port of trade, are proved erroneous by our present further knowledge. In order to do this, I take the trade returns for 1877, and in going over them strive to briefly conjoin such other information as may seem fitted to convey an adequate idea of the existing state of matters, and I would ask you to remember that although these returns purport to refer to the whole nine months of 1877, they may in reality be looked on as chiefly showing the trade of the first happy four months immediately following the opening of the port.

The import trade was almost entirely confined to piece goods and a little opium, coming chiefly from Shanghai, although some were shipped to Ningpo.

The value in all amounted to £73,600.

Opium—Of Malwa, there were imported thirty-nine chests, and of Patna ten. The average price for the former being $644 per picul, and for the latter $653.

Owing to a failure of the poppy crop in this province in the autumn of 1877, Indian drug would undoubtedly have obtained high rates; but unfortunately a similar catastrophe seems to have occurred in India, and there was little or no attempt made to respond to the demand. In December, 1878, the price offered for Malwa had risen to $750 per picul.

Patna, quoted at $670, was not however so much wanted. In starting the direct import of opium to this place, there are many obstacles to be overcome, and one was the absence of local capital, which enables the immediate purchases to dispense with long credit. Again, hitherto all drug coming here has been sent overland from Ningpo, the native guilds of which place have been able to grant the necessary facilities. By this method of forwarding stock, apart from the arrangements which it would appear they are able to make with the Ningpo *lekin* officials—it seems possible for a good deal of opium to evade the tax altogether.

The whole amount consumed in Wenchow itself is only about 115 chests per annum, so perhaps it may be thought possible or convenient to postpone operations on this portion of the trade, devoting their efforts to gain the custom of those outlying districts at present supplied by Ningpo, but which would probably come to our port favoured as it is by its geographical and other advantages.

For instance, there are many districts in Fohkien infinitely more accessible from Wenchow than from Ningpo, and these would I think be sure to buy the drug from the former place and most probably seek to barter tea for it.

The *lekin* on Opium is extremely high at Foochow, whereas that paid here may be regarded as being similar to that imposed at Ningpo, viz.: Tls. 33 or Tls. 34 per picul; besides which the difference in cost of transport leaves a larger margin for profit. To give an idea of what the demand for opium is in Chekiang and a large portion of Fohkien, I have the best authority for stating that at least from thirty to forty per cent of the population smoke a mixture containing Taicheng (native drug) and Malwa, the former preponderating.

The most important factor, however, in diminishing the foreign opium trade is the increasing native cultivation of the poppy in this province, the crops from which supplying Chekiang and a large portion of Fohkien furnish exports to Formosa, Shanghai and other places. The total yield in the prefectures of Taichow and Wenchow is estimated at about 7, 000 chests per annum.

Last year from various causes the crop of opium failed to about half of its usual amount. In August and September when first it realizes about $200 per picul, running up from that time through December (when it attains about $350 per picul), from $400 up to $450 in February and March, at which time its further value is regulated by the prospects of the crop to be gathered in the following May. Last year through the failure before mentioned, native opium kept up to about $450 per picul, and but for the contemporary high price of Malwa (which is said to be double the strength), the latter would have quite monopolized the market. Speaking generally then, it may be said (in view of the partiality shown for the Indo-Chinese mixture in those parts of Keangsi and Fokien more easily approached from this,) that should attempts be made to supply the demand for foreign drug through this port it is probable a result would be obtained profitably commensurate with the energy and capital expended; and if, as seems by no means improbable, opium be accepted at the tea districts in exchange for their products, a condition of trade likely to prove specially favourable to foreigners would be established, with this advantage, that whereas the barter of drug for leaf which may now go on in Foochow passes through independent middle men; and thus is not so readily amenable to profitable foreign manipulation as perhaps could be arranged here where foreigners might come in more direct contact with the consumers, or at any rate be more "au-courant" with the transaction. Tea thus obtained if brought down under transit pass would of course be quite independent of *lekin* fluctuations.

Cotton Piece Goods.—In the months of April, May, June, and July, 1877, that is during the period when trade was progressing, there were imported 35,000 pieces gray shirtings, 41,900 pieces T-Cloths, 12,624 pieces drills, all of which found a satisfactory market. That Wenchow should be the source from which a large area ought to draw their supplies of piece goods is suggested by reference to the Customs records for 1876, of cotton goods sent from Ningpo under transit pass to the following districts, all within easy reach of us: —

	Grey Shirtings, pieces.	White Shirtings, pieces.	T-Cloths, Pieces.	Drills & Jeans, pieces.
Chü-chü	23,038	4,650	32,339	5,830

Wenchow	39,657	2,337	29,681	9.326
Kü-chow	37,917	2,905	77,238	10,868
Chuan-chow	2,700	—	2,320	—
Chien-ming	1,380	350	2,370	560
Total	104,692	10,242	143,948	26,584

Besides the above, large quantities were also sent up under *lekin* pass issued by the foreign piece goods guild at Ningpo, and of which no exact record can be obtained. If in spite then of all the difficulties of transit and increased distance, these places furnish so considerable a demand, how much more may be looked for when the access of goods is stimulated by the facilities offered by a direct water route from the places of the manufacture to the seats of consumption. Such a line of communication Wenchow opens up not only to these places, but to others in the South and South-east; and until the abrupt closure of trade took place we had practical evidence of its tendency to diverge into the new and more natural route. In Ping-yung district, to the South of this, a cloth celebrated for its durability and strength is made, the greater portion of which is used on the spot, although some is exported to Shanghai and Hangchow. For its manufacture there is an import of 100,000 bales of raw cotton, annually, much of which no doubt ought to supply lucrative employment to foreign bottoms, as the present mode of transport by junk is tedious and the freight nearly half as high again as that which would pay our vessels.

Woollen Goods—Soon after the period when the demand for this description of goods commenced, the blow fell on trade, and therefore beyond noting the fact of there being a fair promise of good market there is but little to remark. The supply, however, to the districts with which Wenchow is in more immediate contact went on as briskly as usual through the old Ningpo route. The actual quantities imported during the short time our port had an opportunity of engaging in the trade, were as follows:—Camlets 900 pieces, Spanish Stripes 762 pieces, Long Ells 600 pieces, Lastings 510 pieces, and Lustres 1,500 pieces.

When it is remembered that it is only towards the later and colder part of the year (during the greater portion of which Wenchow was almost entirely shut out), that the demand for this class of goods becomes marked, perhaps the figures given may be thought more re-assuring than would otherwise be the case. The import trade with the Straits Settlements before alluded to as being formerly concentrated at Wenchow, consists in great part of rattans and mangrove bark; this though now disposed over the numerous small points of entry below the city, still goes on and offers opportunities to those interested in shipping.

Of metals imported, Japan copper, 364 piculs, stands first. Iron (nail-rod or wire) 88 piculs, Lead 102 piculs, Tin 81 piculs; 60 piculs of steel remaining unsold were re-exported. Kerosine Oil is in great and ever increasing demand. In this part of Chehkiang a good deal of sugar is consumed, giving lively employment to junks during the season. This trade also, although at present scattered, may undoubtedly be centralized at Wenchow with advantage to both merchants and shipowners.

Exports.—So little effort has been made for developing or rather diverting the trade into foreign channels, or perhaps it may be more correct to say so little opportunity has been given for making any such attempt, and so much has been done to thwart all enterprise, that from the bare returns little or nothing can be gathered as to the possibilities of the trade. The returns simply show a total value of £5,435 for 1877; but as my object is to show what could be done under less extraordinary circumstances, I will take each article offering or likely to offer the export and give such information concerning it as may be obtainable.

Facile princeps stand Tea; and although for reasons already given but a small quantity of Congou (278 piculs) actually came here in 1877, we have good reason to believe that in the season of 1878, the teamen were willing and anxious to send their produce down; and that had there been even a limited competition, in spite of all late obstacles, the effort to make this a port of sale would have been renewed; although of course in the absence of that action on the spot to which I have before referred, less leaf would spontaneously find its way here than would be the case if efforts were made to stimulate and instruct the producers as to the advantages of the new market.

Separated as a great part of the finest tea-producing districts are from Foochow by long ranges of mountains, traversed by difficult passes; and in direct water communication with them as we are, it is obvious that but little need be done to attract the produce to this its natural outlet. To give a practical idea of the advantages offered by this route, I may mention that it is reliably estimated that tea can be put on the Wenchow market at $2 per picul less for transport alone than if taken to Foochow. The nearest tea district in Ping-yang, distant about 34 miles, where however the annual crop of fine tea for the foreign market is only about 30,000 piculs, although there is about 70,000piculs of a coarser kind produced, the greater part of which is for native consumption.

The great tea-producing district is that which includes the portion popularly known as Pak-hun, but properly Pei-ling, and it is this part of the country generally that is hoped may in future be induced to send the tea here in exchange for piece goods and opium. Pei-ling is to some extent, and would probably become entirely, the centre for concentration, not alone for the produce of the country strictly covered by its name, but also for the parts immediately adjacent, the route to which is good and easy, about half consisting of canal and river. The other tea districts are Yo-ching to the North of Wenchow, where a very fine green tea is grown, Tai-shun and Sui-yan. The products of these two latter, however, are sent through Ping-yang, and are therefore included under that head. Could it be possible for foreign shipping to get hold of the coarser or unfired teas, which are annually exported through Wenchow, either for native consumption or to be fired for the foreign market, a considerable amount of freight might thus be obtained; but unfortunately the duty levied at the native Custom House is about half less than that imposed by the foreign Customs. Mr. Hobson, some time before he left, represented the matter with a view to modify the tariff, and some months after his departure it was arranged that a discount of 20 percent from the actual weight of the teas when shipped should be granted as allowances for future loss in weight from firing or other causes. I would seem, however, that even this concession is inadequate to approximate the two duties, and therefore the tea will probably continue to be shipped in junks. It has been suggested that if the same rule were applied to the native tea sent from Wenchow as obtains with that imported from Japan, and a duty of 4 percent *ad valorem* constitute the whole import, the desired result might be brought about. On the other hand, such an alteration it is thought might prove inconvenient in relation to the general Customs tariff. There can be no doubt then that Wenchow ought by reason of its geographical and other advantages to prove of some importance in relation to the tea-trade alone; but when it is remembered that in doing this Foochow must be materially affected, and the great interests (foreign and native) at present vested in that port considerably influenced, the reluctance which has been shown to take advantage of the opportunities offered here can be readily understood. Obstacles, however, which are based only on prejudice or individual interests, and are in opposition to natural laws, will most likely be overcome in the end, so it would seem tolerably certain that the development of Wenchow into a considerable market for teas is merely a matter of time.

Oranges grown and exported from Wenchow enjoy considerable celebrity; and in ordinary times form a large item in the export return. Last year, a continuation of that run of ill-luck which so often interfered with the progress of trade, it happened that all the Tientsin steamers by which the great bulk of the oranges go from Shanghai were so entirely engaged transporting rice that it was found impossible to get room for the Wenchow freight. The Europe had taken away from this a large cargo of fruit; and this as the first great export shipment in foreign bottom was naturally regarded in the light of a test venture; but for the reasons given the cargo had to be sold at a loss in Shanghai, to the disappointment not only of the shippers, but of all those who had hoped this would prove an efficient introduction to people who, as is well known, look more to present result than to future possibilities.

The general products and manufactures of the districts of Wenchow are as follows:—

Copper,	Charcoal,	Umbrellas,
Furniture,	Iron Wire,	Pulse,
Nankeens,	Gauzes,	Hemp,
Matting,	Iron-ware,	Wheat,
Coir,	Silver,	Bamboos,
Pine Wood,	Opium,	Tea,
Indigo,	Silk,	Paper,

Also seventeen different varieties of medicines.

All these are exported in sufficient quantity to furnish considerable employment for shipping; but in order to divert the trade from the junks it will be necessary for the owners of ships or their agents (at any rate at first) to enter the competition prepared to offer the same facilities that the junk-masters or owners are in the habit of giving. First amongst these is the necessity of making an advance against cargo shipped to one-third or one-half its value; for the people here, luxurious and extravagant in their habits, with but few exceptions do not care to or are not able to wait any time for the pecuniary equivalent of their produce, preferring to adopt that mode of disposing of it which gives the least trouble and seems to show the speediest return in money.

Taking advantage of this, the junk owners and supercargoes are able to secure high freights and otherwise good investments for their money. It is probable that at first unless represented by responsible agents who are prepared to make all these arrangements in anticipation of arrival of sailing ships, having more time at their disposal, will find the system less inconvenient than would steamers. There can be no doubt, however, that but a short process of nursing, such as I have indicated, would bring the trade into a condition more tangible for both kinds of vessels; and this remark applies no more to shipping than to other departments of trade.

Charcoal ought of itself to form a large item of export available for foreign craft; and if as merchants and others assert, it is by treaty entitled to pass free at the foreign Customs, would undoubtedly have proved a very valuable source of revenue to ships; as when passing through the native Custom-house it has to pay export duty. The Foreign Customs here, however, exact a duty of 5 percent *ad valorem*, which with the 2½ percent imposed at destination makes a total impost of 7½ percent; but as the whole subject is at present sub-judice, I need do no more than refer to it, merely adding that as the imposition is not levied at all the treaty ports (Foochow where the largest export takes place being, I am told, one of the exempt) it would seem possible that Wenchow may hope for similar facilities. Warned by the results of their last year's escapade, and doubtless more or less influenced by pressure of a higher order, the *lekin* here at present is undoubtedly more favourable than at any other Treaty port. The "rules and regulations" to which I have already alluded have been withdrawn and allowed to sink into the oblivion they merit, and the present staff seem really anxious to work entirely in an opposite direction to their predecessors and so attract foreigners and foreign trade to the place. Steps have been taken and arrangements made which would seem to render the *lekin*-farming guild system of monopoly (such as has ruined the hopes and chances of foreigners at Ningpo) an impossibility in the future; and under the *lekin* transit pass which it must be remembered has the advantage of being respected over the province, goods can be sent into the interior at a considerably less rate than even that demanded by the Foreign Customs.

Coupled with this is the tendency or willingness to engage in a barter trade, which at least with regard to tea may be thought worthy of encouragement by foreigners. In a word, the demands of the districts which it would seem Wenchow ought naturally to supply, are undoubtedly large, and the facilities at present offered for profitably responding to this call proportionately great.

It may possibly take some time to overcome the prejudice, nay, even incredulity, of foreigners, somewhat justifiably excited by past experience in China; or perhaps it may be considered that there are already a sufficient number of open ports, exclusive of those provided by the Chefoo Convention, for absorbing all the enterprise and capital foreigners are at present or for some time to come able to supply but there seems every reason to believe that should it ever be thought advisable to take advantage of the opportunities here offered, Wenchow will be found capable of taking a high stand as a seat of brisk and probably remunerative trade.

Exchange.—The average rate during 1877, was for 150 clean Mexican dollars, Haikwan Tales 100. For clean Carolus 1,350 and for clean Mexican 1,170 *cash* were given, in consequence of which the export of *cash* promised to be pretty brisk; but strong official pressure being put on, it soon declined.

There are many counterfeit dollars in circulation at Wenchow, chiefly coined at Ningpo, Lu-chao, and Tai-chow, some are nearly up to standard, while others are 52 percent below.

In concluding this portion of my paper, I append a table showing the most important districts of this and other provinces likely to be supplied by or send exports through Wenchow, with a description of their chief products:—

Chekiang Province

Products

Tai-chow.—Opium, tea, iron, saltfish, bamboo shoots, gauze.

Chü-chow.—Tea, varnish, mushrooms, and stone for seats.

Chin-hua.—Varnish, tea, dates of high quality, hams, paper.

Kü-chow.—Tea, paper.

Ping-yang.—Tea, iron.

Tai-shun.—Tea, iron.

Fohkien Province

Products

Pei-lin.—Tea.

Kien-ming.—Tea.

Yen-hing.—Tea, copper, iron.

Shao-wu.—Tea, bamboo shoots.

Kiangsi Province

Products

Kuang-sin.—Tea, rattans, paper, hemp.

Fu-chow.—Grass cloth, sugar.

Man-chang.—Tea, grass cloth.

Chien-chang.—Tea, grass cloth.

General.—There is yet one class of possible visitors to whom some further information may be acceptable. I allude to missionaries.

The attractions offered by Wenchow to these gentlemen are two-fold. As looked on from a layman's point of view, the field would seem peculiarly susceptible of development, while in a secular sense the discomforts or hardships attending its culture appear considerably less than those which, by all accounts, accompany the labour in other parts. In proof of the first I would simply allude to the deeply devotional spirit shown by the people; they are gross idolaters, but at the same time unremittingly attentive to the calls of their religion.

Apart from the innumerable temples scattered all over the city, the streets are not less studded with altars to "Baal" than shrines to Cloacina, close adjacent to each of which latter one of the former is generally found. One hopeful conclusion, however, that may be drawn from this tendency to subordinate themselves to religion teaching is that if directed into the proper channel it is not improbable the people would be found to be unusually pious and therefore satisfactory converts. As to secular attractions, I would refer to my remarks on the climate, and also the good and cheap living to be obtained here. There are numerous sites which would afford ample accommodation for building the most stately mansions, if necessity arose, but supposing that circumstances should not favour such operations, or a place of temporary residence were needed whilst the permanent ones were undergoing erection, then many of the native houses themselves, even if untouched, would be capable of affording comparatively comfortable and undoubtedly spacious dwellings, and whatever their owners may be, as I have before shown, with very few foreign additions they could be readily converted into something highly satisfactory. In a word I may say that under whatever exigencies a missionary settled down here it would be impossible for him to be subjected to the miserable shifts for house accommodation, and other necessities of life, which we find so often accompanies residence elsewhere.

Throughout the city there are several very nice commodious disused shops or dwellings, which, absolutely, without any expense, could be readily utilized as Chapels or Preaching Halls. The people, as I have shown, are naturally quite adverse to disturbance, therefore annoyance or trouble need not be looked for. Itinerating trips up country could be accomplished through all the surrounding districts, with a total absence of all those great hardships and toils which it would seem accompanies them in other parts; for on canal and river ply house boats, to travel in which need cause but little diminution in the ordinary comforts to be obtained at home.

For the last ten years, the China Inland Mission has been represented by two of its members with their wives, and within the last year a missionary, belonging to the English Free Methodist Church, established himself here. I believe the former has been able to enroll 40 or 50 members under their church. The Roman Catholics also have been established for a year or two, and it is said—with what accuracy I know not—that their church at this place has secured upwards of 600 converts.

During the time we have been deprived of steam communication with the outer world, we have had to fall back on couriers for sending and receiving mails. One system, which Mr. H.E. Hobson took the chief part in organizing, ran with the utmost regularity once a week for seven months. Unfortunately, however, the native establishments dispatching them too umbrage at some fines which had been inflicted, and refused to go any longer. The Customs then attempted to organize a special system for itself, but his after lingering for a week or two came to an untimely end. We were then constrained to patronize the regular native post, leaving this about every other day for Ningpo; taking, however, eight days to accomplish the journey between the two places instead of the four days in which the trip used to be done under the Hobson-Warren system; but notwithstanding this slight delay, our mails would appear to go and come with safety and regularity.

The North – China Herald and Supreme Court & Consular Gazette, April 29, 1879

Wenchow

WENCHOW.

Since last writing, the port has made considerable progress in the matter of trade.

The *Yung-ning*, running as she has with the support of the most influential natives, and trip after trip with improved and improving results, seems now to have almost attained to that point where if more offered it would of necessity become merely a tantalising superfluity. As has been often surmised, the impetus given by regular and speedy means of shipment has brought to the front export of all kinds.

The prospects for tea being shipped from this place for the Shanghai market would seem to be good, if we may believe the somewhat confident statement that a goodly quantity has already been promised to the steamers.

Wenchow

Since last writing, the port has made considerable progress in the matter of trade.

The *Yung-ning*, running as she has with the support of the most influential natives, and trip after trip with improved and improving results, seems now to have almost attained to that point where if more offered it would of necessity become merely a tantalizing superfluity. As has been often surmised, the impetus given by regular and speedy means of shipment has brought to the front export of all kinds.

The prospects for tea being shipped from this place for the Shanghai market would seem to be good, if we may believe the somewhat confident statement that a goodly quantity has already been promised to the steamers.

But apart from this, a batch of Ningpo men, connected with a new establishment at that place for the preparation of black tea, have arrived, and proceeded to the districts with a view of purchasing unfired leaf for treatment at Ningpo.

It so came about that one of the very few individuals who attempted last year to sell his tea here, but through some defect in the packing was not able to obtain the price he wanted from the only foreign buyer in Wenchow, shipped his produce to Shanghai on his own account, at which place he happened to effect a very remunerative sale. This has, of course, stimulated not only him, but his neighbours, and, if rumour speaks truly, will have some influence on the tea export this season. It will be recollected how impossible it has seemed in the past to overcome the opposition of Ningpo and obtain a market for opium imported direct. Beginning with one chest by the *Yung-ning*'s first trip, the importation has steadily increased, until last voyage seven were brought down. This demand is due in some measure to the favouring efforts of the *lekin* officials; and it is an undoubted fact that propositions have been made to them by certain native merchants here, which, if accepted, will result in the latter *guaranteeing to pass at least two chests of opium per diem*.

It is not improbable that some such arrangement may be come to; but be this as it may, the fact of such an offer being made (and it by no means implies any impracticable concession,) speaks volumes for the capabilities of the place.

Of course this large consumption can only be effected by taking over those districts at present supplied through Ningpo, but which are infinitely more easy of access from this.

Speaking broadly, the general trade returns for the past quarter will be found to show an increase of about four times the extent of those for the corresponding one last year; and there can be no doubt but that should things go on as they are at present, the next will be still more satisfactory.

One foreign merchant has opened a house here, but with this exception, natives are at present reaping all the benefits of the improved state of affairs.

We hear, strange to say from Chinese sources, that in the event of Indian tea competing strongly with Chinese leaf, Wenchow will come prominently forward as a market, its position and other advantages permitting of the necessary reduction in price being made. This is accounted for by the very marked difference in cost of transport as compared with Foochow, and the possibility when opening a new market of putting an end to certain "customs and squeezes" which are said to have attained the force of law in that port.

I give the last reason as it comes to me, and leave it to those of your readers better qualified to judge what is meant; merely adding that, as far as I can learn, official malfeasance is not particularly alluded to.

Apropos of officials, I would remind you that although Chinese are at present undoubtedly getting the full benefit of progressing trade here, as well as enjoying privileges which have been granted entirely in the hope of attracting foreigners and originally for them alone, still nothing has been done to invalidate those precautions which at the very outset were taken to prevent the creation of similar combinations and monopolies to those which have acted so disastrously on foreign merchants in Ningpo.

Workmen are busy converting a portion of one of the temples on Conquest Island into a temporary Consulate, which, however, I assume, will have to do duty until the port has attained sufficient importance to justify, first, the selection of a permanent site for the Settlement, and, secondly, the erection of one of those substantial mansions in which we are wont to find H.M.'s representatives housed.

I am still unable to report any man-of-war's arrival; but in case there should be uneasiness on our account, I may mention that the people continue to exhibit the same friendly and neighbourly disposition; and as the ducks have fled, I fear the only inducement we can offer our nautical friends is the very hearty welcome they are sure to receive, whenever the exigencies of the service permit of their looking in. (19th April)

The North – China Herald and Supreme Court & Consular Gazette, June 10, 1879

Wenchow

Wenchow

The disaster to the *Yungning,* says our correspondent, caused a great deal of consternation amongst the shippers, especially those teamen who had opend to get their leaf on the Shanghai market before either Hankow or Foochow opened. By shipping via Wenchow it will always be possible to get tea down at least a fortnight before the earliest could reach Foochow; and this fact, it is hoped, will eventually prove an additional attraction to our port.

WENCHOW.

The disaster to the *Yungning,* says our correspondent, caused a great deal of consternation amongst the shippers, especially those teamen who had hoped to get their leaf on the Shanghai market before either Hankow or Foochow opened. By shipping viâ Wênchow it will always be possible to get tea down at least a fortnight before the earliest could reach Foochow; and this fact, it is hoped, will eventually prove an additional attraction to our port.

When the first news of the fatal ending of the *Yungning's* "blow-up" reached us, it was feared that a marked effect would be visible on the native passenger lists of the future; but the fact of the engines being now put in charge of a foreigner has gone far to restore confidence, and as long as the engineer is retained on board all will probably go well.

When the first news of the fatal ending of the *Yungning*'s "blow-up" reached us, it was feared that a marked effect would be visible on the native passenger lists of the future; but the fact of the engines being now put in charge of a foreigner has gone far to restore confidence, and as long as the engineer is retained on board all will probably go well.

It certainly seems "penny wise and pound foolish" to trust the machinery to men who at best can only be persons who have proved themselves special adepts at shoveling coals or lubricating bearings; and that this confidence is misplaced, surely the fact of its being palpable to the Chinese themselves is tolerably good evidence.

If rumour speaks truly, another steamer is suffering from the want of that foreign supervision which as far as machinery is concerned seems so essential to the general welfare. However, as the evil is remedied in our direction, we have no reason to be solicitous about others.

The Customs House was the scene of some most unusual and lively transactions today, as the tea was being examined. The Chinese have not got into the routine as yet, and this leads to more bustle than will probably exist later on.

In consequence of the rain, the steamer's departure had to be postponed and the shipment, examination, &c., concentrated in the few hours of fine weather fortunately available.

The *Yungning* takes away about 1,200 chests and there are about 500 or 600 to follow on the lorcha. More is expected to arrive for the steamer on her next trip, and if that now sent turns out well, I fancy the shipments will be more continuous than is perhaps expected at present.

Things certainly look brighter for the place, and there can be no doubt but that much if not all of this improvement is due to the steps taken by the C. M. S. N. Co. Let us hope they will continue to preserve and prosper in, for them, so good a work.

Apropos of these good wishes, why are the Company so mild and conciliatory towards natives and yet so awfully hard and exacting towards foreigners? Freights charged to the latter are tremendously high. To give an instance, the other day a member of the community got down six ordinary chairs, value, say, about $7.5, and they were charged upwards of $5 freight. I may remark that not being the victim alluded to, no personal soreness prompts reference to the matter. Again, the passage money is surely out of all proportion to the services rendered and the rates demanded from Chinese.

Notwithstanding all this growl, however, and the cause of grumbling, foreigners here, one and all, wish well to the Company, and would be only too glad to do all that in them lies to further the view of those who, alone and unaided, have so effectively come forward to help our port in her struggles to obtain that position which must be hers some day. (30th May)

The North – China Herald and Supreme Court & Consular Gazette, December 31, 1879

Wenchow

WENCHOW.

We have actually had a little excitement here to vary the dull monotony of our humdrum life. It appears that the existence of a Hua Hui (Flowery Meeting) or, as we should call it, a lottery, conducted by Wênchow men at Cha Shan, a place about 30 *li* from this, was lately discovered by the Prefect, who immediately instructed the District Magistrate to seize the proprietors, some thirty in number. The Magistrate, accordingly, arrested the ringleaders on the night of the 15th instant, capturing among others a certain Chien-tsung or Captain, named Ying. The soldiers were exasperated at what they looked upon as an insult to their cloth, and, after spending the 16th in grumbling, they finally decided on taking active measures on the morning of the 17th, when they seized and closed all the city gates. By 11 a.m. the Taotai had succeeded in pacifying the soldiers to the extent of allowing the gates to be opened, and, as far as the public were concerned, the "great rebellion" was at an end.

Wenchow

We have actually had a little excitement here to vary the dull monotony of our humdrum life. It appears that the existence of a Hua Hui (Flowery Meeting) or, as we should call it, a lottery, conducted by Wenchow men at Cha Shan, a place about 30 li from this, was lately discovered by the Prefect, who immediately instructed the District Magistrate to seize the proprietors, some thirty in number. The Magistrate, accordingly, arrested the ringleaders on the night of the 15th instant, capturing among others a certain Chien-tsung or Captain named Ying. The soldiers were exasperated at what they looked upon as an insult to their cloth, and, after spending the 16th in grumbling, they finally decided on taking active measures on the morning of the 17th, when they seized and closed all the city gates. By 11 a.m. the Taotai had succeeded in pacifying the soldiers to the extent of allowing the gates to be opened, and, as far as the public were concerned, the "great rebellion" was at an end. Rumour says, however, that the Chentai is far from satisfied with the action of the civil authorities in seizing one of his subordinates without his permission, and that both parties have petitioned the higher officers at Hangchow on the subject.

The inhabitants, peaceful by nature, seemed to consider the matter as not very serious, and, in fact treated it as rather a joke. Still most of the shops were practically closed all day and the crowds of people wandering about without any apparent object showed that something unusual was "up." No disturbances took place, however, and the roughs contented themselves, during the time that the gates were shut, with firing volleys of chaff at those who, having urgent business outside the city, rushed frantically from gate to gate, vainly seeking exit.

Wen Taotai, who has for some months been doing duty as Judge at Hangchow, has returned, and the Acting Taotai Liang left on the 20th by the gunboat *Fu Po*.

The river here is well stocked with wild fowl, and the Sui An river, about twelve miles off, is said to teem with ducks and geese, while even swan are to be found “rari nantes in gurgite vasto.” What a chance for a sporting chaasze to combine business with pleasure in the off-season!

The China Merchants' Co.'s steamer *Yung-ning* now runs regularly between this port and Shanghai, making the round-trip in twelve days. Thus, by staying over one trip, an energetic chaasze would be able to interview the native merchants, to make an excursion into the Tea district, about three days' journey from this by boat, and would yet have ample time for some good sport amongst the ducks and geese before returning to this desk with his lungs filled with ozone and his brain enriched by the knowledge of the fact that it is impossible to appreciate the capabilities of a place until you try them. *Verbum Sap.*

The weather here is delightful, though hardly cold enough to be seasonable. (22nd December)

The North – China Herald and Supreme Court & Consular Gazette, January 22, 1880

Wenchow

Wenchow

As might be expected there is little or no news here. Owing to the absence of produce and the approach of the Chinese New Year business is somewhat slack, indeed the winter bamboo shoot will be the only article on the market. I am told, however, that in spite of this our fortnightly steamer continues to take away a full cargo every trip. After New Year the spring bamboo shoots will be in season and the second crop of oranges will be shipped, so in the course of another month a somewhat brisker trade may be looked forward to.

Our oranges, the bulk of which are destined for Tientsin, do not ripen much before the middle of November, consequently only the more forward fruit can be picked and shipped in time to catch the last steamer from Shanghai to the north. The remainder, or so called second crop is stored on wooden floors and covered over with straw, by which process the fruit is preserved until the opening of the Peiho permits of its shipment.

We are still without a doctor and seem likely to remain so. The pecuniary inducements are, I fear, small, but the variety of diseases, particularly those of the eye, which are daily brought to one's notice, would seem to promise a grand field to the philanthropic medicus.

For the last month the weather has been fine and not too cold, but now a change seems to be impending. At the present moment there is an unsettled appearance about the sky that would have puzzled Old Moore himself. (14th January)

WENCHOW.

As might be expected there is little or no news here. Owing to the absence of produce and the approach of the Chinese New Year business is somewhat slack, indeed the winter bamboo shoot will be the only article on the market. I am told, however, that in spite of this our fortnightly steamer continues to take away a full cargo every trip. After New Year the spring bamboo shoots will be in season and the second crop of oranges will be shipped, so in the course of another month a somewhat brisker trade may be looked forward to.

Our oranges, the bulk of which are destined for Tientsin, do not ripen much before the middle of November, consequently only the more forward fruit can be picked and shipped in time to catch the last steamers from Shanghai to the north. The remainder, or so called second crop is stored on wooden floors and covered over with straw, by which process the fruit is preserved until the opening of the Peiho permits of its shipment.

The North – China Herald and Supreme Court & Consular Gazette, February 19, 1880

Wenchow

WENCHOW.

The New Year festivities are over and the inhabitants of the so-called "Cathedral City" have put away their store-clothes till next year. The rejoicings were conducted with quietness and decorum, the proper quantity of nastiness was eaten, and the usual amount of tomtomming and fireworks was indulged in; in fact, everything was done in accordance with "olo custom." On New Year's Eve most of the shops in the principal thoroughfares were prettily illuminated with coloured lamps, and bonfires were lighted in nearly all the streets of the city and suburbs. That this dangerous amusement did not result in a general conflagration is simply miraculous, and the immunity is by all right-thinking persons attributed to the special intervention of Zen Tien Ta Ti, the great Lord of Blazing Heaven, or some other benevolent deity, though here, as elsewhere, scoffers are to be found who point to the saturated condition of everything or to some other such commonplace reason. Now all that remains of the

Wenchow

The New Year festivities are over and the inhabitants of the so-called "Cathedral City" have put away their store-clothes till next year. The rejoicings were conducted with quietness and decorum, the proper quantity of nastiness was eaten, and the usual amount of tomtomming and fireworks was indulged in; in fact, everything was done in accordance with "olo custom." On New Year's Eve most of the shops in the principal thoroughfares were prettily illuminated with coloured lamps, and bonfires were lighted in nearly all the streets of the city and suburbs. That this dangerous amusement did not result in a general conflagration is simply miraculous, and the immunity is by all right-thinking persons attributed to the special intervention of Zen Tien Ta Ti, the great Lord of Blazing Heaven, or some other benevolent deity, though here, as elsewhere, scoffers aer to be found who point to the saturated condition of everything or to some other such commonplace reason. Now all that remains of the great annual festival is, on the part of the natives, a general disinclination to return to labour, and in the streets a grand display of placards, once bright coloured and gay, but now sadly dimmed and washed out by the unremitting exertions of Jupiter Pluvius.

During the holidays the gunvessel *Chao-Wu* was in port and dressed ship in true man-o'-war fashion, while the merchant marine was ably represented by that noble steamer the *Yungning*. But alas, the apparently innocent name of the latter vessel awakens in the breast of the Wenchow exile the sad recollection that the China Merchants' Company have raised their fares, and that a trip to

Shanghai now costs the same number of hard-earned Mexicans as a voyage from Shanghai to Hongkong. This is indeed unkind, nay more it is unfair, especially considering the accommodation, or rather want of it, on board the *Yungning*, which is only made bearable by the extreme courtesy of her commander. There are also rumours of increased rates for native passengers, which it is to be hoped are without foundation. Of course such a change would not directly affect the foreign community, but it is the general opinion that it would be suicide on the part of the Company, and most injurious to the prospects of the port. Neither the trade nor the passenger traffic by steamer are yet firmly established here, and, although the advantages of employing foreign bottoms are beginning to be appreciated, all that the native merchants have hitherto done has been to put out feelers in the shape of small ventures. It is, therefore, generally to be feared that any immediate increase in the rates of freight or passage would arouse all the conservative feelings of the shippers and cause them to revert to the good old slow and sure junk trade, patronized by their ancestors from time immemorial.

The cold weather has left us and with it have gone most of the ducks and geese. A general moistness prevails and umbrellas and waterproofs are being patched up in anticipation of the regular spring deluge. (14th February)

The North - China Herald and Supreme Court & Consular Gazette, November 8, 1881

Wenchow

WENCHOW.

The *Yung-ning* arrived later than was expected. She was delayed by want of coolies to unload, all those needful aids to commerce being in hiding on her arrival, in consequence of the arrival at the same time of the Governor of Chêh-kiang on a tour of inspection. The coolies fearing impressment and poor pay retired for the time being from public life. Pirate news is in course of preparation. It does not promise fair for Huang. Five hundred Hupeh braves have been landed on the coast of the southern part of Tai-chou, and the same number on the coast of the northern part of Wenchow, which forces, with a fleet of gunboats, must bring his adventures to a close. It is said he is suffering from a wound, but is undismayed.

Wenchow

The *Yung-ning* arrived later than was expected. She was delayed by want of coolies to unload, all those needful aids to commerce being in hiding on her arrival, in consequence of the arrival at the same time of the Governor of Cheh-kiang on a tour of inspection. The coolies fearing impressment and poor pay retired for the time being from public life. Pirate news is in course of preparation. It does not promise fair for Huang. Five hundred Hupeh braves have been landed on the coast of the southern part of Taichou, and the same number on the coast of the northern part of Wenchow, which forces, with a fleet of gunboats, must bring his adventures to a close. It is said he is suffering from a wound, but is undismayed.

The North – China Herald and Supreme Court & Consular Gazette, April 22, 1882

Dr. Macgowan's Medical Report on Wenchow

Dr. Macgowan's Medical Report on Wenchow

Dr. Macgowan in his Medical Report on Wenchow has, to use an American expression, spread himself out over the wholes subject of the health, pestilence, famines, and topography of the place. Thirty-six closely printed pages have not sufficed to relieve him of his whole burden of knowledge, for at the beginning of his paper he says that he reserves the medical topography for another occasion; but so varied are the matters of which he has treated, and so successfully have they been jumbled together, that we should scarcely have missed such a trifle as that from his paper. He begins with a description of the district in which Wenchow is situated, and passing on to the climate he draws a picture of it which ought to induce invalids to give it a trial. It possesses, he says, the climate of Nice without a mistral. It offers tiger-hunting to the vigorous, as it appears that those creatures are as troublesome to the people there, as they are under the Equator or on the banks of the Amoor. But unfortunately neither patients nor sportsmen are attracted to the port, as there is no suitable accommodation for them. In propitious seasons the Wenchow district seems to be a happy and smiling laud, but it has its times of trial, when it is subject to floods from the mountains, cyclones from the ocean, and storms that cause of famine and pestilence. A record is given of the storms, floods, droughts, and famines which have occurred in the district and the maritime portions of Chekiang and part of Fohkien, from the year 291 down to 1858. Further on there is a table giving a record of epidemics in the province of Chekiang from the year 95 down to 1864; which is followed by an account of some of them. But instructive as these doubtless are, we prefer Dr. Macgowan on epidemic frenzies to the same learned gentleman

DR. MACGOWAN'S MEDICAL REPORT ON WENCHOW.

DR. MACGOWAN in his Medical Report on Wenchow has, to use an American expression, spread himself out over the whole subject of the health, pestilence, famines, and topography of the place. Thirty-six closely printed pages have not sufficed to relieve him of his whole burden of knowledge, for at the beginning of his paper he says that he reserves the medical topography for another occasion; but so varied are the matters of which he has treated, and so successfully have they been jumbled together, that we should scarcely have missed such a trifle as that from his paper. He begins with a description of the district in which Wenchow is situated, and passing on to the climate he draws a picture of it which ought to on leprosy or Asiatic cholera. The story of the delusions to which all classes of Chinese have yielded themselves up from time to time, is more entertaining to the general reader than a treatise on infection, or fevers, or smallpox. Not that there are not little passages in the midst of the Doctor's learned disquisitions which are entertaining enough. For instance there is the account of Pie Chiao, the earliest Medicine Prince to whom a temple was erected. This physician lived BC 468 to 440 and he had the good fortune to meet a spirit who advised him to take a certain medicine daily for a month. This he did, and became so spiritualized and sharpsighted that he was able "to see through a stone wall," and consequently by his vision to penetrate the human system and observe the viscera. Modern physicians can see on further through a stone wall than can other men, and can get no nearer observation of the viscera than an inspection of the condition of the patient's tongue. This highly gifted practitioner receiver 20,000 mow of laud as a fee on one occasion, and remembering this, and the distinction which his talents and skill had won for him, we are scarcely surprised to learn that the Court physician procured his assassination soon afterwards. Quoting from a work published in 1876, by a benevolent gentleman of Chaug-chau, Kiangsi, Dr. Macgowan states that periods of frenzy occurred in the writer's part of the country in 1464, 1529, 1596, 1657, and 1753, and this leads to an amusing account of the various sorcerers from which the Chinese have suffered, and of the remedies which they have employed, down to the famous queuecutting craze of 1876. We are then introduced to the Supreme Pontiff of Taoism, who is applied to by the people. Dr. Macgowan says that the word demon in Chinese is to be understood, not in the medieval, but, in the classical sense but we cannot recall at the moment an classical writer who attributed to demons, familiars, or guardians the malicious or evil propensities which distinguish the demons of this land in an especial degree. The doings of the Taoist Pope are thus described:

> This hereditary potentate who is supposed to exercise authority over demons appear on occasions like the present in an official capacity: he met the current emergency by the reissue of a charm or amulet which he had used against a cholera epidemic in 1862. There was scarcely a house door that was not protected by the charm, hardly an individual who did not wear the amulet under cap or in sleeve. In times of excitement, particularly when disease is rife, every house door will be found to have a charm, and foreigners may thereby know that the public mind is in a state of ferment either from bodily or mental suffering.

Plates of the above charms are given, and Dr. Macgowan describes their nature, and translates the central characters on one of them, which is less satisfactory than if he had rendered into plain English the charm which is supposed to be in the six demon characters on the sides, and of which he merely says that they are said to mean urgent and imperative commands. Dr. Macgowan says he made the acquaintance of his Holiness when he was on a visit to the faithful at the coast from his seat on Dragon Tiger mountain, where he lives a retired life surrounded by innumerable sealed jars in which he keeps his demons and the imps he has captured. Dr. Macgowan found him to be a simple-minded, unpretentious character. The whole subject of these delusions is treated at great length, and the Doctor, either warmed by righteous wrath, or by the theme, indulges himself occasionally in language that is not strictly professional. We can understand, and almost honour, his indignation at a literary graduate who threw the inhabitants of Wenchow into a panic, by saying he had discovered that the city was to be invaded by a fleet of vessels filled with foreign women, of hideous mien and with long carrotty beards. The Doctor did well to be angry at this, and some may think he has not gone too far in calling the libeller of foreign women a wily scoundrel and a scalawag. Still the use of such epithets is a departure from the calm philosophical spirit which characterizes the rest of his discourse. There is room for regret in this; and if he should again wish to release himself for a moment or two from the restraints of formalism, we do not know that we can do better than recommend him to read the Medical Report which follows his own. There he will find both the death rate last year and the proportion of deaths among females in this Settlement airily ascribed to chance. We cannot attempt to criticize the medical part of Dr.Macgowan's report; that will be done no doubt with frankness by this professional friends. But we may mention that his conclusions as to the nonexistence of colour-blindness among the Chinese are not shared by some, at least, of the doctors here.

The North - China Herald and Supreme Court & Consular Gazette, June 2, 1882

Dr. Macgowan on Wenchow

DR. MACGOWAN ON WENCHOW.

To the Editor of the

NORTH-CHINA DAILY NEWS.

SIR,—I observe in Dr. Macgowan's Medical Report for Wênchow recently issued, that I am incorrectly put down as giving the average daily consumption of opium at 4½ mace and Mr. Douthwaite at 3.2 mace. The figures should be transposed, which a reference to Mr. Douthwaite's table on the opposite page renders apparent. My views elsewhere published do not substantiate this high average.

Yours,

J. DUDGEON.

Peking, 24th May.

Dr. Macgowan on Wenchow

To the Editor of the

North-China Daily News

SIR,—I observe in Dr. Macgowan's Medical Report for Wenchow recently issued, that I am incorrectly put down as giving the average daily consumption of opium at mace and Mr. Douthwaite at 3.2 mace. The figures should be transposed, which a reference to Mr. Douthwaite's table on the opposite page renders apparent. My views elsewhere published do not substantiate this high average.

Yours,

J. Dudgeon.

Peking, 24th May.

The North – China Herald and Supreme Court & Consular Gazette, December 6, 1882

Wenchow

(From Our Own Correspondent)

Wenchow

(From Our Own Correspondent)

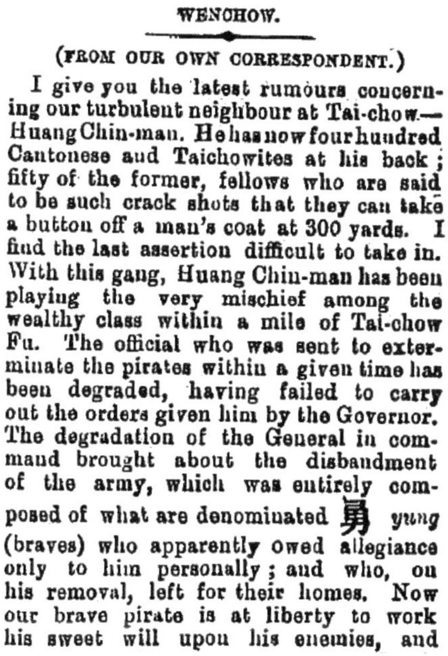

WENCHOW.

(FROM OUR OWN CORRESPONDENT.)

I give you the latest rumours concerning our turbulent neighbour at Tai-chow.—Huang Chin-man. He has now four hundred Cantonese and Taichowites at his back; fifty of the former, fellows who are said to be such crack shots that they can take a button off a man's coat at 300 yards. I find the last assertion difficult to take in. With this gang, Huang Chin-man has been playing the very mischief among the wealthy class within a mile of Tai-chow Fu. The official who was sent to exterminate the pirates within a given time has been degraded, having failed to carry out the orders given him by the Governor. The degradation of the General in command brought about the disbandment of the army, which was entirely composed of what are denominated 勇 *yung* (braves) who apparently owed allegiance only to him personally; and who, on his removal, left for their homes. Now our brave pirate is at liberty to work his sweet will upon his enemies, and

I give you the latest rumours concerning our turbulent neighbor at Tai-chow Huang Chin-man. He has now four hundred Cantonese and Taichowites at his back; fifty of the former, fellows who are said to be such crack shots that they can take a button off a man's coat at 300 yards. I find the last assertion difficult to take in. With this gang, Huang Chin-man has been playing the very mischief among the wealthy class within a mile of Tai-chow Fu. The official who was sent to exterminate the pirates within a given time has been degraded, having failed to carry out the orders given him by the Governor. The degradation of the General in command brought about the disbandment of the army, which was entirely composed of what are denominated (braves) 勇 *yung* who apparently owed allegiance only to him personally; and who, on his removal, left for their homes. Now our brave pirate is at liberty to work his sweet will upon his vengeance. But if the rumour concerning the Cantonese be ture, is it not very significant? In my opinion the government will have something more than a mere handful of pirates to deal with ere long. The presence of southerns at Taichow strikes me that the movement is fast becoming of political importance. The history of past revolution is this country teaches us that they all had such a beginning, and among the same class.

There is a dearth of local news down here at present. The only thing that has occurred which may be of interest to you is as follows:—A military official at Foochow had two wives, upon the younger of whom he lavished all his wealth and affection. The “boss” wife did not take this kindly, and determined to make things hot for her rival. She did so, and made life for her, at least in that locality, unbearable. The young lady determined to elope. Selecting two soldiers to accompany her, she dressed herself as a brave, and with her companions came to Wenchow, where they put up at an inn near the west gate. They remained there three days, during which time she was afraid to speak in the presence of strangers for fear of betraying her sex. The people of the house remarked her strange conduct and concluded there was something wrong, so reported the matter to the District Magistrate, who had the parties arrested and brought before him. The matter has not yet been fully settled; in the meantime the three runaways are in durance vile awaiting the verdict.

The weather lately has been simply abominable, warm and wretched. To-day, however, is cold, and our sporting friends are rubbing their hands gleefully, anticipating big bags.

The officials are making anxious enquiries about our recent visitor, the comet, being anxious to know if it is not ominous of down-fall or other calamity to this on some other nation. (28th Nov., 1882)

The North - China Herald and Supreme Court & Consular Gazette, February 28, 1883

Earthquakes in China in 1882

EARTHQUAKES IN CHINA IN 1882.

To the Editor of the

NORTH-CHINA DAILY NEWS.

SIR,—Having prepared a record of the earthquakes that occurred during the past year in China, with an account of their accompanying phenomena, and apprehensive that the seismial list is far from being complete, I beg through your columns to solicit the assistance of observers. The list, omitting details is as follows :—

March 19th—Formosa, J. N. Hardy.
May 27th—Formosa, Honkong papers.
June 3rd—Foochow, *Foochow Herald.*
July 24th—Chungking, Pére Dechevren.
August 11th—Ningpo, *Shênpau.*

Earthquakes in China in 1882

To the Editor of the

North-China Daily News

Sir,—Having prepared a record of the earthquakes that occurred during the past year in China, with an account of their accompanying phenomena, and apprehensive that the seismial list is far from being complete, I beg through your columns to solicit the assistance of observers. The list, omitting details is as follows:

March 10th–Formosa, J. N. Hardy.

May 27th–Formosa, *Honkong papers.*

June 3rd–Foochow, *Foochow Herald.*

July 24th–Chungking, Pere Dechevren

August 11th–Ningpo, *Shenpau.*

September 12th–Wenchow, Natives.

22nd–Amoy, *Amoy Gazette.*

23rd–Ningpo, *Shenpau.*

October 7th–Foochow, *Foochow Herald.*

14th–Taiyuen, General Mesney, *Daily News.*

December 1st–Shenchau, Imperial Edict.

9th–Formosa and Mainland, Hongkong, Amoy and Foochow papers, T. W. Kingsmill and Consul Jamieson.

The accounts for the most part are defective, particularly as regards precise time, direction and accompanying phenomena. Being desirous of transmitting the record to Professor Zuck, in time for his Annual Earthquake Record. I beg an early response to this solicitation.

Respectfully,

D. J. Macgowan.

Wenchow, 17th February

The North – China Herald and Supreme Court & Consular Gazette, May 30, 1884

Wenchow

(From A Correspondent)

Wenchow

(From A Correspondent)

An employé of the British Consulate at Wenchow came to his death a few days ago by falling from the upper part of a pagoda. He was attempting to rob the nest of a Brahmin kite, (which was in an orifice outside of the pagoda) and was attacked by the parent bird which by its wings and beak compelled him to act on the defensive, and while fighting the bird with one hand and supporting himself with the other he fell, and survived the shock but a short time. (22nd May)

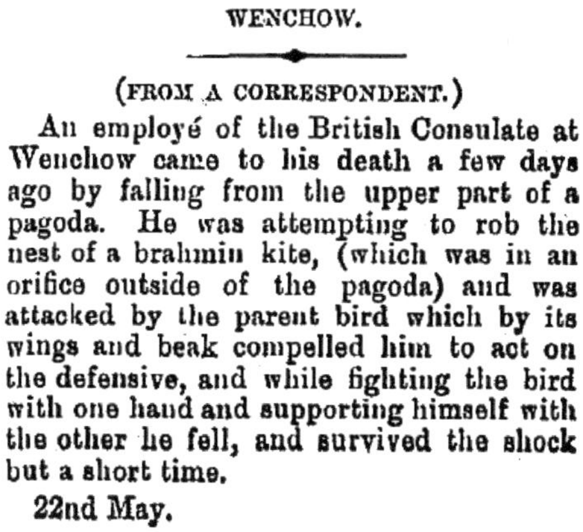

WENCHOW.

(FROM A CORRESPONDENT.)

An employé of the British Consulate at Wenchow came to his death a few days ago by falling from the upper part of a pagoda. He was attempting to rob the nest of a brahmin kite, (which was in an orifice outside of the pagoda) and was attacked by the parent bird which by its wings and beak compelled him to act on the defensive, and while fighting the bird with one hand and supporting himself with the other he fell, and survived the shock but a short time.

22nd May.

The North - China Herald and Supreme Court & Consular Gazette, September 12, 1884

Wenchow

(From Our Own Correspondent)

WENCHOW.

(FROM OUR OWN CORRESPONDENT.)

The *Yungning*, on entering Wenchow river, observed some straggling poles connected with strawropes, the remains of a vast number that were driven into the sands to prevent the enemy's vessels entering. Had they resisted the current they would have been as useless as fish-stakes. A proposition that was made to choke the channel has been abandoned, but not until a panic was created by a proclamation requiring every family to bring for the mandarins a basket of stones. Foreigners feel as secure as if they had an ironclad for protection; the authorities being so very solicitous for their safety. Some vagabonds threw missiles, and others cried "kill, kill," but they were bambooed, and the excitement that followed the news from Foochow passed quietly away.

7th September.

Wenchow

(From Our Own Correspondent)

The *Yungning*, on entering Wenchow river, observed some straggling poles connected with strawropes, the remains of a vast number that were driven into the sands to prevent the enemy's vessels entering. Had they resisted the current they would have been as useless as fish-stakes. A proposition that was made to choke the channel has been abandoned, but not until a panic was created by a proclamation requiring every family to bring for the mandarins a basket of stones. Foreigners feel as secure as if they had an ironclad for protection; the authorities being so very solicitous for their safety. Some vagabonds threw missiles, and others cried "kill, kill," but they were bambooed, and the excitement that followed the news from Foochow passed quietly away. (7th September)

The North – China Herald and Supreme Court & Consular Gazette, October 15, 1884

No Title

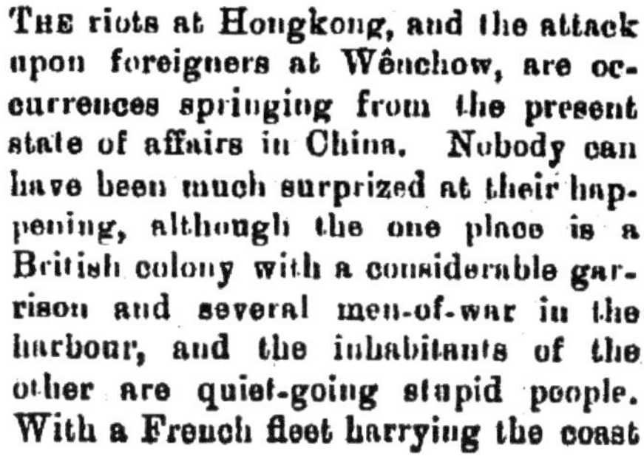
THE riots at Hongkong, and the attack upon foreigners at Wênchow, are occurrences springing from the present state of affairs in China. Nobody can have been much surprized at their happening, although the one place is a British colony with a considerable garrison and several men-of-war in the harbour, and the inhabitants of the other are quiet-going stupid people. With a French fleet harrying the coast

No Title

The riots at Hongkong, and the attack upon foreigners at Wenchow, are occurrences springing from the present have been much surprised at their happening, although the one place is a British colony with a considerable garrison and several men-of-war in the other are quiet-going stupid people. With a French fleet harrying the coast and Formosa, the ignorant people on the mainland will always be liable to sudden gusts of passion, and encouraged by some of better position, they will make indiscriminate attacks upon the foreigners who are within their reach. The Chinese laboring classes in and near the other Treaty ports are probably not more intelligent than those who last week rose upon the foreigners at Wenchow. Nor is it likely that the knowledge of foreigners which a Hongkong coolie has acquired, enables him to discriminate between Frenchmen, whose Government is making war upon his country, and other alien people. In the eyes of the uneducated Chinese all foreigners are pretty much alike, and all are, we should say, looks upon as inimical to China at the present moment, Nor is it unlikely that some of the educated classes in the districts where foreigners are living are taking advantage of their ignorant countrymen. To the gentry and literati, and to the priesthood, the presence of foreigners is, we know, thoroughly distasteful, while to the officials of every degree a more malignant feeling may be attributed without doing great injustice to their order. There are no doubt exceptions, but we are writing of the official class in general. We believe that as yet no particulars have been received here of the manner in which the riots at Wenchow originated, but the accounts that have reached us show that everything must have been well planned beforehand. Now, that could scarcely be done by a crowd composed of such materials as that which attacked the foreign residents in Wenchow. The coolies and rowdies were no doubt assisted by men in a better position in rioters proceeded to act in the manner usual to mobs in all parts of the world, which start upon and act upon a prearranged programme. That is, we think, the account of the Wenchow riots will draw, and if, unfortunately, any further disturbances of the same kind occur in other places, we shall be prepared to find that the mob has been incited into riot by those privileged classes of their countrymen who have always been most hostile to foreigners.

Judging from an article in a recent number of the *Daily Press*, we should say that there was a very strong opinion among the community of Hongkong that the strikes and riots which lately occurred there were assisted and controlled by some Chinese of position. Our contemporary says that there was a very general belief in the colony that certain wire-pullers, who stood carefully in the background, prolonged, if they did not excite, the strikes and riots. Further, our contemporary states that it was generally reported among the lower class natives that the troubles ended because the leading Chinese had "so willed it," and that the Tung Wah Hospital, or some of the Guilds, or a mixture of both, have been "first inciting to disorder, and then usurping the functions of government." The last charge refers to an attempt made by a number of Chinese of standing to dictate to the Government what it should do. These persons began by modestly desiring the Colonial Secretary to meet them at the Tung Wah Hospital in order to discuss the situation, and when they found themselves obliged to carry their suggestions and opinions to the Government offices, some of them assumed a tone to the Secretary which was scarcely respectful. The *Daily Press* also says that the proposals made by some of the Chinese at the meeting, and the past actions of the Tung Wah Committee, are evidence that a portion of the Chinese residents of position desired to usurp the functions of government. No doubt that was their intention, and we see the same desire shown in the attempt of the Kuangtung shopkeepers in this Settlement to obtain the sanction of the Municipal Council to the formation of a Volunteer Corps among their assistants and dependents. Both the Hongkong and the Shanghai Chinese with to interfere in matters which appertain solely to foreigners, and the feelings which prompt them are probably not very different from those of the literati and gentry.

The professions of goodwill towards non-belligerent foreigners which are made in the Edicts from the Throne, and the proclamations of officials, do not carry much assurance to us when we see that wherever an outbreak of the populace takes place the local authorities become utterly useless. The demoralization that fell upon the mandarins of Foochow and Wenchow will fall upon their class at every port where foreigners are attacked. Residents at the ports must be protected by foreign men-of-war until the return of peace. It will not do to subject other places to the risk which was incurred at Wenchow. Foreigners will require to exercise vigilance as well as prudence, for there is one most noticeable thing in the accounts of the riots at Wenchow in the fact that, almost up to the moment when the mob begun the attack, there had been nothing in the demeanour of the people to excite suspicion, and that although many Chinese must have known what was intended by the mob, none of them gave any hint of what was going to happen to the community. The lesson to be learned from that is, that we must rely entirely on the protection of our own Governments and on our own efforts. The present state of affairs has apparently already weakened the authority of the mandarins, and law will be less respected and the disorderly classes become border as the war continues. It is difficult to say whether the success or defeat of the Chinese arms would expose foreign communities to most danger from the mob; but anyway foreign authorities are bound to do everything in their power to protect their people from outrage. The agreement among the great Western nations for the protection of foreigners in China, which was come to last year, surely confers ample powers on their representatives out here; and we hope they will use them. The Chinese fleet is useless for the protection of foreigners in China, which was come to last year, surely confers ample powers on their representatives out here; and we hope they will ues them. The Chinese fleet is useless for the protection of foreigners, even when, as at Wenchow, most of the residents are in Government employment; for at that six out of the thirteen foreign residents at the beginning of this year were Customs employer.

The North – China Herald and Supreme Court & Consular Gazette, October 15, 1884

Riot at Wenchow

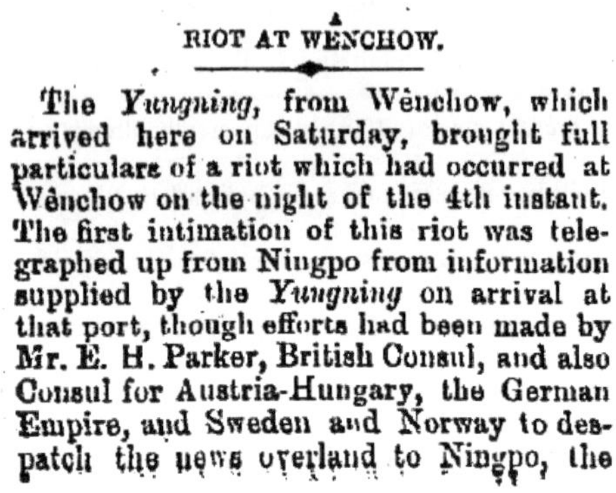

RIOT AT WÊNCHOW.

The *Yungning*, from Wênchow, which arrived here on Saturday, brought full particulars of a riot which had occurred at Wênchow on the night of the 4th instant. The first intimation of this riot was telegraphed up from Ningpo from information supplied by the *Yungning* on arrival at that port, though efforts had been made by Mr. E. H. Parker, British Consul, and also Consul for Austria-Hungary, the German Empire, and Sweden and Norway to despatch the news overland to Ningpo, the

Riot at Wenchow

The *Yungning*, from Wenchow, which arrived here on Saturday, brought full particulare of a riot which had occurred at Wenchow on the night of 4th instant. The first intimation of this riot was telegraphed up from Ningpo from information supplied by the *Yungning* on arrival at that port though efforts had been made by Mr. E. H. Parker, British Consul, and also Consul for Austria-Hungary, the German Empire, and Sweden and Norway to dispatch the news overland to Ningpo, the nearest port; but the messengers refused to go, or according to anther report, were forcibly prevented from going. Wenchow has always been considered a quiet place, the natives appearing too stupid to be able to cause any rows or excitement, and in fact this newly opened port has been considered the most dead-and-alive place of all the open ports of China. A foreign steamer, the *Yungning*, pays the port a visit about once in eight days, and on very rare occasions indeed does a foreign man-of-war put in an appearance, such a visit being considered quiet an event in the history of place. It is quiet a considerable time since a foreign man-of-war paid Wenchow a visit, it being an out-of-the-way place, and, probably owing to the reputation of the inhabitants, the various naval commanders have neglected to send one of their vessels there, though under the circumstances of the riot we are recording it is quiet possible that the more frequent visits of men-of-war would have had no effect on preventing the disturbances. Opinions are divided as to whether the riot was a well-planned scheme, or whether it originated on the spur of the moment, though the subsequent actions of the rioters incline us to the belief that it was planed; be this as it may, the rioters acted more like wild beasts than human beings throughout the night of Saturday and Sunday morning-the 4th and 5th instant-and their demoniacal fury gathered strength as the work of destruction proceeded. From several sources we have obtained the following particulars. The first intimation of the riot came upon the foreign residents "like a flash of lightning" as one correspondent informs us. Everything had been quiet, the people had performed their daily occupations, and not the slightest sign of ant ill-feeling was noticed, by even the most observant, and such an event as a riot never entered the thoughts of any of the residents; but they were greatly deceived. On Saturday evening, at about 9 o'clock, the Rev. W. E. Soothill of the English Methodist Free Church Mission conducted his usual prayer meeting with the ordinary converts, at his chapel on a street in the western part of the city, apparently with closed doors. About an hour before this, a crowd of rowdies had congregated in front of the building, idling about. They began to talk among themselves and then wanted to enter the place by force. A proclamation had been issued by the authorities promising protection to foreigners, and this was shown to the crowd. Instead of being overawed, and while the services were being held, some one went and kicked at the doors of the chapel; and the crowd outside becoming more demonstrative, Mr. Soothill sent a man out to enquire the cause. This man was the gate-keeper, and on his opening the door, the noise-makers dispersed. Again the noise commenced, and again the gate-keeper expostulated with the crowd. This occurred three times, and on its repetition, the missionary went himself to the gate and arrested one of the rioters. This act was like pouring oil on the fire. The mob, by this time considerably re-inforced, attempted to rescue their comrade and made a more determined attack on the mission premises, which they surrounded, and in about ten minutes they succeeded in bursting into the building from the rear, but not till the converts had escaped. Having obtained possession, they immediately proceeded to set fire to the buildings, and in a few short minutes the place was in flames. Having wreaked their vengeance here, they next proceeded to the residence of the Rev. Mr. Jackson, who is connected with the China Inland Mission. They attacked his house, and in a very short time it was in flames too. While this was going on, the foreigners living in the city were making efforts to escape to an island in the river, several hundred yards distant. Those living in the city consisted of Messrs. E. H. Grimani, S. J. Hanisch, Dr Macgowan and the Revs. Stott, Soothill, Jackson and Paccare, the latter an Italian priest in charge of the Roman Catholic Mission. The British Consul, and Messrs. Martin and Cunniffy of the Customs and Mr. Compton of the Consulate, and his family, lived on Pagoda Island, while Mr. Sharnhorst, also of the Customs, was stationed at the Lower Anchorage, eleven miles distant from the city. Mr. E. H. Grimani, Clerk-in-charge of the Customs, and Mr. S. J. Hanisch, clerk, were together, and they proceeded escape by the rear of the building one of them lived in. They scaled the walls of the city and succeeded in finding a sampan into which they got and pushed off into the stream. They were fortunate in doing so, for the boat had no sooner got into the stream, than the mob caught sight of them and rushed down to the water's edge after them, yelling and shouting like furies. If these foreigners had fallen into their hands, there is no doubt their lives would have been sacrificed. The Congsulate is on the island and the foreigners made tracks for it, and while they were doing so, the mob were proceeding with the work of destruction, the foreigners from their place of comparative safety viewing the proceedings. After the two Protestant Mission premises had been burnt, the rioters went to the Roman Catholic Mission and destroyed that; Mr. Stott's house was the next to go, and after that his chapel. Mr. Stott was at home, and the mob vented their fury on him also. Being a cripple, having lost one of his legs, and walking on crutches, he had a hard job to escape, and it was only with the assistance of Dr. D. J. Macgowan of the Customs, who is, we believe, over seventy years of age, that he got away. After destroying the whole of the various. Missionary premises, it was thought that the mob would desist. Not so, however, for the fury of the rioters only made them all the more eager for a still further exercise of their destructive capabilities. True, there was a lull, but it was only while the mob gathered greater strength, and the foreigners on the island heard murmur growing louder and longer, ending in a yell which appears to have been the signal for an onslaught on the residence of Mr. Grimani, which was soon in a blaze. A few minutes later, and Mr. Hanisch's place was in flames. So far as the city was concerned, this finished the work of the mob, who again rested from their labours. Having somewhat recovered from the fatigue, they again sallied forth and this time the Custom House became the centre of attraction. This place they sacked, but as it was in a temple they did not burn it. They contented themselves with tearing down the ceilings and pulling up the floors. They collected furniture, and all the official documents they cold lay hands upon, and made a big bonfire of them. Still they were not satisfied. They still wanted more work to do, and in their implacable and demoniacal rage, they tried to get to the island and still further continue the destruction. But they did not succeed, as the fates were against them. They tried to obtain boats, and failing these constructed rafts. One account is that they were unable to reach the island owing to the wind and tide. Had the mob succeeded in reaching the island, there is no telling what the result might have been, as the foreigners had but slight means of defence. When the residents saw the mob constructing rafts, they got into boats and went down the river, all except the Consul, who dressed himself in his Consular uniform and awaited the rowdies. The foreigners on the mainland had gone to the mainland had gone to the Yamens for protection, but the Italian priest did not turn up till two days afterwards, as he had been in hiding somewhere. The mandarins, as soon as quiet was restored, escorted the Reproduced with permission of the copyright owner. Further reproduction prohibited without permission. Foreigners at their Yamens, to Pagoda Island. The reason the mob could obtain no boats was that the authorities had ordered them some time previously to go over to the right bank of the river. The foreigners who went own the river afterwards returned under the protection of a Chinese war junk.

The *Yungning* arrived at Wenchow lower anchorage on as Sunday afternoon and proceed to Wenchow on Monday morning. She left again on Thursday when all appeared to be quite, though the authorities considered it advisable to station a guard of soldiers round the Customs officials.

Such had been the rage and fury of the mob during the riot, that they burnt two dogs belonging to foreigners, and tried to do the same with Dr. Macgowan's pony, but the animal succeeded in getting away form them. The rioters attempted to break open an iron safe, but their efforts were unavailing, notwithstanding that they battered it about and tried to barn it.

The authorities appear to have been demoralized by fear, as they only succeeded in making five arrests, the excuse given being that they could not "distinguish the bad form the good."

We take the following extracts from the Hu Pao of 12th instant:

When Mr. Soothill found that he could not expel the crowd, he proceeded to the District Magistrate's yamen and asked for assistance in suppressing the mob. The Magistrate who was trying some cases at the time, immediately adjourned his court and processed with a number of soldiers to the scene of the riot, and as he left his yamen, the sky was red with the reflection of burning houses. The Taotai having also been informed of the riot, proceeded to the spot also, and got there first, as his yamen was close by. The Prefect, the commander of the troops, the commander of the city and the General of the Reserves and all the civil and military mandarins turned out too, but the people were like mountains and seas and the officials could not force their way through them. The Magistrates and runners could not distinguish the good from the bad, and so made no arrests; all they could do was to try and quiet the excited populace. At about 0 p.m. the fire went out the fire went out and all the officials returned home. Suddenly the French church was discovered to be on fire; another Protestant Missionary's home was also in a blaze; shortly after a second Missionary's place was on fire a little later another house and the night was turned into day, while the voice of the people was like the roaring of the waves. The crowd because more boisterous, and the fire engines which turned out made but feeble effort to extinguish the flames. It is fortunate that there was little wind on that night, otherwise other houses might have caught fire too. At midnight, the people began to be more quiet, but scare half an hour elapsed before the crowd rushed to the house of the first clerk on the hill and burnt it down. They then went to the residence of the Temple of the God of Fire, took out all the effects and piled them up on a vacant lot and made a big bonfire of them. The foreigners being burnt out of house and home sought only to save their lives; and some went to the Tao-t'ai's yamen and others to that of the District Magistrate for protection. At 6 a.m. on Sunday, some of the incendiaries stole out of the city by the Western Water Gate and went to the Custom House. Here they acted in the same way that they had done at the Commissioner's and burnt everything. They even cut down the Custom's flagstaff and burned the Dragon flag. By the time the commandant the city troops had destroyed everything they could find at the Custom House. As there were no boats on the river，the mob could not get the British Consulate on Pagoda Island.

On enquiry at the British Consulate General we informed that no particulars had been receives respecting the origin of the riot, and no details beyond the fact of the burning of the six missionary establishments and of the property of the Custom House officer, and the consequent destitute state of the sufferers who had fled to the British Consulate.

H. M. S. *Zephyr* would probably be now at Wenchow. We understand that Sir Harry Parkes has telegraphed to express his sympathy with the sufferers and to state that he has seen the Prince and Ministers who immediately telegraphed orders to the Governor of Chekiang to punish the offenders.

The North – China Herald and Supreme Court & Consular Gazette, December 17, 1884

Wenchow

(From Our Own Correspondent)

Wenchow

(From Our Own Correspondent)

Mr. Stronach was welcomed back to Wenchow as its Consul on the 12th inst, Mr. Parker taking leave on a new departure, having first secured the last instalment of the indemnity that the authorities agreed to pay for losses sustained by foreigners in the recent disturbances. To ascribe Mr. E. H. Parker's success in giving general satisfaction to foreigners and native authorities in regard to the questions raised by the riot to good luck, would be unjust to that accomplished officer. It was tact that effected an amicable settlement.

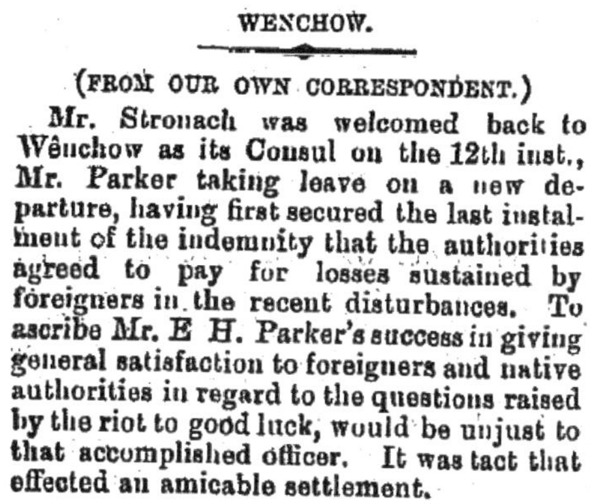

WENCHOW.

(FROM OUR OWN CORRESPONDENT.)

Mr. Stronach was welcomed back to Wênchow as its Consul on the 12th inst., Mr. Parker taking leave on a new departure, having first secured the last instalment of the indemnity that the authorities agreed to pay for losses sustained by foreigners in the recent disturbances. To ascribe Mr. E H. Parker's success in giving general satisfaction to foreigners and native authorities in regard to the questions raised by the riot to good luck, would be unjust to that accomplished officer. It was tact that effected an amicable settlement.

The North - China Herald and Supreme Court & Consular Gazette, March 18, 1885

Railways in China

RAILWAYS IN CHINA.

To the Editor of the
NORTH-CHINA DAILY NEWS.

SIR,—Although the subject of railways in China was ably discussed at a late meeting of the Shanghai Literary and Debating Society the question was not so exhaustively treated as to preclude me from offering a small contribution, assuming that it will not be unacceptable to those who desire the prosperity of this hoary (but not senile) Empire.

Considered topographically, it must be conceded to those who think the introduction of railways premature, that there are extensive regions where it may be questioned if they are needed; for example, Kiangsu and northern Chêkiang are reticulated by watercourses, and where labour is so cheap, it is doubtful if the locomotive could successfully compete with sail and scull. (It was urged that railways might be employed by an invader, but so can the rivers of China, which have been well termed her glory.) There

Railways in China

To the Editor of the

North-China Daily News

Sir,—Although the subject of Railways in China was ably discussed at a late meeting of the Shanghai Literary and Debating Society the question was not exhaustively treated as to preclude me from offering a small contribution, assuming that it will not be unacceptable to those who desire the prosperity of this hoary (but not senile) Empire.

Considered topographically, it must be conceded to those who think the introduction of railways premature, that there are extensive regions where it may be questioned if they are needed; for example, Kiangsu and northern Chekiang are reticulated by watercourses, and where labour is so cheap, it is doubtful if the locomotive could successfully compete with sail and scull.(It was urged that railways might be employed by an invader, but so can been well termed her glory.)There are however more or less favoured regions to which that means of communication would be an inestimable boon to the north, so often scantily supplied with food, and to the south, which frequently has superfluous harvest of the Chinese staff of life .But it is neither north nor south that most needs railways; there is a China beyond the rapids of the Yangtsze and the adjacent mountain region, which is separated from the rest of the empire more effectually than if a wide tempestuous ocean intervened. Ultramontane China, constituting the extensive and rich provinces of Szechuan and Yunnan, is physically isolated, enhancing enormously the cost of imported commodities. Were they to be tapped by a railway (or, where ponies abound, by tramways) east to west would be reciprocally enriched.

But great as the commercial and social advantages are that would be derived from uniting the physically discovered portions of China by railways, those benefits would be inconsiderable compared to the strategic importance of facile means of communication. And enemy in command of the Red River, possessed of modern applications of war, would be able to invade and subjugate Yunnan and Szechuan ere troops from the East could make the tedious foursome and perilous ascent of rapids, or scale passes to offer resistance; and if the invader should find in his march hosts of co-religionists as unpatriotic as those of Tongking, how great would be the peril to the Empire at large! It is not on the north that China is most vulnerable, but on the west. Szechuan was subjugated in the first instance by transforming a bridle-path into a road (by Ts'in, 329 B.C), and now, after a lapse of more than demanded for its due development, and for its retention as an integral portion of the Empire.

Yours obediently,

D. J. Macgowan.

Wenchow, 4th February, 1885

The North – China Herald and Supreme Court & Consular Gazette, December 22, 1886

Riot at Wenchow

Riot at Wenchow

A serious riot occurred at Wenchow on the 9th instant, and the C. M. S. N. Co.'s office was gutted by the mob after the *Kiangpiau* had left for Shanghai on her previous trip. The people did not want any rice to be exported; because, although there was plenty stored up in the granaries, they thought the price would go up, and so they posted up placards intimating that no rice should be exported.

RIOT AT WENCHOW.

A serious riot occurred at Wênchow on the 9th instant, and the C.M.S.N. Co.'s office was gutted by the mob after the *Kiangpiau* had left for Shanghai on her previous trip. The people did not want any rice to be exported; because, although there was plenty stored up in the granaries, they thought the price would go up, and so they posted up placards intimating that no rice should be exported.

At this stage of affairs, the Agent of the C.M.S.N. Co. bought up some 3,000 bags or 4,500 piculs of rice for exportation to Canton and as soon as this information became public, the price of rice immediately jumped up thirty cents a picul. This made the poor people more dissatisfied, and the Tao'tai, to allay the discontent, issued a proclamation to the effect that no more rice was to be exported. Later on, the Agent went to the Tao-t'ai and told him he had previously

At this stage of affairs, the Agent of the C. M. S. N. Co. bought up some 3,000 bags or 4,500 piculs of rice for exportation to Canton and as soon as this information became public, the price of rice immediately jumped up thirty cents a picul. This made the poor people more dissatisfied, and the Tao'tai, to allay the discontent, issued a proclamation to the effect that no more rice was to be exported. Later on, the Agent went to the Tao'tai and told him he had previously purchased a large quantity of rice and that he had chartered a steamer to take it away, and that if he were not allowed to ship it, he would have to pay the charter money and would still have the rice on his hands. The *Meefoo* arrived from Shanghai to take the Agent's rice away, and then the people got more angry, upon which the Tao'tai issued another proclamation to the effect that only a certain quantity of rice was to be exported. The angry feeling of the poor people, when this proclamation appeared, knew no bounds. The rice was put into boats to be sent to the *Meefoo* when the mob collected and attacked the offices of the C. M. S. N. Co. Fortunately for the Agent, he lived with his family elsewhere, for if the mob had caught him they would have killed him. When they did find not the Agent, they set to work to demolish the office, the lower floor of which was also used as a store, and such was their fury that they left nothing but two of the walls standing. They pulled the roof off the house, destroyed the books, smashed up everything inside the building, stole some opium and money, and took away the iron safe with all the papers and documents it contained.

In the midst of the hubbub, the District Magistrate appeared upon the scene, and the fury of the mob was directed towards him. Seeing this, his chair bearers took to their heels, leaving their master to take care of himself, and he consequently had a rough time of it. He was dragged out of his chair which was smashed into small pieces, he was unmercifully beaten and cut about the head with stones, the soldiers in the meantime rendering him no assistance. At the same time, some of the soldiers joined the mob in looting the rice, part of which was in cargo boats and some at the Customs where it was being examined. One of the foreign offices had a narrow escape, as the mob appeared to be about to vent their feelings on him, but he fortunately got into a boat and went over to the island. The mob then took the rice away into the city, hauling it over the walls from the boats. The C. M. Co.'s Agent finding how matters had turned out, ran away from Wenchow and went overland to Ningpo, reporting what had occurred. The Ningpo authorities immediately despatched the *Chao Wo* to Wenchow to render assistance, but by the time she arrived, the danger was all over, though the poor just then, because the rich men had been despoiled and the poor had plenty of rice.

On the 10th instant, the mob, numbering many thousands, found some boats ladon with rice, and under a guard of soldiers. Thinking this was to be sent away by the *Meefoo*, they seized it, but when they found it was not for exportation they allowed the soldiers to take it to the granaries.

The family of the Agent, fearing the mob might attempt to wreak their vengeance on them, very wisely concluded to come up to Shanghai, which they did in the *Kiangpiau* yesterday, the Agent joining them at Ningpo.

It is strange, that although the *Meefoo* arrived at Hongkong on the 14th instant, no account of the riot appears in the papers of that place.

The North - China Herald and Supreme Court & Consular Gazette, April 6, 1887

Hart's Peak—Wenchow

(From A Correspondent)

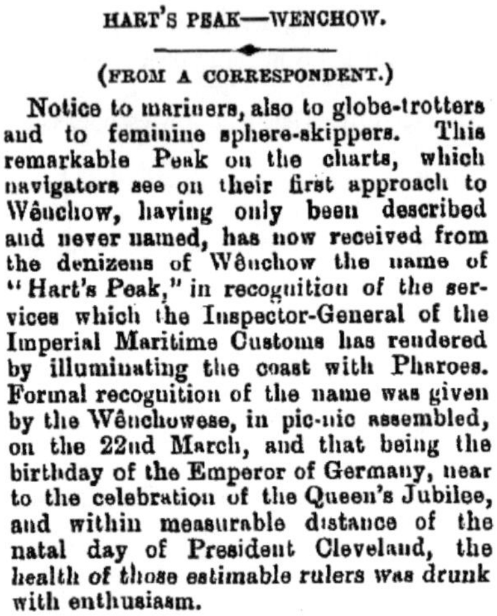

HART'S PEAK—WENCHOW.

(FROM A CORRESPONDENT.)

Notice to mariners, also to globe-trotters and to feminine sphere-skippers. This remarkable Peak on the charts, which navigators see on their first approach to Wênchow, having only been described and never named, has now received from the denizens of Wênchow the name of "Hart's Peak," in recognition of the services which the Inspector-General of the Imperial Maritime Customs has rendered by illuminating the coast with Pharoes. Formal recognition of the name was given by the Wênchowese, in pic-nic assembled, on the 22nd March, and that being the birthday of the Emperor of Germany, near to the celebration of the Queen's Jubilee, and within measurable distance of the natal day of President Cleveland, the health of those estimable rulers was drunk with enthusiasm.

Hart's Peak—Wenchow

(From A Correspondent)

Notice to marines, also to globe-trotters and to feminine sphere-skippers. This remarkable Peak on the charts, which navigators see on their first approach to Wenchow, having only been described and never named, has now received from the denizens of Wenchow the name of "Hart's Peak," in recognition of the services which the Inspector-General of the Imperial Maritime Customs has rendered by illuminating the coast with Pharoes. Formal recognition of the name was given by the Wenchowese, in pic-nic assembled, on the 22nd March, and that being the birthday of the Emperor of Germany, near to the celebration of the Queen's Jubilee, and within measurable distance of the natal day of President Cleveland, the health of those estimable rulers was drunk with enthusiasm.

A Taoist shrine on the summit of the Peak is approached, a large part of the way, by a flagged path, and the ascent is not difficult. Like all other elevations on sea coasts, Hart's Peak presents views of grandeur and beauty; the most striking feature of the scenery is the unique appearance of the terraces beneath, which alone are highly picturesque. The ocean and the islands on one side, and mountains on the other, enclosing the rich plains of Wenchow, carpeted with golden *brassica* and green wheat, reticulated with silvery watercourses, in strong contrast with the sombre city which seems to smirch the landscape, afford scenes of surpassing beauty, which were regarded with more in interest from the endearing names which salient points bear—Grace Mount, Mount Jenny, Lucy Range, Dorothy Peak and Evelyn Terrace. (April 1st)

The North – China Herald and Supreme Court & Consular Gazette, June 17, 1887

Wenchow

(Communicated)

Wenchow

(Communicated)

The scene of devastation that met our eye on entering the river of Wenchow was appalling. For miles the country was flooded. One vast expanse of water broken by homesteads crowded with cattle. A murky sky and frowning background of lofty hills made a most depressing and mournful picture. We passed too quickly to pourtray it save by the pen. Women and children stood in groups, doubtless talking over their heavy losses while the men were busy in their boats. In some places where the bridges were still standing only the upper portion of their arches was visible looking like mirages—water above, below and around them! Great indeed must have been the downpour to have caused such an inundation. It was a comforting change to turn one's gaze from the immersed country to the numberless fishermen pursuing their calling as if no such thing as home troubles existed. The flooded country passed, it was pleasing to note the approaching attractions of the picturesque scenery—so unlike what is generally to be met with in the Northern parts of China. As the sky cleared the lights and shadows passed continuously over the hills—now bringing out some hitherto unperceived bright spot, now plunging into semi-obscurity some retreating valley, with here and there a mountain stream rushing impetuously down the face of the rocks. The absence of all foreign craft in the port, and not a foreign building visible, brings out the more forcibly the essentially Chinese character of the place. The air was pure and invigorating without that oppressiveness one generally experiences, in a warm atmosphere, after heavy rains.

Well would it repay the traveler in search of health to spend a few days in this lovely spot! Rare and beautiful ferns abound, every nook and cranny being clothed with them. Who but those who

WENCHOW.

(COMMUNICATED.)

The scene of devastation that met our eye on entering the river of Wênchow was appalling. For miles and miles the country was flooded. One vast expanse of water broken by homesteads and graves, and here and there mounds crowded with cattle. A murky sky and frowning background of lofty hills made a most depressing and mournful picture. We passed too quickly to pourtray it save by the pen. Women and children stood in groups, doubtless talking over their heavy losses, while the men were busy in their boats. In some places where the bridges were still standing only the upper portion of their arches was visible looking like mirages—water above, below and around them! Great indeed must have been the downpour to have caused such an inundation. It was a comforting change to turn one's gaze from the immersed country to the numberless fishermen pursuing their calling as if no such thing as home troubles existed. The flooded country passed, it was pleasing to note the have seen them can express the grandeur of the City Wall or the summits the hills—each crowned with a resting-place roofed in and supported by stone pillars. Temples and Pagodas abound, the latter, more or less, in course of decay and in many instances surmounted by a tree in lieu of roof. We regretted our stay was all too short; nothing could exceed the kind hospitality shown us or the assistance rendered in visiting the various places of interest. Such a trip as we made in the old *Nautilus*, alias *Kiangpiau*, would dissipate many ailments. The epicure need not fear but that he would be entertained as sumptuously as at his own board, while the care and attention of Capt. Graham and his officers could not be surpassed.

The North - China Herald and Supreme Court & Consular Gazette, February 10, 1888

Notes of A Trip to Wenchow and Its Neighbourhood

NOTES OF A TRIP TO WENCHOW AND ITS NEIGHBOURHOOD.

Chêkiang is noted for its varied and picturesque beauty, and Wênchow, the city of pagodas, kittysols and oranges, may be taken as a favourable example. The entrance to it—the city being some twenty miles from the mouth of the river Ou—is grand in the extreme. Mountain and valley, river and sea, islet and cliff, unite in forming a picture that to our eyes, fresh from the unvarying plains of Kiangsu, was most charming. We dropped anchor between the city and a fairylike island, famous alike for its beauty and historical associations. Afterwards we found that viewed from the top of a distant peak it resembled in shape a river steamer, and needed but smoke from the twin pagodas to make the illusion complete.

Wênchow is unusually clean for a Chinese city, and one may walk through the streets without meeting much that is offensive to the sight or smell; there are several canals which appear to be effective as a system of drainage. A pleasant and interesting walk

Notes of A Trip to Wenchow and Its Neighbourhood

Chekiang is noted for its varied and picturesque beauty, and Wenchow, the city of pagodas, kittysols and oranges, may be taken as a favourable example. The entrance to it—the city being some twenty miles from the mouth of the river Ou—is grand in the extreme. Mountain and valley, river and sea, islet and cliff, unite in forming a picture that to our eyes, fresh from the unvarying plains of Kiangsu, was most charming. We dropped anchor between the city and a fairylike island, famous alike for its beauty and historical associations. Afterwards we found that viewed from the top of a distant peak it resembled in shape a river steamer, and needed but smoke from the twin pagodas to make the illusion complete.

Wenchow is unusually clean for a Chinese city, and one may walk through the streets without meeting much that is offensive to the sight or smell; there are several canals which appear to be effective as a system of drainage, A pleasant and interesting walk is to be had by going round the city walls which can be done comfortably in a couple of hours, They extend over several small hills and at the summit of each there is a Ting'rh or rest-house, affording a good view of the city and surrounding country. One in particular is used as a look-out for vessels coming up the river and is a great resort of the foreign residents, as from this point is first sighted the steamer from Shanghai ,the advent of which is an event that causes no little excitement. Here and there rusty old cannon lie dismounted ,and ferns of many varieties flourish luxuriantly.

The foreign residents live for the most part in rooms in the native temples, which after a thorough cleaning and some little Europeanising are made comfortable enough. Worship regularly goes on in the adjoining rooms. It is whispered that the only billiard table in the place is under the guardianship of a venerable old “joss” bricked up in the wall!

The lower reaches of the river abound in waterfowl amongst which we spent some time and cartridges before making a more extensive trip up the river.

Houseboats as they exist at Shanghai are unknown in Wenchow, but a very passable substitute is found in a native boat about 35 by 10 feet and drawing eight inches of water. These easily accommodate four foreigners with servants and boatmen, and being of such light draught, are admirably adapted for the numerous shallows and rapids in the upper reaches of the river.

Leaving the city with the commencement of the flood tide on a January morning, we were accompanied by a large number of other boats, great and small, all bound up-river for wood. They kept us company for several hours, and by frightening away the waterfowl, prevented us from getting as much shooting as we otherwise might have done. After several miles the water's edge, and covered with trees and shrubs. This was the general character of the river valley as far as our journey extended, Towards evening we arrived at a lager village called Wen-ch'i which is about 90 *li* from Wenchow, and as we were now above the tide the water became beautifully clear, and sand and pebbles replaced mud and reeds, Another few *li b*rought us to the first rapid where our lowdah decided to wait for daylight before attempting to ascend. Early next morning we started; a pole was fixed on the prow of the boat so that about four feet projected on either side, this the boatmen used as a lover to raise the hull off the bottom, at the same time pushing us slowly up, while we and our servants assisted by poling. This rapid was the first of many and gave us considerable difficulty in surmounting as the water was very low.

There were a number of smaller woodboats working their way over, and their method of doing so struck us as being a very sensible one. In the majority the captain and crew consist of but one man, and it would need a ruinous expenditure of time and trouble were he to go up alone; so, waiting till several boats have collected, the men assist each other and with their united strength take up one at a time until all are over.

We passed a city called Ching-tien during the morning , which appears to be fairly large; the walls extend for about a quarter of a mile along the river bank and enclose a portion of a high hill, the upper part of which covered with four trees, forms a marked contrast to the squalid houses and ruinous walls at its foot. Judging from the number of large pole and bamboo rafts about here, the trade in wood must be enormous. As we passed by, numbers of natives flocked to the walls and with the occupants of the numerous boats below regarded us with evident astonishment. Here we were able to purchase some excellent fish, not unlike trout, for six if which we paid the modest sum of fifty cash,-not dear by any means. A short distance above, there were numbers of fishing cormorants, which appeared to be more successful than their brethren on the waters in the neighbourhood of Shanghai.

The river about here wound through some lovely scenery which our slow progress gave us ample time to enjoy. In some places a temple would be situated high above us on a hill, surrounded by a grove of trees and overlooking the river, while various picturesque looking hamlets were dotted here and there wherever there was any shelter, The houses above Ching-tien were much better in appearance than those at and near Wenchow.

We reached our goal-Shih-men-tung 洞石門 (literally Stone-gate-cavern) in the course of the next afternoon; it is said to be about 85 miles from Wenchow. For several miles before this the rapids were less frequent, for which we were not sorry, as it became monotonous being constantly stopped by them; the river too wound through loftier hills and grander scenery than we had hitherto seen, At a narrow gap in the range of hills on the left bank of the river we landed, and walking through, suddenly found ourselves in a most lovely glen with branching valleys spreading in all directions, the beauty of which baffles description. Numerous streams found their way down the sides of the mountains, here and there taking wild plunges over the rocks and cliffs. Five minutes' walk from where we landed brought us to an old ruined monastery and just beyond to a waterfall about 200 feet high; there was not much water falling at the time, owing, no doubt, to the late drought, and in the cavern worn away in the rock below, the water was frozen hard enough in some places to bear our weight. Many kinds of trees covered the hills, whose sides and feet were adorned by a profusion of ferns, which, strange to say, were as green as if it were June instead of January.

About 50 li above Shih-men-tung there is a large city called Ch'u-chow, which time prevented us from visiting. A good trade is done with it in wood and bamboos. Which are brought down in immense rafts.

Our return voyage was as much unlike the journey up, as the coming down a toboggan slide is to the slow process of mounting. The rapids which had so much tried our patience and endurance on the upward course now made amends by forwarding us at extra speed in the opposite direction. People with weak nerves should not shoot rapids. As you approach the first, you see rocks ahead apparently anger for your destruction, which too seems to be the sole aim and object of the boatmen, for at something like half-a-mile a minute you speed onwards. Holding on tight with both hands, your breath comes in shore gasps, for you are apparently doomed to be dashed to atoms, but just as the prow of the boat seems to touch the rocks, you are saved by vigorous use of the pole and glide by into comparatively smooth water. Then your heart gradually resumes its accustomed beat, and after a few more such experience you get used to it and feel the excitement most exhilarating.

On the second afternoon after leaving Shih-men-tung there was a strong breeze against us which necessitated our stopping at a small village. Here we landed, and walked though the village up to an old pagoda and monastery on the top of a hill close by, from where we had one of the finest views we saw during the whole excursion. On our return, we were met by a crowd of villagers headed by some ancient dames and one small boy, who held out two cups of tea for us. After such a greeting, it was not long before we had some thirty boys running races for cash, and fully initiated into the mysteries of handicapping. The natives everywhere were most friendly. Next day, coming into some likely country, we got some shooting, and on our sixth day out arrived once more at Wenchow, where we found the C.M.'s steamer *Haechang* from Shanghai awaiting us with letters and news.

So hospitable had been our reception by the harmonious little knot of foreign residents, that it was with unfeigned reluctance we were compelled to turn our backs on their pleasant compelled to turn our backs on their pleasant company and charming scenery, and set our faces northwards.

The North – China Herald and Supreme Court & Consular Gazette, March 2, 1888

Chinese New Year Holidays At Wenchow

Chinese New Year Holidays At Wenchow

Foreigners and Chinese at Wenchow enjoyed in part the holiday season conjointly.

The closing exercises of Mrs. Stott's school for Chinese girls, and Mr. Soothill's for boys, consisted first, of a distribution of presents which had been provided in the former case by their kind mistress (now at home). They were embowered in a large illuminated New Year tree and being useful things, rather than perishable gimcracks and gewgaws, were highly appreciated.

Then that never failing source of instruction and amusement, a magic lantern, the first seen in Wenchow, was exhibited by Mr. Acting Commissioner Brazier. The scenes were witnesses with pleasurable wonderment by the children and their parents, who never before learnt so much in so short a time, nor enjoyed more delight.

Rumours of the magical performances were bruited abroad, which led Mr. Brazier to repeat the exhibition in the Chapel of the Inland Mission, which was attend by the high officials, or their deputies, and many of the literati, and subsequently the instrument did duty in the chief Yamen, for the mandarinate, their staff and families.

Now the happy thought has struck the active brain of the Taotai's weiyuen, to have an exhibition in Mr. Stott's chapel for the well-to-do among the citizens, who are to be charged for admission, the proceeds to be appropriated to the fund for relief of sufferers on the Yellow River, the genial and clever Aberdonian being lecturer. Mr. Donovan, through whose good offices the use of the magic lantern was obtained from Dr. Williamson, is thanked as well as that learned and

CHINESE NEW YEAR HOLIDAYS AT WENCHOW.

Foreigners and Chinese at Wênchow enjoyed in part the holiday season conjointly.

The closing exercises of Mrs. Stott's school for Chinese girls, and Mr. Soothill's for boys, consisted first, of a distribution of presents which had been provided in the former case by their kind mistress (now at home). They were embowered in a large illuminated New Year tree and being useful things, rather than perishable gimcracks and gewgaws, were highly appreciated.

Then that never failing source of instruction and amusement, a magic lantern, the first seen in Wênchow, was exhibited by Mr. Acting Commissioner Brazier. The scenes were witnessed with pleasurable wonderment by the childrens and their parents, who never before learnt so much in so short a time, nor enjoyed more delight.

urbane gentleman, for that means of enlightenment and goodfellowship which this lean, land and drowsy port has just enjoyed.

Finally, the annual distribution of candies and cakes at the extensive native orphan asylum came off. Its inmates, blind, mute, idiotic, paralytic, rickety, deformed children, each received a packet, some three hundred in numbers, and a few oranges. At the close these was an amusing scramble among the nurses, attendants and urchins (street Arabs who had forced themselves in) for that luscious, toothsome, quinine-flavoured fruit, the Wenchow orange.

For one hour at least the hapless inmates of that humane institution experienced joyful emotions, the recollection of which and anticipations of its recurrence will soothe and beguile many weary hours in the interim.

As usual and natural in affairs of this sort, the graceful and humanizing, compassionate sex was prominent throughout. Women do not need to be told, they instinctively know, that in striving to diffuse happiness and mitigating sorrow through life's thorny path they accumulate uncolyable pleasure, stores of heart treasure, sources of enjoyment of which its possessors can never be bereft. (Wenchow, February, 1888)

The north – China Herald and Supreme Court & Consular Gazette, October 19, 1888

Wenchow

(From A Correspondent)

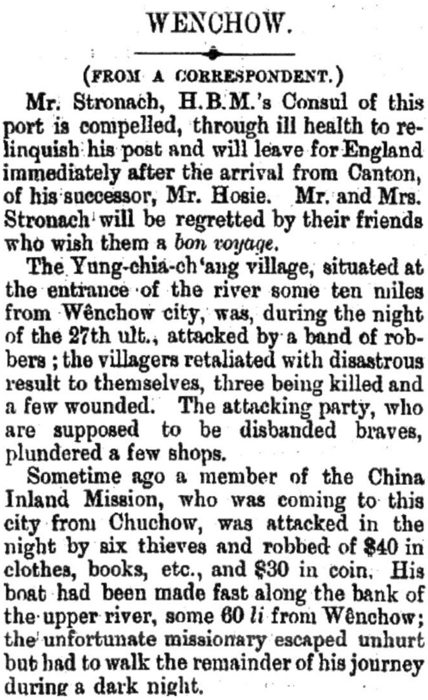

WENCHOW.

(FROM A CORRESPONDENT.)

Mr. Stronach, H.B.M.'s Consul of this port is compelled, through ill health to relinquish his post and will leave for England immediately after the arrival from Canton, of his successor, Mr. Hosie. Mr. and Mrs. Stronach will be regretted by their friends who wish them a *bon voyage*.

The Yung-chia-ch'ang village, situated at the entrance of the river some ten miles from Wênchow city, was, during the night of the 27th ult., attacked by a band of robbers; the villagers retaliated with disastrous result to themselves, three being killed and a few wounded. The attacking party, who are supposed to be disbanded braves, plundered a few shops.

Sometime ago a member of the China Inland Mission, who was coming to this city from Chuchow, was attacked in the night by six thieves and robbed of $40 in clothes, books, etc., and $30 in coin. His boat had been made fast along the bank of the upper river, some 60 *li* from Wênchow; the unfortunate missionary escaped unhurt but had to walk the remainder of his journey during a dark night.

Wenchow

(From A Correspondent)

Mr. Stronach, H. B. M.'s Consul of this port is compelled, through ill health to relinquish his post and will leave for England immediately after the arrival from Canton, of his successor, Mr. Hosie, Mr. and Mrs. Stronach will be regretted by their friends who wish them a bon voyage.

The Yung-chia-ch'ang village, situated at the entrance of the river some ten miles from Wenchow city, was, during the night of the 27th ult., attacked by a band of robbers; the villagers retaliated with disastrous result to themselves, three being killed and a few wounded. The attacking party, who are supposed to be disbanded braves, plundered a few shops.

Sometime ago a member of the China Inland Mission, who was coming to this city from Chuchow, was attacked in the night by six thieves and robbed of $40 in clothes, books, etc., and $30 in coin. His boat had been made fast along the bank of the upper river, some 60 li from Wenchow; the unfortunate missionary escaped unhurt but had to walk the remainder of his journey during a dark night.

The Chinese man-of-war *Yuan-kai* left on the 5th instant for your port having the family of Wang Taotai on board, this vessel has been in our deserted harbor for a whole week and was a pleasant sight to the community.

No further intelligence has been received with regard to our regular trader, the s. s. Haechang, calling, on her way down, at Sheipoo and Hai-men, it is said that the passenger traffic and the export of treasure form those places will prove quite remunerative.

The Roman Catholic Mission is building a very pretty church; this edifice will be the highest and prettiest in the city.

The German gunboat *Wolf*, arrived today from Ningpo and will leave again on the 12th for Foochow, it is now over two years since a foreign man-of–war visited this port. (10th October, Ahtram)

The North－China Herald and Supreme Court & Consular Gazette, October 26, 1888

Wenchow

(From A Correspondent)

Wenchow

(From A Correspondent)

We were agreeably surprised to-day to see a British steamer enter the river, which proved to be the Fookching, a small iron vessel of 77 tons. Mr. Kaw Hong Take of Hong Kong is the owner; it is his intention to keep that vessel on the Foochow and Wenchow line, and should meet with success. This is quite a new departure and will, no doubt, cause the junk owners to grumble. A rumour is afloat that another steamer is to run between Foochow, Wenchow, Ningpo and Shanghai; if this comes to be true, Wenchow will no longer be an isolated port.

Cholera is prevalent amongst the natives and a good many deaths have occurred during the last few days. The German gunboat *Wolf* left on the 12th instant for Canton via Foochow and Swatow.

(20th October)

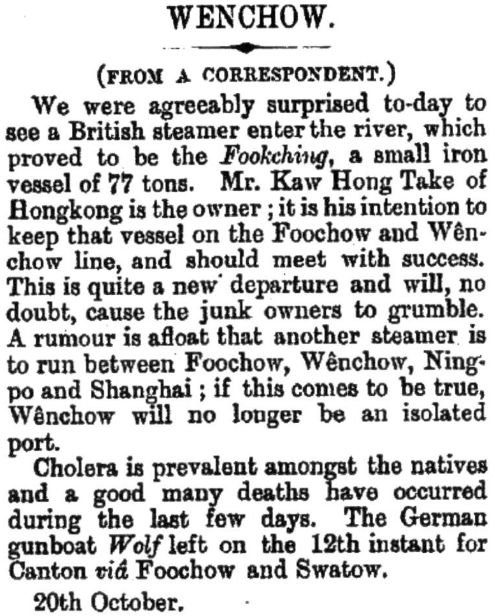

WENCHOW.

(FROM A CORRESPONDENT.)

We were agreeably surprised to-day to see a British steamer enter the river, which proved to be the *Fookching*, a small iron vessel of 77 tons. Mr. Kaw Hong Take of Hongkong is the owner; it is his intention to keep that vessel on the Foochow and Wênchow line, and should meet with success. This is quite a new departure and will, no doubt, cause the junk owners to grumble. A rumour is afloat that another steamer is to run between Foochow, Wênchow, Ningpo and Shanghai; if this comes to be true, Wênchow will no longer be an isolated port.

Cholera is prevalent amongst the natives and a good many deaths have occurred during the last few days. The German gunboat *Wolf* left on the 12th instant for Canton *viâ* Foochow and Swatow.

20th October.

The North - China Herald and Supreme Court & Consular Gazette, November 16, 1888

Wenchow

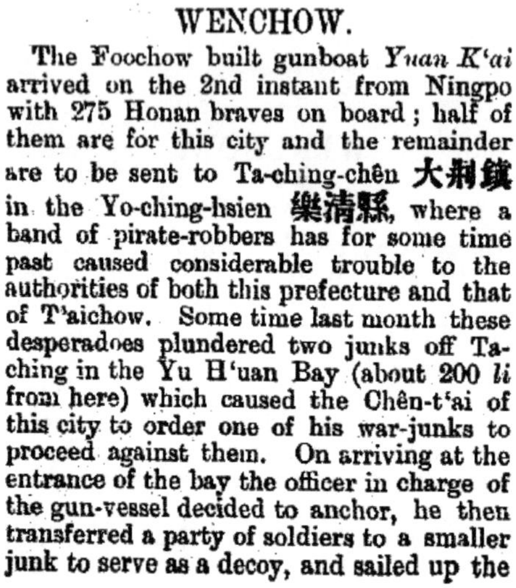

WENCHOW.

The Foochow built gunboat *Yuan K'ai* arrived on the 2nd instant from Ningpo with 275 Honan braves on board; half of them are for this city and the remainder are to be sent to Ta-ching-chên 大荆鎮 in the Yo-ching-hsien 樂清縣, where a band of pirate-robbers has for some time past caused considerable trouble to the authorities of both this prefecture and that of T'aichow. Some time last month these desperadoes plundered two junks off Ta-ching in the Yu H'uan Bay (about 200 *li* from here) which caused the Chên-t'ai of this city to order one of his war-junks to proceed against them. On arriving at the entrance of the bay the officer in charge of the gun-vessel decided to anchor, he then transferred a party of soldiers to a smaller junk to serve as a decoy, and sailed up the

Wenchow

The Foochow built gunboat *Yuan K'ai* arrived on the 2nd instant from Ningpo with 275 Honan braves on board; half of them are for this city and the remainder are to the sent to Ta-ching-chen 大荊鎮 in the Yo-ching-hsien 樂清縣, where a band of pirate-robbers has for some time past caused considerable trouble to the authorities of both this prefecture and that of T'aichow. Some time last month these desperadoes plundered two junks off Taching in the Yu H'uan Bay (about 200 li form here) which caused the Chen-t'ai of this city to order one of his war-junk to proceed against them. On arriving at the entrance of the bay the officer in charge of the gun-vessel decided to anchor, he then transferred a party of soldiers to a smaller junk to serve as a decoy, and sailed up the bay; this ruse proved a success; the robbers thinking that it was a trading junk immediately bore down upon it; when they were near, the soldiers rushed on deck and received them with a volley, but in this case the words of Byron do not apply:

"Each volley tells that thousands ceased to breathe."

And the pirates, finding that they had been ensnared took to fight; three of the piratical craft succeeded in making their escape, but one was pursued and captured. Out of the ten pirates that manned it, six were there and then beheaded, and four brought to this city to be executed.

In the early part of last month I reported to you that a band of robbers had attacked a village at the entrance of the river; since then considerable consternation prevails here, and the city gates are closed punctually at nine o'clock.

Form Ningpo I hear that the Chinese there circulate various rumours about this place being unsafe, etc. Etc. These are exaggerations; the authorities are wide awaken and Wenchow is quite safe.

The *Yuan K'ai* left for Ningpo on the 4th, and the Training-ship *Ching Yuan* arrived on the 7th from Foochow and left for Shanghai on the 8th. (10th November, Ahtram)

The North - China Herald and Supreme Court & Consular Gazette, February 22, 1889

Wenchow

(From Our Own Correspondent)

Wenchow

(From Our Own Correspondent)

The foreigner who would like to see one of the most remarkable sides of Chinese character could not do better than visit a city during the Chinese New Year festivities; there, in the midst of them, he would certainly acquire a knowledge of domestic life of the various class. Here these festivities have lasted the customary length of time, taking into consideration that not one merchant has settled his accounts by an act of incendiarism and that no failures have taken place; this augurs well for this secluded port.

As in other Chinese cities there exists here a refuge for blind and crippled children. Our benevolent Doctor made the usual annual distribution of cakes, oranges, etc., to the poor creatures who number somewhat over two hundred; the joy to which these poor children give way on these but too rare occasions, amply repays our Doctor for his good work.

The new Roman Catholic church is approaching completion; this magnificent edifice will be ready for Easter and will be consecrated by the Bishop of this province, Monseigneur Reynaud.

Rumours have been rife to the effect that the s. s. *Smith* (or *Cass*) is to run between Formosa and Shanghai *via* Amoy, Foochow, Wenchow and Ningpo, and we shall hail the pioneer of the line with delight.

The weather has been very unsettled since the early part last month; rain and snow visited us a little too often and the natives agree in saying that this has been the severest winter for some years.

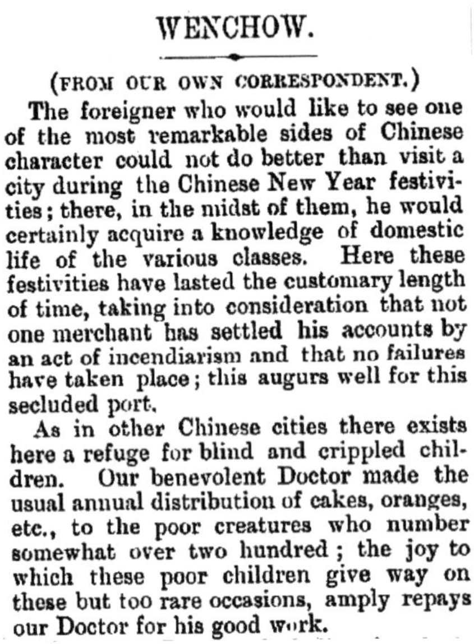

WENCHOW.

(FROM OUR OWN CORRESPONDENT.)

The foreigner who would like to see one of the most remarkable sides of Chinese character could not do better than visit a city during the Chinese New Year festivities; there, in the midst of them, he would certainly acquire a knowledge of domestic life of the various classes. Here these festivities have lasted the customary length of time, taking into consideration that not one merchant has settled his accounts by an act of incendiarism and that no failures have taken place; this augurs well for this secluded port.

As in other Chinese cities there exists here a refuge for blind and crippled children. Our benevolent Doctor made the usual annual distribution of cakes, oranges, etc., to the poor creatures who number somewhat over two hundred; the joy to which these poor children give way on these but too rare occasions, amply repays our Doctor for his good work.

A serious conflagration which caused the destruction of the largest pawnshop in this city occurred last week; this was caused, as in the majority of cases, by the upsetting of a lamp. The destruction of such an important establishment caused some trouble to the officials who were compelled to seek military protection from the anger of the Yung-chia Hsien had promised the payment of their claims in full that they dispersed, and further trouble was thus avoided. (7th February)

The North – China Herald and Supreme Court & Consular Gazette, July 3, 1891

The Disturbance At Wenchow

(From A Correspondent)

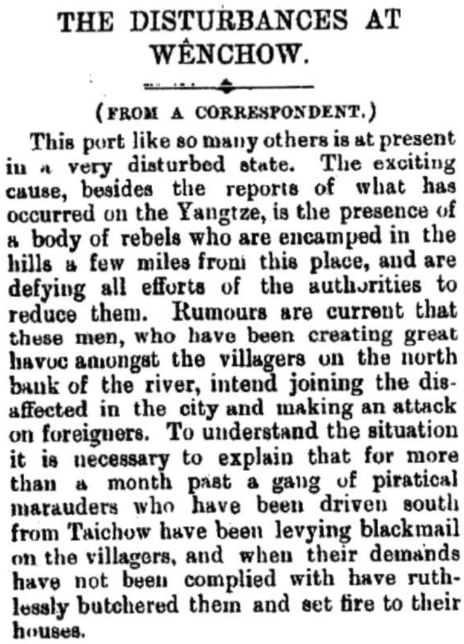
THE DISTURBANCES AT WÊNCHOW.

(FROM A CORRESPONDENT.)

This port like so many others is at present in a very disturbed state. The exciting cause, besides the reports of what has occurred on the Yangtze, is the presence of a body of rebels who are encamped in the hills a few miles from this place, and are defying all efforts of the authorities to reduce them. Rumours are current that these men, who have been creating great havoc amongst the villagers on the north bank of the river, intend joining the disaffected in the city and making an attack on foreigners. To understand the situation it is necessary to explain that for more than a month past a gang of piratical marauders who have been driven south from Taichow have been levying blackmail on the villagers, and when their demands have not been complied with have ruthlessly butchered them and set fire to their houses.

The Disturbance At Wenchow

(From A Correspondent)

This port like so many others is at present in a very disturbed state. The exciting cause, besides the reports of what has occurred on the Yangtze, is the presence of a body of rebels who are encamped in the hills a few miles from this place, and are defying all efforts of the authorities to reduce them. Rumours are current that these men, who have been creating great havoc amongst the attack on foreigners. To understand the situation it is necessary to explain that for more than a month past a gang of piratical marauders who have been driven south from Taichow have been levying blackmail on the villagers, and when their demands have not been complied with have ruthlessly butchered them and set fire to their houses.

A week or two ago they arrived in this district and made a raid on a village twenty miles off. They went to the house of the richest man in the village and demanded money; there being some delay in satisfying them they killed the owner, his father, and two wives, and also shot three of the neighbours who came up on hearing the noise: they then looted the house and others adjoining, set fire to them and completely destroyed them. On the news reaching the city the Magistrate at once proceeded with all the soldiers at his command to the scene of the outrage, but after being away some days the force returned without accomplishing anything. The officials say that their troops were outnumbered by the rebels, who are variously estimated at from 200 to 500 strong and are well armed with foreign guns, etc. Since then the city gates have been closed from 8 o'clock at night till 4 in the morning and soldiers are stationed at various places in the city keeping armed night patrols.

On the 21st inst. The rebels made a raid on another village some 30 *li* away with the like result as on the first occasion. Now the surrounding villagers who have anything to lose are deserting their houses and flocking into the city; and it is said that the brigands have posted placards in the neighbouring villages threatening to attack them if they do not send them money: and it is rumoured that foreigners also are menaced with attack. The city officials are greatly alarmed as their soldier will not face the rebels. It is said that the failure of the magistrate's expedition has caused a large number of bad characters to join the rebels, besides making them more bold. On the 23rd some suspicious looking characters were observed in the city; on being questioned by the *yamen* runners they tried to escape, but one was caught and on his person were found two revolvers and a dirk. On the 24th he was examined by the magistrate when he boldly said he was a spy sent by the rebel band: he said if they killed him the rebels would shortly have their revenge. It is said the authorities are sending for troops from Hangchow; and that the Viceroy regarding the serious outlook. What with the rebels on the north bank and the disaffected in the city, the tranquility of this place is by no means assured. Meantime foreigners are quietly making preparations and getting their arms furbished up and in readiness so as to be prepared should any trouble break out.

The presence of a gunboat would be of some service down here. About half the foreigners live in the city, the rest on an island in the middle of the river about 400 yards from either shore. We live so far apart and our numbers are so few that we are in a most critical position. (25th June)

Since writing the above the British gunboat *Redpole* has arrived, and as long as she remains with us we shall feel quite safe. (26th June)

The North - China Herald and Supreme Court & Consular Gazette, February 26, 1892

Persecution of Christians At Wenchow

PERSECUTION OF CHRISTIANS AT WENCHOW.

Serious trouble has broken out at one of the mission stations in the neighbourhood of Wênchow. Only a week before the troubles began the popular feeling in favour of Christianity was most encouraging. During the visit of the Rev. W. E. Soothill nearly a thousand people assembled to hear the preaching. It took nearly a quarter of an hour for them to settle down to quiet and order. Addresses lasting for about three hours were kept up. When most of the outsiders had taken their departure, the remaining enquirers and Christians had a meeting for prayer, and over one hundred knelt down. Sixty-six have given in their names as enquirers, although the work in that locality is only fifteen months old. Six were examined and baptised, and the day's work appeared to be most satisfactory.

Persecution of Christians At Wenchow

Serious trouble has broken out at one of the mission stations in the neighbourhood of Wenchow. Only a week before the troubles began the popular feeling in favour of Christianity was most encouraging. During the visit of the Rev. W. E. Soothill nearly a thousand people assembled to hear the preaching. It took nearly a quarter of an hour for them to settle down to quiet and order. Addresses lasting for about three hours were kept up. When most of the outsiders had taken their departure, the remaining enquirers and Christians had a meeting for prayer, and over one hundred knelt down. Sixty-six have given in their names as enquirers, although the work in that locality is only fifteen months old. Six were examined and baptized, and the day's work appeared to most satisfactory.

On the 14th instant, however some of the villagers came down in haste Wenchow to report that while holding the usual Christian service about 70 of the more disaffected among them had come to the chapel and smashed up lamps, furniture and everything they could lay hands on. The hymn books and Testaments were taken out and burned and the Christians were brutally attacked, one being kicked most severely and left senseless on the ground.

On the 15th instant further persecutions were reported. The two leading men of the village led their adherents out again and this time every Christian house was despoiled. Only four were injured the previous day. The inmates were driven out young and old, and the doors closed and sealed up. Those families who denied having anything to do with Christianity were unmolested.

Nearly twenty houses were thus closed and the people left without homes. In one case the wind blew a door open and the marauders thought its owner had open and the marauders thought its owner had opened it to show he was a convert to Christianity. The house was attacked, and the occupant maltreated while his property was destroyed, although he had not accepted Christianity at all.

While the English Missionary was writing to his Consul on the subject, another deputation of converts came to say that in four other villages near Wenchow a similar attack had been made on a house, of which the Christian owner had refused to make a feast for the idols on the occasion of his wedding. The rowdies poured filth into his rice pans, broke everything they could find, knocked his wife down, and threatened to leave nothing standing the next evening.

In both these cases the motive seems to be that the tendency of Christianity is to displace idolatry, and thus the idols and temples will be neglected. The prosperity of the place being supposed to depend on these idolatrous arrangements, which have been kept up for ages, it is feared that if idols or temples are neglected the heaviest public calamities will be the result. These persecutions show however that the work of the missionary is progressing.

The North - China Herald and Supreme Court & Consular Gazette, December 30, 1892

News From Wenchow

NEWS FROM WENCHOW.

During a fierce gale which raged at Wenchow about a fortnight ago, several serious disasters occurred, attended in many cases with lost of life. Four large junks, laden with poles, were upset and many others dragged anchor or sustained other injuries, whilst a great number of small fishing craft suffered a worse fate. The villagers on the coast showed great barbarism. Instead of affording succour, they busied themselves with picking up wreckage thrown ashore. In the worst cases they even wrested the poles away from the shipwrecked people, who in their exhausted state were made to yield the logs to the merciless people. Owing to the unusually cold weather at Wenchow there is considerable suffering amongst the poorer classes, who are not provided with extensive wardrobes, and especially amongst those who have a precarious living.

News From Wenchow

During a fierce gale which raged at Wenchow about a fortnight ago, several serious disasters occurred, attended in many cases with lost of life. Four large junks, laden with poles, were upset and many others dragged anchor or sustained other injuries, whilst a great number of small fishing craft suffered a worse fate. The villagers on the coast showed great barbarism. Instead of affording succour, they busied themselves with picking up wreckage thrown ashore. In the worst cases they even wrested the poles away from the shipwrecked people, who in their exhausted state were made to yield the logs to the merciless people. Owing to the unusually cold weather at Wenchow there is considerable suffering amongst the poorer classes, who are not provided with extensive wardrobes, and especially amongst those who have a precarious living.

The North – China Herald and Supreme Court & Consular Gazette, July 21, 1893

Death of Dr. Macgowan

Death of Dr. Macgowan

Dr. Daniel Jerome Macgowan, the oldest foreign resident in Shanghai, and one of the best-known men in China, passed away quietly yesterday morning, at his residence in Boone Road, in his 79th year. Born in Fall River, Mass, he first came to Ningpo, as a missionary doctor, exactly fifty years ago. During the Civil War in the United States, he served as a surgeon with the northern armies, and made himself much respected at Washington. He returned to China in 1865 as the agent of a syndieate that proposed to build a telegraph line to China by way of Bering and from that time made Shanghai his headquarters. His wife, who was equally popular with himself, died about 1878, and he was never quite the same man after her death. He leaves only one child, a daughter, the wife of Sir Chaloner Alabaster, whom lie had intended soon to rejoin in English. Sir Robert Hart gave him an appointment in the Customs in 1879, and he served in served in Shanghai and in Wenchow, at which latter port he had full scope to pursue his studies in folk-lore and natural history. He was a man of vast and various information which he was always anxious to add to, and to impart to others, and he was a contributor to our columns from the first, as well as to numerous other missionary, scientific, and literary publications. He was a thoroughly genial, kind-hearted man, at home in any company, and always with something fresh to tell, a man of unfailing energy in the pursuit of knowledge, and who bore his years wonderfully, as his recent long and arduous trip in Siberia showed. He only returned from a visit to Peking and Tientsin on Saturday last, and, had been ailing, but refused for some time to consult a doctor. He was expecting from the Viceroy Li Hung-chang letters of introduction to the new Minister to the United States, etc. Yang Ju, to whom the Viceroy recommended him for the post of adviser to the

DEATH OF DR. MACGOWAN.

Dr. Daniel Jerome Macgowan, the oldest foreign resident in Shanghai, and one of the best-known men in China, passed away quietly yesterday morning, at his residence in Boone Road, in his 79th year. Born in Fall River, Mass., he first came to Ningpo, as a missionary doctor, exactly fifty years ago. During the Civil War in the United States, he served as a surgeon with the northern armies, and made himself much respected at Washington. He returned to China in 1865 as the agent of a syndicate that proposed to build a telegraph line to China by way of Bering Straits, and from that time made Shanghai his headquarters. His wife, who was equally popular with himself, died about 1878, and he was never quite the same man after her death. He leaves only one child, a daughter, the wife of Sir Chaloner Alabaster, whom he had intended soon to rejoin in England. Sir Robert Hart gave him an appointment in the Customs in

Legation at Washington. He took to his bed on Tuesday and Dr. Jamieson was sent for, but on Wednesday he got up and dressed himself preparatory to going out. He was persuaded to return to bed, where he died quite quietly, just as milk was being given him, of exhaustion and old age, at 10:30 a.m. yesterday. A telegram announcing his death was at once sent to Lady Alabaster in England. The funeral is to take place at the New Cemetery at 5:30 p.m. today.

The North – China Herald and Supreme Court & Consular Gazette, December 15, 1893

Piracy Near Wenchow

Piracy Near Wenchow

Notwithstanding the recent additions to the war junks cruising after pirates along the war junks cruising after pirates along the Min-Che sea coast, it seems that the pirates of Fukien and Taichow are still as numerous and as savage as ever. A junk and its consort bound from Ningpo to Foochow laden with rice and sundries were recently attacked near Wenchow by a couple of pirates, who boarded the merchants and having ransacked everything of value from the latter, left them with twenty-five killed and seriously wounded Strict order have been issued by the Governor-General, Tan, for the capture of war junks is now out, but it seems to be the universal opinion that the quest will be unsuccessful.

PIRACY NEAR WENCHOW.

Notwithstanding the recent additions to the war junks cruising after pirates along the Min-Chê sea coast, it seems that the pirates of Fukien and T'aichow are still as numerous and as savage as ever. A junk and its consort bound from Ningpo to Foochow laden with rice and sundries were recently attacked near Wênchow by a couple of pirates, who boarded the merchants and having ransacked everything of value from the latter, left them with twenty-five killed nd seriously wounded Strict orders have been issued by the Governor-General, T'an, for the capture of the pirates and quite a large fleet of war junks is now out, but it seems to be the universal opinion that the quest will be unsuccessful.

The North – China Herald and Supreme Court & Consular Gazette, July 13, 1894

Wenchow

(From A Special Correspondent)

WÊNCHOW.

(FROM A SPECIAL CORRESPONDENT.)

A TYPHOON.

On Friday, 29th June, a typhoon passed in very close proximity to this port. From 5 a.m. the barometer began to fall and continued to do so until 5 p.m., when it began to rise—the lowest reading was at that hour, 28.95. The wind blew from N.W. the whole time. Other barometer observers made the lowest reading at 5 p.m. All through Friday everyone was anxious as to the safety of the *Taian* which left this port at daylight on Thursday. She took away as passengers from us Consul Mansfield and Commissioner Novion (the latter only bound on a pleasure trip to Shanghai, the former to take up his appointment at Foochow).

SAFETY OF THE "TAIAN" REALISED.

Everyone hoped the ship would have been able to get into safe anchorage before the force of the typhoon was felt. All thoughts of the typhoon had almost passed until late last night (Monday, 2nd July), when Messrs. Mansfield and Novion appeared once more in our midst.

Wenchow

(From A Special Correspondent)

A Typhoon

On Friday, 29th June, a typhoon passed in very close proximity to this pot. From 5 a.m. The barometer began to fall and continued to do so until 5 p.m., when it began to rise-the lowest reading was at that hour, 28.95. The wind blew from N.W. The whole time. Other barometer observers made the lowest reading at 5 p.m. All through Friday everyone was anxious as to the safety of the Taian which left this port at daylight on Thursday. She took away as daylight on Thursday. She took away as passenger from us Consul Mansfield and Commissioner Novion (the latter only bound on a pleasure trip to Shanghai, the former to take up his appointment at Foochow).

Safety of the "Taian" Realised

Everyone hoped the ship would have been able to get into safe anchorage before the force of the typhoon was felt. All thoughts of the typhoon had almost passed until late last night (Monday, 2nd July), when Messrs. Mansfield and Novion appeared once more in our midst.

Story of the Passengers

Their story was soon told. After the Taian left on Thursday morning the engines became disable after steaming 35 miles, and the ship was compelled to anchor in a very bad anchorage between Quangta and Cliff Island .On Friday all the force of the typhoon was felt and the three anchors down dragged at least two miles towards the dangerous shore off Cliff Island; fortunately the anchors at anchors at last found holding ground and the helpless craft was saved. The lowest read of the barometer was 28.31. On Sunday the Chinese gun-vessel *ChaoWu* hove in sight coming from Wenchow. She was signalled and asked to tow the helpless ship into safer anchorage. Her commander, after being very rude, made a futile attempt to tow the ship-then ran up the signal "Can't tow you" and steamed off in the direction of Ningpo, the sea then being perfetectly calm and all signs of the typhoon done. Energy was not wanting on the *Taian*, for the engineers worked with a will to try and patch up, not only the engines, but the rudder gear, which become damaged during the typhoon; and later on Sunday she was able to crawl to White Rock, a very safe anchorage.

A Humane Official

On Monday the Chinese gun-vessel *Yuankai* came in sight and she was signalled and asked for help. She, too, had an official passenger on board, the late Wenchow Chentai. Nothing could exceed his kindness; he directed that gear, etc, wanted should be immediately lent, and he took the passengers both foreign and Chinese in the Yuankai to Wenchow. The Taian when left hoped to Wenchow. The Taian when left hoped to try and make her way to Shanghai even if she only did tow knots.

Sufferers

The tea and other cargo is much damaged by water. All the Chinese passengers lost their luggage as it had to be thrown overboard. Notwithstanding the fact that they pay full passage fare they are only given deck accommodation, their quarters proper below being used for cargo. It is to be hoped the China Merchants' Co. will recompense them for their loss, but too much sympathy cannot be expected form the Company. Since ever the Taian has been running on the line, it has been known that the engines were very defective and feeble. There is no steam windlass on the Taian and she does not carry enough sailors to heave anchor; when she leaves Wenchow, coolies from the shore have to be hired to help in getting the anchors up. On Sunday after the typhoon all passengers had to be roped in to heave up the anchors. The stearing gear is very primitive, ropes instead of iron rods connecting the rudder with the wheel. The telegraph from the bridge to the engine room is broken and the orders have to be carried verbally by a sailor. What would the British Board of Trade say to a ship like this being at sea?

It goes without saying that the whole community rejoice with Messrs. Mansfield and Novion in their miraculous escape, and from their remarks it is not likely their experience on the Taian will quickly be forgotten.

A Word of Praise

Both gentlemen speak in high terms of Captain Frigast, his officers and engineers. Nothing could possibly be more trying to a Captain, then to have a disabled ship in a bad anchorage in a typhoon and to be able to do nothing. Had the anchors not at last found holding ground, the ship must have gone on the rocks off Cliff Island. Twice the Captain summoned Messrs, Mansfield and Novion on the deck for he feared the ship was drifting nearer to the rocks.

Weather

It is very hot here now, and we long for a teamer to come and bring us news from the outer world.

Result of the Typhoons

Very little damage has been done locally; even the “MacW. buildings” have not suffered from the typhoon. (3rd July)

The North – China Herald and Supreme Court & Consular Gazette, December 28, 1894

Wenchow

(From A Correspondent)

Wenchow

(From A Correspondent)

In the absence of our one steamer, the "Universal Benefactor", there is little to disturb the normal quiet of our sleepy hollow. Since its last departure, however, the perilous adventures of two estimable lady members of the community have supplied considerable stimulus to conversation. The two ladies went on Thursday evening, the 6th, to a small village just on the borders of the port limits to spend the night at the house of some Christian natives with whom they held an evening service. Retiring to rest in due course, unsuspicious of danger, imagine their alarm about midnight on finding the room filled with a dozen or more fierce looking men armed with guns and spears, and carrying flaming torches. The air was full of the screams of women from whom bangles and earrings were being torn. The ladies themselves, in endeavouring to keep on their coverings, were roughly used and struck with bamboos, everything they had, bedding, clothes, were seized, and had it not been for the presence of mind if a native Bible woman who pushed through bandits to the side of the ladies and dragged them off through a neighbor's house, they would more than likely have been carried off and been held to ransom. As it was, they sped up the hillside barefooted, and there in the cold night air, clad in nothing but sleeping clothes, their feet torn, bruised and bleeding, they sat shivering for a long time till the discharge of guns, and the retreat of the torches told them the bandits had disappeared. Then they discovered that not only themselves,

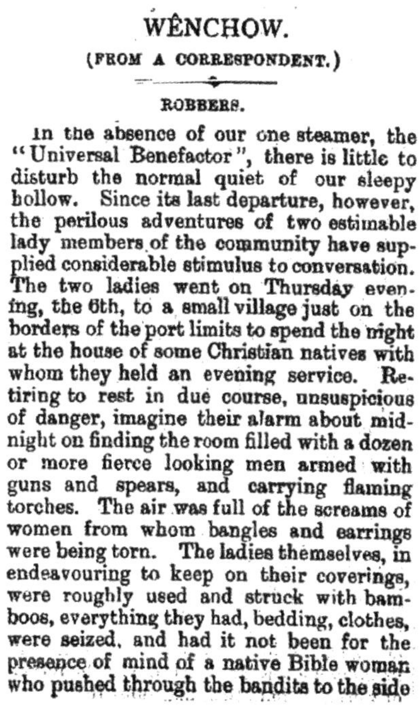
WÊNCHOW.

(FROM A CORRESPONDENT.)

ROBBERS.

In the absence of our one steamer, the "Universal Benefactor", there is little to disturb the normal quiet of our sleepy hollow. Since its last departure, however, the perilous adventures of two estimable lady members of the community have supplied considerable stimulus to conversation. The two ladies went on Thursday evening, the 6th, to a small village just on the borders of the port limits to spend the night at the house of some Christian natives with whom they held an evening service. Retiring to rest in due course, unsuspicious of danger, imagine their alarm about midnight on finding the room filled with a dozen or more fierce looking men armed with guns and spears, and carrying flaming torches. The air was full of the screams of women from whom bangles and earrings were being torn. The ladies themselves, in endeavouring to keep on their coverings, were roughly used and struck with bamboos, everything they had, bedding, clothes, were seized, and had it not been for the presence of mind of a native Bible woman who pushed through the bandits to the side but the villagers had lost almost everything that was moveable, and that three men, their servant included, had been carried off. With difficulty they next day reached the city and reported the matter to the Consul.

Captured

Three of the bandits have since been caught by the villagers but two have got away; the third is now in the magistrate's yamen. The names of the robbers are known, and one of their houses has been visited by some of the villagers. The magistrate has made a pretence of going to enquire into the matter; as a matter of fact he did not go near the place, but contented himself by sending a few runners who further extorted their travelling expenses from the already impoverished people.

The Officials Afraid

The officials do not seem to know their power; certainly they seem afraid to exert it. The cowardice of the officials, and the withdrawal of the soldiers from the district to fight the Japanese have left the neighbourhood at the mercy of any band of men who care to league themselves together to prey upon their fellows.

Strange Statement About the Consul

The Consul here has sent in a representation to the Taotai but has, we hear, at the same time told him that all ladies' passports are withdrawn and any found travelling outside the port limits are to be brought back by soldiers!

The North - China Herald and Supreme Court & Consular Gazette, February 22, 1895

Wenchow

(From Our Own Correspondent)

WÊNCHOW.

(FROM OUR OWN CORRESPONDENT.)

RUMOURS AND RUMOURS

and of the usual Chinese style fill the air hereabouts. The improbable is firmly believed, the probable never thought of, and that which has happened they haven't the least conception of. Tell a native south of the Yangtze that Port Arthur has fallen and both eyes and mouth gape open with an "A-a-h?" He doesn't even know that there ever has been such a place as Port Arthur. Tell him that Têng-chow is invested, he has no idea of its whereabouts or the importance of the statement. But—the British Fleet happens to pay a visit to the Chusan Islands; a month or two passes by, the fleet goes up to Chefoo, and forgets the existence of Chusan—*then* all is flutter in the Chinese dovecote; it is the Japanese who are at Chusan flying the British flag, and sure enough, they are going to honour Slocum-podgum with a visit.

Wenchow

(From Our Own Correspondent)

Rumours and Rumours

and of the usual Chinese style fill the air hereabouts. The improbable is firmly believed, the probable never thought of, and that which has happened they haven't the least conception of. Tell a native south of the Yangtze that Port Arthur has fallen and both eyes and mouth gape open with an "A-a-h?" He doesn't even know that there ever has been such a place as Port Arthur. Tell him that Tengchow is invested, he has no idea of its whereabout or the importance of the statement. But—the British Fleet happens to pay a visit to the Chusan Islands; a month or two passes by, the fleer goes up to Chefoo, and forgets the existence of Chusan—then all is flutter in the Chinese dovecote; it is the Japanese who are at Chusan flying the British flag, and sure enough, they are going to honour Slocum-podgum with a visit.

The North – China Herald and Supreme Court & Consular Gazette, March 1, 1895

Wenchow

(From Our Own Correspondent)

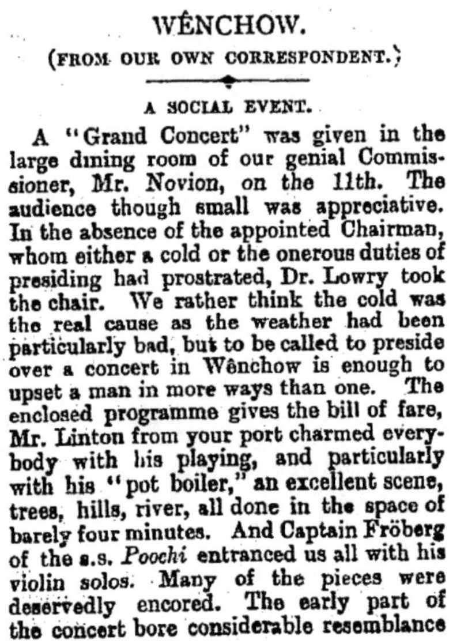

WÊNCHOW.

(FROM OUR OWN CORRESPONDENT.)

A SOCIAL EVENT.

A "Grand Concert" was given in the large dining room of our genial Commissioner, Mr. Novion, on the 11th. The audience though small was appreciative. In the absence of the appointed Chairman, whom either a cold or the onerous duties of presiding had prostrated, Dr. Lowry took the chair. We rather think the cold was the real cause as the weather had been particularly bad, but to be called to preside over a concert in Wênchow is enough to upset a man in more ways than one. The enclosed programme gives the bill of fare, Mr. Linton from your port charmed everybody with his playing, and particularly with his "pot boiler," an excellent scene, trees, hills, river, all done in the space of barely four minutes. And Captain Fröberg of the s.s. *Poochi* entranced us all with his violin solos. Many of the pieces were deservedly encored. The early part of the concert bore considerable resemblance

Wenchow

(From Our Own Correspondent)

A Social Event

A "Grand Concert" was given in the large dining room of our genial Commissioner, Mr. Novion, on the 11th. The audience though small was appreciative. In the absence of the appointed Chairman, whom either a cold or the onerous duties of presiding had prostrated, Dr. Lowry took the chair. We rather think the cold was the real cause as the weather had been particularly bad, but to be call to preside over a concert in Wenchow is enough to upset a man in more ways than one. The enclosed programme gives the bill of fare, Mr. Linton from your port charmed everybody with his playing, and particularly with his "pot boiler," an excellent scene, trees, hills, river, all done in the space of barely four minutes. And Captain Froberg of the s. s. *Poochi* entranced us all with his violin solos. Mandy of the pieces were deservedly encored. The early part of the concert bore considerable resemblance to a funeral party, until Mr. Heywood happily convulsed both the audience and himself by reading Mark Twain's affecting account of "Aurelia's Unfortunate Young Man." Such an important event, not likely to be repeated for a decade, marks an epoch in the history of Wenchow, The following is programme:—

Part I

1.—Opening Overture.—*Lieder ohne uorte*—Violins, Messrs. Hogg & Heywood.

2.—Song—*The Charge of the Light Brigade*......Dr. Lowry.

3.—Song—*True till Death*. Mr. Lamond.

4.—Piano—*Carmen*......Mr. Linton.

5.—Song—*The Holy City*. Mrs. Soothill.

6.—Reading—*Aurelia's unfortunate Yong Men*. Rev. Mr. Heywood.

7.—Violin Solo—*Auld Robin Gray*......Capt. Fröberg.

8.—Recitation—*The Prayer of a Mariner's Mother*. Mr. Ljunglöf.

9.—Song—*Bedouin Love Song*......Rev. Mr. Soothill.

10.—Reading—*A discususion on Humour*......Dr. Hogg.

Part II

1.—Opening Overture. Violins, Messrs. Hogg & Heywood

2.—*The Song of the Brush*. Mr. Linton.

3.—Song......Mr. Lamond.

4.—Song—*Good Company*. Mr. Soothill.

5.—Violin Solo—*The Gondoliers* (Fantasia).......Dr. Hogg.

6.—Reading—*Buttous*......Rev. Mr. Soothill

7.—Piano—*Mikado*......Mr. Linton.

8.—Song—*The Vicar of Bray*......Mr. Heywood.

9.—Violin Solo—*Blue Danube*......Capt. Fröberg.

10.—Song—*Four Jolly Smiths*......Mr. Lamond.

Violins and Piano—Finale—

La Marseillaise.

God Save the Queen

An Epidemic

A severe epidemic of smallpox (neither cause of nor cause by the concert) has been scouring this district for months. Thousands have died, mostly children; in fact the disease has in a remarkable manner confined itself almost entirely to children and young people. In the city of Yokts'ing over 1,000 die; in a large village near there 200, and such is the story all over the prefecture. It seems of late to have somewhat exhausted itself, and cases now attacked recover more readily.

Defensive Operation

The "big hill" is in the possession of a band of soldiers who have been lately hard at work at the ting-r, levelling the ground evidently with the intention of planting cannon there. The gates, too, are all guarded by soldiers with the evident purpose of giving the Jape a warm reception should they venture here.

Fengshui

In the city the people are civil enough and we are able to go about without fear. Considerable animosity, however, is still felt by the literati of the place because of the new Consulate. Europeans merely look upon it as a piece of perhaps necessary vandalism; it has ruined the beauty of the island. But the natives consider the fengshui of Wenchow has been seriously interfered with by it. At the last examination at the provincial capital not a single scholar from the prefecture of Wenchow obtained a degree. Such a disgrace has not fallen to the lot of Wenchow for ages. What can have cause it? Lack of devotion on the part of the examiners? Scamping on the part the examiners? Nothing of the kind. The cause lies in the soil of the sacred isle having been disturbed by the Western barbarian. Last year an M.A. standing on the bank opposite to the new Consulate, inveighed with all his strength against it and called on the people to pull it down. More recently it was seriously proposed to request the British authorities to have it removed; even yet grumblings are heard, but the Union Jack floats calmly on and heedeth not.

Official Obstruction

The war has considerable affected Mission work by rousing the people against the native Christians, who are called *fa-nang* (barbarians) because they are supervised by English missionaries. Last Sunday week a band of rowdies broke up a service up country at which about a hundred Christians were present. Bibles and hymn books were gathered together and made a bonfire of, women had their clothing torn off, and their ornaments stolen, and men were beaten. The magistrate has been appealed to; he promises fair and of course does absolutely nothing. This is but one out of several recent instances of severs persecution. One of the missions having found if necessary to enlarge its premise, has bought a piece of ground adjoining its present compound. Now the Taotai has ordered the magistrate to send for the vendor and the local registrars; the latter has abused them roundly for allowing land to be sold to foreigners to deprive the registrars of their office, and order that in future before any foreigner completes the purchase of property he, the intending vendor, all the neighbours must also or press their willingness, and any new buildings must be of one storey! Such a thing has never occurred here before, and if the magistrate is allowed to have his way, the purchase of property will become absolutely impossible, for no

Chinaman will dare to sell. It looks as if we are to have all the bad old days of official bullying and interference over again even in the open ports .In troublous times like these one naturally looks for official conciliation, and it is rather a rude shock to find irritating opposition taking its place. Such is the spirit that will write "*Mene, mene, takel, upharsin*" over the portals of this empire.

The North – China Herald and Supreme Court & Consular Gazette, March 8, 1895

Wenchow

(From Our Own Correspondent)

WÊNCHOW.

(FROM OUR OWN CORRESPONDENT.)

A QUIET TIME.

Here in Wênchow we become past-masters in the art of living either on pleasures that are gone, or on those which the future has in store. To some of us, however, the daily round of duties often proves a hard enough nut to crack, and we are ready wearily to exclaim "Oh, where can rest be found." But in spite of a dearth of solid facts to report we have a feeling that the womb of the future has events in store for us, though like all wise prophets we will not prophecy till after their fulfilment.

THE "POOCHI"

had a bad trip down this time, fog the whole way, resulting in a three days' journey. And the news she brought is almost as intangible as our own. The armistice had not yet been proclaimed, nor had Li Hung-chang gone to Japan. We shall have to possess our souls in patience for a fortnight, or even three weeks, as our steamer makes a run to Tientsin before she again "returns to bless."

Wenchow

(From Our Own Correspondent)

A Quiet Time

Here in Wenchow we become past-masters in the art of living either on pleasures that are gone, or on those which the future has in store. To some of us, however, the daily round of duties often proves a hard enough nut to crack and we are ready wearily to exclaim "Oh where can rest be found." But in spite of a dearth of solid facts to report we have a feeling that the womb of the future has events we will not prophecy till after their fulfilment.

The "Poochi"

had a bad trip down this time, fog the whole way, resulting in a three days' journey. And the news she brought is almost as intangible as our own. The armistice had not yet been proclaimed, nor had Li Hung-chang gone to Japan. We shall have to possess our souls in patience for a fortnight, or even three weeks, as our steamer makes a run to Tientsin before she again "returns to bless." Pity our darkness in the meantime and tell our tourist friends that the plain is now gay with whole sheets of fragrant rape-flower, that the bright sun shines (it rained the whole of yesterday) and that the cool breezes invite them.

Military Preparation

Our few constitutionals have become circumscribed. Soldiers infest the favourite hill of the community, and are rude to solitary ladies, and jocose to gentlemen. That bright outlook, the tingerh, has become encircled by earthworks—which prophets of evil say a good shower will lay low—and to which in the daylight there in no open sesame; its gun, said to be new, has been planted there, though it has been suggested that the man who fires it will run more risk than the one in front of it. The Taotai is the new broom which has swept all this earth up to the top of the *tingêrh*; two gates have been erected there, for what reason it is hard to say, unless a whole park of artillery is to be imported.

Robbers

We hear of a forced trip the city magistrate had to make up the creek the other day. A party of bandits attacked a village 150 *li* up early one morning. The villagers made a plucky defence, being armed with home-made guns. The battle continued all day, and at night when the bandits withdrew at least one of their number and two of the villagers were numbered among the slain .The *Hsien* went up with a posse of soldiers to inspect the village, and returned to probably relapse again into the normal state of *laissez-faire*. Poverty is the cause assigned by those who know for the spread of this outlawing. (3rd March)

The North – China Herald and Supreme Court & Consular Gazette, March 29, 1895

Wenchow

(From Our Own Correspondent)

Wenchow

(From Our Own Correspondent)

The Cold Snap

Even this port has not escaped the blizzard. Aged Chinese do not remember for decades past such a phenomenon as a heavy fall of snow late in the second moon, preceded by such furious thunderstorms as we had. It is feared the earlier fruits will have suffered, and as the season was an early and warm one the tea crop may be affected, but the orange blossoms are not yet out so that crop should not be any the worse.

Our New Broom,

the Taotai, together with the Chentai, inspected the forts and troops the other day in preparation for the visit of the Provincial Judge, who comes in place of the Governor. The Taotai has, we hear, been bringing strong pressure to bear on the military authorities to put an end to brigandage and piracy, urging that if order could not be maintained within it would be hopeless to maintain it without. Report has it that the telegraph survey is actually to be made, but as the surveyor had to go round borrowing his instruments the result will be looked for with interest.

WÊNCHOW.
(FROM OUR OWN CORRESPONDENT.)
THE COLD SNAP.
Even this port has not escaped the blizzard. Aged Chinese do not remember for decades past such a phenomenon as a heavy fall of snow late in the second moon, preceded by such furious thunderstorms as we had. It is feared the earlier fruits will have suffered, and as the season was an early and warm one the tea crop may be affected, but the orange blossoms are not yet out so that crop should not be any the worse.
OUR NEW BROOM,
the Taotai, together with the Chentai, inspected the forts and troops the other day in preparation for the visit of the Provincial Judge, who comes in place of the Governor. The Taotai has, we hear, been bringing strong pressure to bear on the military authorities to put an end to brigandage and piracy, urging that if order could not be maintained within it would be hopeless to maintain it without. Report has it that the telegraph survey is actually to be made, but as the surveyor had to go round borrowing his instruments the result will be looked for with interest.

Ignorant About the War

It would be amusing to listen to the ignorant remarks of the common people with reference to the war, did they not reveal what utter darkness invests the native mind on everything outside their own immediate field of vision. “They say the foreigners are rebelling,” was remarked in our hearing the other day, "but it must be mere talk," to which statement the other parties assented.

Wanting Money

A proclamation requesting loans to the Emperor at 7 per cent per annum has, we hear, been posted up. We have not yet seen a copy but the man in the street is saying with a sneer, "How poor the Emperor has become that he must go round begging; and who's going to lend him money anyhow?" It is common talk among the yamen people here that last week a man entered the Chentai's yamen and left a letter saying it was from the Titai. He was allowed to depart and on the letter being opened it professed to be from the Titai and stated that the Emperor was unable to run the Empire, that he wished to abdicate and that he begged his officers of rank to choose a more suitable occupant of the Throne. The letter seems to have caused considerable commotion throughout the yamens and indeed throughout the district.

Fearing the People

The great third month festival has been this year forbidden by special proclamation. The people generally do not like this prohibition and a man pretending to be a medium of the gods has been going about in chains threatening divine displeasure at this slight.

The Treaty, A Dead Letter

The famous "Missionary Circular", in which the Tsungli Yamen gave orders that no property should be transferred to foreigners till it had first been inspected by the local officials to see that the feng-shui of the neighbourhood would not be disturbed, is being brought from the abstract to the concrete here. More than a hundred notices have been sent out to the various land registrars, tipaos, etc., instructing them that no land may be transferred to Europeans, until the native lessor has petitioned and got the consent of the Magistrate. The effect of this is to make native landowners afraid to deal because the yamen leeches immediately begin to attach themselves, to the distress and possible ruin of the owners. Strong representations have been made to H.B.M.'s representative; he has ineffectually protested, the Oriental continues the even tenour of his way, and H.B.M.'s subjects might just as well be without a treaty. It is a pity that these anti-foreign orders from the Tsungli Yamen are not dealt with in Peking. These orders are now for the first time being put in force in Wenchow, with the evident intention of preventing any farther leases of land to foreigners. The Chinaman could buy acres in England without opposition; here in a treaty port with people anxious to sell, the official steps in with his Tsungli Yamen orders, and the man who dares to sell is sent for by the Magistrate or Taotai or both, bullied in open court, fleeced by the underlings, and any farther transfer of property thus effectually prevented.

Two Interesting Events

have occurred here during the *Poochi*'s absence. On the 12th inst. Mrs. Stott of the China Inland Mission, completed her fiftieth year and on the same day the twenty-fifth anniversary of her arrival in China. Such a unique experience has probably not fallen to the lot of any one else in China. To suitably celebrate the event, the Rev. W. E. Soothill, on behalf of the Wenchow missionaries, presented Mrs. Stott with a beautiful gold watch. About 300 Chinese guests, most of whom had also been invited to services and dinner, signalised the event by the presentation of a large and very handsome satin scroll which cost nearly $70, also many other smaller scrolls, pictures, candlesticks, etc., etc. All these gifts came as a great surprise to Mrs. Stott who had been kept in ignorance of the preparations. The Church was crowded on the occasion and impressive services were held.

Another

event of a somewhat similar though more convivial nature, was held on the 18th, in the celebration of the birthday of another missionary. It would be impossible for our genial doctor not to suitably commemorate the Pious and Immortal memory of Saint Patrick. Mrs. Lowry arranged an excellent programme and supper for the occasion. A debate in the "Bones Hall" with the doctor's operating table as desk opened the proceedings. "Women's Rights" was the subject. Dr. Hogg took the affirmative and Mr. Soothill the negative. Musical proverbs, a concert, telephone exchange, likenesses while you sit, letter kenning, etc., etc., followed by the supper agreeably occupied the time till midnight.

Consular Change

We hear that our Consul, Mr. Fraser, has received an intimation that his leave will be granted at an early date. As it is considerably overdue doubtless the "relief" will be hailed with considerable pleasure by Mr. Fraser. Speculation is busy with his probable successor, one of the Mr. Allens being mentioned as likely to succeed Mr. Fraser. (19th March)

The North – China Herald and Supreme Court & Consular Gazette, April 11, 1895

Wenchow

(From Our Own Correspondent)

WÊNCHOW.

(FROM OUR OWN CORRESPONDENT.)

CAPTURE OF THE PESCADORES CONFIRMED.

The *Peking* came in on Friday, the 29th, from Amoy, bringing word that she had been unable to go to Formosa as the Japanese are in possession of the Pescadores, and the Channel. She also brought the news of the murderous attack on Li Hung-chang, which is now the common talk of all the people here and has caused much excitement. If the brave old man gets safely over his wound this incident ought to be of some service to him, in raising him in the estimation of his own countrymen, and in stilling much of the prejudice his long maintained attitude in favour of peace has raised against him.

THE "PEKING" ON FIRE.

The *Peking* had the misfortune to catch fire on the way up from Amoy, and in consequence part of her cargo of oil had to be jettisoned. Through the prompt and energetic measures of her officers the fire was speedily got under. thought not before considerable damage had been done.

Wenchow

(From Our Own Correspondent)

Capture of the Pescadores Confirmed

The *Peking* came in on Friday, the 29th, from Amoy, bringing word that she had been unable to go to Formosa as the Japanese are in possession of the Pescadores, and the Channel. She also brought the news of the murderous attack on Li Hungchang, which is now the common talk of all the people here and has caused much excitement. If the brave old man gets safely over his wound this incident ought to be of some service to him, in raising him in the estimation of his own countrymen, and in stilling much of the prejudice his long maintained attitude in favour of peace has raised against him.

The "Peking" on Fire

The *Peking* had the misfortune to catch fire on the way up from Amoy, and in consequence part of her cargo of oil had to be jettisoned. Through the prompt and energetic measure of her officers the fire was speedily got under thought not before considerable damage had been done.

A Robbers' Ruse

The banditti have been busy again, and one hundred and twenty two of them dressed as the Futai's soldiers all carrying guns or other weapons, marched out from Nanch'i a week ago. One of their number was bound with chain as a prisoner, and then the Captain rode in a chair. They represented themselves as being in charge of the prisoner and were talking him to Hangchow. Travelling across the hills they came to a large village called T'alu, beyond the city of Ts'ingt'ien, which they attacked by night. The villagers resisted bravely but in vain, the village was ransacked, and everything portable was carried off. The Methodist Mission here has a station at T'alu and lost several articles of minor valuc. The bandits returned by another road and the following night made a further attack on a village in Sich'i called Sunt'sa; their number here had been reduced to 94, probably rest had been detailed to transfer the booty their lair.

Hungry Robbers

We are told of half a dozen of them attacking a lonely house in the hills, where they seized the husband, tied him up in a tree, bound the other members of the family together, killed the poor man's pig, cooked the edible internal organs, and carried off the rest, leaving the poor folks to shift as best they could and to lose pig which to them was as valuable as his horse is it the small farmer at home. No wonder the wealthier residents of Sich'i and Nanch'i keep armed men on guard all night for fear of attack, nor that many villages are being fortified with gates, their walls being strengthened, and firearms bought. In a country where the materials for making power are contraband, the question naturally suggests itself, Where do the people and the banditti get their powder from? And Echo answers Where?

A Typical Case

The *Hsien* was met by one of our community 1,500 feet up one of the northern hills the other day on his way to hold an inquest on the body of a deceased Chinaman; the charge is of causing his death and is laid against several of the well-to-do residents in the village. We have it on excellent authority that the facts of the case are as follows :Last autumn the deceased man knew where his uncle had stowed $184; he informed a man from a distant village, arranged for the latter to do the stealing and for both parties to share. The transaction was effected, as arranged, but the thief was tracked. He fled; his wife was taken, brought before the magistrate, tried, and dismissed. She was kept imprisoned by the runners, but the husband got her out by a bribe of eighty dollars. In the meantime she had revealed the author of the crime; the uncle's party enquired into it, found the charge true, and in usual Chinese fashion went and smashed his house, and his *lares et penates*. The family is known to be a bad one anyhow. Two months after the man is taken ill, and in due course dies, whereupon his relatives come down to the city, lay a charge against the uncle and other well-to-do men of harassing the man to death. As the charge is laid against men of means the *yamen* harpies take the matter up with avidity; the Magistrate, no doubt, at their instigation, travels up a two days' journey with about ten chairs and 60 followers. All the followers must be fed, the chair bearers paid, and the harpies satisfied and the end of it all is ruination to the thrifty, and injustice all round.

The North - China Herald and Supreme Court & Consular Gazette, April 19, 1895

Wenchow

(From Our Own Correspondent)

Wenchow

(From Our Own Correspondent)

Quite a Scare

prevails here just now. The Japanese are coming, so 'tis said. And those who lay value enough on their *lares et penates*, which phrase to a Chinaman means his goods rather than his gods, are seriously contemplating their removal to regions more remote. The chief obstacle to many seems to be the fear that escaping the Scylla of shot and shell may only land them on the Charybdis of banditti or dishonest relatives. In the meantime the officials are placing insurmountable difficulties in the way of any Japanese entry into this hub of the universe. The foe will first of all run the risk of being blown sky high by electric torpedoes; the ships that escape these will stand little chance of passing the batteries along the banks of the river; the small remains that battered and shattered crawl past these will be blown to splinters by the new gun on the hill, and by the way of making assurance doubly sure all the ancient guns of Ta Ming or later periods, are now being furbished up to utterly annihilate whatever fragments of the Japanese fleet may still remain. These ancient guns, the more valuable that, having been cast in almost pre-historic times, and having well and safely guarded the city walls for so many ages, they are evidently chock-full of the indomitable spirit of generations of ancestors, not like the modern productions which cannot boast of ancestry and inches of rust—mere *parvenus*. So for the small consideration of fifty Mexicans these honoured but hitherto much neglected spit-fires around and over which the grass has sprung up and withered year after year

WÊNCHOW.

(FROM OUR OWN CORRESPONDENT.)

QUITE A SCARE

prevails here just now. The Japanese are coming, so 'tis said. And those who lay value enough on their *lares et penates*, which phrase to a Chinaman means his goods rather than his gods, are seriously contemplating their removal to regions more remote. The chief obstacle to many seems to be the fear that escaping the Scylla of shot and shell may only land them on the Charybdis of banditti or dishonest relatives. In the meantime the officials are placing insurmountable difficulties in the way of any Japanese entry into this hub of the universe. The foe will first of all run the risk of being blown sky high by electric torpedoes; the ships that escape these will stand little chance of passing the batteries along the banks of the river; the small remains that battered and shattered crawl past these will be blown to splinters by the new gun on the hill, and by way of making assurance doubly sure all the ancient guns of Ta Ming or later periods are now being furbished up to utterly annihilate whatever fragments of the Japanese fleet may still remain. These from time immemorial, are now roasted with charcoal on the Commissioner's drill ground, so as to clear off the rust and bake the ancestral spirit well in the iron. Then they are to be carried back and remounted—and woe be it to any Japanese ship that escapes the other dangers to fall at last within the range of these ancient and honourable weapons. "It is blood that tells," even with guns; but it has been suggested the blood will be that of the man who fires the gun.

Art

All these preparations seen to make no impression on the spirits of the foreign community. To-day a pleasant diversion was given us by Mr. Linton from your port, by an exhibition on board the s. s. *Poochi* of paintings made by him during his stay in Wenchow. Two of his local pictures, one of the famous "Shihment'ung Waterfall," another of the falls across the river were very much admired. A third, "A sunrise on the river," attracted much attention and was by some deemed the best picture in the room. The "Interior of a Temple" is and imposing work and whoever obtains it will have a striking reminder of life in China. Figure painting was also well represented, and numerous unfinished sketches promising effective results when complete, bore testimony to the artist's diligence and well known ability. Mr. Linton Promises to effect more than the merchants have hitherto done to bring this port into prominence, and to materially increase the influx of visitors, with or without palette and easel.

The North - China Herald and Supreme Court & Consular Gazette, May 10, 1895

Wenchow

(From Our Own Correspondent)

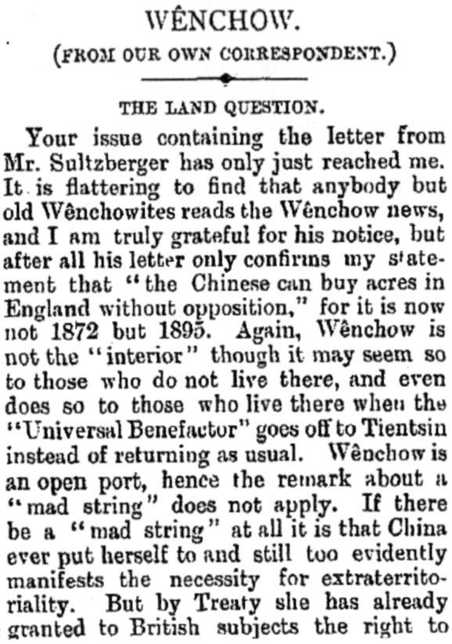

WÊNCHOW.

(FROM OUR OWN CORRESPONDENT.)

THE LAND QUESTION.

Your issue containing the letter from Mr. Sultzberger has only just reached me. It is flattering to find that anybody but old Wênchowites reads the Wênchow news, and I am truly grateful for his notice, but after all his letter only confirms my statement that "the Chinese can buy acres in England without opposition," for it is now not 1872 but 1895. Again, Wênchow is not the "interior" though it may seem so to those who do not live there, and even does so to those who live there when the "Universal Benefactor" goes off to Tientsin instead of returning as usual. Wênchow is an open port, hence the remark about a "mad string" does not apply. If there be a "mad string" at all it is that China ever put herself to and still too evidently manifests the necessity for extraterritoriality. But by Treaty she has already granted to British subjects the right to

Wenchow

(From Our Own Correspondent)

The Land Question

Your issue containing the letter from Mr. Sultzberger has only just reached me. It is flattering to find that anybody but old Wenchowites reads the Wenchow news, and I am truly grateful for his notice, but after all his letter only confirms my statement that "the Chinese can by acres in England without opposition," for it is now not 1872 but 1895. Again, Wenchow is not the "interior" though it may seem so to those who do not live there when the "Universal Benefactor" goes off to Tientsin instead of returning as usual. Wenchow is an open port, hence the remark about a "mad string" does not apply. If there be a "mad string" at all it is that China ever put herself to and still too evidently manifests the necessity for extraterritoriality. But by Treaty she has already granted to British subjects the right to lease land without let or hindrance from the officials, and the least she can do is to lease land without let or hindrance from the officials, and the least she can do is to maintain this arrangement until she is in a position to make a fresh one-especially seeing that China's own subjects, on Mr. Sultzberger's own admission, are able not only to lease, but actually to purchase in England, to say noting of those more advanced continental nations he mentions, to the full extent of purse or credit. This, too, without let or hindrance, whereas the treaties are now so much dead letter here, and in other places in China, that no registrar dare part with a certificate to a British subject until the lessor has petitioned the magistrate and obtained his permission before signing the deeds. Anyone whose experience has not been confined to Shanghai, and who knows the attitude of mandarindom towards Europeans, readily understands the deeper meaning of this. Lessors hesitate to sign transferences, except either on exorbitant terms or on a guarantee to cover *yamen* expenses, which expenses may be serious or otherwise as the *yamen* harpies decide. It is all very well to say that European Ministers have not accepted these riders of the Tsungli Yamen, but the fact remains that they(the Ministers) know of them, and to ignore what is almost forced on the attention is to give a tacit acceptance, for "silence gives consent."

The Terms of Peace

are considered very humiliating here by those who know them; but the news of peace dose not seem to spread so rapidly as did that of the loss of Penghu and Formosa. Two hundred millions is a term incomprehensible to the ordinary native—he merely gasps, and would like to say *putung*, but daren't.

On the Defensive

In consideration of the presence of the Japs so near as Formosa the militia has been called up in the shape of the firemen who keep watch at night in brilliant uniform but with borrowed spears and tridents; these are strengthened by the various tradesmen, etc., of the city who take duty one evening in three. Probably the news departure, for the officials will not care to pay the tradesmen would mush rather stay at home.

Several Pirates

were beheaded here the other day. A man was treated at the Methodist Mission Hospital for a gunshot wound received during an attack by pirates near the mouth of the river. Dr. Lavy (in the absence of Dr. Hogg) excised the bullet, and the man is progressing admirably. Dr. Hogg has since extracted a bullet from the left temple of another native which was received from pirates three months ago. The man had a narrow escape of his life. To pursue this chapter of horrors a little further I may as well mention here that on Sunday, the 21st of April, an overcrowded boat had only left the East Gate jetty a short distance, when a gust of wind capsized it. Out of 26 occupants only seven were saved; amongst the drowned being two Christian women belonging to the China Inland Mission who were returning home from service.

The First Tea

The *Poochi* carries up the first tea of the season—about 3,000piculs—and with other merchandise she has a full cargo this trip.

The North－China Herald and Supreme Court & Consular Gazette, June 7, 1895

Wenchow

(From Our Own Correspondent)

Wenchow

(From Our Own Correspondent)

Hideous Torteires

Our chief local official is distinguishing himself again, and winning the admiration of the people. The pirates are to be put down. Now nobody except the pirates will object to this, but a comparison of methods really seems to show up the pirate as a mere tyro in barbarity as compared with our local archetype of China's civilization. This gentleman, aided by his son, we are told, daily examines a couple of pirates unfortunate enough not to be beheaded when caught. The sight of a wretched looking prisoner being half carried through the streets yesterday laden with chains, prompts us to give your readers through the medium of these pirates another little peep behind the scenes. The usual place for examinations of this kind is the magistrate's Yamén; H.E. (whose name we might call "Thorough" had we not observed that the New Fort erected only a month or two ago on the top of the hill has suffered severely during last week's heavy rain) fearing apparently that the magistrate would not exhibit energy enough, has had the magistrate's inquisitorial instruments brought over to his own *Yamén*. There the two poor wretches are daily made to kneel on chains, a bar of wood is passed behind the flexure of the knees, the back fixed firmly against an uptight by pulling the queue through a hole in it, the arms are stretched out and fastened to a cross-piece, and the thumbs tied with stretched cords; the machine is set to work, the sufferer's bones start from their sockets, excruciating agony racks his every limb, unconsciousness happily relieves him, and to bring him to his senses his tormentors beat him with long canes, and dash water over him. He is taken away for that day cast into a loathsome dungeon, to be brought

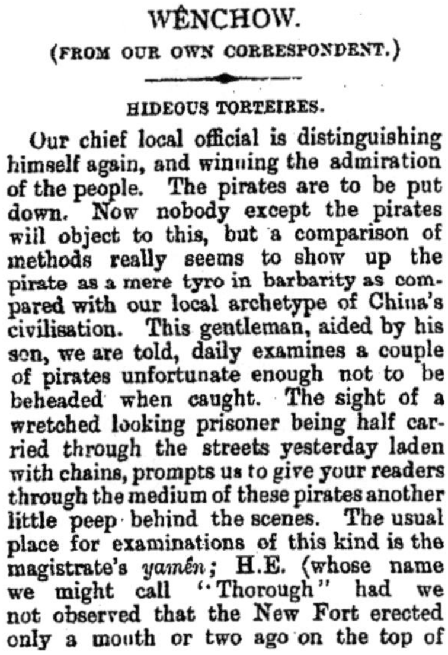
WÊNCHOW.

(FROM OUR OWN CORRESPONDENT.)

HIDEOUS TORTEIRES.

Our chief local official is distinguishing himself again, and winning the admiration of the people. The pirates are to be put down. Now nobody except the pirates will object to this, but a comparison of methods really seems to show up the pirate as a mere tyro in barbarity as compared with our local archetype of China's civilisation. This gentleman, aided by his son, we are told, daily examines a couple of pirates unfortunate enough not to be beheaded when caught. The sight of a wretched looking prisoner being half carried through the streets yesterday laden with chains, prompts us to give your readers through the medium of these pirates another little peep behind the scenes. The usual place for examinations of this kind is the magistrate's *yamên*; H.E. (whose name we might call "Thorough" had we not observed that the New Fort erected only a month or two ago on the top of up again next day for a repetition of the process. The dark ages are not past yet; those who want work need not want long. What ended the Spanish Inquisition can end this.

Floods

There were heavy floods in the river last week, coffins, buffaloes, furniture, everything was floating down to the sea. For many hours the river was impassable. A junk got loose near the west gate; in trying to anchor again it broke loose a raft of bamboos, there in turn careered down the river, and colliding with two Taichow junks sunk them, drowning eleven poor fellows who were on board.

An Accident

As two of our community were last week crossing the creek, 30miles away, they were hailed by a native military officer and his men. They wished to know if there were any expeditious way of recovering the body of a comrade drowned six hours before. It appeared they had walked to this point by noon, the ferry boat was on the opposite bank with no one in sight. The young soldier, a Honan man, stripped and attempted to swim across for the boat; but when half way "a devil seized him by the feet, and dragged him instantly down." His distressed comrades had spent the whole afternoon fruitlessly dragging for the body with brambles sunk by means of stones.

Is This Laziness?

A "communicated" article in an issue of yours a fortnight or more ago contrasting the Japanese very favourably with the Chinese rather astonished some of us here by calling the Chinese lazy. It so happened that on the day we read it we had been stopped up the by the tide and had been compelled to get out and hires chairs. The men who carried us in had been tapping opium from two in the morning till sunrise, and transplanting rice or pumping water till we hired them at 4 o'clock; they brought us in the rain 30 *li* into the city, took their money and ate some rice, etc., walked the 30 *li* back at once, reaching home after 11, and would be up at work again at 2 in the morning. All over the south of China the farmer is working at this time of the year from least daybreak to sunset, and bard work it is. A building is being erected near us; the masons and carpenters are at work by 6 o'clock, having breakfasted; their midday meal is taken before eleven; they are at work again before one, and they work till 6:30 with a lunch at 4 taken standing. Such is the native workman, except that those who work in shops generally open till seven or later in the evening, the assistants rarely finishing before 8 or 9. Schools open soon after seven, and a diligent student makes the late night and the too, too early morning hideous with his howls. What the Shanghai “boy” may be I cannot say from prolonged experience, but depend upon it if he is lazy it is the fault of his master. Slow he may be, inert in character if you like, lazy by no means.

The North - China Herald and Supreme Court & Consular Gazette, June 14, 1895

Wenchow

(From Our Own Correspondent)

WÊNCHOW.

(FROM OUR OWN CORRESPONDENT.)

CONFESSING UNDER TORTURE.

Two of the men we wrote about last charged with piracy and suffering torture under the Taotai's vigorous hand, have we hear confessed to the charge. Another man has been brought in and seeing the terrible nature of the torture said it was better to die than endure those agonies, so admitted the charge at once—and wisely too we should say, for the choice lies between being tortured to confession and then being put to death or being put to death without the torture. Confession means death, refusal to confess means torture continued till the poor wretch does confess.

EVEN A WORM WILL TURN.

Another case is exciting some interest in the city, arising out of the big fire last December. A merchant owns property adjoining a small canal; another small merchant had a shop over this canal. A few years ago a proclamation was posted for-

Wenchow

(From Our Own Correspondent)

Confessing under Torture

Two of the men we wrote about last charged with piracy and suffering torture under the Taotai's vigorous hand, have we hear confessed to the charge. Another man has been brought in and seeing the terrible nature of the torture said it was better to die than endure those agonies, so admitted the charge at once—and wisely too we should say, for the choice lies between being tortured to confession and then being put to death or being put to death without torture. Confession means death, refusal to confess means torture continued till the poor wretch does confess.

Even A Worm Will Turn

Another case is exciting some interest in the city, arising out of the big fire last December. A merchant owns property adjoining a small canal; another small merchant had a shop over this canal. A few years ago a proclamation was posted for bidding the construction or reconstruction of any buildings over the public canals—a law as carefully carried into effect as Chinese laws generally are, as witness new buildings over canals in various parts of the city, erected through the influence on various yamenites of the almighty dollar. Merchant number on, thinking to oust merchant two and thus get a little more elbow room, accused the owner of two's shop of reconstructing over a public canal. The magistrate cast out the petition, as did the perfect later—but not so the Taotai—consequently the shop had to be pulled down without a cent of compensation. Merchant number one, inflated with success, now turned his attention to a man on the opposite side of the street; a poor man who had small erection over the canal in which he baked and sold small cakes. This man he also forced into pulling down his reconstructed building. A mat-shed took its place and despite the entreaties of the poor baker to allow him to earn a bowl of rice for himself and family, he was compelled to remove the mat-shed and all. Filled with resentment and brooding over his wrongs he happened to meet his oppressor the other day, all dressed in holiday clothes. Seizing him in his strong arms he pushed him time and again into one of those beds of hidden violets which obtrude themselves so on the attention in every southern city. The sequence is that the oppressor has had his pride effectually humbled for a lifetime, while the oppressed having no money to fight with has taken to his heels, and we can't help hoping he will succeed in keeping out of sight.

Double Dealing

Apropos of the recent Tsung-li Yamen circular abrogation the demand that the local officials must be consult before land was transferred to foreigners, our local officials a few weeks ago sent out as I then told you hundreds of notices to the various land registrars in accordance with the old order. For the evident purpose of creating difficulty in certain districts these notices have been publicly posted up. This face having been brought to the notice of our energetic Consul, he has communicated with the authorities to ask if they are aware of the new regulations abrogating the necessity for consulting the local officials. The reply came that they received such counter instructions after the private notifications to their clerks had been issued. Mr. Fraser is now rightly demanding that inasmuch as these “private” notices have been public. In this we trust in the interests of Europeans generally, and for the prestige of H.B.M.’s Minister he will be successful.

A Reported Calamity

We hear that during the recent hoods two villages were destroyed and over 200 lives lost, but have not yet been able to get definite confirmation of the report. (5th May)

The North - China Herald and Supreme Court & Consular Gazette, June 21, 1895

Wenchow

(From Our Own Correspondent)

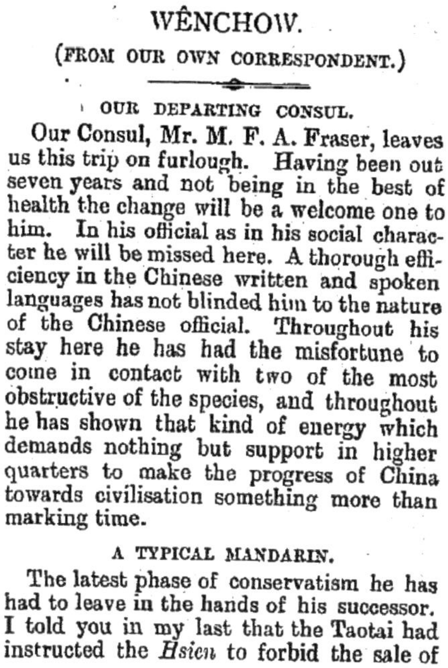
WÊNCHOW.

(FROM OUR OWN CORRESPONDENT.)

OUR DEPARTING CONSUL.

Our Consul, Mr. M. F. A. Fraser, leaves us this trip on furlough. Having been out seven years and not being in the best of health the change will be a welcome one to him. In his official as in his social character he will be missed here. A thorough efficiency in the Chinese written and spoken languages has not blinded him to the nature of the Chinese official. Throughout his stay here he has had the misfortune to come in contact with two of the most obstructive of the species, and throughout he has shown that kind of energy which demands nothing but support in higher quarters to make the progress of China towards civilisation something more than marking time.

A TYPICAL MANDARIN.

The latest phase of conservatism he has had to leave in the hands of his successor. I told you in my last that the Taotai had instructed the *Hsien* to forbid the sale of

Wenchow

(From Our Own Correspondent)

Our Departing Consul

Our Consul, Mr. M. F. A. Fraser, leaves us this trip on furlough. Having been out seven years and not being in the best of him. In his official as in his social character he will be missed here. A thorough efficiency in the Chinese written and spoken languages has not blinded him to the nature of the Chinese official. Throughout his stay here he has had the misfortune to come in contact with two of the most obstructive of the species, and throughout he has shown that kind of energy which demands nothing but support in higher quarters to make the progress of China towards civilisation something more than marking time.

A Typical Mandarin

The latest phase of conservatism he has had to leave in the hands of his successor. I told you in my last that the Taotai had instructed the *Hsien* to forbid the sale of land to foreigners until the local officials had notified their assent. These notices were publicly posted in the rural districts, though not in the city, against this violation of treaty rights Mr. Fraser strongly protested, and pointed out the new Tsungli Yamên orders. We hear that the Taotai has acknowledged the receipt of these orders, but has definitely declined to publicly abrogate the notices already published, on the extraordinary ground that he does not think the Tsungli Yamên ever intended their new orders to become public property! We are told too that he frankly cites, of all people, the antiforeign

Ruler of Szechuan, the promoter of the recent riots there, as his ensample in this his present attitude. The matter, we hear, has been referred to the Provincial Governor and to Peking for adjudication, whence we hope such orders will come as will bring this representative of the official class, whose delight it is to sit and torture prisoners, to a sense of what is right. The attitude of deliberate opposition maintained by certain mandarins towards foreigners, and this despite China's recent defeat, in only to be accounted for on the ground of a deliberate attempt to embarrass the Manchu Emperor with a view to something more serious in the near future. *Gallia omnis est in tres partes divisa, quarum unam, etc.* Such men as these may hasten the application of this phrase to a country not so far way as Gaul. (17th June)

The North – China Herald and Supreme Court & Consular Gazette, July 12, 1895

Wenchow

(From Our Own Correspondent)

WÊNCHOW.

(FROM OUR OWN CORRESPONDENT.)

ANOTHER RIOT.

Now that the war is over, and the necessity no longer exists for the native to sit on the hedge waiting to see if he must don a foreign yoke, he is relieving his feelings as was to many foreseen, by rejoicing and huzzaing in the shape of riots. The news of the Szechuan trouble had already reached here, and now the whole district is further and more violently disturbed with exaggerated rumours of a recent riot at Pingyang, a China Inland Mission station 100 *li* south of here. The case is bad enough, without any additions.

THE ALLEGED CAUSE.

A fortnight ago, during the Dragon Boat Festival, boats belonging to two villages 30 *li* from Pingyang had a contest. One of them had to lose the day, and of course did. But what could be the cause? A Taoist priest was called in, who discovered an eyeless idol! Who could have gouged these eyes out if not a Christian? A "medium" confirmed the theory under

Wenchow

(From Our Own Correspondent)

Another Riot

Now that the war is over, and the necessity no longer exists for the native to sit on the hedge waiting to see if he must don a foreign yoke, he is relieving his feelings as was to many foreseen, by rejoicing and huzzaing in the shape of riots. The news of the Szechuan trouble had already reached here, and now the whole district is further and more violently disturbed with exaggerated rumours of a recent riot at Pingyang, a China Inland Mission station 100 *li* south of here. The case is bad enough without any additions.

The Alleged Cause

A fortnight ago, during the Dragon Boat Festival, boats belonging to two villages 30 *li* from PINGYANG had a contest. One of them had to lose the day, and of course did. But what could be the cause? A Taoist priest was called in, who discovered an eyeless idol! Who could have gouged these eyes out if not a Christian? A "medium" confirmed the theory under the influence of a certain god. A band of roughs went along to the house of a prominent Christian, and threatened that if the boat failed again his house would be destroyed. That was Thursday, the 27th of June. The Magistrate was duly informed of the threat. On Saturday they began with a newly erected chapel, which was soon burnt to the ground. A literary gentleman who had been urging the mob against the Christians now fearful of the consequence regretted the step he had taken and almost on his kness begged the rioters to desist. There blood was up, it was too late. From one house they went to another, until not one of the Christians' houses was left standing. Everything was deliberately taken outside, and bonfired; where the house adjoined others it was destroyed, where it stood alone it was given over to the devouring element. The Christians had to flee to the city of Pingyang to the care of the missionary. Next day the rioters sought out other Christians in other villages and continued.

The Work of Destruction

On Monday the Magistrate and the Wenchow Taotai's Weiyuan who happened to be in Pingyang went off with soldiers. Before reaching the spot a river had to be crossed. "Thousands" of people were waiting on the opposite bank; they had taken possession of the ferry boats. Later the two officials got cross in other boats leaving the soldiers behind. They had a difficult task before them so they soon give it up and returned, after making the gentry responsible for order.

Threaten to Spread

But order is not yet restored. Monday, Tuesday, Wednesday, saw more houses destroyed; Friday another and Saturday another. Every Christian house that side of the river is destroyed, and the rioters are still massed together. Twenty houses are gone, twenty families driven out, and fifty-one homeless natives are residing in the missionary's house and looking to him for help. The rioters now threaten to cross the river and carry the attack further afield. Our Consul, Mr. Fox, has made strong representations to the Taotai, who sent off, it is said, 400 soldiers on Saturday morning. They had not reached Ping-yang on Sunday evening. Though it is only a 12 hours' journey, and report, says they are resting part way, or according to another report, have been refused a passage across the Jiuan river.

The Force of Example

The people in this city and neighbourhood extol the valour of the Pingyangites in thus boldly attacking the foreigner and his religion, and the attitude both of young and old here has during the past week become very decidedly antipathetic to every foreigner they see. The youngsters do ten times as much shooting as heretofore, and their elders are much bolder and more abusive. If the infection is not too spread prompt steps will have to be taken. Some suspect a more serious basis for the riots than mere anti-foreign prejudices.

Sympathy

The heart of every member of this community throbs in deepest sympathy with our respected Customers Doctor and his dear little daughter in their recent distressing bereavement. (8th July)

The North – China Herald and Supreme Court & Consular Gazette, July 26, 1895

Wenchow

(From Our Own Correspondent)

Wenchow

(From Our Own Correspondent)

A Better State of Affairs

There has been happily for us, no further extension of the Pingyang riot, but the whole district is still seething with excitement; a spark would set the heather blazing, and bring woe to perhaps some thousands of Christians hereabouts. Our Consul Mr. Fox, is a gallant standard-bearer, and even the Taotai is beginning to recognize that H.B.M.'s flag flutters within the scope of observation. Another little aid to any deficiency of vision in this respect will be the news that Sir Nicholas O'Conor has, as we are told, obtained the promise of the Tsungli Yamen to order the withdrawal of the obnoxious notices which forbade the sale of land to foreigners without official consent first had and obtained, The withdrawal of these by the substitution of others of us an opposite nature will, we trust be graciously carried into execution. Can one wonder at riots when the highest local authority threaten severe punishment on any one selling land to Europeans without official consent, and also threatening the dismissal and punishment of yamen employees, who permit such transfers to take place?

WÊNCHOW.

(FROM OUR OWN CORRESPONDENT.)

A BETTER STATE OF AFFAIRS.

There has been, happily for us, no further extension of the Pingyang riot, but the whole district is still seething with excitement; a spark would set the heather blazing, and bring woe to perhaps some thousands of Christians hereabouts. Our Consul, Mr. Fox, is a gallant standard-bearer, and even the Taotai is beginning to recognise that H.B.M.'s flag flutters within the scope of observation. Another little aid to any deficiency of vision in this respect will be the news that Sir Nicholas O'Conor has, as we are told, obtained the promise of the Tsungli Yamên to order the withdrawal of the obnoxious notices which forbade the sale of land to foreigners without official consent first had and obtained. The withdrawal of these by the substitution of others of an opposite nature will, we trust, be graciously carried into execution. Can one wonder

A Suggested Remedy

Some of the destroyed houses are already been rebuilt, and promise have been given that all shall be restored. This is excellent as far as it goes, but not till an example is made of a few of the gentry will such frolics as these be put a stop to. The young men of the villages enjoy it, and knowing they will not be held responsible in any way, are not loth to act on suggestions from the village authorities. A “button” or two less after a riot would ensure a diminution of the riots.

In this case of a trail (better termed a fiasco) has been held by the Pingyang, magistrate. Despite the fact that he had promised to ask the Mission before arresting Christians, he sent and in broad daylight dragged one of them through miles of country and a jeering populace to the city. There in a yamen so crowded with people, so crowded that a native preacher was unable to obtain access, the poor fellow, in all has crowded solitariness, was “examined” by the Magistrate. The charges made against him were of taking out an idol’s eyes and internal arrangements, but no accuser was brought to face him. It appears that two days after the riots began, the local tipao went to this Christian’s house, pointed to the ancestral incense bowl, and asked: “if you are a Christian, what’s this here for?” Then lifting up his pipe he hooked it’s lower and into the censer and pulled it to the ground, and on to the floor rolled an idol’s intestines, consisting of bits of paper put there by the subscribers to the idol’s erection. “What are these?” said he. “Why; so you are the iconoclast!” It was a very evident “plant;” the Christian denied the charge, but this same tipao has now come forth with his scandalous charge. Such is the latest phase of the Pingyang riots. In the meantime the fifty-one people are still homeless and absolutely dependent on their fellow Christians, native and foreign, for food and everything; the early rice is now ready for reaping, and they cannot go to reap it. The notion that it is easy for the Chinaman to be a Christian is a very mistaken one; all suffer ostracism more or less, many lose their employment, some suffer severe persecution in home and village, and others are called upon to suffer as the Szechuan and Pingyang Christians are now doing; the astonishing thing is the patience manifested by them under such trying experiences.

An Influx of Soldiers

The garrison here has been strengthened by the arrival of 500 solders brought from Ningpo on Sunday by H. I. M. S. *Yuankai*. We are waiting to know the why and the wherefore of this. (18th July)

The North – China Herald and Supreme Court & Consular Gazette, August 2, 1895

Wenchow

(From Our Own Correspondent)

WÊNCHOW.

(FROM OUR OWN CORRESPONDENT.)

A TIMELY PROCLAMATION.

Our Taotai put out an excellent proclamation two or three days ago; as it may interest some of your readers here is a translation of it:—

"I, Tsung, Taotai-in-charge of the Wên and Chu perfectures, etc., etc., in compliance with orders received from Provincial-Governor Liao, make this proclamation. The Provincial Governor, obedient to urgent orders from the Board of War, announces that in accordance with an Imperial decree, the Tsungli Yamên commands all local officials to assemble their military subordinates with a view to instituting a secret watch, and a minute enquiry, to ascertain if there be cases of wrongful treatment of Christians, and that any such cases be immediately settled, and punishment administered, and thus trouble be nipped in the bud. Moreover,

Wenchow

(From Our Own Correspondent)

A Timely Proclamation

Our Taotai put out an excellent proclamation two or three days ago; as it may interest some of you readers here is a translation of it:—

"I, Tsung, Taotai-in-charge of the Wen and Chu perfectures, etc., etc., in compliance with orders received from Provincial-Governor Liao, make this proclamation. The Provincial Governor, obedient to urgent orders from the Board of war, announces that in accordance with an Imperial decree, the Tsungli Yamen commands all local officials to assemble their military subordinates with a view to instituting a secret watch, and a minute enquiry, to ascertain if there be cases of wrongful treatment of Christians, and that any such cause be immediately settled, and punishment administered, and thus trouble be nipped in the bud. Moreover, that enquiries be made as to the whereabouts of the local preaching halls, and proclamation posted there, so warning all lawless parties that they may know to stand in fear, ad to realize that they will not be allowed to create disturbances. Should insufficient precautions be taken, then all the local officials concerned, both civil and military, including also Taotais and Prefects, will without mercy be dismissed form office."

"These plain orders received from the Provincial Governor are to the intent that all matters be settled, the people pacificated, and order maintained. Now recently in the *hsien* of Pingyang disturbances have occurred in connection with a preaching hall. Along with the Chentai therefore I sent soldiers to guard that district, the village rioters are known, they do not belong to the literary or intelligent classes, and already a willingness exists to compensate. In (the district of) Juian also rowdies have circulated evil rumours and soldiers have been despatched there to search for and arrest them. In Wenchow itself since the riot of (1884) all classes know of the danger thereof and of the proper restitution made, and the people and the Christians have lived (ever since) harmoniously. Now according to the exceeding stringent orders of the Govern it is incumbent on me to adopt extraordinary precautions, and I therefore punish this proclamation looking to all you gentry and scholars both in town and country to make yourself thoroughly acquainted with these facts. The desire of Foreign Mission is truly to exhort people to goodness, and upon these who do not desire to become Christians no compulsion is brought; moreover when people do become Christians they still remain the subjects of China, and in regard to the rights or wrongs of any matter when they are brought before my notice they will be adjudicated on their merits and with strict impartiality. You therefore of experience must teach the ignorant populace that peace means happiness, then serious affairs will become trifling, and trifling affairs will disappear altogether. Let each attend to his own occupation, and see that the peace is kept. Should there be any lawless people whose object it is to call down trouble, and who finding excuse for acting against Christians wildly say: ‘it is better to punish them ourselves rather than send them to the officials for punishment,’ such fellows are the foes of our people. The responsibility laid on the Taotai, the Perfect, and the local officials is exceedingly heavy, and we are under the necessary of maintaining the law and severely administering punishment. Don’t repent too late. Let everybody obey. 6th moon 4th day.”

Credulous Chinese

This is the best proclamation we have seen published hereabouts and ought to clam the minds of the people, who at present and much disturbed by rumours in connection with Pingyang riots, the Szechuan riots, and the Japanese in Formosa. In connection with the last it is universally credited here that 40 gunboats, 38 Japanese and 2 British, were sunk recently by the Flack Flags .We are told that Liu Yung-fu’s men floated oil down by night, covered the oil with chaff (!) and sent divers below who bound the propellers of the gunboats which then become an easy prey to the Black Flag torpedoes; the whole 40 ships were sunk and tens of thousands of Japanese perished. We are told to that Liu Yung-fu having caught a Japanese prince holds him to ransom for 300 million tales of silver. High-coloured cartoons showing the trial and execution of Japanese

Viceroys and other high officers, the sinking of Japanese vessels, and the defeat of their troops, are meeting with a ready sale in this city, which cartoons do not tend much to the pacification of the populace. (27th July)

The North - China Herald and Supreme Court & Consular Gazette, August 16, 1895

Wenchow

(From Our Own Correspondent)

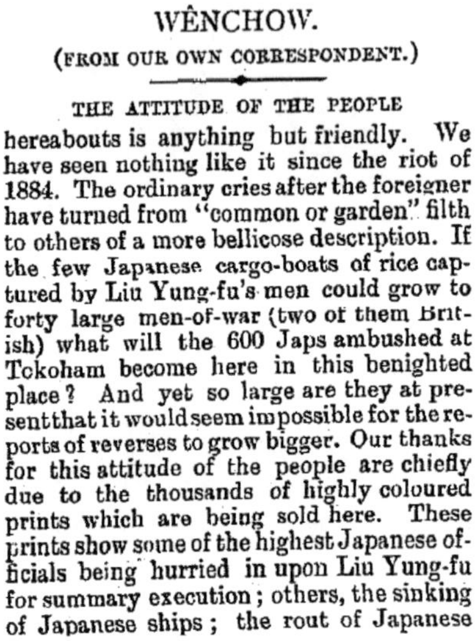
WÊNCHOW.

(FROM OUR OWN CORRESPONDENT.)

THE ATTITUDE OF THE PEOPLE hereabouts is anything but friendly. We have seen nothing like it since the riot of 1884. The ordinary cries after the foreigner have turned from "common or garden" filth to others of a more bellicose description. If the few Japanese cargo-boats of rice captured by Liu Yung-fu's men could grow to forty large men-of-war (two of them British) what will the 600 Japs ambushed at Tokoham become here in this benighted place? And yet so large are they at present that it would seem impossible for the reports of reverses to grow bigger. Our thanks for this attitude of the people are chiefly due to the thousands of highly coloured prints which are being sold here. These prints show some of the highest Japanese officials being hurried in upon Liu Yung-fu for summary execution; others, the sinking of Japanese ships; the rout of Japanese

Wenchow

(From Our Own Correspondent)

The Attitude of the People

hereabouts is anything but friendly. We have seen nothing like it since the riot of 1884. The ordinary cries after the foreigner have turned from "common or garden" filth to others of a more bellicose description. If the few Japanese cargo-boats of rice captured by Liu Yung-fu's men could grow to forty large men-of-war (two of them British) what will the 600 Japs ambushed at Tokoham become here in this benighted place? And yet so large are they at present that it would seem impossible for the reports of reverses to grow bigger. Our thanks for this attitude of the people are chiefly due to the thousands of highly coloured prints which are being sold here. These prints show some of the highest Japanese officials being hurried in upon Liu Yung-fu for summary execution; others, the sinking of Japanese ships; the rout of Japanese troops, etc. Etc, and almost every house in the city has one or more of these prints prominently posted. Hence the whole country around is alive with a too appreciable war spirit. A Britisher was this every morning vigorously stoned, as he pass a city twenty miles from here, by a large crowed of man and youth who followed him for a mile or two. A mission service was effectually stopped only two miles from the threatened trouble several days before.

Worse Still

a week ago, despite appeals to the Taotai made six days before for protection, he allowed a serious attack to be made on an important mission station up country. Seven families are now homeless, the very boards being torn up from their floors and not a cash worth of anything left about the place. H. B. M.'s Consul has made vigorous representation to the Taotai who responded by sending the smallest military officer he could find to make enquiries; six *yamen* runners were also sent, only two of whom reached the place, posted up a proclamation, and did nothing. The promoters of the riot are well known, openly boast of their names were early sent in to the Taotai, but of course nothing has been done. The riot in this place runs a very good chance of spreading all over the district in a few days, and its causes are first the notices freely posted at the Taotai command forbidding selling land to Europeans, which notice despite the orders of the Tsungli Yamen he refuses to withdraw, secondly the Pingyang riots and thirdly the prints already spoken of

Strange Incidents.

Two days ago a man calling himself a cotton pedlar endeavoured to commit suicide at the door of a mission house. Fortunately he was discovered in time, through not before bleeding from the nose had set in as the result of the cord he had tightly bound round his neck. His story was that he had been robbed that morning by a stranger of all his stock-in trade. His story may be true but it is singular that in times to disturbed as the present such a hitherto unknown attempt should take place. Fortunately the street is a quiet one or serious trouble might have ensued .An 0ther strange experience hitherto not gone through here was the death of a servant on European premises. He is said to have eaten three water-melons one after the other, each then to have lain fell in torrents and did not weak him still he was chilled to the marrow. Dysentery of a violent description set in and he died. His father, not from heart-broken grief for his son, but because the place was not given to another brother, absorbed more wine than was good for him, went to the foreigner's of poisoning his son, but before the tipao's arrival discretion urged the man to retire from the filed. Such are a few of the incident which keep the foreigner here in Wenchow from dying of ennui during the dog days, which by the way this year are treating us very coolly.

The Weather

The early rice is after all turning out a poor crop, the fields are parched for lack of rain, and the farmers are lamenting. (5th August)

The North - China Herald and Supreme Court & Consular Gazette, August 23, 1895

Wenchow

(From Our Own Correspondent)

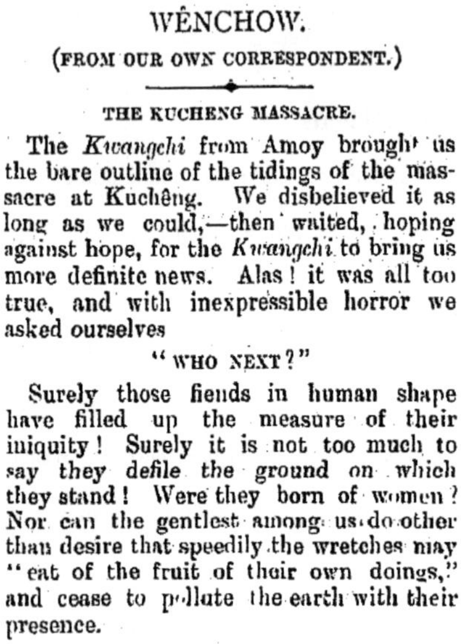

WÊNCHOW.

(FROM OUR OWN CORRESPONDENT.)

THE KUCHENG MASSACRE.

The *Kwangchi* from Amoy brought us the bare outline of the tidings of the massacre at Kuchêng. We disbelieved it as long as we could,—then waited, hoping against hope, for the *Kwangchi* to bring us more definite news. Alas! it was all too true, and with inexpressible horror we asked ourselves

"WHO NEXT?"

Surely those fiends in human shape have filled up the measure of their iniquity! Surely it is not too much to say they defile the ground on which they stand! Were they born of women? Nor can the gentlest among us do other than desire that speedily the wretches may "eat of the fruit of their own doings," and cease to pollute the earth with their presence.

Wenchow

(From Our Own Correspondent)

The Kucheng Massacre

The *Kwangchi* from Amoy brought us the bare outline of the tidings of the massacre at Kucheng. We disbelieved it as long as we could,—then waited, hoping against hope, for the *Kwangchi* to bring us more definite news. Alas! It was all too true, and with inexpressible horror we asked ourselves.

"Who Next?"

Surely those fiends in human shape have filled up the measure of their iniquity! Surely it is not too much to say they defile the ground on which they stand! Were they born of women? Nor can the gentlest among us do other than desire that speedily the wretches may "eat of the fruit of their own doings," and cease to pollute the earth with their presence.

Public Indignation

Kathleen Stewart is 12 years old. Our hearts bleed when we think of the awful memories which must henceforth darken her life, and haunt her footsteps! Our community is as the heart of one man in horror and abhorrence of this almost unparalleled deed of darkness and devilry. We are also one in profound sympathy with the survivors of that reign of terror on the Kucheng hills.

The Right Course

We look upon it as the duty of every Englishman in China to do his utmost to bring pressure to hear upon his home government to now have these barbarities stopped. Personally we are writing to several papers, and to several members of Parliament of our acquaintance to arouse public opinion on this matter.

The White Lily

If the White Lily sect are chargeable with this butchery then there are plenty of them in this neighborhood; they are in the city, and in the whole surrounding district.

The Pingyang Case

is settled. Four thousand dollars are to be paid for the destruction of foreign and native property, which is 1,200 dollars less than was demanded. The Feng-lin persecution case still hangs fire. (17th August)

The North - China Herald and Supreme Court & Consular Gazette, September 6, 1895

Wenchow

(From Our Own Correspondent)

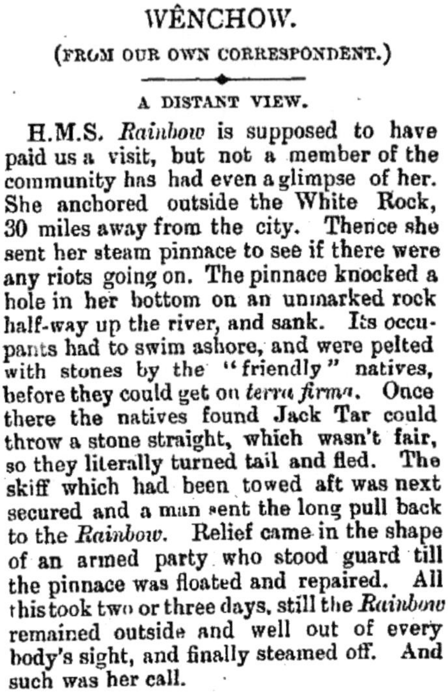

WÊNCHOW.

(FROM OUR OWN CORRESPONDENT.)

A DISTANT VIEW.

H.M.S. *Rainbow* is supposed to have paid us a visit, but not a member of the community has had even a glimpse of her. She anchored outside the White Rock, 30 miles away from the city. Thence she sent her steam pinnace to see if there were any riots going on. The pinnace knocked a hole in her bottom on an unmarked rock half-way up the river, and sank. Its occupants had to swim ashore, and were pelted with stones by the "friendly" natives, before they could get on *terra firma*. Once there the natives found Jack Tar could throw a stone straight, which wasn't fair, so they literally turned tail and fled. The skiff which had been towed aft was next secured and a man sent the long pull back to the *Rainbow*. Relief came in the shape of an armed party who stood guard till the pinnace was floated and repaired. All this took two or three days, still the *Rainbow* remained outside and well out of every body's sight, and finally steamed off. And such was her call.

Wenchow

(From Our Own Correspondent)

A Distance View

H. M. S. *Rainbow* is supposed to have paid us a visit, but not a member of the community has had even a glimpse of her. She anchored outside the White Rock, 30 miles away from the city. Thence she sent her steam pinnace to see if there were any riots going on. The pinnace knocked a hole in her bottom on an unmarked rock half-way up the river, and sank. Its occupants had to swim ashore, and were pelted with stones by the "friendly" natives, before they could get on terra firma. Once there the natives found Jack Tar could throw a stone straight, which wasn't fair, so they literally turned tail and fled. The skiff which had been towed aft was next secured and a man sent the long pull back to the *Rainbow*. Relief came in the shape of an armed party who stood guard till the pinnace was floated and repaired. All this took two or three days, still the *Rainbow* remained outside and well out of every body's sight, and finally steamed off. And such was her call.

The Taotai's Behavior

This is the more to be regretted as the Taotai is behaving obnoxiously. For instance, after the *Forfait* left here a short time ago, he had the pilot arrested who had brought her to the Lower Anchorage. Representations were privately made to him that this was a breach of treaty right, whereupon he released the man, who one may be sure had been in the meantime pretty well fleeced by the *yamen* runners by which means a warning was effectually given against any more steamers being piloted in. Now comes the Rainbow, and, as luck has it, she refuses to come into the river at all though there is no lack of water. It is astonishing how all the natives know that a British cruiser has been at the mouth of the river. Of course, the natural inference to them is that the Taotai would not allow her to come in. The effect on the Taotai himself is what might be expected; he does not intend a foreign gunboat to come in without his permission first had and obtained, and the non-entrance of the Rainbow into the river seems to have wonderfully inflated him. Only to-day we are told he has refused to honour one of the bills given in the Pingyang compensation unless the matter be acknowledged as now settled, whereas not a man has been arrested, nor are the Christians yet allowed to rebuild their houses. He has completely also changed his views to the detriment of British interests on another important matter or two, but these we leave in anticipation of further development.

An Unusual Incident

occurred on the 26th. Quite an army (for Wenchow) of British subjects, eight in all, were coming into the city. One of them, holding a roll of paper, as suddenly attacked by a Chinaman, who seized him by the legs, tried to throw him. Snatched the roll of paper from his hand and fled. Needless to say he was followed, and (what is not so easy) caught hiding under a bed in a house not far away. Subsequently he found lodging in the *hsien*'s *yamen*, where he still remains. Report says he is mad. It is strange that such incidents as these never happened in peaceful times.

Rain

has fallen heavily for 48 hours, to the relief of the farmers, who were looking forward to something like a famine. Cholera and dysentery are raging round us and the death rate is rising rapidly. (27th August)

The North-China Herald and Supreme Court & Consular Gazette, September 20, 1895

Wenchow

(From Our Own Correspondent)

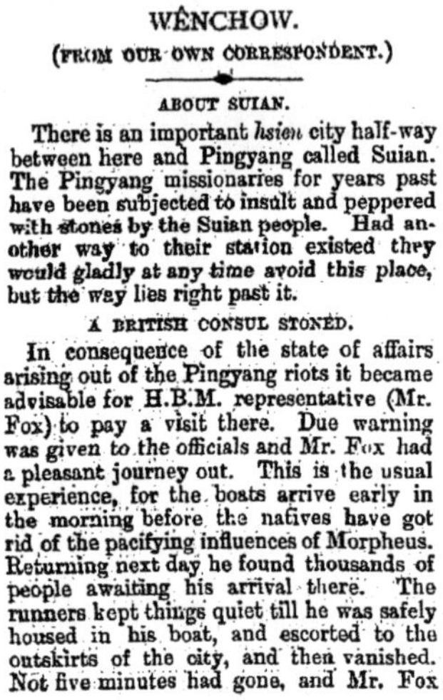

WÊNCHOW.

(FROM OUR OWN CORRESPONDENT.)

ABOUT SUIAN.

There is an important *hsien* city half-way between here and Pingyang called Suian. The Pingyang missionaries for years past have been subjected to insult and peppered with stones by the Suian people. Had another way to their station existed they would gladly at any time avoid this place, but the way lies right past it.

A BRITISH CONSUL STONED.

In consequence of the state of affairs arising out of the Pingyang riots it became advisable for H.B.M. representative (Mr. Fox) to pay a visit there. Due warning was given to the officials and Mr. Fox had a pleasant journey out. This is the usual experience, for the boats arrive early in the morning before the natives have got rid of the pacifying influences of Morpheus. Returning next day he found thousands of people awaiting his arrival there. The runners kept things quiet till he was safely housed in his boat, and escorted to the outskirts of the city, and then vanished. Not five minutes had gone, and Mr. Fox

Wenchow

(From Our Own Correspondent)

About Suian

There is an important *hsien* city half-way between here and Pingyang called Suian. The Pingyang missionaries for years past have been subjected to insult and peppered with stones by the Suian people. Had another way to their station existed they would gladly at any time avoid this place but the way lies right past it.

A British Consul Stoned

In consequence of the state of affairs arising out of the Pingyang riots it became advisable for H.B.M. representative (Mr. Fox) to pay a visit there. Due warning was given to the officials and Mr. Fox had a pleasant journey out. This is the usual experience, foe the boats arrive early in the morning before the natives have got ride of the pacifying influence of Morpheus. Returning next day he found thousands of people awaiting his arrival there. The runners kept thing quiet till he was safely housed in his boat, and escorted to the outskirts of the city, and then vanished. Not five minutes had gone, and Mr. Fox was probably beginning to think the missionaries needlessly excitable, when volley after volley of stones was hurled upon the boat. With true British pluck he went out to face the foe, but was speedily glad to find a refuge inside again, urged there to by the entreaty of his people and Sundry other consideration. Some dollar's worth of damage was done to the boat and to our worthy Consul's crockery. Fortunately the tipao turned up again and with his arrival the showers of stoned abated. We hear that representation and apologies have been made. But there is only one remedy for these attacks. The suffering ought to be one-sided. A month's cangue is the best preventive of the repetition of such pranks.

The Fenglin Outrage

is still unsettled. An interesting item has just turned up. Some weeks ago when a request was made that the *hsien* be sent to Fenglin to make enquiries on the spot; we are told the reply came that a *hsien* never went to Fenglin, the roads were so bad. That of course was Chinese diplomacy, in other words.

A Deliberate Lie

It so happened that last week a murder case turned up a day's journey further on than Fenglin, and the *hsien* had to go .On the way he called at Fenglin, and enquiries are being put in the right quarters how it is, seeing that the magistrate never goes to Fenglin, he yet can call in on his way to a place twice the distance further on. To call there now six weeks after the outrage is absurd.

Pleasant Comments

However he did call, the gentry met him; he understood the dialect, and happened to overhear certain derogatory remarks made some of the gentry in the background: — "This fan jên kuan (mandarin for the barbarians)." "Let us drop him into the pit," etc. etc. His worship's ire was roused and he made a fuss about being thus insulted. The reply made was the as that originally advanced concerning the perpetration of the outrage: "It was only children." His comments hereupon became violent, and he wound up by saying that if that was the way in which they treated him, their *fumu kuan*, he could readily believe they had treated the Christians as the Christians stated .If he will only act accordingly , there is hope of a settlement. Query, will he?

A Word to The Shanghai Authorities

What are the Model Settlement fathers thinking of in allowing so many manifest incentives to riot, pillage, and murder to emanate from your metropolis ?What with cartoons, brochures, and the Sinwanpao, the whole south of China will soon be in a big blaze. I have two booklets before me evidently printed in Shanghai, from steoreotypes, full of mendacity expressed in the very best classical style. Here is a free translation of one of the statements: "The Japs fled for their lives, but in vain, those who did not die by fire perished in the water, so that by mid-day their losses amounted to 20 men-of-war and 20,000 men, and the damage done to warship of other nationalities was by no means small." Can you really do nothing to stop the publication of stuff such as this which is mild indeed in comparison with other items? Here with the two booklets. (9th September)

The North - China Herald and Supreme Court & Consular Gazette, September 27, 1895

Wenchow

(From Our Own Correspondent)

Wenchow

(From Our Own Correspondent)

The Fenglin Outrage

Since my last a most flagrant travesty of justice has taken place in the Fenglin persecution case. Four of the Christians have been cast into prison and tortured, while the opposing ringleaders have been sent home rejoicing and encouraged to continue their tactics. I gave you a short account of the outrage at the time. Warning reached here a week beforehand that some trouble was brewing. Mr. Fox with his usual promptitude informed the Taotai, who did nothing. In due time the attack was made, the Christians driven forth, their homes destroyed and property carried off.

Official Prevarication

Numerous efforts were made by the Consul to get the Taotai to send up a responsible official. He refused to send the *hsien*, saying the latter never travelled to such out of the way places as Fenglin, a deliberate lie, for, after this city, it is the most important town in his *hsien*. A month later the *hsien* had to go to a place a day's journey further on than Fenglin. He called in on his return journey and reported (as ordered by the Taotai) that no damage had been done. As a matter of fact $300 will not cover the losses of the Christians.

And Worse

WÊNCHOW.

(FROM OUR OWN CORRESPONDENT.)

THE FÊNGLIN OUTRAGE.

Since my last a most flagrant travesty of justice has taken place in the Fênglin persecution case. Four of the Christians have been cast into prison and tortured, while the opposing ringleaders have been sent home rejoicing and encouraged to continue their tactics. I gave you a short account of the outrage at the time. Warning reached here a week beforehand that some trouble was brewing. Mr. Fox with his usual promptitude informed the Taotai, who did nothing. In due time the attack was made, the Christians driven forth, their homes destroyed and property carried off.

OFFICIAL PREVARICATION.

Numerous efforts were made by the Consul to get the Taotai to send up a responsible official. He refused to send the *hsien*, saying the latter never travelled to such out of the way places as Fênglin, a deliberate lie, for, after this city, it is the most important town in his *hsien*. A mouth

Under orders from the Futai the Taotai at last ordered the trial to take place, and put a relative of his own in to try the case. So on Friday last, the 13th, the case came on and for five hours the four Christians were bullied and threatened in a most violent manner. They were kept kneeling the whole five hours on the hard stone floor and the runners, seeing the attitude of the officials, denied them the relief allowed even to the worst criminals of resting their hands on the floor. When the *weiyuan* could find nothing to lay hold of to torture them or put them in person, he called for documents to be written out to the effect that the Christians acknowledged having laid a false accusation against the gentry of the town, also that they had received back all their goods, and that they promised to hold no more Christian services at Fenglin. This the accused (i.e. the rioters) were first asked to sign, which they naturally did with joy, praising the discrimination of the judge. The Christians were then ordered to sign it, but firmly refused to do so. The Judge was exceedingly violent and several times ordered them to be beaten—but finally instead asked: "Does Christianity teach you to smoke opium?" "No, it forbids any dealing with it." "To gamble?" "Decidedly not." "To drink?" "Only in moderation." "To pay your debts?" "Certainly." "Then you owe Imperial land taxes. Take them to prison." And the four poor fellows, who had lost pretty well everything, were taken to prison. There the gaolers tied them up, each with a chain round his neck passed beneath a pair of handcuffs and drawn together to a beam overhead. Thus they were kept standing at their utmost stretch for eight hours. The Consul happened to have just gone away for the week-end, nobody dreaming of such developments as occurred. Appeals were made in vain to the gaolers, and later to the *hsien*. At midnight a bribe to the gaolers loosed the chains a few inches and the poor fellows were able to stand properly, and thus they were kept standing till noon next day, by which time frequent appeals had been made to this end.

A message had been sent after the Consul and he came back with all spend; the incoming tide caught him up river, but he walked the 10 miles so as to get into the Taotai on Sunday night. His appeal was in vain; their release was refused, and they are still in prison. The charge at first was unpaid land taxes; payment and bail were both rejected. As a matter of fact one owe nothing, the second actually had a balance to the good, the third owed a very small sum, and the fourth could only reckon up his to a couple of dollars or so. When asked next day to put his reply in writing the Taotai shuffled, offered to release three "on payment of taxes", but the fourth must be kept on a charge of laying a false accusation.

Firm Action Needed

The whole affair is the Taotai's and the following facts will prove this. These four men had their crops destroyed last year; the case was settled up by a payment of one-third of their losses, but only after a contretemps between Messrs. Frazer and the Taotai in which the latter came off the worse of the two. He never forgot it. Later when a British subject bought land here he put every possible obstacle in the way of its completion. Then he issued notices all up the Fenglin district forbidding the sale of land to foreigners—when asked to withdraw them he refused for the British though he sent out private orders withdrawing for the French. Being ordered from Peking to withdraw them openly he set about it in a dilatory manner, and in the Fenglin district they are not yet withdraw. The Consul's request a week before the disturbance for immediate relief was absolutely ignored, and after the outrage no attempt was made to settle the matter up. There is evidence that (apart from the actual riot) the whole case has been worked up in the Taotai's *yamen* and the unfortunate *hsien* has had to submit everything for the Taotai's inspection and approval. The weiyuan who tried the case is a relation of the Taotai, and has been in almost daily consultation with him. The first runners who went up reported serious damage, but on the morning of the trial this weiyuan made them rewrite all their evidence, asking how they dare report damage when the *hsien* himself had reported to the contrary.

Will There be Further Trouble

Is it to be wondered at that the whole district is in a ferment? It will be a marvel if we have not further riots to report next time. In the meantime Mr. Fox is working might and main to uphold the honor of his flag. If the *Rainbow* had not further inflated the Taotai's self-esteem by remaining outside we should have had a different lesson to write than this. There has been no gunboat since February. (18th September)

There Men Released

P. S. —We here that the four Christians have just been allowed to pay their landtax. There have been released, but the fourth is kept imprisoned on the charge of false accusation. It is feared there are clauses in the documents signed which were not explained to the Christians and which may somewhat compromise them.

The North – China Herald and Supreme Court & Consular Gazette, October 18, 1895

Wenchow

(From Our Own Correspondent)

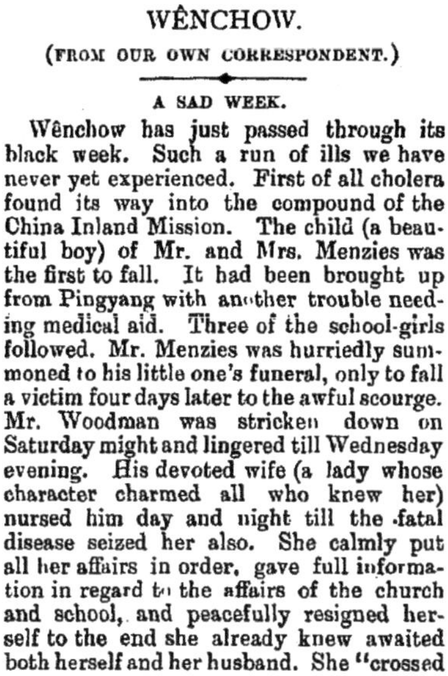
WÊNCHOW.

(FROM OUR OWN CORRESPONDENT.)

A SAD WEEK.

Wênchow has just passed through its black week. Such a run of ills we have never yet experienced. First of all cholera found its way into the compound of the China Inland Mission. The child (a beautiful boy) of Mr. and Mrs. Menzies was the first to fall. It had been brought up from Pingyang with another trouble needing medical aid. Three of the school-girls followed. Mr. Menzies was hurriedly summoned to his little one's funeral, only to fall a victim four days later to the awful scourge. Mr. Woodman was stricken down on Saturday might and lingered till Wednesday evening. His devoted wife (a lady whose character charmed all who knew her) nursed him day and night till the fatal disease seized her also. She calmly put all her affairs in order, gave full information in regard to the affairs of the church and school, and peacefully resigned herself to the end she already knew awaited both herself and her husband. She "crossed

Wenchow

(From Our Own Correspondent)

A Sad Week

Wenchow has just passed through its black week. Such a run of ills we have never yet experienced. First of all cholera found its way into the compound of the China Inland Mission. The child (a beautiful boy) of Mr. and Mrs. Menzies was the first to fall. It had been brought up from Pingyang with another trouble needing medical aid. Three of the school girls followed. Mr. Menzies was hurriedly summoned to his little one's funeral, only to fall a victim four days later to the awful scourge. Mr. Woodman was stricken down on Saturday might and lingered till Wednesday evening. His devoted wife (a lady whose character charmed all who knew her) nursed him day and night till the fatal disease seized her also. She calmly put all her affairs in order, gave full information in regard to the affairs of the church and school, and peacefully resigned herself to the end she already knew awaited both herself and her husband, She "crossed the bar" on Wednesday morning, her husband following towards evening. They were buried together in the same grave in our little God's acre. All that medical skill could do was done for them. In addition to Dr. Hogg of the Methodist Mission and Dr. Lowry of the Customs, Dr. Penney of H. M. S. *Firebrand* rendered kindly assistance so that the sufferers were never without the presence of a medical man of experience.

Shipping Accident

Our next misfortune came in the stranding of the *Kwangchi*, about which you have probably already received information. She bumped on an unmarked and covered rock near Montagu about 8.30 on the evening of the 5th.There was a swell on at the time, and it seems likely that she toughed the rock while in the hollow between two waves, for she lifted right off at once and seemed none the worse at the time. Evidently, however, the rivets had given way for she almost immediately began to make water in the stoke hole. Her officers acted with promptitude and found their way in through an unknown and dangerous passage to a spot where she was comfortably beached. In the meantime Mr. Adair, the engineer, together with the only fireman who was willing to remain below, worked up to their waists in water bravely keeping the upper fire going, though the lower one was already under water; another five minutes or less would have put out even this fire and the vessel must have gone down. Under the unfortunate circumstances every praise seems due to the officers and engineer for their prompt and brave conduct. We hear that the chief officer was in charge at the time of the accident, and much sympathy is felt here for him, as he is considered to be a very capable seaman, and well versed in the intricacies of this awkward bit of coast.

Fire

The third misfortune came in the shape of a big fire, biggest known here for years. Another long stretch of the main street was destroyed by fire, and over 1,000 people rendered homeless. The fire at one time seemed likely to attack the premises of the Methodist Mission, bur its progress was checked in time. Such has been our black week, may we never have another like it.

The “Firebrand” Arrives

The *Firebrand* has been here for ten days; she came in without the Taotai’s permission, much, no doubt, to this disgust. The protest on the Admiral’s part against the Taotai’s outrageous attitude ought to be a lesson to him.

The Christian Persecution

The Fenglin Christian who was so shamefully incarcerated by the Taotai’s orders is still in prison. We hear that several promises of release have been made, but when the time for fulfillment came demands were made that he should sign away all further claims and perjure himself by admitting that all his case was a base concoction; the man pluckily prefers incarceration to such disgraceful terms. A promise has now been made to release him tomorrow without these terms. Whether this is a further put-off on the Taotai’s part we await tomorrow to see.

Sport

The terrible outbreak of the community to make the *Firebrand’s* visit as festive as it might have been, but a concert was given by the men on Saturday, and the community did its best to return the compliment by getting up an excellent set of sports today. Our Consul took the lead in the matter and the sports were held in his grounds. The events consisted of a hundred yards flat race, a sack race, egg and spoon race, obstacle race (all round the Island), potato and bucket race, boxing, fencing, tug of war, etc. etc. All passed off well and some interesting and valuable reminiscences of Wenchow are now in the hands of the *Firebrand's* men.

A Departure

We lose today a valued member of our community. Dr. J. H. Lowry leaves by the *Haeshin* for your port en route for England with his little daughter. While here his skill has ever been freely at the command of all who needed it, whether Europeans or natives. He has rendered much assistance to both the missions, who will greatly miss his kindly aid. He has taken a warm interest in all that concern the welfare of the community, by whom his loss will be keenly felt. Should fortune ever direct his steps back again he will meet with a most hearty welcome. (14th October)

The North – China Herald and Supreme Court & Consular Gazette, November 1, 1895

Wenchow

(From Our Own Correspondent)

Wenchow

(From Our Own Correspondent)

A Reviewer Reviewed

Your reviewer who kindly corrected the quotation I made from the native books sent you a month or so ago has laid me under an obligation; certainly the character 誤 ought now to be indelibly grafted in my memory. But really the absence of this little word seems to have dragged the main aim of my remarks below the surface of his observation. That aim was to draw attention to the fact that books were (and still are) emanating from Shanghai, beautifully printed, containing the wildest fabrications in regard to the doings of Liu Yung-fu in Formosa; and that these fabrications were endangering the safety of foreigners in the South of China.

The book I quoted states that Liu Yung-fu, in a manner impossible to anybody save of course a Chinaman, had the propellers of the Japanese fleet fastened with wire; he then sent down fire rafts of a formidable order, the Japanese fleet endeavouring to avoid them discovered too late that their ships were immovable and were then subjected by the Chinese to a terrific cannonade on every side. Entrapped in this fashion, unable to advance or withdraw, the Japanese all perished either by fire or by water. In this manner twenty Japanese warships and more than 20000 men perished, and not a few warships of other nationalities were accidentally injured. This word "accidentally" was accidentally omitted from my letter, but seeing that not a single Japanese warship, not even a Japanese sailor, much less a warship of any other nationality came to any grief at all, one fails to see how the omission of the word "accidentally" (or mistakenly) can affect the intention of my letter. I am unable to refer to the exact words used but I know my wish was to call attention not so

WÊNCHOW.
(FROM OUR OWN CORRESPONDENT.)
A REVIEWER REVIEWED.
Your reviewer who kindly corrected the quotation I made from the native books sent you a month or so ago has laid me under an obligation; certainly the character 誤 ought now to be indelibly grafted in my memory. But really the absence of this little word seems to have dragged the main aim of my remarks below the surface of his observation. That aim was to draw attention to the fact that books were (and still are) emanating from Shanghai, beautifully printed, containing the wildest fabrications in regard to the doings of Liu Yung-fu in Formosa; and that these fabrications were endangering the safety of foreigners in the South of China.
The book I quoted states that Liu Yung-fu, in a manner impossible to anybody save of course a Chinaman, had the propellers of the Japanese fleet fastened with wire; he then sent down fire rafts of a

much that the report of the destruction of foreign ships was arousing the war spirit of the people, as that the publication by some Shanghai firm of such outrageous lies concerning the destruction of the Japanese fleet only adds fuel to fire already too warm for comfort. The Japs, like ourselves, are foreigners to the Chinese, whose ignorance of geography has almost passed into a proverb, and he South of China will not be safe for foreign residence so long as the natives are led to believe that Liu Yung-fu is wiping the Japs off the face of the earth. Only last week, with thousands of students here for the examinations, I saw a crowd round a stall near the examination hall on which were exposed vivid cartoons and booklets of the nature already referred to, all calculated to seriously prejudice the interests and safety of foreigners in this country, and to rouse the spirits of men of the Whasang order.

Official Tactics

The Fenglin Christian has at last been released, but in a most scurvy manner. He was brought before his tormentor, the Taotai's *weiyuan*, last Saturday, bullied, threatened, and the bamboos produced to beat him; a thousand blows were ordered, the man said "ten thousand, if you will, but I can never sign the document you demand." This document was to the effect that all the charges he had made were false. The beating did not take place, but at the orders of this *weiyuan* runners seized the Christian, held him kneeling on the ground, some stretched out his left arm to its full extent, other his right, one held his hand which he had clenched, another prized open his finger, rubbed it with ink, pressed the document against it, and thus he was made to sign away his character! Such is the justice of mandarindom to those they are instructed to protect under threat of losing their buttons! The Chinese will make any outward show our Consuls ask for in the way of proclamations, but it all ends there. In the meantime the Taotai is blandly proposing to negotiate the case with the British Consul, with what success remains to be seen.

An Invitation

The *Poochi* is put on this run again and we all hope she will be kept on. If any of you Shanghai people need a short change you won't find a more beautiful and convenient trip on the coast of China than the run down to Wenchow. (23rd October)

The North - China Herald and Supreme Court & Consular Gazette, November 22, 1895

Wenchow

(From Our Own Correspondent)

WÊNCHOW.

(FROM OUR OWN CORRESPONDENT.)

A HORRIBLE MURDER

was perpetrated a few days ago. When the outrage took place nobody seems to know, and there is absolutely no clue to the perpetrator. It was only discovered yesterday morning by the body floating to the surface of the blind canal, the equivalent to Wênchowites of your Bubbling Well Road. The head was almost severed from the body, and the corpse was partially disembowelled; it is stark naked, so that nothing is left to trace him by, and as he is supposed to be either a Shantung or a Canton man there is little probability of his identification. Thousands have flocked to see the body and with the exception of a few women have evinced the callousness of the usual Chinese mob.

MORE PERSECUTION.

Once more the Fênglin Christian has been arrested and thrown into prison at the command of the Taotai. Released three weeks ago he went home and Christian

Wenchow

(From Our Own Correspondent)

A Horrible Murder

was perpetrated a few days ago. When the outrage took place nobody seems to know, and there is absolutely no clue to the perpetrator. It was only discovered yesterday morning by the body floating to the blind canal, the equivalent to Wenchowites of your Bubbling Well Road. The head was almost severed from the body , and the corpse was partially disemboweled; it is stark naked, so that nothing is left to trace him by, and as he is supposed to be either a Shantung or a Canton man there is little probability of his identification. Thousands have flocked to see the body and with the exception of a few women have evinced the callousness of the usual Chinese mob.

More Persecution

Once more the Fenglin Christian has been arrested and thrown into prison at the command of the Taotai. Released three weeks ago he went home and Christian services were soon commenced. The people of the place made no opposition whatever, but after the second Sunday seemed to accept Christianity as a settled fact; when to everybody's astonishment runners arrived to carry off the chief Christian. He was examined by two Taotai's weiyuans and the *hsien*, confronted with the document to which before his release his signature was by muscular force compelled, and asked why he had recommenced Christian services. His reply was that he had let his house to the

Mission and the Mission held services. Being asked to withdraw his permission to the services being held he firmly refused, and was thrown once more into the inner prison where he now lies with banditti, thieves, men charged with murder, and all kinds of bad characters.

The Treaty Defied

The Consul has made strong representations to the Taotai, but in vain. He refuses to release him unless a promise is given that no more Christian services will be held in Fenglin. If this is not open defiance of the Treaty, to say nothing of common justice, it is hard to know what is! There is absolutely no charge laid against the Christian beyond that of holding service in his own house. Two of his neighbors have been brought down to say that the services are an annoyance to them and to others; for this they are receiving the generous sum of 10 cents a day from the officials. These men state privately that they have no objection to Christianity, indeed they proved it by protecting the Christians during the attack, moreover, that they would like to return home to their fields, but dare not resist the commands of the mandarins. As to compensation for the damage done or the arrest of the rioters the case is *in statu quo ante*. The simple fact remains that the Chinese mandarins have not been humiliated one whit by recent events. Indeed we believe there is evidence more than enough in the Consular records of the immediate present and all over China to prove that they are more arrogant, more insulting, and more opposed to foreigners than has been the case for decades. (13th November)

The North - China Herald and Supreme Court & Consular Gazette, December 13, 1895

Wenchow

(From Our Own Correspondent)

Wenchow

(From Our Own Correspondent)

The Harvest

The late rice crop this year has turned out far from satisfactory; in some districts it is quite a failure. There is no fear of a famine in the Wenchow prefecture, though rice is pretty sure to go up in price. A rise in price always presses hard on the lower classes, an advance of 5 cash a pint making a difference of nearly a quarter of their food supply to families of say half-a-dozen "mouths."

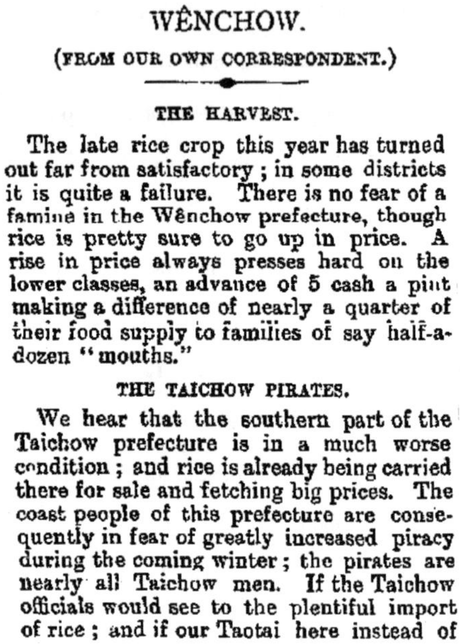
WÊNCHOW.

(FROM OUR OWN CORRESPONDENT.)

THE HARVEST.

The late rice crop this year has turned out far from satisfactory ; in some districts it is quite a failure. There is no fear of a famine in the Wênchow prefecture, though rice is pretty sure to go up in price. A rise in price always presses hard on the lower classes, an advance of 5 cash a pint making a difference of nearly a quarter of their food supply to families of say half-a-dozen "mouths."

THE TAICHOW PIRATES.

We hear that the southern part of the Taichow prefecture is in a much worse condition ; and rice is already being carried there for sale and fetching big prices. The coast people of this prefecture are consequently in fear of greatly increased piracy during the coming winter ; the pirates are nearly all Taichow men. If the Taichow officials would see to the plentiful import of rice ; and if our Taotai here instead of

The Taichow Pirates

We hear that the southern part of the Taichow prefecture is in a much worse condition; and rice is already being carried there for sale and fetching big prices. The coast people of this prefecture are consequently in fear of greatly increased piracy during the coming winter; the pirates are nearly all Taichow men. If the Taichow officials would see to the plentiful import of rice; and if our Taotai here instead of persecuting Christians would expend a little of his superfluous energy in arming a steam launch and sending it to patrol the Yohtsing coast he would attain a fair amount of popularity at a small cost in money.

Persecution

As it is, he still keeps the Fenglin Christian in prison, where he has been seriously ill. There is absolutely no cause for the imprisonment except that the Christian had services held in his own house. Even the Taotai makes no other charge against him, and offers to release him if guarantees be given for the cessation of services there. This open and flagrant defiance of the treaty is only another evidence that the Imperial, Viceregal, and other proclamations so profusely posted in town and country are only for the purpose of making a show to quiet the pestiferous barbarian. Representations have been again made to Peking and to Hangchow, and it is to be hoped the poor fellow who has borne so bravely be released and compensation made for the serious loss and damage at Fenglin.

A Vain Attempt

Last Sunday at a village opposite the city on the other side of the river the China Inland Mission endeavoured to hold a service in the house of a native Christian. Despite the promise of the Taotai to render due protection the service was completely prevented, and considerable damage done to the property. "Feeling from this city to another" they found to be of no avail either, for the next village, where service has often been held before, said: "If the other village can turn you out we can," and they did so.

The Taotai and the "Lion"

We had a visit from the French gunboat *Lion* on the 26th of November. She spent two nights and a day here, leaving on the 28th. The Taotai has been having a few old cannon put on the city wall, and hearing the *Lion* fire a gun each sundown, he gave orders, and a gun with a strong charge was fired an hour or so later! What his object was nobody seems to know; the firing was strictly limited to the two evenings when the *Lion* was in port! (3rd December)

图书在版编目(CIP)数据

《北华捷报》温州史料编译. 1876－1895 年 / 温州市档案局（馆）译编. -- 北京：社会科学文献出版社，2018.11

ISBN 978－7－5201－3458－3

Ⅰ.①北… Ⅱ.①温… Ⅲ.①温州－地方史－史料－1876－1895 Ⅳ.①K295.53

中国版本图书馆 CIP 数据核字（2018）第 210114 号

《北华捷报》温州史料编译（1876～1895 年）

译　　编 / 温州市档案局（馆）

出 版 人 / 谢寿光
项目统筹 / 王玉敏
责任编辑 / 赵怀英　王玉敏　张文静

出　　版 / 社会科学文献出版社・独立编辑工作室(010) 59367153
地址：北京市北三环中路甲 29 号院华龙大厦　邮编：100029
网址：www.ssap.com.cn
发　　行 / 市场营销中心（010）59367081　59367083
印　　装 / 三河市东方印刷有限公司

规　　格 / 开　本：787mm×1092mm　1/16
印　张：27.25　字　数：447 千字
版　　次 / 2018 年 11 月第 1 版　2018 年 11 月第 1 次印刷
书　　号 / ISBN 978－7－5201－3458－3
定　　价 / 159.00 元

本书如有印装质量问题，请与读者服务中心（010－59367028）联系